BELIZE
HANDBOOK
SECOND EDITION

BELIZE
HANDBOOK
SECOND EDITION

**CHICKI MALLAN
PHOTOS BY OZ MALLAN**

MOON
PUBLICATIONS INC.

BELIZE HANDBOOK
SECOND EDITION

Published by
Moon Publications, Inc.
P.O. Box 3040
Chico, California 95927–3040, USA

Printed by
Colorcraft Ltd.

Please send all comments,
corrections, additions,
amendments, and critiques to:

**BELIZE HANDBOOK
c/o MOON PUBLICATIONS, INC.
P.O. BOX 3040
CHICO, CA 95927–3040, USA**

Printing History
1st edition—January 1991
Reprinted—June 1991
2nd edition—August 1993
Reprinted—May 1994
Reprinted—February 1995

Library of Congress Cataloging in Publication Data
Mallan, Chicki, 1933 –
Belize Handbook / Chicki Mallan. —2nd ed.
p. cm.
Includes bibliographical references and index.
ISBN 0-918373-95-6 : $14.95
1. Belize—Guidebooks. I. Title.
F1443.5.M35 1993   92–21235
917.28204'5—dc20   CIP

Editor: Gina Wilson Birtcil
Copy Editors: Deana Corbitt, Asha Johnson
Production & Design: David Hurst, Carey Wilson
Cartographers: Bob Race, Brian Bardwell
Index: Asha Johnson, Gina Wilson Birtcil, Pauli Galin

Front cover photo by Bill Boehm
All photos by Oz Mallan unless otherwise noted.

Printed in Hong Kong

CONTENTS

MAPS

MAP SYMBOLS

———— HIGHWAY	○ LARGER TOWN OR CITY
——— ROAD	○ VILLAGE OR TOWN
— — ROAD SURFACE UNDETERMINED	▲ MOUNTAIN
— — INTERNATIONAL BORDER	■ POINT OF INTEREST
·····— DISTRICT BORDER	WATER
REEF	

GAS
AIRPORT
ARCHAEOLOGICAL SITE OR RUIN
BRIDGE

CHARTS

SPECIAL TOPICS

ACKNOWLEDGEMENTS

It's almost impossible to remember everyone who helps with the making of a guidebook! First, the people of Belize are sensational. Everyone was willing to take a few minutes to answer questions and give generously of their personal knowledge. Thanks to the Fort George Hotel and Paul Hunt, and Avis Car Rental in Belize City for their considerations. Thanks also to the many people who share our enthusiasm for Belize: Steve Cox and Nancee DePuy at International Expeditions in Helena, Alabama.

The entire Moon staff pulled it off again. First, what would any writer do without a sharp, sensitive editor—that's Gina Wilson Birtcil. It's been a pleasure working with her. She continually caught my glitches and was always ready with productive ideas. Thanks, Gina. Moon took my words, Oz Mallan's pictures, Kathy Sanders's and Bob Race's outstanding drawings, and Bob Race's and Brian Bardwell's maps, to make another beautiful book.

IS THIS BOOK OUT OF DATE?

We strive to keep our books as up to date as possible and would appreciate your help. If you find that a resort is not as we described, or discover a new restaurant or other information that should be included in our book, please let us know. Our mapmakers take extraordinary effort to be accurate, but if you find an error, let us know that as well.

We're especially interested in hearing from female travelers, RVers, outdoor enthusiasts, expatriates, and local residents. We are always interested in hearing from the tourist industry which specializes in accommodating visitors to Belize. Happy traveling! Please address your letters to:

Belize Handbook
c/o Moon Publications, Inc.
P.O. Box 3040
Chico, CA 95927-3040, USA.

ABOUT THE PRICES IN THIS BOOK

As numbers go, relatively few people have shared the wonderful secret of Belize over the years. But as it happens, the secret is out—more and more adventurers, divers, sun-worshippers, and curiosity-seekers are discovering Belize. All of this attention is bringing about rapid changes to the country. Please use the prices given only as a guideline; they too are apt to change. We've tried to furnish accurate addresses as well as fax and telephone numbers where you can verify these facts. If you find the numbers have changed, we would appreciate knowing about that as well. All prices are in U. S. dollars.

ABBREVIATIONS

a/c—air conditioned	**4WD**—four-wheel drive	**RT**—round trip
BZE$—Belize dollars	**MAP**—modified American	**RV**—recreational vehicle
C—centigrade	plan	**s**—single occupancy
d—double occupancy	**OW**—one way	**t**—triple occupancy
F—Fahrenheit	**p/d**—per day	**tel.**—telephone number
FAP—full American plan	**pp**—per person	**YH**—youth hostel

BELIZE TELEPHONE SERVICE AND USE

Belize has a fine, modern telephone system that enables visitors to make contact with the rest of the world quickly and efficiently with direct dial service. Belize country code is 501 and the area codes follow. The number of digits varies from city to city.

AREA CODES

2	Belize City	4	Corozal	7	Punta Gorda
8	Belmopan	5	Dangriga	92	San Ignacio
93	Benque Viejo	6	Independence	4	San Joaquin
3	Blue Creek	25	Ladyville	26	San Pedro
28	Burrell Boom	3	Orange Walk Town	8	Spanish Lookout
22	Caye Caulker	6	Placencia		

KATHY ESCOVEDO SANDERS

INTRODUCTION

When you say "Belize" many people think of unbelievably clear blue water and diving along a protected reef rich with brilliant sealife. Amen! But that's just part of Belize's treasure. Along with a polyglot of people who have maintained a variety of traditions and cultures over hundreds of years, this isolated country has not cemented over nature's wonders. Generally speaking, Belize is ecotourism in action.

Early recorded comments, following Columbus's fourth voyage to the New World, led the Spaniards to hastily conclude that the swampy shoreline was unfit for human habitation. Today this little-known destination is stepping quietly into the world of tourism. The government has recognized priorities and is establishing clear guidelines as the country welcomes more and more visitors. "Our tourism is based on our wildlife, the forests, the flora and fauna," proclaims Victor Gonzalez, permanent secretary of Belize's Ministry of Tourism and the Environment. The country, on the cutting edge of the ecotourism phenomenon, actively protects its natural resources: wildlife, tracts of rainforest and unsullied swamplands, innumerable Maya archaeological sites, varied cultural heritages,

and the largest barrier reef in the Western Hemisphere.

Geographically located in Central America, Belize is considered part of the Yucatán Peninsula and the region called **Mundo Maya,** home to the Maya for 3,000 years. An English-speaking country, Belize was called British Honduras from 1862 until 1973, when it once again became Belize in anticipation of its independence from England.

Belize was the favored hideout for pirates until pirating went out of style. Then these hard-drinking, high-seas robbers discovered an even more lucrative profession: stripping the forests of trees to fill the holds of their ships, and later fetching high prices at home in England. Fortunately, it was selectively done, removing only a couple of species of trees.

Today Belize has one of the most peaceful, stable governments in all of Central America. It has a growing population of about 200,000 (22.6 people per square mile), a quarter of whom live in Belize City. Edging the unspoiled Western Caribbean, it only recently realized its enormous potential for tourism. Divers, the first visitors to the tropical country, have quietly enjoyed the

BELIZE

BELIZE DISTRICTS

MEXICO

CHETUMAL

COROZAL TOWN

SARTENEJA

PROGRESO

SHIPSTERN LAGOON

CUELLO

ORANGE WALK TOWN

NEW RIVER

COROZAL DICTRICT

AMBERGRIS CAYE

SAN PEDRO

BLUE CREEK VILLAGE

SAN FELIPE

SHIPYARD

CAYE CAULKER

ORANGE WALK DISTRICT

GALLON JUG

BERMUDIAN LANDING

BURRELL BOOM

CAYE CHAPEL

CHAN CHICH

RANCHO DELORES

INTERNATIONAL AIRPORT

BELIZE CITY

NORTHERN TWO CAYE

LIGHTHOUSE REEF

SPANISH LOOKOUT

ROARING CREEK

GUANACASTE PARK

BELIZE DISTRICT

TURNEFFE ISLANDS

BLUE HOLE

SAN IGNACIO

GEORGEVILLE

BELMOPAN

MANATEE RIVER

BLUEFIELD RANGE

HALF MOON CAYE

LONG CAYE

BENQUE VIEJO

BLUE HOLE

HIDDEN VALLEY FALLS

MOUNTAIN PINE RIDGE

MIDDLESEX

CAYE BOKEL

MELCHOR DE MENCOS

AUGUSTINE

POMONA

STANN CREEK DISTRICT

DANGRIGA

GLOVER'S REEF

CAYO DISTRICT

COCKSCOMB RANGE

JAGUAR RESERVE

HOPKINS

LONG CAYE

VICTORIA PEAK (3675 ft)

MAYA CENTER

SOUTHWEST CAYE

MAYA MTNS.

MANGO CREEK INDEPENDENCE

MAYA BEACH SEINE BIGHT VILLAGE

BIG CREEK

PLACENCIA

TOLEDO DISTRICT

SOUTHERN HWY.

MONKEY RIVER TOWN

BELIZE BARRIER REEF

SAN PEDRO SAN ANTONIO

BIG FALLS

CARIBBEAN SEA

PUSIL HA

BLUE CREEK VILLAGE

PUNTA GORDA

SAPODILLA CAYES

BARRANCO

GUATEMALA BELIZE

BELIZE GUATEMALA

0   30 mi

0   30 km

© MOON PUBLICATIONS, INC.

NEW RIVER

RIO HONDO

NORTHERN HWY.

WESTERN HWY.

BELIZE RIVER

SIBUN RIVER

HUMMINGBIRD HWY.

BELIZE DISTRICTS (inset)

COROZAL TOWN

COROZAL DISTRICT

ORANGE WALK TOWN

ORANGE WALK DISTRICT

BELIZE DISTRICT

BELIZE CITY

BELMOPAN

CAYO DISTRICT

DANGRIGA

STANN CREEK DISTRICT

PLACENCIA

TOLEDO DISTRICT

PUNTA GORDA

Belize Reef for decades—thanks, Jacques Cousteau! Independent travelers and special interest groups (birdwatchers, archaeologists, and nature buffs) are beginning to take note of the country's beautiful cayes (meaning "islands," pronounced KEES) lying off the Caribbean coast, as well as inland rainforests and a vast number of archaeological centers. More and more middle-aged travelers from the U.S. are looking into Belize as a viable, warm-weather, budget location to spend their retirement years. And at the same time, foreign industries are finding the Belizean government cooperative and willing to make tax concessions in order to attract outside investments. This in turn provides jobs for the locals, which the emerging country desperately needs.

The people of Belize are very aware of the importance of treasuring the pristine natural treasures in their own back yard. They realize these natural resources must be protected and they have opted for a long-term investment in a tourism that attracts people curious about natural history. Today thousands of rainforest acres have been declared reserves, hunting certain animals (which in other parts of the world are already extinct) is illegal, and the lavish coast with miles of reef has strict regulations. The beautiful atolls and surrounding underwater marine world that is considered second to none in the world have also been declared reserves.

NATURE RESERVES AND SANCTUARIES OF BELIZE

Belize Zoo and Tropical Research Education Center
Blue Hole National Park
Cockscomb Basin Wildlife Sanctuary
Community Baboon Sanctuary
Crooked Tree Wildlife Sanctuary
Guanacaste Park
Half Moon Caye Natural Monument
Mountain Pine Ridge Forest Reserve
Shipstern Nature Reserve

THE BELIZE NATIONAL ANTHEM

LAND OF THE FREE

O, Land of the Free by the Carib Sea,
Our manhood we pledge to thy liberty!
No tyrants here linger, despots must flee
This tranquil haven of democracy
The blood of our sires which hallows the sod,
Brought freedom from slavery oppression's rod,
By the might of truth and the grace of God.
No longer shall we be hewers of wood.

Arise! ye sons of the Baymen's clan,
Put on your armours, clear the land!
Drive back the tyrants, let despots flee—
Land of the Free by the Carib Sea!

Nature has blessed thee with wealth untold,
O'er mountains and valleys where prairies roll;
Our fathers, the Baymen, valiant and bold
Drove back the invader; this heritage bold
From proud Rio Hondo to old Sarstoon,
Through coral isle, over blue lagoon;
Keep watch with the angels, the stars and moon;
For freedom comes to-morrow's noon.

THE LAND

Belize lies on the eastern coastline of Central America. Its 8,866 square miles of territory are bordered on the north by Mexico, on the west and south by Guatemala, and on the east by the Caribbean Sea. From the Rio Hondo border with Mexico to the southern border of Guatemala, Belize's mainland measures 180 miles long. Its widest section measures 68 miles wide, roughly the same size as the state of Massachusetts. Offshore, Belize has more than 200 cayes. Both the coastal region and the northern half of the mainland are flat, but the land rises in the south and west in the Maya Mountains to over 3,000 feet above sea level. Much of the humid coastal plain is covered by mangrove swamps. The Maya Mountains and the Cockscombs form the coun-try's backbone, rising 3,675 feet to Victoria Peak, Belize's highest point.

In the west, the Cayo District contains the **Mountain Pine Ridge Preserve,** which was at one time a magnificent pine forest. Destroyed in the lower plains over the decades by fires and lumber removal, only a few straggler pine trees remain in the arid foothills. However, the upper regions of Mountain Pine Ridge provide spectacular scenery, and thick forest encompasses the **Macal River** as it tumbles over huge granite boulders. **Hidden Valley Falls** plunge 1,000 feet to the valley below. The **Rio Frio** cave system offers massive stalactites and stalagmites to the avid spelunker. The diverse landscape includes limestone-fringed granite boulders.

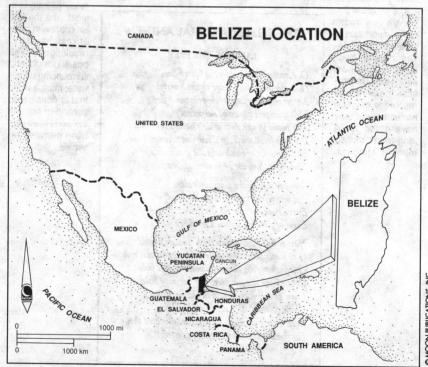

BELIZE LOCATION

CANADA

UNITED STATES

ATLANTIC OCEAN

BELIZE

MEXICO

GULF OF MEXICO

YUCATAN PENINSULA

CANCUN

PACIFIC OCEAN

0   1000 mi

0   1000 km

GUATEMALA   HONDURAS

EL SALVADOR

NICARAGUA

CARIBBEAN SEA

COSTA RICA

PANAMA   SOUTH AMERICA

© MOON PUBLICATIONS, INC.

Over thousands of years, what was once a sea in the northern half of Belize has become a combination of scrub vegetation and rich tropical hardwood forest. Near the Mexican border much of the land has been cleared, and it's here that the majority of sugar crops are raised, along with family plots of corn and beans. Most of the northern coast is swampy with a variety of grasses and mangroves attracting hundreds of species of waterfowl. Rainfall in the north averages 60 inches annually and it's generally dry Nov.-May.

Significant rainfall in the mountains washes silt and nutrients into the lower valleys to the south and west, forming rich agricultural areas. In southern Belize it rains most of the year, averaging 150 inches or more. The coastal belt attracts large farms that raise an ever-expanding variety of crops. A dense rainforest thrives in this wet humid condition with thick ferns, lianas, tropical cedars, and palms.

WATERWAYS OF BELIZE

Heavy rains, deluging the mountains strung across the center of Belize, feed the rivers and waterways that flow from the mountains to the sea. For decades the rivers were the highways of the country; a few are deep enough to be navigable and are still used for hauling logs. These rivers are: **Blue Creek, Rio Hondo, New River, Belize River, Sibun River, Macal Deep River, Rio Grande, Moho River, Tumex River,** and **Sarstoon River.**

THE WEATHER

The climate in Belize is subtropical with a mean annual temperature of 79° F, so you can expect a variance between 50-95° F. There are definite wet and dry seasons. The dry season generally lasts Nov.-May and the wet season June-November. **Note:** In the tropics it's not unusual to have rain in the dry season, maybe just in shorter spurts. The amount of rainfall varies widely from north to south. Corozal in the north receives 40-60 inches while Punta Gorda in the south averages 160-190 inches with an average humidity of 85%. Occasionally

buttress root

during the winter months "northers" sweep down from North America across the Gulf of Mexico, bringing rainfall, strong winds, and cooling temperatures. Usually lasting only a couple of days, they often interrupt fishing and influence the activity of lobster and other fish. Fishermen invariably report increases in their catch several days before a norther.

The "mauger" season is generally in August, when the air is still and the sea is calm; it can last for a week or more. All activity halts while locals stay indoors as much as possible to avoid the onslaught of ferocious mosquitoes and other insects.

Hurricanes

Belize is in a hurricane belt. Though this powerful phenomenon seldom occurs, Belize has had firsthand experience with three in recent history (over a period of 60 years), and since 1787, 21 hurricanes have hit the small country in varying degrees of intensity. In 1931, 2,000 people were

WEATHER INFORMATION

	JAN.	FEB.	MARCH	APRIL	MAY	JUNE
AVERAGE INCHES OF RAINFALL (BELIZE CITY)	2.98	1.45	1.68	0.04	5.41	14.01
	JULY	AUG.	SEPT.	OCT.	NOV.	DEC.
	4.59	8.18	10.41	8.40	4.58	7.0
AVERAGE INCHES OF RAINFALL (PUNTA GORDA)	JAN.	FEB.	MARCH	APRIL	MAY	JUNE
	10.32	2.51	0.09	0.28	3.74	13.13
	JULY	AUG.	SEPT.	OCT.	NOV.	DEC.
	28.67	25.38	27.32	14.50	2.60	9.10
MEAN HIGHS AND LOWS IN DEGREES FAHRENHEIT	JAN.	FEB.	MARCH	APRIL	MAY	JUNE
	82/66	83/66	85/68	87/71	87/72	85/72
	JULY	AUG.	SEPT.	OCT.	NOV.	DEC.
	85/72	87/73	85/72	84/70	82/68	81/66
HUMIDITY	JAN.	FEB.	MARCH	APRIL	MAY	JUNE
	73%	68%	67%	74%	75%	85%
	JULY	AUG.	SEPT.	OCT.	NOV.	DEC.
	82%	82%	82%	67%	75%	89%

Hurricanes may occur during the period June-Nov., but are most likely to occur in Aug. and September.

killed and Belize City was almost totally destroyed. The water rose nine feet in some areas, even onto Belize City's Swing Bridge. Though forewarned by Pan American Airlines that the hurricane was heading their way, most of the townsfolk were unconcerned, believing that their protective reef would keep massive waves away from their shores. They were wrong! The next weather devastation came with Hurricane Hattie in 1961. Winds reached a velocity of 150 mph, with gusts of 200 mph; 262 people drowned. It was after Hurricane Hattie that the capital of the country was moved from Belize City (just 18 inches above sea level) to Belmopan. Then in 1978, Hurricane Greta took a heavy toll in dollar damage, though no lives were lost.

THE SEA

Running parallel to the coast is the Belize Reef, the longest in the Western Hemisphere and fifth longest in the world. Scattered offshore and protected by the reef are more than 200 cayes and three of the Caribbean's four atolls: **Glover's Reef, Turneffe Islands,** and **Lighthouse Reef.** An atoll is a ring-shaped coral island surrounding a lagoon, always beautiful, and almost exclusively found in the South Pacific. The three types of cayes seen by the visitor vary from **wet cayes** that are submerged part of the time and can support only mangrove swamps, to **bare coral outcroppings** that are equally uninhabitable, to **sandy islands** with palm trees, jungle shrubbery, and their own set of animals. The inhabited cayes are in the north and include Caye Caulker, Ambergris Caye, St. George's Caye, and Caye Chapel.

THE REEF

The sea is a magical world. Man is just beginning to learn of the wonders that take place within its depths. Some dreamers predict that a time is coming when the world's oceans will provide humans with all the nutrients we need, and that people will live comfortably side by side with the fish in the sea. For now, men and women are content just to look at what's there, often through a small round window on a diving mask.

Coral

The Belize Reef is so extraordinarily clear that looking through your mask brings you into a world of color. The myriad hues of coral are rainbowlike: pale pinks, flashy reds, deep purples, flamboyant greens, and a multitude of colors in between.

Coral is a unique limestone formation that grows in innumerable shapes, such as delicate lace, trees with reaching branches, pleated mushrooms, stovepipes, petaled flowers, fans, domes, heads of cabbage, and stalks of broccoli. Corals are formed by millions of tiny carnivorous polyps that feed on minute organisms and

live in large colonies of flamboyantly colored individual species. These small creatures can be less than half an inch long or as large as six inches in diameter. Related to the jellyfish and sea anemone, polyps need sunlight and clear salt water not colder than 70° F to survive. Coral polyps have cylinder-shaped bodies. One end is attached to a hard surface (the bottom of the ocean, the rim of a submerged volcano, or the reef itself), and the mouth end is encircled with tiny tentacles that capture its minute prey with a deadly sting.

Coral reefs are formed when polyps attach themselves to each other. Stony coral, for example, connects with a flat sheet of tissue between the middle of both bodies. They develop their limestone skeletons by extracting calcium out of the seawater and depositing calcium carbonate around the lower half of the body. They reproduce from buds or eggs. Occasionally small buds appear on the adult polyp; when the buds mature they separate from the adult and add to the growth of existing colonies. Eggs, on the other hand, grow into tiny forms that swim away and settle on the ocean floor. When developed, these begin a new colony.

A Reef Grows

As these small creatures continue to reproduce and die, their sturdy skeletons accumulate. Over aeons, broken bits of coral, animal waste, and granules of soil all contribute to the strong foundation for a reef that will slowly rise toward the surface. To grow, a reef must have a base no more than 82 feet below the water's surface. In a healthy environment it can grow

---

LONGEST REEFS IN THE WORLD

Great Barrier Reef, Australia	1,600 km
S.W. Barrier Reef, New Caledonia	600 km
N.E. Barrier Reef, New Caledonia	540 km
Great Sea Reef, Fiji Islands	260 km
Belize Reef	250 km
S. Louisade Archipelago Reef, PNG	200 km

CORAL MEDICAL REPAIR

Medical researchers have recently discovered that sections of coral can be placed in the body where a piece of bone is missing and the body's bones readily graft themselves onto the strong coral.

one to two inches a year. One small piece of coral represents millions of polyps and many years of construction.

Reefs are divided into three types: atoll, fringing, and barrier. An **atoll** can be formed around the crater of a submerged volcano. The polyps begin building their colonies on the round edge of the crater, forming a circular coral island with a lagoon in the center. Thousands of atolls occupy the world's tropical waters. A **fringing reef** is coral living on a shallow shelf that extends outward from shore into the sea. A **barrier reef** runs parallel to the coast, with water separating it from the land. Sometimes it's actually a series of reefs with channels of water in between. This is the case with some of the larger barrier reefs in the Pacific and Indian oceans.

The Belize Reef extends from the tip of Mexico's Isla Mujeres to Sapodilla Caye in the Bay of Honduras. This 180-mile-long reef is known by various names (Belize Reef is the most common). The beauty of the reef attracts divers and snorkelers from distant parts of the world to investigate the unspoiled marinelife.

The Meaning Of Color

Most people interested in reefs already know they're in for a brilliant display of colored fish. In the fish world, color isn't only for exterior decoration. Fish change hues for a number of reasons, including anger, protection, and sexual attraction. This is still a little-known science. For example, because of their many colors, marine biologists are uncertain how many species of groupers exist—different species or different moods? A male damselfish clearly imparts his aggression and his desire for love by turning vivid blue. Some fish have as many as 12 different recognizable color patterns that they can transform into within seconds. These color changes, along with other body signals, combine to make communication simple between species. Scientists have discovered that a layer of color-bearing cells lies just beneath a fish's transparent scales. These cells contain orange, yellow, or red pigments; some contain black, others combine to make green or other hues. A crystalline tissue adds white, silver, or iridescence. Color changes when the pigmented cells are revealed, combined, or masked, creating the final result. Fish communicate in many other surprising ways, including electrical impulses and flashing bioluminescence (body light). If fish communication intrigues you, read Robert Burgess's book *Secret Languages Of the Sea* (Dodd, Mead and Company).

exploring the caves along the Macal River

OZ MALLAN

PROTECT THE MARINE HERITAGE

To ensure that the waters of Belize, particularly the reefs, remain healthy for everyone's enjoyment, please respect the following protective regulations:

1. No person shall buy, sell, export, or attempt to export black coral in any form, except under a license obtained from the Fisheries Administrator.

2. No person shall have in his possession any turtle from 1 June to 31 Aug., take any turtle found on the shores of Belize, export any turtle or articles made from turtle otherwise than under a license granted by the Minister.

3. No person shall take fish (mollusk, scale, crustacea) using scuba equipment, except under a special permit from the Fisheries Administrator.

4. No person shall take, buy, sell or have in possession crawfish, 15 March-14 July, or conch, 1 July-30 September.

5. No person shall take, buy, or sell any coral at any time.

Conservation

The Belizean government has strict laws governing the reef, to which most divers are more than willing to comply in order to preserve this natural phenomenon and its inhabitants. However, there are always a few who care only for their own desires. Recently, an American purchased Hatchett Caye; he has remodeled it and (some say) dynamited part of a nearby reef to better fit his idea of a tropical hideaway for tourists. This is still rumbling in the legal offices of Belize.

It takes hundreds of years to form large colonies of coral, so please don't break off pieces of coral for souvenirs. After a very short time out of water, the polyps lose their color and you have only a piece of chalky white coral—just like the pieces you can pick up while beachcombing. Strict fines await those who remove *anything* from the reef; spearfishing is also against the law.

FAUNA

Nature lovers will find a fantasyland in Belize. A walk through the jungle brings you up close to myriad animal and bird species many of which are almost extinct in other Central American locations—and the world. Tread softly—more than likely you won't see many of the beasties mentioned here since they're experts at hiding in trees, behind thick vines, in old logs, in hidden burrows, or just blending in with their background. But with concerted effort, a light step, and sharp eyes, you might get lucky.

HOWLER MONKEYS

In Creole the howler monkey is referred to as "baboon" and in Spanish called *saraguate,* no close connection to their African relatives. Because the howler prefers low-lying tropical rainforests under 1,000 feet elevation, Belize is a perfect habitat, boasting a healthy family of 1,300 howlers. They are more commonly found near the riverine forests, especially on the Belize River and its major branches. The howler monkey, along with its small cousin the **spider monkey,** also enjoys the foothills of the Maya Mountains. In order to protect the howler monkey, the **Bermudian Landing Community Baboon Sanctuary** was recently organized to help conserve the lands where they live. Thanks to an all-out effort involving local property owners, the **Belize Ministry of Natural Resources,** the **U.S. World Wildlife Fund,** the **Belize Audubon Society,** and the **Peace Corps,** the land that provides for the howler will be saved. The monkey lives only in Belize, southern Mexico, and parts of Guatemala. In many areas it's in danger of disappearing altogether. The sanctuary is an ideal place for researchers to study its habits and hopefully discover the key to its survival among encroaching humans. Concentrations of the howler are reasonably accessible to visitors in Belize.

The adult howler monkey is entirely black and weighs 15-25 pounds. Their most distinct trait is a roar that can be heard up to a mile distant. This unusual roar is caused by a bone in the throat that acts as an amplifier; the cry sounds much like that of a jaguar. The unforgettable bark is said by some to be used to warn other troops away from their territory. Locals, on the other hand, say the howlers roar when it's about to rain, to greet the sun, to say goodnight, or when they're feeding.

The howlers live in troops that number four to eight and no more than 10, consisting of one adult male and the rest females and young. Infants nurse for about 18 months, making the space between pregnancies about 24 months. Initially, "mom" carries her young clutched to her chest; once they're a little older, they ride piggyback. The troop sleeps, eats, and travels together. The howlers primarily eat leaves, but include flowers and fruit in their diet (when available). Highly selective, they require particular segments of certain trees and blossoms: sapodilla, hog-plum, bay cedar, fig, and buket trees.

After ecologists spent much time studying the Belizean "baboon," it became obvious that with the destruction of the riverine sections of the forest the howlers in Belize would go the way of their cousins in southern Mexico and northern Guatemala (nearly extinct). As a result, the people that live in an 18-square-mile area have joined together, voluntarily, and agreed to do or not to do certain things in order to encourage the lifestyle of the howler monkey. Thanks to the forward-thinking Bermudian Landing villagers, the **Community Baboon Sanctuary** has evolved. The villagers in this area maintain strips of forest between fields and along rivers and preserve the food trees of the baboon. The locals even put up with the monkey's occasional invasion of cashew trees. Although the baboon has a couple of natural predators—the jaguar and the harpy eagle—its worst foe is deforestation by man. An unexpected boon to the area has been the reappearance of other small animals and bird species also taking advantage of the protected area.

If you wish to visit the Community Baboon Sanctuary, contact the manager at the small interpretive museum in the village. Be aware that the trails are on private land and visitors should not infringe on private property. A trail is maintained and it's advised that all who visit have a guide for orientation. The Sanctuary employs two full-time guides. The trails are marked with

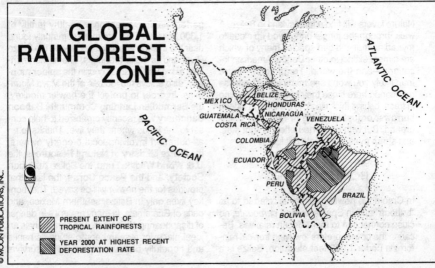

GLOBAL RAINFOREST ZONE

ATLANTIC OCEAN

PACIFIC OCEAN

MEXICO
BELIZE
HONDURAS
GUATEMALA
NICARAGUA
COSTA RICA
VENEZUELA
COLOMBIA
ECUADOR
PERU
BRAZIL
BOLIVIA

PRESENT EXTENT OF TROPICAL RAINFORESTS

YEAR 2000 AT HIGHEST RECENT DEFORESTATION RATE

© MOON PUBLICATIONS, INC.

numbered signs that correspond with information provided in a (good) book, *Community Baboon Sanctuary,* available in most gift shops or through the sanctuary. It's always a thrill to watch the bright-eyed black monkey as it sits within five feet of you on a wild-lime tree branch, happily munching the leaves. They seem to know they're protected here. Group trips and/or guides from local hotels are available (see p. 113). Ask at Bermuda Landing about locals who provide home-cooked meals and informal accommodations; in Belize City ask at the Audubon Society Office, 12 Fort St., tel. (02) 35-004, (02) 34-987; fax (02) 34-985.

CATS

Jaguars

Seven species of cats are found in North America; four are distributed tropically. The jaguar is heavy chested with sturdy, muscled forelegs, small rounded ears, and a relatively short tail. Color ranges from tan on top with white on the underside to pure black. The male can weigh 145-255 pounds, females 125-165 pounds. Largest of the cats in Central America and third-largest cat in the world, the jaguar is about the same size as a leopard. It is nocturnal, spending most daylight hours snoozing in the sun. The male marks an area of about 65 square miles and spends its nights stalking deer, peccaries, agoutis, tapirs, monkeys, and birds. If hunting is poor and times are tough, the jaguar will go into the rivers and scoop fish with its large paws. The river is also a favorite spot for the jaguar to hunt the large tapir when it comes to drink. Females begin breeding at about three years, and generally produce twin cubs.

For years the rich came to Belize on safari to hunt the jaguar for its beautiful skin. Likewise, hunting margay, puma, ocelots, and jaguarundis was a popular destructive sport in the rainforest. All of that has changed. Hunting any endangered species in Belize is not allowed. In order to preserve the cats, as well as other unique animals including the tapir, paca, and dozens of bird species, approximately 155 square miles have been designated as **Cockscomb Basin Jaguar Preserve** (see p. 210).

While much of the wildlife in the preserve is nocturnal, signs of animals are found by those that trek along the old logging tracks, or climb up into the Cockscomb Range, including the highest peak in Belize, Victoria Peak (3,675 feet). South Stann Creek and the Swasey branch of the Monkey River both flow through the preserve and are good stop-offs for a cooling swim while hiking the basin. When planning a visit go

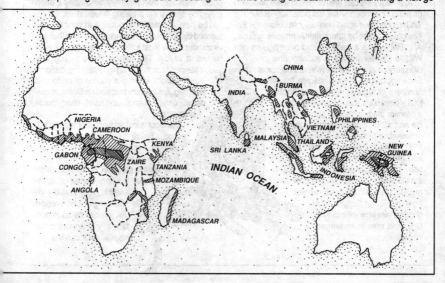

to Maya Center (a small town) first and ask about a guide, who might also take you to a minor Maya ceremonial center within the preserve. The Cockscomb Basin Jaguar Preserve can be reached from the Southern Highway, which parallels the coast between Dangriga and Placencia. Sadly, the jaguar is still illegally hunted for its skin. The animal's greatest predator is man. Hopefully by establishing Cockscomb Preserve and preserves like it, the big cat will be around for many centuries to come.

Pumas

The other cats found in Belize are the **puma, ocelot, jaguarundi,** and **margay.** The largest of these, the puma, is also known as the cougar or mountain lion. The adult male measures about 6.5 feet in length and weighs up to 198 pounds. It thrives in any environment that supports deer, porcupine, or rabbit. The puma hunts day or night.

Ocelots

The ocelot is another of nature's great works of art, with a beautiful striped and spotted coat. Average weight is around 35 pounds. A good climber, the cat hunts in trees as well as on the ground. Its prey includes birds, monkeys, snakes, rabbits, young deer, and fish. Ocelots usually have litters of two but can have as many as four.

Margays

The smallest of the Belizean cats is the margay, usually weighing in at around 11 pounds and marked by a velvety coat with exotic designs, beautifully patterned eyes, and a bushy tail. A shy animal, it is seldom seen in open country, preferring the protection of the forest. It hunts mainly in the trees, satisfied with birds, monkeys, and insects as well as lizards and figs.

JAGUARS 1, HUNTERS 0

Jaguars, the biggest predators in the new world, need lots of space to roam. So it's ironic that Belize, a country so small it would fit into the hip pocket of Texas, claims to have the greatest concentration of jaguars on earth.

Apparently the cats are hanging in there and even growing in numbers. After the possibility of hunting the big cats once again was brought before the Belize government by international hunting groups, Alan Rabinowitz, a leading authority on jaguars with Wildlife Conservation International (the foreign service arm of the New York Zoological Society), helped them to decide that the numbers of jaguars were not enough to justify hunting. It was Rabinowitz who did a premier study a decade ago on the big cat and at that time encouraged the government to protect the animals. Since 1981, hunting jaguars has been banned and thousands of acres of forest have been set aside for the big cat; 102,000 in the Cockscomb Basin Wildlife Sanctuary. Jaguars, which once ranged from the Grand Canyon to Argentina, are now extinct in the U.S. and rare or endangered elsewhere.

Changes in the countryside have made the jaguar more popular, such as a decline in cattle ranching. Pastures have been replaced by citrus orchards, and fruit is now the country's number two export, after sugar. For jaguars at least, citrus farmers make better neighbors than ranchers, who have a deep prejudice against the prowling meat-eaters.

The new appreciation, pride, and concern expressed by Belizeans about their wildlife and their environment is the most striking change that has occurred in Belize. The image of the jaguar has changed from that of a night-stalking, dangerous, livestock killer to a source of pride and awe. Jaguars are now featured on Belizean currency, postage stamps, and nearly every tourist brochure.

The most vocal advocates of jaguar protection in Belize are people involved in the country's escalating tourism business. Rabinowitz strongly advises the government to maintain its moratorium on jaguar hunting. His report is reassuring and sees the increasing public support for jaguars as an important ally in ensuring the majestic cat's survival.

BOB RACE

Jaguarundis

Larger and not nearly so catlike as the margay, this black or brown feline has a small flattened head, rounded ears, short legs, and a long tail. They hunt by day for birds and small mammals in the rainforests of Central America.

OTHER MAMMALS

Peccaries

Next to deer, peccaries are the most widely hunted game in Central America. Other names for this piglike creature are musk hog and javelina. Some compare these nocturnal mammals to the wild pigs found in Europe, though, in fact, they are native to America.

Two species found in Belize are the collared and the white-lipped peccary. The feisty collared peccary stands one foot at the shoulder and can be three feet long, weighing as much as 65 pounds. It is black and white with a narrow semi-circular collar of white hair on the shoulders. In Spanish *javelina* means "spear," descriptive of the two spearlike tusks that protrude from its mouth. This more familiar peccary is found in deserts, woodlands, and rainforests, and travels in groups of 5-15.

Also with tusks, the white-lipped peccary is reddish-brown to black and has an area of white around the mouth. This larger animal, which can grow to four feet long, is found deep in tropical rainforests and at one time lived in herds of 100 or more.

Tapirs

The national animal of Belize, the South American tapir is found from the southern part of Mexico to southern Brazil. It is stout-bodied, with short legs, a short tail, small eyes, and rounded ears. Its nose and upper lip extend into a short but very mobile proboscis. Totally herbivorous, tapirs usually live near streams or rivers in the forest. They bathe daily and also use the water as an escape when hunted either by man or by its prime predator, the jaguar. Shy, unaggressive animals, they are nocturnal with a definite home range, wearing a path between the jungle and their feeding area. The tapir is said to have bad eyesight and if attacked, it lowers its head and blindly crashes off through the forest; they've been known to collide with trees and knock themselves out in their chaotic attempt to flee! "April the Tapir" is a star attraction at the Belize Zoo. A birthday celebration is held for her each year to the delight of hundreds of Belizean schoolchildren. April gets her vegetarian "cake," and the children get the real thing as well as a good visit with the national animal. Many people attend the party that doubles as a popular fundraiser to help support the zoo.

SNAKES

Snakes roam the Belize jungles and plains. The much-maligned animal is shunned by most humans, and in some cases that's a wise move. Belize has six poisonous snakes that I know of. Many others are harmless, and anyone who will be wandering in the bush should try to learn the difference. Pick up the Audubon Society's booklet, *Snakes Of Belize.* It's full of good information from herpetologist Dora Weyer, and detailed drawings by Ellen McRae, who lives in Caye Caulker.

Coral Snakes

Coral snakes are found only in the New World, mostly Central and South America, with a few in the southern U.S. In all there about 50 species. The coral snakes found in Belize average about 31 inches long. The true coral is highly poisonous and a bite is usually fatal. The harmless false coral is also found in the country. Its body is slender, with no pronounced distinction between head and neck. Here in Belize the true coral snake is banded in a red-yellow-black-yellow-red sequence (this is not the case in other countries). If you don't know for sure, don't approach a banded snake with those colors. Remember, red means stop! One jingle says: "Red and yellow kill a fellow; red and black, a friendly Jack." Usually nocturnal, coral snakes spend the day in mossy clumps under rocks or logs.

They don't look for trouble and seldom strike, but will bite if stepped on; their short fangs, however, can be stopped by shoes or clothing. Even though the locals call this the "20-minute snake" (meaning if you are bitten and don't get antivenin within 20 minutes, you'll die), it's actually more like a 24-hour period. It's mostly children who are reportedly bitten.

Chances of the average tourist being bitten by a coral (or any other snake) are slim. However, if you plan on extensive jungle exploration, check with your doctor before you leave home. Antivenin is available, doesn't require refrigeration, and keeps indefinitely. It's wise to be prepared for an allergic reaction to the antivenin—bring an antihistamine and Adrenalin. The most important thing to remember if bitten: *don't panic and don't run.* Physical exertion and panic cause the venom to travel through your body much faster. Lie down and stay calm; have someone carry you to a doctor (see "Simple First-aid Guide").

Fer-de-lance
Another treacherous Belize snake is the fer-de-lance, called a yellow-jawed tommygoff, a nocturnal pit viper that comes from the same family as the cascabel (tropical rattler), water moccasin, and the jumping viper. The fer-de-lance can be found anyplace: in thick jungle, savanna grass, or out in the open chasing prey. This nasty specimen will grow to be 8.5 feet long. It comes from litters of up to 75, and until it reaches adolescence it sports a prehensile tail and can and will swing and jump from any tree. As it matures it comes to the ground and pretty well stays there. It attacks with two fangs from either a coiled or extended position and will attack more than once if given the opportunity. The adult has an arrow-shaped head, is thickset, and its dorsal coloring ranges from dark brown to olive to gray to red. It has 30 paired triangles along its sides, lighter in color and edged in black, which form a row of dark diamonds the length of the snake's back. The underside is cream or yellow beneath the jaw to the throat. The mouth is large and contains two hollow, retractable fangs, larger in proportion to its size than any other snake's. Its venom is highly poisonous and should be treated immediately. Carrying a **Cutters Snake Bite Kit** is a possible last-ditch effort when there's nothing else, but be advised that most doctors discourage cutting the wound. Do not use a tourniquet and do not ingest alcoholic beverages. If you ask advice from a rural local about where to go if bitten, he/she might suggest a snake doctor who is little more than a healer. However, there are those Belizeans who say, "Do not *ever* go to a snake doctor!" In a desperate situation you must make a choice.

For more information *Poisonous Snakes Of The World* is available from the Superintendent of Documents, U.S. Government Printing Office, Washington D.C.

LIZARDS

You'll see a great variety of lizards, from a skinny two-inch miniature gecko to a chameleon-like black anole that changes colors to match the environment, either when danger is imminent or as subterfuge to fool the insects it preys upon. At mating time, the male anole puffs out its bright red throat fan to make sure all female lizards will see it. Some lizards seen are brightly striped in various shades of green and yellow; others are marked with earthy colors that blend with the gray and beige limestone dotting the landscape. Skinny as wisps of thread running on hind legs or chunky and waddling with armorlike skin, the variety is endless—and fascinating! And don't forget the entertaining Jesus Christ lizard, who runs along the surface of water.

Iguana
One species found all over Central America—lizards of the family Iguanidae—includes various large plant-eaters, typically dark in color. They come in many sizes with slight variations in color. The young iguana is bright emerald green. This common lizard grows to three feet long, has a blunt head and long flat tail. Bands of black and gray circle its body, and a serrated column reaches down the middle of its back, almost to its tail. During mating season it's common to see brilliant bright orange males on a sunny branch hoping to attract a girlfriend.

Very large and shy, the lizard uses its forelimbs to hold the front half of its body up off the ground while the two back limbs remain relaxed and splayed alongside its hindquarters. However, when the iguana is frightened, its hind legs do everything they're supposed to, and the iguana crashes quickly (though clumsily) into the brush searching for its burrow and safety. This reptile is not aggressive, but if cornered will bite and use its tail in self-defense. The iguana mostly enjoys basking in the bright sunshine along the

Caribbean. Though they are herbivores, the young also eat insects and larvae. Certain varieties in some areas of southern Mexico and Central America are almost hunted out—for example, the spiny-tailed iguana in the central valley of Chiapas, Mexico. A moderate number are still found in the rocky foothill slopes and thorn-scrub woodlands. It is not unusual to see locals along dirt paths carrying sturdy specimens by the tail to put in the cook pot.

From centuries past, recorded references attest to the medicinal value of this lizard, partly explaining the active trade of live iguanas in the marketplaces of some parts of Belize. Iguana stew is believed to cure or relieve various human ailments, such as impotence. Caught before the nesting season, unlaid eggs are considered a delicacy. Another reason for their popularity at the market is their delicate white flesh, which tastes much like chicken. If someone says they're having "bamboo chicken" for dinner, know that they are dining on iguana.

Several other species of iguana are seen in Belize, from the small to a gargantuan six feet long. Their habits are much the same, however. They all enjoy basking in the sun, sleeping in an old hollow tree at night, and eating certain tender plants. The female can lay up to a hundred eggs, and when they emerge from the rubbery egg skin they scoot about quickly, pale green or tan in color. One of the iguana's serious predators is the hawk. If the iguana sights a winged shadow while sunbathing on a high tree limb, it flings itself from the tree either into a river below or the brush, skittering quickly into hiding. However, man remains its most dangerous predator.

BATS

Honduran White Bats

A sight that most people will never see is the two-inch Honduran white bat. It lives only in the jungles of Central America. It's actually a cuddly looking little creature, white and furry with pink ears and nose. Like most bats, they feed at night on the local fruit trees found in the jungle or in a farmer's back yard. During the day, they sleep in groups of 2-15 in a "tent" they fashion by biting through the veins of a *heliconia* leaf (much

like a large banana leaf) near the midrib until the sides droop. The result is a tent where they cluster under the midrib while hanging upside down by their feet. The drooping leaf protects them from the sun and rain as they sleep. The leaf also creates a perfect camouflage against predators. During the day the bright sunlight filters through the leaf, bathing the bats' fur in green hues. The green tone makes it hard for enemies, such as monkeys and snakes, to spot the bats.

MANATEES

Probably the most unusual mammal, the manatee is an elephantine creature of immense proportions with gentle manners and the curiosity of a kitten. Though today seldom seen, this enormous animal, often referred to as the sea cow, at one time roamed the shallow inlets, bays, and estuaries of the Caribbean in large numbers. The manatee is said to be the basis of myths and old seamen's references to mermaids. In South America this particular mammal is revered by certain indigenous tribes. The Maya hunted the manatee for its flesh, and its image is frequently seen in ancient Maya art. In modern times, the population has been reduced by the encroachment of large numbers of people in the manatees' habitats along the riverways and shorelines. Ever-growing numbers of motor boats inflict often deadly gashes on the nosy creatures.

At birth the manatee weighs 60-70 pounds; it can grow up to 13 feet long and weigh more than a ton. Gray with a pinkish cast and shaped like an Idaho potato, it has a spatulate tail, two forelimbs with toenails, pebbled coarse skin, tiny sunken eyes, numerous fine-bristled hairs scattered sparsely over its body, and a permanent Mona Lisa smile. The head of the mammal seems small for its gargantuan body, and its preproboscidean lineage includes dugongs (in Australia), hydrax, and elephants. The manatee's truncated snout and prehensile lips help to push food into its mouth. As the only aquatic mammal that exists solely on vegetation, the manatee grazes on bottom-growing grasses and other aquatic plantlife. It ingests as much as 495 pounds per day, cleaning rivers of oxygen-choking growth. It is unique among mammals in that it constantly grows new teeth—worn teeth fall out and are replaced. Posing no threat to any other living thing, it has been hunted for its oil, skin, and flesh, which is said to be tasty.

The mammal thrives in shallow warm water and has been reported (infrequently, however) in shallow Belize bays. One recent spring evening in the bay in front of the Adventure Inn at Consejo Shores in Belize, a curious manatee spent about an hour lazily swimming the cove, lifting its truncated snout, and often its entire head, out of the water about every four minutes. The few people (this author included) who were standing on a small dock in the bay were thrilled to see the shy animal. They are around, just keep looking. Belize reportedly has the largest population of manatees in the world, except perhaps for the Florida Sanctuary in the United States.

In neighboring Guatemala, the government is sponsoring a manatee reserve in Lago de Izabal. In the U.S. the mammal is found mostly at

MANATEE BREEDING PROGRAM

The state of Florida, under the auspices of the Miami Seaquarium and Dr. Jesse White, has begun a captive-breeding program hoping to learn more about the habits of the manatee and to try to increase the declining numbers. Several manatees have been born in captivity; they along with others that have recuperated from injury or illness will be or have been released into Florida's Crystal River where boat traffic is restricted. They are tagged and closely observed. Florida maintains a 24-hour hotline for people to report manatees in néed of help for any reason. Rescues can include removing an adult male from a cramped storm drain or rushing to the seaquarium newborns that somehow managed to get separated from their mothers and have washed ashore. These newborns are readily accepted by surrogate-mother manatees and are offered nourishment (by way of a thumb-sized teat under the front flipper) and lots of TLC. Medical aid is given to mammals that have been slashed by boat propellers as a result of cruising boats. The manatee has a playful curiosity and investigates anything found in its underwater environment, many times sustaining grave damage.

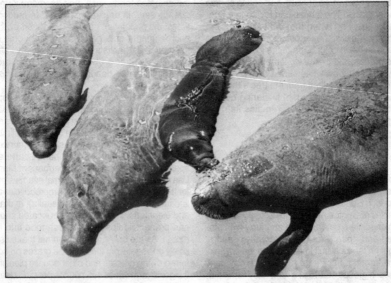

OZ MALLAN

inshore and estuarine areas of Florida. It is protected under the Federal U.S. Marine Mammal Protection Act of 1972, the Endangered Species Act of 1973, and the Florida Manatee Sanctuary Act of 1978. It is estimated that their total population numbers about 2,000.

BIRDS OF BELIZE

motmot

LOUISE FOOTE

Since a major part of Belize is still undeveloped and covered with trees and brush, it isn't surprising to find exotic, rarely seen birds across the landscape. The Belizeans are beginning to realize the great value in this (almost) undiscovered treasure trove of nature (attracting both scientists and laymen) and are making rapid progress in protecting natural habitats. The birds in Belize have until recent years been free of pest sprays, smog, and encroaching human beings. If you're a serious birdwatcher, you know all about Belize. Change is coming as more people intrude into the rangeland of the birds, exploring these still undeveloped tracts in the wilderness areas of Belize. Still, there are more birds to watch here than in almost any other location in Central America.

Belize, with its marsh-rimmed shores and lakes, nearby cornfields, and tall, humid forest, is worth a couple of days to the ornithologist. One of the more impressive birds to look for is the spectacularly hued keel-billed toucan. This is the national bird of Belize and is often seen perched high on a bare limb in the early hours of the morning. Others include chachalacas (held in reverence by the Maya cult), screeching parrots, and occasionally, the oscellated turkey. A good book that zeros in on the birds and animals of Belize is called, *Jungle Walk, Birds And Beasts of Belize,* by Katie Stephens. No color, but along with sketches of the creatures, she

gives good down-to-earth descriptions of their habits. The book is available through International Expeditions, US$4.95 plus tax, postage, and handling; to order call (800) 633-4734. At the Audubon Society Office in Belize City at 29 Regent St., pick up a copy of the *Checklist of the Birds of Belize,* by Wood, Leberman, and Weyer, published by the Carnegie Museum of Natural History, Pittsburgh, Pennsylvania. Another excellent bird book that deals with the *entire* Yucatán Peninsula is *Common Birds of the Yucatán Peninsula,* with full-color photos, written by Barbara MacKinnon. It's available through Amigos de Sian Ka'an (Apto Postal 770, Cancun, Quintana Roo 77500, Mexico).

Jabiru Stork
The largest flying bird in the Americas is the jabiru stork, which grows four to five feet tall and has a wing span of 9-12 feet. Though few in number in the rest of the Western Hemisphere, Belize boasts a healthy community of breeding storks. Building the nest is a major construction job. The brooding nest is generally built on a high tree in an open area above the rainforest; a favorite spot is in the Crooked Tree Wildlife Sanctuary. The cumbersome birds weave a platform from large branches measuring as much as 10 feet across. The hatchlings (two to four) are an indiscriminate gray color that eventually changes into the adult coloration of black beak, white body and black head, with a bright red band below the neck. Occasionally seen in a farmer's field, from a distance it looks like a bent old man wearing a red tie. The birds feed in and around swamps and ponds, preferring snails, frogs, small mammals, fish, and especially reptiles.

Sooty Terns
The sooty tern is not the only seabird that lacks waterproof feathers, but it is the only one that will not land and rest on passing ships or drifting debris. The bird feeds on tiny fish and squid that swim close to the surface of the sea. While hovering close to the water they snatch their unsuspecting prey. The birds nest April-Sept., and if left undisturbed, a colony can raise 150-200 chicks in a summer. Man is the sooty tern's only predator. If frightened the parent birds panic, leaving the eggs exposed to the hot

BIRDS OF BELIZE

Marsh Birds
white ibis
roseate spoonbill

Wading Birds
American flamingo

Water Birds
fulvous tree-duck
black-bellied tree-duck
white-fronted goose

Lowland Birds
rufous-tailed hummingbird
violaceous trogon
blue-crowned motmot
keel-billed toucan
golden-olive woodpecker
barred antshrike
masked tityra
boat-billed flycatcher
social flycatcher
kisadee flycatcher
olivaceous flycatcher
white-tipped brown jay
spotted-breasted wren
clay-colored robin
singing blackbird
yellow-throated euphonia
blue tanager
crimson-collared tanager
black-headed saltator

Birds In The Dense Forest
little tinamou
jabiru stork
spotted wood-quail
short-billed pigeon
white-fronted dove
ruddy quail dove
white-bellied emerald
collared trogon
violaceous trogon
keel-billed toucan
acorn woodpecker
golden-olive woodpecker
lineated woodpecker
brown woodpecker
flint-billed woodpecker
olivaceous creeper

sulphur-bellied flycatcher
green jay
spotted-breasted wren
lowland wood-wren
white-throated robin
gray-headed vireo
golden-crowned warbler
red-crowned tanager
black-faced grosbeak

Birds At Beaches, Bays, And Adjacent Ocean
brown pelican
magnificent frigate bird
black vulture
spotted sandpiper
laughing gull
black tern
least tern
sooty tern
royal tern

Birds Seen At Lagoons, Tidal Flats, Shallow Estuaries, And Mangrove Swamps
olivaceous cormorant
magnificent frigate bird
great blue heron
little blue heron
reddish egret
common egret
snowy egret
Louisiana heron
yellow-crowned night heron
American widgeon
black vulture
American coot
jacana
killdeer
spotted sandpiper
laughing gull
royal tern
mangrove swallow
mangrove warbler
great-tailed grackle

Birds Seen In Villages And Overgrown Fields
black vulture
common ground-dove

ruddy ground-dove
groove-billed ani
Vaux's swift
tropical house wren
tropical mockingbird
clay-colored robin
singing blackbird
gray saltator

Birds Seen At Partially Cleared Archaeological Sites, Woodland Edge, Or Scrubby, Deciduous Woodland
plain chachalaca
white-winged dove
common ground-dove
ruddy ground-dove
white-fronted dove
Aztec parakeet
groove-billed ani
ferruginous pygmy owl
lesser nighthawk
pauraque
golden-fronted woodpecker
laughing creeper
rose-throated coptinga
masked tityra
tropical kingbird
boat-billed flycatcher
social flycatcher
olivaceous flycatcher
yellow-billed elaenia
cave swallow
Yucatán jay
white-browed wren
spotted-breasted wren
white-bellied wren
blue-gray gnatcatcher
white-lored gnatcatcher
peppershrike
mangrove vireo
red-eyed cowbird
altamira oriole
hooded oriole
black-headed saltator
gray saltator
blue-black grassquit

tropical sun, or knocking the young out of the nest where they cannot fend for themselves.

Quetzals

Though the ancient Maya made abundant use of the dazzling quetzal feathers for ceremonial costume and headdress, they hunted other fowl in much larger quantities for food; nonetheless, the quetzal is the only known bird from the pre-Columbian era and it is almost extinct. Though the colorful bird is not found in Belize, we mention it because birdwatchers continuing on into Guatemala or Costa Rica will want to visit their habitats. The Guatemala government has established a quetzal sanctuary not too far from the city of Coban. The beautifully designed reserve is open to hikers, with several miles of good trails leading up into the cloud forest. For the birder this could be a worthwhile detour to search out the gorgeous quetzal. The Coban tourist office, INGUAT, hands out an informative leaflet with a map and description of the quetzal sanctuary. If in Costa Rica, take a trip into the Monteverde Cloud Forest Reserve for a possible glimpse of these shy, beautiful birds.

The Acorn Woodpecker

This bright little creature lives an ingenious lifestyle. It's most well known for storing its supper in individual holes burrowed into tree trunks, allowing the nut to dry out without fermenting. As part of a "commune," the male birds share the breeding females who then lay their eggs in a communal nest. The young hang around the nest for several years "helping out at home" before leaving to raise their own families. The woodpecker has black and white feathers with a red patch on the top of its head.

Marshy Havens

Estuaries play host to hundreds of bird species. A boat ride into one of them will give you an opportunity to see a great variety. The lakes of Belize (such as those at Crooked Tree) are wintering spots for many flocks of North American duck species. Among others, you'll see the blue-winged teal, northern shoveler, and lesser scaup, along with a variety of wading birds feeding in the shallow waters, including numerous types of heron, snowy egret, and (in the summer) white ibis. On a recent trip to Crooked Tree, we

quetzals

BOB RACE

watched a peregrine falcon hunt. First it slowly circled high above the lake watching its prey and then plunged to attack a flock of American coots. Seconds before the falcon reached the ducks they spotted it and began squawking loudly, warning the whole family and diving into the water (where the falcon will not follow). After watching the falcon dive for the ducks over and over again, we moved on in our boat, but at that point the score was ducks "8," falcon "0."

INSECTS AND ARACHNIDS

Any tropical jungle has literally tens of thousands of insects. Some are annoying (mosquitoes and gnats), some are dangerous (black widows, bird spiders, botflies, and scorpions), and others can cause pain when they bite (red ants). Many, however, are beautiful (butterflies and moths), and *all* are fascinating studies in evolved socialization and specialization.

Fireflies

The poor firefly is really a misnomer. It's not a fly and it surely has no fire. Quite the contrary, it's a beetle that turns on a glow on the underside of its abdomen when nature's cycle brings together certain chemicals. When you see a tree in the forest literally *aglow* with tiny flashing lights, you know that it's mating season. Both males and females locate each other by flashing an on/off pattern special to their genus. However, sometimes in a hunger frenzy, females fool the mates of other species by imitating their flashing pattern and when the poor love-struck male approaches, she eats him! Even in the larval stage, the young can glow, perhaps to scare away predators. Occasionally fireflies eat each other, but most other jungle predators, like birds, toads, and others searching for supper, stay away from them because the chemicals in their body taste sooooo bad.

Butterflies And Moths
Belize has an abundance of beautiful moths and butterflies. Of the 90,000 types of butterflies in the world, a large percentage are seen here (see "Shipstern Wildlife Reserve and Butterfly Farm," p. 166). You'll see, among others, the magnificent blue morpho, orange-barred sulphur, copperhead, cloudless sulphur, malachite, admiral, calico, ruddy dagger-wing, tropical buckeye, and emperor. The famous monarch is also a visitor during its annual migration from the Florida peninsula to the Central American mountains and Mexican highlands where it spends the winter. Trying to photograph a but-

---

DIFFERENCES BETWEEN MOTHS AND BUTTERFLIES

1. Butterflies fly during the day; moths fly at dusk and during the night as well.

2. Butterflies rest with their wings folded straight up over their bodies; most moths rest with their wings spread flat open.

3. All butterflies have bare knobs at the ends of both antennae (feelers); moths' antennae are either plumy or hairlike and end in a point.

4. Butterflies have slender bodies; moths are plump. Both insects are of the order Lepidoptera—lepidopterists bring your nets!

---

terfly (live) is a testy business. Just when you have it in your cross hairs, the comely critter flutters off to another spot!

FLORA

Belize is a Garden of Eden. Four thousand species of native flowering plants include 250 species of orchids and approximately 700 species of native trees. It is one of the few countries where thousands of acres of forest are still in a semi-pristine condition. The country is divided into several ecological life zones: subtropical moist, subtropical lower Montane moist, subtropical lower Montane wet, subtropical wet, tropical moist-transition to subtropical, and tropical wet-transition to subtropical. A botanist can recognize the life zones by the type of natural vegetation that occurs. The determining factor of these zones is the amount of rain that falls. Even the common mangrove grows differently depending on which life zone it is in. Those trees in the subtropical moist forest along the northern coast are shorter than those growing in the wetter zones in the south. The tallest mangroves occur in the tropical wet forest-transition to subtropical in the southern Toledo district.

Rainforests Of Belize
Most of the country's rainforests have been logged off and on for more than 300 years. The areas closest to the rivers and coast were the

hardest hit because boats could be docked and logs loaded and taken farther out to sea to the large ships used to haul the precious timber. For years small patches were burned for use as *milpas* (cornfields) by the Maya. Today, the government is trying to educate the people about the advantages of using other farming methods. However, it will take a long time to break a tradition that goes back millennia.

Flying over the countryside gives you a view of the patchwork landscape of cleared areas and secondary growth. Belize consists of four distinct forest communities: pine-oak, mixed broadleaf, riverine, and cohune palm forests. Pine ridge forests are found in sandy dry soils. Also in these soils large numbers of mango, cashew, and coconut palms are grown near homes and villages. The mixed broadleaf forest is a transition area between the sandy pine soils and the clay soils found along the river. Often the mixed broadleaf forest is broken up here and there and doesn't reach great height; it's species-rich but not as diverse as the cohune forest. The cohune forest area is characterized by the cohune palm and is found in fertile clay soil where a moderate amount of rain falls

EMERGENT TREE LAYER
HARPY EAGLE
MORPHO BUTTERFLY
SWALLOWTAIL HUMMINGBIRD

CANOPY LAYER
SCARLOT MACAW
THREE TOED SLOTH
HOWLER MONKEY
EMERALD TREE BOA
CHESTNUT-MANDIBLED TOUCAN

MIDDLE LAYER
QUETZAL
WOOLLY OPOSSUM
OCELOT

SHRUB LAYER
SPOT-BACKED ANTBIRD
HELICONIUS BUTTERFLY
LEAF-CUTTING ANT

GROUND LAYER
TAPIR
JAGUAR
CORAL SNAKE

BOB RACE

throughout the year. The cohune nut was an important part of the Mayan diet. Archaeologists have a saying: when they see a cohune forest they know they'll find evidence of the Maya.

The cohune forest gives way to the riverine forest along river shorelines, where vast amounts of water are found year-round both from excessive rain and from the flooding rivers. About 50-60 tree varieties and hundreds of species of vines, epiphytes, and shrubs grow here. Logwood, mahogany, cedar, and pine are difficult to find along the easily accessible rivers, due to the extensive logging activity. The forest is in different stages of growth and ages. To find virgin forest it's necessary to go high into the mountains that divide Belize. Because of the rugged terrain, lack of roads, and distance from the rivers, these areas were left almost untouched. Even in the 1990s few roads exist. If left undisturbed for many, many years, the forest will eventually regenerate itself.

Among the plantlife of Belize look for mangroves, bamboo, and swamp cypresses, as well as ferns, vines, and flowers creeping from tree to tree, creating a dense growth. On topmost limbs, orchids and air ferns reach for the sun. As you go farther south you'll find the classic tropical rainforest, including tall mahoganies, *campeche*, *sapote,* and *kapok,* thick with vines.

Palms

A wide variety of palm trees and their relatives grow in Belize: short, fruited, even oil producers. Though similar, various palms have distinct characteristics. Royal palms are tall with smooth trunks. Queen palms are often used for landscaping and bear a sweet fruit. Thatch palms are called *chit* by the Maya; the frond of this tree is used extensively for roof thatch. Coconut palms serve the Belizeans well. One of the 10 most useful trees in the world, it produces oil, food, drink, and shelter. The tree matures in six to seven years and then for five to seven years bears coconuts, a nutritious food also used for copra (dried coconut meat that yields coconut oil) and valued as a money crop by the locals.

From Fruit To Flowers

Central America grows delicious sweet and sour oranges, limes, and grapefruit. Avocado is abundant, and the papaya tree is practically a

Cohune nuts look like miniature coconuts. They're rich in oil and the shells make perfect fuel for cooking.

OZ MALLAN

weed. The *sapote* (mammey) tree grows tall (50-65 feet) and full, providing not only welcome shade but also an avocado-shaped fruit with brown fiber on the outside and a vivid salmon pink flesh that makes a sweet snack (the flavor is similar to a sweet yam). It also produces chicle, the sap formerly used for chewing gum. Another unusual fruit tree is the *guaya* (part of the litchi nut family). This rangy evergreen thrives on sea air and is commonly seen along the coast and throughout Belize. Its small, green, leathery pods grow in clumps like grapes and contain a sweet, yellowish, jellylike flesh—tasty! The calabash tree, a friend to the indigenous people for many years, provides a gourd used for containers.

The tall ceiba is a very special tree to those close to the Maya religious cult. Considered the tree of life, even today it remains undisturbed whether it has sprouted in the middle of a fertile Maya *milpa* (cornfield) or anywhere else. When visiting in the summer, *flamboy-anes* (royal poinciana) are everywhere. As its name implies, when in bloom it is the most flamboyant tree around, with wide-spreading branches covered in clusters of brilliant orange-red flowers. These trees line sidewalks and plazas and when clustered together present a dazzling show.

Orchids

While traveling through remote areas of Belize one of the more exotic blooms, the orchid, is often found on the highest limbs of tall trees. Of the 71 species reported in Belize, 20% are terrestrial and 80% are epiphytic, attached to a host plant (in this case trees) and deriving its moisture and nutrients from the air and rain. Both species grow in many sizes and shapes: tiny buttons, spanning the length of a long branch, large-petaled blossoms with ruffled edges, or intense, tiger-striped miniatures. The lovely flowers come in a wide variety of colors, some subtle, some brilliant. The black orchid is Belize's national flower. All orchids are protected by strict laws, so look but don't pick.

Nature's Hothouse

In spring, flowering trees are a beautiful sight—and sound—attracting hundreds of singing birds throughout the mating season. While wandering through the jungle landscapes you'll see, thriving in the wild, a gamut of plants we so carefully nurture and coax to survive in a pot on a windowsill at home. Here in its natural environment, the croton exhibits wild colors, the pothos grows one-foot-long leaves, and the philodendron splits every leaf in gargantuan glory.

White and red ginger are among the more exotic herbs that grow in Belize. Plumeria (called frangipani in the South Pacific) has a wonderful fragrance and is seen in many colors. Hibiscus and bougainvillea bloom in an array of bright hues. A walk through the jungle will introduce you to many delicate strangers in the world of tropical flowers. But you'll find old friends, too, such as the common morning glory, creeping and climbing for miles over bushes and trees. You'll notice viny coils that thicken daily. Keeping jungle growth away from the roads, utility poles, and wires is a constant job because warm humid air and ample rainfall encourage a lush green wonderland.

EXOTIC FRUITS AND NUTS OF BELIZE

Tamarind

An edible pod about an inch in width and three to eight inches in length, the tamarind is reminiscent of a dark-colored string bean. The pulp around and between the two to six seeds is brown and can be 11% acidic, though as much as 20% sugar. Used in cold drinks, preserves, and chutneys, it is 3.3% protein, high in minerals, and an excellent source of vitamin B. You see stacks of them in public markets and children enjoy them straight from the tree, a healthy snack said to be as high in food value as maize or wheat.

Cacao

Considered a stimulant plant along with coffee, the cacao bean is used to make chocolate products including the world's favorite candy. The pods are yellow to greenish in color and look like a type of squash hanging from the tree. If you split the pod you'll find a series of 10-20 seeds surrounded by a white creamy flesh that makes a tasty drink. Children enjoy the seeds fresh from the tree though they must be dried and roasted before they acquire the familiar chocolate flavor that Americans know and love.

Bananas

Bananas come in a variety of shapes and sizes, from the tiny **lady finger** variety that grows in hands of about 75 to the giant **Cavendish**, a plantain used for cooking that produces hands with about 15 fruits. The lady finger grows four to six inches long and weighs about two ounces—they have a wonderful refreshing flavor. Most of the production in Belize is of the large market-size variety. The time from blossom to ripe fruit stage may be as short as 75 days. When the stalk of bananas is harvested, the top of the tree is whacked off and the leaves are dispersed around the base, where a new shoot grows; within eight months it will bear another stem of bananas. The continuous cycle repeats itself for seven years before the entire tree must be replaced.

Pineapple

Tropical fruits have some peculiar family traits. The pineapple, for example, is a bromeliad, which is usually an epiphyte (meaning that it lives on trees and gets its nutrients from what floats around in the breeze). However, a few bromeliads grow on the ground—the pineapple is one of the most famous. Each stem flowers only once and dies after fruiting. But nature in its constant battle to keep going sends up another side shoot that takes over. The plant grows to about three feet tall and the size of the fruit ranges from small (about six to seven inches tall) to the large hybrids (as tall as 12-15 inches). A sweet fruit that personifies the tropics, the pineapple is a favorite all over the world.

The *Sapote*

Also known as the mammey fruit, it grows on a tall tree which for hundreds of years has been a sacred tree to the Maya. Historians say this was the fruit that kept Cortés and his army alive on their march from Mexico City to Honduras. The oval fruit is three to six inches long and covered with a brown fibrous skin. The flesh is a beautiful salmon pink and surrounds an avocado-like seed. The "taste" of the fruit must be "acquired" by most outsiders. The texture is somewhat like a sweet potato, and the flavor reminds *me* of a chestnut—but taste is in the tongue of the taster. It is used in a thick jam called *crema de mamey colorado*, while the seed's commercial value becomes greater when roasted and mixed with cacao in making chocolate.

The Cashew Nut

The amazing diversity among tropical botanical relatives continues to confuse many people. For instance, did you know that the mango is a relative of the cashew nut? Actually, the family comprises some 400 species in about 60 genera around the world, but mostly in the warm-weather countries. It is said that the cashew tree furnishes food and remedies to the poor, provides a refreshing beverage to the sick, a sweetmeat for tables of the affluent, and good timber and resin for industrial use. The cashew tree is a large, spreading evergreen that grows up to 40 feet in height, often with crooked trunk and branches. The fruit is bizarre: The fleshy fruit portion is called the cashew apple; the nut (the true fruit) is a kidney-shaped bean that hangs from the bottom of the

BOB RACE / 3

"apple." It is about an inch long and covered with a thick shell. The shell contains acid substances that severely burn the skin at the touch. The cashew is roasted and then peeled to reveal a white kernel of delicate flavor. The cashew apple is a soft fleshy fruit that gives a zesty juice. It is made into jam and a wonderfully flavorful wine.

BOB RACE / 2

The Sapodilla Fruit

The sapodilla tree at one time was highly prized for its milky latex, which was used for many years in the production of chewing gum. It bears a fruit prized by the locals from southern Mexico, Central America, and northern South America. Fruits grow two to three inches in diameter, the skin is rough to the touch and brown in color, and the flesh is yellowish brown, granular, and very sweet. Unless it is well ripened, granules stick to the teeth and feel like chewing gum. This is another "taste" that must "grow" on you.

The Passion Fruit

The name and the flower of the passion fruit may be more familiar to people than the actual fruit. Again this beautiful purple-flowered fruit has several unlikely relatives: papaya, pumpkin, and melon. Actually there are both purple and yellow passion fruit. Both have high acidic content and are generally used for juice. Many people grow the tree strictly as an ornament because of its colorful, unusual flowers.

HISTORY

THE ANCIENTS

Earliest Man

During the Pleistocene Epoch, when the level of the sea fell (around 50,000 B.C.), people and animals from Asia crossed the Bering land bridge into the American continent. For nearly 50,000 years man continued his epic trek southward. It is believed that the first people reached Tierra del Fuego, at the tip of South America, in approximately 1000 B.C.

As early as 10,000 B.C., Ice Age man hunted woolly mammoth and other large animals roaming the cool, moist landscape of Central America. Between 7000 and 2000 B.C., society evolved from hunters and gatherers to farmers. Such crops as corn, squash, and beans were independently domesticated in widely separated areas of Mesoamerica after about 6000 B.C. The remains of clay figurines from the pre-Classic period, presumed to be fertility symbols, marked the rise of religion in Mesoamerica, beginning around 2000 B.C.

Around 1000 B.C. the Olmec culture, believed to be the earliest, began to spread throughout Mesoamerica. The large-scale ceremonial centers grew along Gulf Coast lands, and much of Mesoamerica was influenced by the Olmecs' often sinister religion of worshipping strange jaguarlike gods. They also developed the New World's first calendar and an early system of writing.

Classic Period

The Classic period, beginning about A.D. 300, is now hailed as the peak of cultural development among the Maya. Until A.D. 900, phenomenal progress was made in the development of artistic, architectural, and astronomical skills. Impressive buildings were constructed during this period, and codices (folded bark books) were written and filled with hieroglyphic symbols that detailed complicated mathematical calculations of days, months, and years. Only the priests and the privileged held this knowledge, and continued to learn and develop it until, for some unexplained reason, there was a sudden halt to this growth.

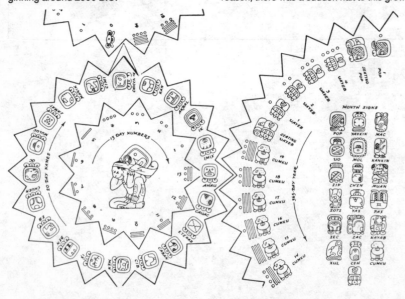

Post-Classic
The end of the most artistic era occurred around A.D. 900 and resulted in the birth of a new militaristic society built around a blend of ceremonialism, civic and social organization, and conquest.

COLONIAL HISTORY

Hernán Cortés
Following Columbus's arrival in the New World, other adventurers traveling the same seas soon found the Yucatán Peninsula. In 1519, 34-year-old Hernán Cortés sailed from Cuba against the authority of the Spanish governor. With 11 ships, 120 sailors, and 550 soldiers he set out to search for slaves, a lucrative business with or without the blessings of the government. His search began on the Yucatán coast and would eventually encompass most of Mexico. However, he hadn't counted on the ferocious resistance and cunning of the Maya. The fighting was destined to continue for many years—a time of bloodshed and death for many of his men. This "war" didn't *really* end on the Peninsula until the Chan Santa Cruz people finally made peace with the Mexican federal government in 1935, more than 400 years later.

Hernán Cortés

Although the Maya in Mérida were a long distance from Belize and not directly bothered by the intrusion of the Spanish, the actions of the Spanish Franciscan priests toward the local Maya would have a great influence on Belize in the years that followed. Ceremonies and all other traces of the Maya cult were being wiped out by Catholic priests, further setting the stage for the bloodshed to come. The ripple effect that followed eventually exploded into the Caste War that, in turn, brought both Maya and mestizos across the borders of Belize.

Diego de Landa was the Franciscan priest who, while trying to gather the Maya into the fold of Christianity, leaned on them and their beliefs with a heavy hand, destroying thousands of Maya idols, many of their temples, and all but four of their books. Because his methods were often cruel, in 1563 he was called back to Spain after colonial civil and religious leaders accused him of "despotic mismanagement." He spent a year in prison, and while his fate was being decided, he wrote a book, *Relaciones de las Cosas de Yucatán,* in defense of the charges. This book gave extensive information about the Maya, their beliefs, the growth and preparation of their food, the structure of their society, the priesthood, and the sciences—essentially a broad insight into the culture that otherwise would have been lost forever. Fortunately, he included in his book a one-line formula that, when used as a mathematical and chronological key, opened up the science of Maya calculations and their great knowledge of astronomy. De Landa returned to the Yucatán Peninsula and lived out his remaining years, continuing his previous methods of proselytizing until his death in 1579.

Catholicism
Over the years, the majority of Maya were indeed baptized into the Catholic faith. Most priests did their best to educate the people, teach them to read and write, and protect them from the growing number of Spanish settlers who used them as slaves. The Maya practiced Catholicism in their own manner, combining

their ancient cult beliefs, handed down throughout the centuries, with Christian doctrine. These mystic yet Christian ceremonies are still performed in baptism, courtship, marriage, illness, farming, house building, and fiestas.

Further Subjugation

While all of Mesoamerica dealt with the problems of economic colonialism, the Yucatán Peninsula had an additional problem: harassment by vicious pirates who made life in the coastal areas unstable. British pirates found the Spanish ships to be great floating treasures from South America, and the bays of Belize were perfect hiding places to lie in wait. Around 1600, when silver production began to wane, the pirates were being put out of business. In other parts of the Yucatán Peninsula the passive people were ground down, their lands taken away, and their numbers greatly reduced by the white man's epidemics and mistreatment.

Caste War

It was inevitable that the Maya would eventually erupt in a furious attack. This bloody uprising in the 1840s was called the Caste War. Though the Maya were farmers, and for the most part, not soldiers, this savage war saw them taking revenge on every white man, woman, and child by means of rape and murder. When the winds of war reversed themselves and the Maya were on the losing side, vengeance on them was merciless. Any Maya, regardless of his beliefs, was killed immediately when encountered by some. Some were taken prisoner and sold to Cuba as slaves; others left their villages and hid in the jungles, in some cases for decades. Between 1846-50 the population of the Yucatán Peninsula was reduced from 500,000 to 300,000. Guerrilla warfare ensued, with the escaped Maya making repeated sneak attacks upon the whites. Quintana Roo, adjacent to Belize along the Caribbean coast, was considered a dangerous no-man's land for more than a hundred years until in 1974, with the promise of tourism, the territory was admitted to the Federation of States of Mexico.

Growing Maya Power

Many of the Maya who escaped slaughter during the Caste War fled to the isolated jungles of Quintana Roo and Belize. The Maya revived the cult of the "talking cross," a pre-Columbian oracle representing gods of the four cardinal directions. This was a religious/political marriage. Three determined survivors of the Caste War— a priest, a master spy, and a ventriloquist—all wise leaders, knew their people's desperate need for divine leadership. As a result of the cult's leadership and advice from the talking cross, the shattered people came together in large numbers and began to organize. The community guarded the location of the cross and its advice made the Maya strong once again.

They called themselves Chan Santa Cruz ("People of the Little Holy Cross"). As their confidence developed so did the growth and power of their communities. Living very close to the Belize (then British Honduras) border, they found they had something their neighbors wanted. The Chan Santa Cruz Maya began selling timber to the British and in return received arms, giving the Maya even more power. During these years of strife, many Maya, mestizos, and Mexicans turned to northern Belize as a new home. Mestizos built small communities, raised corn and vegetables, spoke Spanish, and pretty well lived as they had in Mexico. This was the beginning of the Mexican tradition in Belize, locally referred to as "Spanish tradition." The food is typically Mexican with tortillas, black beans, tamales, squash, and plantain (a type of banana that can be cooked). For many years these mestizos kept to themselves and were independent of Belize City. The colonial administration kept their distance, and the laws were made and kept by a community-appointed headman. Both Hispanic and non-Hispanic Belizeans who live in the northern area speak Spanish. Today, all the towns and cities of Belize come under the jurisdiction of the central Belizean government.

Maya And Spanish

The pre-Columbian history of Belize is closely associated with all of its nearby neighbors: Mexico, Guatemala, and Honduras. The Maya were the first people to inhabit the land referred to as **La Ruta Maya.** They planted corn *milpas,* built ceremonial centers, and established villages with large numbers of people throughout the region.

Cortés passed through the southern part of the country on his trek northward searching for treasure. In 1530 the conquistador Montejo attacked the Nachankan and Belize Maya, but his attempt to conquer them failed. This introduction of Spanish influence did not make the impact on Belize that it did in the northern part of the Caribbean coast until the Caste War.

Pirates

British buccaneers sailed the coast, attacking the Spanish fleet at every opportunity. These ships were known to carry unimaginable riches of gold and silver from the New World back to the king of Spain. The Belizean coast became a convenient place for pirates to hole up during bad weather or for a good drinking bout. And, though no one planned it as a permanent layover, by 1650 the coast had the beginnings of a British pirate lair/settlement. As pirating slacked off on the high seas, British buccaneers discovered they could use their ships to carry logwood back to a ready market in England. These early settlers were nicknamed the Baymen.

In the meantime, the Spanish desperately tried to maintain control of this vast New World they had grasped from across the ocean. But it was a difficult task and brutal conflicts continually flared between the Spanish and either the British inhabitants or the Maya. The British Baymen were continually run out but always returned. Treaties were signed and then rescinded. However, the British relentlessly made inroads into the country, importing slaves from Africa beginning in the 1720s to laboriously thrash through the jungles and cut the timber—work that the fiercely independent Maya resisted with their lives.

In 1763 Spain "officially" agreed to let the British cut logwood. The decree allowed roads (along the then designated frontiers) to be built in the future though definite boundaries were to be agreed upon later. For nearly 150 years the only "roads" built were narrow tracks to the rivers, which became Belize's major highways. Boats were common transport along the coast and somehow road building was postponed, leaving boundaries vaguely defined and countrymen on both sides of the border unsure. This was the important bit of history that later encouraged the Spanish-influenced Guatemalans to believe strongly that Belize, failing to carry out the 1763 agreement, was their turf. Even after Spain vacated Guatemala, Guatemalans tried for generations to assume ownership across the existing Belize borders. Since 1988, however, the boundary disagreement *appears* to have blown over with the Guatemalan threat of a takeover stopping on their side of the frontier. But because no official agreements have been made, most believe this conflict is still unresolved.

Treaty Of Paris

Politically, Belize (or, more to the point, its timber) was up for grabs, and a series of treaties did little to calm the ping-pong effect between the British and the Spanish over the years. One such agreement, the Treaty of Paris, did little to control the Baymen—or the Spanish. With license, British plantation owners continued to divest the forests of logs, leaving Belize with nothing more than a legacy of brutality and tyrannical control over the slaves (who worked under cruel conditions while making rich men of their masters). The Spanish continued to claim sovereignty over the land but never settled in Belize. Efforts to take over continued with Spain sporadically harassing and attacking the Baymen—only to fail each time when the British returned and held on to their settlement.

The Baymen held on with only limited rights to the area until the final skirmish in 1798 on a

BELIZE HISTORY IN A NUTSHELL

The peaceful country of Belize is a sovereign democratic state of Central America located on the Caribbean. The government is patterned on the system of parliamentary democracy and experiences no more political turmoil than any other governments such as Great Britain or the United States.

Important Dates

1862	Became a British colony
1954	Attained universal adult suffrage
1964	Began self-government
1981	Attained full independence

small caye just offshore of Belize City. Courageous Baymen, with the help of an armed sloop and three companies of a West Indian regiment, won the battle of St. George's Caye on 10 Sept., ending the Spanish claim to Belize once and for all. After that battle Belize was ruled by the British Crown until gaining its independence in 1981.

Over the first 400 years after Europeans arrived, nothing much was done to develop the country, not even roads or railroads, and you can count on one hand how many historic buildings are standing (few were ever built). Maya structures don't count—they were here before the British and will be here for many years to come.

Land Rights
In 1807, slavery was *officially* abolished in Belize by England. This was not agreeable to the powerful British landowners though, and in many quarters it continued to flourish. Changes were then made to accommodate the will of the powerful. The local government no longer *gave* land to settlers as it had for years, as the British law now permitted former slaves and other "coloureds" to hold title. The easiest way to keep them from possessing the land was to charge for it—essentially barring the majority in the country from landownership.

The Sugar Industry
Between 1847 and 1850, during the Caste War in neighboring Yucatán, thousands of Maya and mestizo refugees who were fleeing the Spaniards entered Belize. It was the Yucatecans who introduced the Latin culture, the Catholic religion, and agriculture. Though most refugees ultimately returned to their homes in Mexico, some stayed on and began farming the land. This was the first real attempt at much-needed agriculture. Large tracts that had been cleared of trees were empty, and rich landowners were willing to rent acreage (cheaply) to the refugees for farming. Until then almost all foodstuffs had been imported from other countries (and to this day it's not unusual to see many tinned foods from Australia, England, and the States on market shelves).

The mestizos settled mostly in the northern sections of the country, which is apparent by

WHAT'S IN A NAME?

No one knows for sure where the name of Belize originated or what it means. The country was called Belize long before the British took the country over and renamed it British Honduras. In 1973, the locals changed it back to the original Belize as a first step on the road to independence. There are several well-known theories for its meaning. Some say it's a corruption of the name Wallis (pronounced wahl-EEZ), from the pirate (Peter Wallace) who roamed the high seas centuries ago and visited Belize. Others suggest that it's a distortion of the Maya word *belix* which means muddy river. Still others say it could be a further distortion of the Maya word *belikin* (which is also the name of the local beer). And of course it could be another of those mysterious Maya secrets we may never learn.

the names of the cities: Corozal, San Estevan, San Pedro, and Punta Consejo. By 1857, the immigrants were growing enough sugar to supply Belize, with enough left over to export the surplus (along with rum) to Britain. After their success proved to the tree barons that sugarcane could be lucrative, the big landowners became involved. Even in today's world of low-priced sugar, the industry is still important to Belize's economy.

Timber
For 300 years Belize was plundered and neglected—and not just by swashbuckling pirates and hard-living buccaneers. Its forests were denuded of valuable logwood (the heart of which provided rich dyes for Europe's growing textile industry until manmade dyes were developed). When the demand for logwood ceased, plantation owners found a viable substitute for their logging interests—removing mahogany trees from thick virgin forests. For three centuries the local economy depended on exported logs and imported food.

In a 1984 Audubon Society report, it was noted that despite the widespread use of slash-and-burn farming by the Maya a millennium ago, and the more recent selective logging of logwood and mahogany since the 16th century,

Belize still has extensive forests. The large-scale abandonment of farms with the decline of the Maya civilization around A.D. 900 permitted forest regeneration that has attained what plant ecologists consider to be "climax" status. The removal of only logwood had little effect on the forest structure. It's in today's economy that logging can cause serious damage to the forest with the indiscriminate removal of large tracts of trees, no matter the variety, because of modern methods and high-tech equipment.

Independence
In 1862 Belize received the official title of Colony of British Honduras, though it had been ruled by the British crown since 1798. The average Belizean had few rights and a very low living standard. Political unrest grew in a stifled atmosphere. Even when a contingent of Belizean soldiers traveled to Europe to fight for the British in WW I, the black men were scorned. But when these men returned from abroad, the pot of change began to boil. Over the next 50 years, the country struggled through power plays, another world war, and economic crises. But always the seed was there—a growing desire to be independent. The colonial system had been falling apart around the world, and when India gained its freedom in 1947 the pattern was set; many small undeveloped countries soon began to gain their independence and started relying on their own ingenuity to build an economy that would benefit the people.

Belize was dominated by outside influences until Sept. 1981 when it gained its independence from the British Crown. But change comes slowly. This third-world country is learning through hard knocks how to be self-sustaining, self-motivated, self-governing—noncolonial. In the process of finding methods to become financially independent and raising the standard of living, Belizean leaders are discovering that the country's natural assets may indeed hold the key to bringing in dollars in the form of tourism, an industry never before dreamed of. The government is proceeding slowly to design the proper tourist growth to fit into their scheme to preserve the ethnic cultures, the animals, the reef, and the forests. Belize is becoming a role model for other developing countries that need tourism dollars but are not willing to sacrifice their culture and natural resources. In Sept. 1981 the Belizean flag was raised—the birth of a new era! Belize joined the United Nations, the Commonwealth, and the Non-Aligned Movement. Their work is cut out for them.

ECONOMY

One of the exciting aspects of a developing country is watching how the people's creative genius can turn them into entrepreneurs. The U.S. is a great example of this and a good role model for countries just putting their toes into the sea of world commerce. Belize has been independent since 1981, and after a few false starts is beginning to see the *start* of a glowing future. The *Belize Investment Code* states, "Foreign investment is welcome as long as it creates jobs and expands Belizean talent and skills; infuses foreign financial resources and good managerial skills into Belize; produces for export markets; utilizes indigenous raw materials; and engages in environmentally sound projects which make technological advances and increase the capital stock of the nation." Developing and improving the country's infrastructure promises big changes. For example, the government is working on providing electricity to outlying villages, promising that by the end of 1994, 98% of the Belizean population will have power.

However, some critics in the country say Belize should take a hard look at what's going on. These locals are questioning how much of the country they are willing to give away to enter mainstream economics. An editorial in the local paper, *Amandala,* put it succinctly:

What we poor Belizeans have to consider is just exactly what all are we prepared to sell in order to achieve so-called "development." We've been poor for centuries in this country, and while none of us are prepared to sell our mother, we have been selling our motherland. We may not be prepared to sell our children, but we have no problem selling our children's future. We may not think we are selling our souls, but some of us are certainly selling our bodies.

We argue, when we sell our assets, that we have to get into this development race now, but when a nation sells resources which are non-renewable, then it is giving up some of its sovereignty for money—speculative money.

Certainly these are words to ponder for any developing country.

Income

Tourism is gradually heading to the top of the list of money-makers in the country. Both local and outside investors are catching on and the Belizean government is helping by giving tax concessions to legitimate businesses, not just gold-plated Wall Street names. A few Americans who have taken the plunge into the bureaucracy describe a moderate amount of paperwork involved such as establishing residency and obtaining work permits. Although it can take time, it isn't so difficult that it discourages potential investors.

Industry

The economy of Belize was traditionally based on logwood, mahogany, and chicle export. Today's economic growth is finding tourism along with agriculture, fisheries, and small manufactured goods giving the country an important boost. The main exports are sugar, citrus, bananas, lobster, and timber. Thanks to tax concessions given foreign investors, Belize has experienced a diversification of manufacturing industries, such as plywood, veneer manufacturing, matches, beer, rum, soft drinks, furniture, boat building, and battery assembly.

Recently, the **Belize Bank** began offering US$ accounts for their international business corporations. This has been a big factor in attracting foreign investors.

Fishing

Belize has maintained a viable fishing industry. For years Belize fishing co-ops have been exporting rock and spiny lobster to the U.S. At first it was almost a giveaway, but as the fishermen began working together through co-ops, prices have risen and fishermen manage to make a good living. In recent years fishing has been controlled to prevent the "fish-out" of the lobster by closing the season March-July and limiting the size of the lobsters. The main export markets for scale fish are the United States, Mexico, and Jamaica. With the help of Canadian government agencies, Belizean fishermen are trained in many fields of the fishing industry. They are learning modern processing techniques, navigation, and marine engineering.

Mariculture And Aquiculture
Mariculture is a new activity in Belize, still in the pilot stage. Shrimp are being harvested near the Monkey River with two species of shrimp introduced from Ecuador. Another shrimp farm is being developed near Quashie Trap Lagoon in southern Belize District. Another farm in its beginning stages will introduce the American lobster on Turneffe Islands to Caribbean waters in an attempt to stimulate faster growth. At Turneffe Islands' Northern Bogue, the spiny lobster is

OZ MALLAN

bananas

being raised in enclosed submerged pens. Many new "fish-growing" industries are also in the planning stages for Belize. The newest is a shrimp hatchery to be located at Mile 5 on the Western Highway. Taiwan will be providing facilities to rear post larvae (baby shrimps) so that Belize will not be so dependent on imported larvae, a system that has kept the growth of the shrimp industry in slow mode. The Taiwanese will assist in developing the process while training Belizean Fishing Department personnel.

Sugarcane
Another Belize export is sugarcane. Mestizos originally planted sugar in large tracts of land that were left empty after loggers had removed the trees. Within 10 years Belize produced enough sugar to take care of its needs, with a surplus that allowed for exporting and making rum. Sugar has continued throughout the years as the primary money-maker for the country, despite low sugar prices in recent years. England was for years the major export/import partner for Belize. Although Belize exports to other countries, England is still an active importer for Belize, along with the United States.

Bananas
One of the attractive new investments is establishing banana plantations in Belize's southern coastal region; so far the land costs are reasonable. Limestone soil (washed down from the nearby mountains), a warm climate, and an annual rainfall of 130 inches make the area perfect for growing bananas.

Citrus Fruit
Stann Creek offers excellent conditions for raising citrus fruit, first introduced into the country in the early 1920s. Nine hundred grafted trees were imported from Florida and with a great deal of TLC tending them, they won blue ribbons at agricultural shows in England from 1928-1931. But as much as the Europeans were impressed with Belizean oranges, freight costs made shipping the whole fruit impossible and they had to be content with the juice.

Over the years, despite hurricanes that have flattened the trees and fluctuating prices, a combination of external events has given the Belizean citrus industry a big boost. In 1983

This cow dines on tasty water plants during the dry season.

OZ MALLAN

President Reagan removed taxes from Caribbean-grown citrus. Soon after, severe frosts damaged and limited fruit production in Florida and Texas, followed by a canker disease on Florida citrus that dealt another blow for the U.S. citrus industry. This enabled Belize to get a toehold in trading, and it has been climbing ever since.

Cattle

Not too many years ago, beef was either not available, tough and stringy (and therefore "cooked to tenderness"), or "cooked to death" for health reasons. The average Belizean family just didn't put beef on the table much. Beef growing was a depressed business. Most Belizeans grew up eating canned meat, fried chicken, and seafood, and that was just fine. However, a new breed of cattlemen came along (mostly from the U.S.), and showed the locals how cattle should be "rustled." After a lot of hard work, the quality improved and the word was out—hamburgers are good! Government support of the industry has helped. And ranchers are learning the secrets of ranching in Belize. Pastures of higher-protein grasses are being established that can support and fatten one animal per acre for one year. Next time you're in a restaurant in Belize, compliment the chef, or rather the rancher—order a tender, high-quality beefsteak raised in Belize.

The Little Guy Lives

Hot Stuff! That's the best way to describe **Melinda's** hot sauce, one of Belize's newest products. This is a gourmet chile pepper sauce that has found its way from the kitchen of Marie Sharp to restaurants and homes in Belize, and fifteen states in the U.S. including Hawaii. The sauce is made from the notorious *habanero* pepper grown only on the Yucatán Peninsula, primarily in Belize. Pepper lovers the world over agree the *habanero Capsicum chinense* is the hottest pepper known to man. Marie and Jerry Sharp grow their own on their 400-acre plantation in the Maya Mountain foothills just outside Dangriga in southern Belize.

In 1983, Marie planted five acres of peppers. After bringing along a healthy crop she was offered a ridiculous US$.50 a gallon for the peppers. She refused to give her peppers away and began experimenting with recipes to make a hot sauce. After some time she came up with the perfect recipe that includes onions and carrots, pureed raw *habaneros,* lime juice, vinegar, garlic, and salt. With ingredients like that, how could it miss? To get the bright red color she wanted, it was necessary to use only specially cultivated all-red peppers.

After a lot of hard work, including several packaging and marketing classes in the U.S., the label "Melinda's. Proud Product of Belize" is enjoying deserved fame. Originally found only in specialty shops, such as Marshall Fields, and supermarket chains, such as Jewel's, Melinda's sauce should now be more widely available in the United States.

Marie is now working on her delicious fruit jams and spreads, all made of pure, natural ingredients, including fruits raised in the sweet earth of Belize. And, yes, she had to move out of the family kitchen.

THE PEOPLE

THE MAYA

The indigenous people, the Maya, inhabited the area that is now Guatemala, El Salvador, southern Mexico, Honduras, and Belize. Scientists believe that at one time the Maya, the first settlers in what is now called Belize, numbered about a million. The earliest known community in the Maya world was at Cuello, in Belize's Orange Walk District, dating back to 2000 B.C. Here they were pottery makers and farmers. A few of the most powerful Maya ceremonial centers have been uncovered at Altun Ha, Lubaantun, Caracol, and Xunantunich (zoo-nahn-too-NEECH).

The Maya Mystery

For hundreds of years, modern scholars of the world have asked, "What happened to the Maya people?" We know that many Maya descendants survive today, but not the intelligentsia. However, their magnificent structures, built with such advanced skill, still stand. Many carvings, unique statues, and even a few colored frescoes remain. All of this art depicts a world of intelligent human beings living in a well-organized, complex society. It's apparent that their trade and agricultural methods supported the population for many centuries. They used intensive systems of farming by terracing foothill slopes and constructing raised beds in valley bottoms where soil fertility could be enriched by trapping alluvial deposits and adding organic supplements. Scholars agree Mayans were the most advanced of all ancient Mesoamerican cultures. Yet all signs point to an abrupt work stoppage. After around A.D. 900, no buildings were constructed and no stelae, which carefully detailed names and dates to inform future generations of their roots, were erected. So what happened?

Anthropologists and historians do know that perhaps as many as 500,000 Maya were killed by such diseases as smallpox after the arrival of the Spaniards into the New World. But no one really knows for sure what halted the progress of the Maya culture.

A Society Collapses

Priests and noblemen, the guardians of religion, science, and the arts, conducted their ritual ceremonies and studies in the large stone pyramids and platforms found today in ruins throughout the jungle. Consequently, more specific questions arise: What happened to the priests and noblemen? Why were the centers abandoned? What happened to the knowledge of the intelligentsia? They studied the skies, wrote the books, and designed the pyramids. Theories abound. Some speculate about a revolution of the people or decentralization with the arrival of outside influences. Others suggest the people tired of subservience and were no longer willing to farm the land to provide food, clothing, and support for the priests and nobles. Whatever happened, it's clear that the special knowledge concerning astronomy, hieroglyphics, and architecture was not passed on to Maya descendants. Sociologists who have lived with the indigenous people in isolated villages are convinced that this privileged information is not known by today's Maya. Why did the masses disperse, leaving once-sacred stone cities unused and ignored? It's possible that lengthy periods of drought, famine, and epidemic caused the people to leave their once-glorious sacred centers. No longer important in day-to-day life, these structures were ignored for a thousand years and faced the whimsy of nature and its corroding elements.

The Maya question may never be answered with authority. One non-conforming theory suggests that these stone cities were built by people from outer space. Another considers the possibility that today's Maya are no relation to the people who built the structures, made near-perfect astronomical observations, and discovered infinity a thousand years ago.

Modern Maya

Although the Spanish were never successful in annihilating the Maya in Latin America, they destroyed many communities. The Maya wisely left the coastal areas (where most of the outsiders were) and lived deep in the jungle interior of Belize. That, together with the influx of Maya during the Caste War, created a fairly good-sized population of Maya in the country. More recent comers are Guatemala Maya escaping brutal treatment from the upper class. These people make up a large part of the hill areas of the Cayo, Toledo, and Stann Creek districts.

Modern Times

With today's technology, astronauts have seen many wonders from outer space, spotting overgrown structures within the thick uninhabited jungle of La Ruta Maya. These large treasures of knowledge are just waiting to be reopened. But until the funds and plans are in hand, these mounds are left unsung and untouched in hopes that looters will not find them before archaeologists are able to open them up. Looters generally are not interested in the knowledge gained from an artifact; they're primarily interested in the dollars. Not only has much been lost in these criminal actions, but also their heavy-handed methods have destroyed countless artifacts. As new finds are made, the history of the Maya develops new depth and breadth. Archaeologists, ethnologists, art historians, and linguists continue to unravel the ongoing mystery with constant new discoveries of temples and artifacts, each with a story to tell.

Physical Characteristics Of The Maya

Maya men average just over five feet tall, women just under five feet. Muscular bodied, they have straight black hair, round heads, broad faces with pronounced cheekbones, aquiline noses, almond-shaped dark eyes, and eyelids with the epicanthic or Mongolian fold (a prolongation of a fold of the upper eyelid over the inner angle or both angles of the eye).

Stylized Beauty

Bishop Diego de Landa writes in his *Relaciones* that when the Spanish arrived, the Maya still practiced the ancient method of flattening a newborn's head with a press made of boards. By pressing the infant's forehead, the fronto-nasal portion of the face was pushed forward, as can be seen in carvings and other human depictions from the pre-Columbian period; this was considered a very important sign of beauty. Further, they dangled a bead in front of a baby's eyes to encourage cross-eyedness, another Maya beauty mark. Dental mutilation was practiced by filing the teeth to give them different shapes or by making slight perforations and inlaying pyrite, jade, or turquoise. Tattooing and scarification were accomplished by lightly cutting a design into the skin and purposely infecting it, creating a scar of beauty. Adult noblemen often wore a nosepiece to give the illusion of an even longer nose sweeping back into the long flat forehead.

The Maya Bloodline

Isolation of the indigenous people kept the Maya bloodline pure. The resemblance of today's Maya to the people of a thousand years ago is thus understandable, but still amazing! Three distinct Maya groups are found in Belize. Though the languages of these groups are related, they are different enough from each other that even if you know one dialect it's still difficult to understand another dialect. The locals call the Mopan and Yucatecs by the term Maya, and separate the Kekchi as a non-Maya group, although they, too, are Maya. Together the three groups make up about 12% of the entire population of the country. The Maya settlements are found in southwest Toledo, the upper Belize River Valley, and northwest Corozal/northern Orange Walk districts. These villages have a south-to-north pattern of Kekchi-Mopan-Yucatec. The Kekchi migrated from Guatemala to work on sugar plantations. The Yucatec, who have had the most contact with mestizos, have experienced the biggest changes in their culture. A good example is Yo Creek in the Orange Walk District. Once an all-Maya agricultural village, Spanish is the first language and more Yucatecs than ever now work for wages outside the village.

POLYGLOT

Although the first settlers, outlawed pirates, did most of their own logging, it was the second wave of settlers—the British—that changed the face of the landscape now known as Belize. Cheap labor was needed to do the grueling timber work in thick, tall jungles. They failed to force it on the maverick Maya, so slaves were brought from Africa, indentured laborers from India, and Caribs from distant Caribbean islands, as was common in the early 16th and 17th centuries. The Caribs, much like the Maya, were a detached group and never really gave in to slaving in the sugar fields. Much later between 1958-62, a group of Mennonites (originally from 16th-century Switzerland) came looking for religious freedom and began a fine dairy and agricultural tradition. This assortment of nationalities eventually created a handsome group of people of multicolored skin and hair. Although English is the official language, a mixture of Spanish, African dialects, Carib, and English has become a patois called Creole that's pleasant to the ear, though it takes heavy-duty listening to understand. Most of the population of Belize is black-skinned Afro-Creole.

Creoles

The people who call themselves "Creoles" make up 60% of the population of Belize today. All Creoles share two distinctive traits: a degree of African ancestry and the use of the local English-Creole dialect. Skin color runs from very dark to very light, but European ancestry is usually apparent. Most Creoles believe themselves to be "true Belizeans" because their ancestors are thought to have been among the first settlers. This may not have been the case, however. Aside from the claims by resident Amerindians and European Baymen to first occupancy, many Creoles are descended from the immigrants who entered the country years after the Garifuna, Maya, East Indians, and Ladinos. Slaves were traded among the British colonials until slavery was abolished in 1833.

The center of Creole territory is Belize City, and half of the ethnic Creoles comprise more than three-fourths of the city's population. Rural Creoles are located along the highway between Belmopan and San Ignacio, in isolated clusters in northern Belize District, and in a few coastal spots to the south—Gales Point, Mullins River, Mango Creek, Placencia, and Monkey River Town.

Ladinos

Spanish-speaking Belizeans, descended from Amerindians and Europeans, normally are labeled "mestizos." While the term is appropriate in a racial connotation, Ladino better describes the cultural attributes of Mexican and Central American immigrants who have given up the distinct culture of their ancient ancestors. Once the predominant population (following immigration from the Yucatecan Caste War), Ladinos are now the second most populous ethnic group of Belize. They occupy the old "Mexican-Mestizo corridor" that runs along New River between Corozal and Orange Walk. In west central Belize—Benque Viejo and San Ignacio—indigenous people from Guatemala have recently added to the earlier Spanish-speaking immigrants from Yucatán.

The Caribs

The Caribs came to the Caribbean islands around 1300 from South America. These warlike tribes lived mainly in the Amazon River Valley and Guiana lowlands, and it's said the fierce warriors ate their victims. They were experts in building and navigating large plank dugouts, as well as prolific trappers, farmers, and fishermen (they fished with poison darts.) Being wanderers they moved from island to island every couple of years. In the 17th century, Africans who had escaped from slavery intermarried within the Carib groups who lived on the Windward Islands in the east Caribbean. The resulting group of people is called the Garinagu or Garifuna. There are no pure-blooded Caribs left in Belize.

Garifuna

The Garifuna (also called Garinagu) inherited the independent bloodlines of their ancestors and strongly resisted control by the Europeans. However, their arrows were no match for colonial guns, and they were ultimately defeated by the Spanish. In 1796 about 5,000 Garifuna were forced to the Bay Islands off the coast of

*Garifuna drummers,
an important part
of any Garifuna
celebration*

OZ MALLAN

Honduras. Over the years they migrated to the coastal areas of Honduras, Nicaragua, Guatemala, and southern Belize. A small Garifuna settlement grew in Stann Creek, where they fished and farmed. They began bringing fresh produce to Belize City, but were not welcome to stay for more than 48 hours without getting a special permit—the Baymen wanted the produce but didn't want these independent thinkers around the city, fearing they'd help slaves escape or perhaps cause a loss of the tight control the Baymen maintained. They tried to keep them separated from the people of Belize City by any means possible. Rumors were spread about their religious beliefs—that they were devil worshippers and baby eaters. They did have their exotic and often ritualistic ceremonies—some still do—but the dancing and singing weren't always as evil as these manipulating politicians would have one believe. (A certain amount of prejudice and fear still exists today.) The Garifuna tried many times to become part of the Public Meeting (the British governing system), but were effectively refused until November 19, 1832, when they were allowed to join the community. That event, **Garifuna Settlement Day,** continues to be a major national celebration and holiday each year.

Immigrants From India

From 1844-1917, under British colonialism, 41,600 East Indians were brought to British colonies in the Caribbean as indentured workers.

They agreed to work for a given length of time for one "master." After that they could either return to India or stay on and work freely. Unfortunately, the time spent in Belize was not as lucrative as they were led to believe it would be. In some cases they owed so much money to the company store (where they received half their wages in trade and not nearly enough to live on) that they were then forced to "re-enlist" for a longer period. Most of the workers were on sugar plantations in the Toledo and Corozal districts, and many of the East Indian men were assigned to work as local police in Belize City. In a town aptly named Calcutta many of the population today are descendants of the original indentured East Indians. Forest Home near Punta Gorda also has a large settlement. About 47% of the ethnic group live in these two locations. The East Indians have large families and live on small farms with orchards adjacent to their homes. A few trade in pigs and dry goods in ma-and-pa businesses. East Indians normally speak Creole and Spanish. Apparently, no one descended from the original immigrants speaks Hindi. A small number of Hindi-speaking East Indian merchants live in Belize City and Orange Walk Town, but they are fairly new to the country and have no cultural ties with the descendants of earlier immigrants.

The Mennonites

German-speaking Mennonites are the most recent group to enter Belize on a large scale. This very different group of Protestant settlers from the Swiss Alps has wandered over the years to northern Germany, southern Russia, Pennsylvania, and Canada in the early 1800s, and northern Mexico following WW I. For some reason the quiet, staid Mennonites disturbed local governments in these other countries, and restrictions on their isolated agrarian lifestyle have caused a nomadic past. Most of Belize's Mennonites first migrated from Mexico from 1958-62. A few came from Peace River in Canada. They purchased large blocks of land (about 148,000 acres) and began to dig in their roots. Shipyard (in Orange Walk District) was settled by a conservative wing, Spanish Lookout (in Cayo District) and Blue Creek (in Orange Walk District) were settled by more progressive members. In hopes of averting future problems with the government, Mennonites and Belize officials made agreements that guarantee freedom to practice their religion, use their language in locally controlled schools, organize their own financial institutions, and to be exempt from military service. Over the 30-plus years that Mennonites have been in Belize, they have slowly merged into Belizean activities. Although they practice complete separation of church and state (and do not vote), their innovations in agricultural production and marketing have advanced the entire country. Mennonite farmers are probably the most productive in Belize; they commonly pool their resources to make large purchases such as equipment, machinery, and supplies. Their fine dairy industry is the best in the country, and they supply the domestic market with eggs, poultry, fresh milk, cheese, and vegetables.

Rastafarians

Some Johnny-come-latelies are Jamaican Rastafarians. Primarily these people live in Belize City, but a few have made homes in Caye Caulker and other parts of the country. Rastafarians are part of a religion that believes in the eventual redemption of blacks and their return to Africa. They are easily recognizable by their dreadlocks—uncombed and uncut long mats of hair (although not all dreadlock wearers are true Rastas). Their beliefs, according to the biblical laws of the Nazarites, forbid the cutting of their hair. Rastafarians use ganja (marijuana) in their rituals (which gets them in trouble in the wrong neighborhoods) and venerate Haile Selassie I, late emperor of Ethiopia, as their god. Selassie's precoronation name was Ras Tafari Makonnen, hence the name (Ras is simply an honorific title). He allegedly descended from King Solomon and the Queen of Sheba.

LITERACY

At one time only the children of the elite were able to attend school. The Belizeans have put a top priority on education; schools are available throughout the country, and today 90% of the Belizeans are literate. (There is concern that the figure may change with the heavy influx of El Salvadoran refugees.) School is mandatory for Belizean children up to age 14. High school is neither mandatory nor free—most are run by religious groups with aid from the government. As a result, not all families can afford to educate their children beyond grammar school.

ACTIVITIES

The most well-known and publicized activities for visitors to Belize for many years have been diving and snorkeling. Without a doubt the Belize Reef (fifth longest in the world and longest in the Western Hemisphere) offers the diver a fulfilling experience observing the colors and variety of tropical fish and coral.

Not everyone who travels to Belize is a diver or even a snorkeler—at first! But one peek through the "looking glass"—a diving mask—will change that. The Caribbean is one of the most notoriously seductive bodies of water in the world. Turquoise blue and crystal clear with perfect tepid temperature, the protected Belizean coast (thanks to offshore reefs) is ideal for a languid float during hot humid days.

Snorkeling

You'll find that the sea is where you'll want to spend a good part of your trip. So even if you've never considered underwater sports in the past, you'll be willing—no, eager!—to learn. It's easy for the neophyte to learn how to snorkel. Once you master breathing through a tube, it's simply a matter of relaxing and floating. Time disappears once you are introduced, through a four-inch glass window, to a world of fish in rainbow colors of garish yellow, electric blue, crimson, and probably a hundred shades of purple. The longer you look, the more you'll discover: underwater caverns, tall coral pillars, giant tubular sponges, shy fish hiding on the sandy bottom, and delicate wisps of fine grass.

Diving Wonderland

For the diver, there's even more adventure. Reefs, caves, and rugged coastline harbor the unknown. Ships wrecked hundreds of years ago hide secrets as yet undiscovered. Swimming among the curious and brazen fish puts you literally into another world. This is raw excitement!

Expect to see an astounding variety of fish, crustaceans, and corals. Even close to shore, these amazing little animals create exotic displays of shape and form, dense or

PORTUGUESE MAN - OF - WAR

NEEDLE FISH

ELKHORN CORAL

TABLE CORAL

SPONGES

STAGHORN CORAL

ANGEL FISH

CLOWN FISH IN SEA ANEMONE

LOBED STAR CORAL

BRAIN CORAL

BOB RACE

BELIZE LIVE-ABOARD DIVE BOATS

Belize Aggressor 100'
Dive/Sail Belize
Box 9182
Treasure Island, FL 33740
tel. (800) 237-DIVE or
(813) 367-1952
or Aggressor Fleet, Ltd.
P.O. Drawer K
Morgan City, LA 70381
tel.(800) 348-2628 or
(504) 385-2416
fax (504) 384-0817

Belize Explorer 165'
tel. (800) 433-7262 or
(305) 563-1711

Manta IV 54'
San Pedro, Ambergris Caye,
Belize, C.A.
tel. (904) 620-0774
fax (904) 620-0684
in San Pedro (26) 2130

M/V Great Reef 65'
Rt. 3, P.O. Box 214A
Corpus Christi, TX 78415
(800) 255-8503
(512) 854-0247

Ocean Spirit 457'
tel. (800) 338-3483 or
(504) 586-8686

Offshore Express 50'
San Pedro, Ambergris Caye,
Belize, C.A.
tel. (26) 2013
fax (26) 2864

Reef Roamer I (36') and II (50')
Out Island Divers
San Pedro, Ambergris Caye,
Belize, C.A.
Box 3455
Estes Park, CO 80517
(303) 586-6020
(303) 586-0870
(800-BLUE HOLE)
in San Pedro (26) 2151

See pp. 129-130 for more information

delicate depending on species, depth, light, and current. Most need light to survive; in deeper, low-light areas, some species of coral take the form of a large plate, thereby performing the duties of a solar collector. Sponge is another curious underwater creature and it comes in all sizes, shapes, and colors, from common brown to vivid red.

Be Selective

Diving lessons are offered at nearly all the dive shops in the country. Before you make a commitment, ask about the instructor and check his acident record; then talk to the locals or, if you're in a small village, ask at the local bar. Most of these divers are conscientious, but a few are not, and the locals know whom to trust.

Bringing your own equipment to Belize might save you a little money, depending on the length of your trip and means of transportation. But if you plan on staying just a couple of weeks and want to join a group aboard a dive boat by the day, it's generally not much more for tank rental, which will save you the hassle of carrying your own.

Choose your boat carefully. Look it over first. Some aren't much more than fishing boats with little to make the diver comfortable. Ask questions! Does it have a platform to get in and out of the water? How many tanks of air may be used

per trip? How many dives? Exactly where are you going? How fast does the boat go and how long will it take to get there? Remember, some of the best dive spots might be farther out at sea. A more modern boat (though it'll cost a little more) might get you extra diving time.

Detailed information is available for divers and snorkelers who wish to know about the dive sites they plan to visit. *Skin Diver* magazine puts out a very informative issue on Belize at least once a year, usually in June. Many pamphlets and books are available, especially for U.S.-based dive tours; some have been in business for many years; check them out. Wherever diving is good, you'll almost always find a dive shop. On both Ambergris Caye and Caye Caulker, and in Belize City, dive shops offer day-trips.

A few high-adventure dives require an experienced guide—not only recommended but also a necessity.

DIVING HAZARDS

Underwater

A word here about some of the less-inviting aspects of marine society. Anemones and sea urchins are everywhere. Some can be dangerous if touched or stepped on. The long-spined, black sea urchin can inflict great pain and its

EMERGENCY NUMBERS FOR ACCIDENT EVACUATION

Divers Alert Network (DAN)   (919) 684-8111
dial this number for info about
decompression chambers

Air-Evac International
San Diego, California   (619) 278-3822
Florida   (305) 772-0003
Houston, Texas   (713) 880-9767

Life Flight (air ambulance)   (713) 797-4357
Houston, Texas   (800) 231-4357

To get the proper help to you much sooner it's important to have as much of the following information as possible ready to give the emergency service you call:
  name and age of the patient
  the problem
  when it happened
  name and telephone number of the doctor and medical facility
  treating the patient

poison can cause an uncomfortable infection. Don't think that you're safe in a wetsuit, booties, and gloves! The spines easily slip through the rubber and the urchin is encountered at all depths, more abundant in some areas than in others; keep your eyes open. If you should run into one of the spines, remove it quickly and carefully, disinfect the wound, and apply antibiotic cream. If you have difficulty removing the spine, or if it breaks, see a doctor—pronto! Note: Environmentalists discourage divers from wearing gloves to deter touching the fragile coral. In some varieties, just one touch is the touch of death.

First Aid

Cuts from coral, even if just a scratch, will often become infected. Antibiotic cream or powder will usually take care of it. If you should get a deep cut, or if minute bits of coral are left in the wound, a serious and long-lived infection can ensue. See a doctor.

If you should get scraped on red or fire coral you may feel a burning sensation for just a few minutes or up to five days. On some, it causes an allergic reaction and will raise large red welts. Cortisone cream will reduce inflammation and discomfort. While it wouldn't be fair to condemn all red things, you'll notice in the next few paragraphs that many of the creatures to avoid are red!

Fire worms (also known as bristle worms) if touched will deposit tiny cactus-like bristles in your skin. They can cause the same reaction as fire coral. *Carefully* scraping the skin with the edge of a sharp knife (as you would to remove a bee stinger) *might* remove the bristles. Any leftover bristles will ultimately work their way out, but you might be very uncomfortable in the meantime. Cortisone cream helps to relieve this inflammation, too.

Several species of sponges have fine sharp spicules (hard, minute, pointed calcareous or siliceous bodies that support the tissue) that should not be touched with the bare hand. The attractive red fire sponge can cause great pain; a mild solution of vinegar or ammonia (or urine if there's nothing else) will help. The burning lasts a couple of days, and cortisone cream soothes. Don't be fooled by dull-colored sponges. Many have the same sharp spicules.

Protect Your Hands And Feet

Some divers feel the need to touch the fish they swim with. A few beginners want an underwater picture taken of them feeding the fish—bad news! When you offer fish a tasty morsel from your hand (whether gloved or not), you could start an underwater riot. Fish are always hungry and always ready for a free meal. Some of those denizens of the deep may not be so big, but in the frenzy to be first in line, their very efficient teeth have been known to miss the target. Another way to save your hands from unexpected danger is to keep them out of cracks and crevices. Moray eels live in just those kinds of places in a reef. A moray will usually leave you alone if you do likewise, but their many needle-sharp teeth can cause a painful wound that's likely to become infected.

A few sea-going critters resent being stepped on and can retaliate with a dangerous wound. The scorpion fish, hardly recognizable with its natural camouflage, lies hidden most of the time on a reef shelf or the bottom of the sea. If you should step on or touch it you can expect a painful, dangerous sting. If this happens, see a doctor immediately.

Another sinister fellow is the ray. There are several varieties in the Caribbean, including the yellow and southern sting rays. If you leave them alone they're generally peaceful, but if stepped on they will zap you with a tail that carries a poisonous sting that might cause anaphylactic shock. Symptoms include respiratory difficulties, fainting, and severe itching. Go quickly to the doctor and tell him what caused the sting. One diver suggests a shuffling, dragging-of-the-feet gait when walking on the bottom of the ocean. If bumped, the ray will quickly escape, but if stepped on it feels trapped and uses its tail for protection. Jellyfish can also inflict a miserable sting. Avoid particularly the long streamers of the Portuguese man-of-war, though some of the smaller jellyfish are just as hazardous.

Don't let these what-ifs discourage you from an underwater adventure, though. Thousands of people dive in Belize's Caribbean every day of the year and only a small percentage have accidents.

Safety References

Check with your dive master about emergency procedures before your boat heads out to sea. Ask about the decompression chamber in San Pedro; he should also know that there's a decompression chamber in Houston, Texas, and another in Isla Cozumel, Mexico (tel. 2-01-40).

OTHER WATER SPORTS

Depending on where you are, other water sports are available. Because so many of these beaches are protected by the reef that runs parallel to Belize's eastern coast, calm **swimming beaches,** though shallow, are easy to find; finding a *sandy* beach is limited to certain areas. Many

hotels have pools. Glass-bottom boats are well worth the time for the nonswimmer or nonsnorkeler. While staying high and dry it's possible to enjoy the beauties of the underwater gardens.

Kayaking

This is becoming a favorite in Belize. Kayakers have an ideal place to explore the coast in calm water within the reef touching on isolated cayes. Kayaking is one of those off-the-wall activities that's growing all over the world and often in unlikely places. Recently while in Chiapas, Mexico, at Agua Azul (where there are dozens of cascading waterfalls), we watched kayaks literally fly over the edge of these water cliffs. Exciting stuff! For more information about kayaking and camping in Belize (or the cliffs of Agua Azul) contact **Slickrock Adventures,** tel./fax (801) 259-6996 (see "Tour Operators," p. 234.)

FISHING AND HUNTING

Fishing

If you plan on cruising to Belize in your own boat, you must contact the Belize consulate about a permit for your vessel; you can also get current information there on fishing seasons and regulations that vary from area to area. This is a dynamite fishing area. Fishers have a choice of fishing within the reef for tarpon, bonefish, and permit, or deep-sea fishing outside of the reef for the big trophies like marlin, sailfish, giant groupers, tuna, and many more. It's easy to find a boat and guide through your hotel and through many tour operators in the U.S. (see "Tour Operators," p. 234.)

Hunting

Hunting is not the big attraction to Belize that it once was. The locals are beginning to realize that the wild creatures still roaming their lands are precisely what attracts visitors to the country. As a result most big-game animals are now off-limits, with stiff fines imposed for violating the law. Jaguar was the star for many years for hunters from other countries, especially the United States. Now it is against the law to kill these sleek animals, and they even have a reserve called the **Cockscomb Jaguar Sanctuary;** visitors welcome. For the best information contact the **Forestry Department, Ministry of Natural Resources** (Belmopan, Cayo District, Belize, C.A.; tel. 8-22-159). Hunters must preregister their guns (including description) with the **Police Commissioner** before bringing them into the country. For more details contact the **Belizean Embassy,** 2535 Massachusetts Ave. NW, Washington, DC 20008; tel. (202) 332-9636, fax (202) 332-6741.

OTHER ACTIVITIES

Flora And Fauna Watching

Birdwatching is spectacular throughout Belize. From north to south the variety of birds is broad and changes with the geography and the weather (see "Fauna"). Bring binoculars and wear boots and lightweight trousers if you plan on watching in jungle areas. Studying **tropical flora** is also a popular activity. For this you most certainly will be in the backcountry—don't forget bug repellent and be prepared for an occasional rain shower, even in the dry season. For most orchids and bromeliads, look *up* into the trees. Remember, don't take anything away with you except pictures.

The **Belize Audubon Society** is very active; write if you have questions: 12 Fort St., (02) 35-0004, (02) 34-987; fax (02) 34-985.

Photography

For the photographer, a world of beauty awaits: the sea, the people, and the natural landscape of the jungle, waterfalls, rivers, and archaeological sites. For those who want to film *everything,* small planes are available for charter in Belize City. See "Cameras and Picture Taking."

Spelunking

Belize offers the avid caver several opportunities for exploration. About 25 miles south of Belize City two caves, **Ben Lomond** and **Manatee,** are open to the curious. It's necessary to hire a boat to take you across the bar bordering **Southern Lagoon** and then continue hiking for several miles. In Belize City or Dangriga you can find boatmen along the waterfront who know the area and will take you. Belize has one of the largest cave systems in Latin America. If you wish to speak to someone who knows the Belizean caves, call Bill Wildman at Adventure Inn in Consejo Shores, (4) 22-187. Check with your hotel or travel agent for a guided tour of the caves.

Tennis

Tennis courts are scarce but the tennis buff will be happy to know that a few resorts do have them: **Adventure Inn** in Consejo Shores, **Villa Holiday Inn** in Belize City, **Journeys End** on Ambergris Caye, and **Airport Hotel** in Ladyville.

LOUISE FOOTE

FESTIVALS

Come to the party! Certain holidays in Belize are signals to have fun. And the variety of activity on each holiday is vast. This is the time to sample the culture and cuisine of Belize traditions. When a public holiday falls on Sunday, it is celebrated on the following Monday. If you should plan on visiting during holiday time, make advance hotel reservations—especially if you plan on spending time in Dangriga on 19 Nov.—as the area has limited accommodations.

Note: On a few holidays (Easter and Christmas) most businesses close for the day; on Good Friday most of the buses do not run. Check ahead of time.

Baron Bliss Day

On 9 March this holiday is celebrated with various activities, mostly water sports. In memory of English sportsman Baron Henry Edward Ernest Victor Bliss, who remembered Belize with a generous legacy when he died, a day of sailing and fishing was designated in his will. A formal ceremony is held at his tomb located below the lighthouse in the Belize Harbor where he died on his boat. Fishing and sailing regattas begin following the ceremony.

Ambergris Caye Celebrates

If you're wandering around Belize near 26-29 June, hop a boat or plane to San Pedro and join the locals in a festival they have celebrated for decades, **El Dia de San Pedro,** in honor of the town's namesake, St. Peter. This is good fun; advance reservations are suggested.

St. George's Caye Day

On 10 Sept. 1798, at St. George's Caye off the coast of Belize, the British buccaneers fought and defeated the Spaniards over the territory of Belize. The tradition of celebrating this victory is still carried on each year, followed by a week-long calendar of events ranging from religious services to carnivals. During this week the town feels like a carnival with parties everywhere. On the morning of 10 Sept., the whole town parades through the streets and enjoys local cooking, spirits, and music with an upbeat

atmosphere that continues well into the beginning of Independence Day on 21 September.

National Independence Day

On 21 Sept. 1981, Belize gained independence from Great Britain. Each year to celebrate this Belizeans enjoy carnivals on the main streets of downtown Belize City and district towns. Like a giant county fair, displays of local arts, crafts, and cultural activities can be seen, while happy Belizeans dance to a variety of exotic rhythms from *punta rock* to *soka* to reggae. Again, don't miss the chance to sample local dishes from every ethnic group in the country. With this holiday back to back with the celebration of the Battle of St. George's Caye, two weeks of riotous, cacophonous celebrating takes place.

Garifuna Settlement Day

On 19 Nov. Belize recognizes the 1823 arrival and settlement of the first Garifuna (Black Caribs, also called Garinagu) to the southern districts of Belize. Belizeans from all over the country gather in Dangriga and Toledo to celebrate with the Garifuna. The day begins with the reenactment of the arrival of the settlers and continues with dancing to the local Garifuna drums and *punta rock.* Traditional food is available on street

---

HOLIDAYS IN BELIZE

1 January	New Year's Day
9 March	Baron Bliss Day
March or April	Good Friday
March or April	Holy Saturday
March or April	Easter Sunday
March or April	Easter Monday
1 May	Labor Day
25 May	Commonwealth Day
10 September	St. George's Caye Day
21 September	National Independence Day
12 October	Columbus Day
19 November	Garifuna Day
25 December	Christmas Day
26 December	Boxing Day

FEAST OF SAN LUIS

An all-night vigil begins the festival, during which traditional masks and costumes are blessed with smoke from burning incense and food offerings. According to Maya belief a great power resides in the masks and it can be directed toward good or evil.

Drums announce the procession to the home of the prioste (holy man) each of the next nine days. Twelve dancers take part. Leading the marchers is a man dressed as the "holy deer," followed by other characters of the dance including *el tigre* (the jaguar), women portrayed by men, dogs, and finally, the hunters dressed in black. Four men carry a marimba, which will be used during the celebrations. Even while being carried, the marimba is played all the way into the prioste's house and intermittently during occasional respites in the ceremonial dances. Some of the men shake rattles and an ongoing chant adds an exotic tone to the music of the dance.

The Tiger Dance

The ancient legend of the tiger is performed in a square. The four corners and the center of the space represent the Maya's five cardinal directions—north, south, east, west, and the center. Slowly and with grace the story of *el tigre* unfolds. With active movements the tiger chases and is chased by the men in red from each of the four corners and around the center. Were they the bacabs, the Maya guardians of the directions? As a clown, the tiger impishly teases the hunters throughout the dance, stealing their hats or their rattles. At the finale the tiger is captured and killed; the hunters pantomime the killing and skinning of the tiger while the dancer steps out of his costume and runs away. Though performed with exaggerated elements of sincerity, it's a comedic performance, a warm-up of more serious things to come.

The Holy Deer Dance

The story of the holy deer, on the other hand, is performed with reverence instead of comedy, and continues for several days. The festivities include a lively procession to the San Antonio village church. The deer dances proudly, head high, acknowledges each of the other dancers, and then disappears into the forest. Enter the dogs sent by the hunters to seek out the deer. After a while the frightened deer/dancer is chased back by the dogs and with great drama the hunters kill the noble animal.

The Greased Pole

Preparations for the finale start two days ahead of time with an all-night vigil for the men who will cut down a tall tree the next day to be used in the pole-climbing festivities. The pillar is about 60 feet long and made from a special tree, called sayuc in Maya. The tree is trimmed and the dancing continues, drawing larger and larger audiences. A great procession follows as the huge pole and a statue of San Antonio (which has been residing in the prioste's home) are carried to San Antonio's church on the top of the hill. Occasionally the long line of people stops and lays the pole on the ground. In silence and great solemnity the pole is "blessed" by the statue of San Antonio while women manipulate dangling urns of burning incense, sending wisps of aromatic smoke wafting around the pole. Once at the church, saints are traded. The statue of San Antonio is returned to its place, more prayers are said, and the statue of San Luis, under a protective colorful canopy and flanked by a dozen flags, is carried out on a wooden platform to "bless" the pole. The procession of people, including the statue, then makes its way to the prioste's house for another night of social dancing.

The Finale

It's 25 Sept., the climax day—and end of the celebration. Preparations for raising the pole begin early in the morning to the steady, low beat of a drum. Under the watchful eyes of many anxious children, bars of soap are flattened with rocks, broken into small pieces, and dissolved in buckets of water. Next, melted lard is added and thoroughly mixed. The oily compound is then generously spread on the pole. How anyone could accomplish an upward movement on this mess is a mystery, although the first would have the most slip. Prizes that have been stored at the prioste's house—a generous hand of bananas, a bottle of rum, and a small sum of money—are placed at the top of the pole for the climber who makes it all the way— he will earn it!

After a slow procession, eating, dancing, and more blessings, the grand finale (under the watchful eye of the saint) is about to begin.

The pole raising brings a still moment, the low beat of the drums and the aroma of incense. Fifty men hold ropes while others hold forked sticks and the pole slowly begins to rise, but not without a few slippery sways that bring gasps from the anticipating crowd. Finally the long pole slips neatly into the hole.

Now the fun begins— at least for the onlookers. The tiger and the hunter characters are the first to attempt to climb the pole, followed by a dozen other men—and to make it more difficult each has his feet tied together. Everyone has a good laugh watching the slipping and sliding. Finally a successful challenger with great determination inches his way to the top and reaches for his prize; the crowd cheers and the church bells ring out, a happy ending to an often serious ceremony.

There is no question that this celebration is symbolic, but of what? It's doubtful that anyone really knows. So much of the ancient traditional culture has been mixed with the Christian religion that even the Maya aren't sure. The men in the village take turns as the religious caretaker for special statues of the church. This is a privilege that includes bearing the expense for most of the ceremonies for the year; a costly honor.

---

stands and local cafes. The language is called Garifuna and both words, Garifuna and Garinagu, are interchangeable.

MUSIC OF BELIZE

Like many Central American countries the music has been heavily influenced by the rhythmic, exotic syncopations of Africa. This is toe-tapping, hip-swinging, hand-clapping music, and anyone who can just sit still and listen must be in a coma. If you manage to get to Belize in September during the festivals of the Battle of St. George's Caye and National Independence Day, you'll have an introduction to the raucous happy music of a **jump up** (a street dance), **punta rock** (a spin-off from the original *punta,* a traditional rhythm of the Garifuna settlers in the Stann Creek District), **reggae** (everyone knows the beat of the steel drums adapted from the Trinidad cousins), **soka** (a livelier interpreta-

tion of reggae), and **brukdown** (a cadence begun in the timber camps of the 1800s, when the workers, isolated from civilization for months at a time, would let off steam with a full bottle of rum and begin the beat on the bottle—or the jawbone of an ass, a coconut shell, a wooden block; anything that made a sound. Add to that a harmonica, guitar, and banjo, and you've got *brukdown*). **Creole** folk songs tell the story like it is, sad or happy, with lyrics in the Creole patois of the people.

In the southern part of Belize in Toledo District, you'll likely hear the strains of ancient Maya melodies played on homemade wooden instruments designed before memory: Kekchi harps, violins, and guitars. In the west in Cayo District listen for the resonant sounds of marimbas and wooden xylophones—from the Spanish influence across the Guatemala border. In Corozal and Orange Walk districts in the north, the infatuations of old Mexico are popularized with romantic lyrics and the strum of a guitar.

Tapes And Recordings

The music recording business is developing in Belize in its own original way—watch out Hollywood! If you want to hear Belizean music but can't get away, send for a catalog of cassette tapes available for overseas sales from **Sunrise Productions** (P.O. Box 137, Belmopan, Cayo District, Belize, C.A.). Look for marimba music, Kekchi harp music, and the everloving **Waribagabaga and Children of the Most High,** combining their music of drums, turtle shells, and vocals sung in Garifuna. Also offered are typical jump up music and *punta rock* rhythms.

DANCES OF THE MAYA

If you happen to be one of the lucky travelers in Belize on 25 Sept., you should make an effort to visit **San Antonio Village** in the Toledo District. There's a good chance you may see the **deer dance** performed by the Mopan and Kekchi Maya villagers. Dancing and celebrating begins around the middle of August, but the biggest celebration begins with a *novena* nine days before the feast day of San Luis.

Actually, this festival was only recently revived. The costumes were burned in an accidental fire some years back at a time when (coincidentally) the locals had begun to lose interest in the ancient traditions. Thanks to the formation of the **Toledo Maya Cultural Council,** the Maya once again are realizing the importance of recapturing their past. A grant from **Video Incorporated** broadcast company enabled the people to make new masks and costumes. In return the broadcasting company was granted permission to tape the festivities—a big concession for the secretive Maya. Before you decide to attend this days-long event, remember just that—it gets long. Ask the headman before you take any pictures.

ACCOMMODATIONS

In Belize basic budget rooms are still fairly easy to find; small modern lodgings are adding more rooms to alleviate the growing shortages, and several upscale hotels have been built in Belize City in the last few years. Scattered about the rest of the countryside and coastal regions, small hotels and delightful intimate guesthouses range from Spartan cottages with kerosene lanterns on the riverbank to luxury cabañas built of rich tropical hardwoods and surrounded by the rainforest, glorious gardens, and well-manicured grass. The rooms offer access to thousands of acres of rainforest, nature reserves, rivers, waterfalls, beautiful flowers, wild animals, colorful birds, and modern Maya villages along with ancient ceremonial sites of their ancestors. On tiny cayes just offshore, simple cabins are located in perfect locations for easy-access scuba diving and snorkeling as well as world-class permit and bonefishing. Or for those interested in turtles, live-aboard boats are available that offer accommodations and the opportunity to comfortably cruise to offshore cayes. Most of the hostelries in the country are small and intimate, which, in keeping with the small country, is what the tourist majority prefers.

As you look through the listings for hotels in this book, remember that in most cases you must add 5% tax, usually 10% service charge, and in some cases an extra few percent for the use of credit cards. If you decide to stay in one of the low-key budget hotels, bring cash; most don't accept credit cards. In the more isolated areas, many of them also don't have hot water, electricity, or telephones. Adventurers won't let that stop them.

FOOD

Many of the crops now produced by U.S. farmers were introduced by the indigenous people of Mesoamerica, including corn, sweet potatoes, tomatoes, peppers, squash, pumpkin, and avocados. Many other products favored by Americans are native to the area: papaya, cotton, tobacco, rubber, vanilla, and turkey.

PRE-COLUMBIAN AGRICULTURE

Enriching The Soil

Scientists believe Maya priests studied celestial movements. A prime function performed in the elaborate temples (built to strict astronomical guidelines) may have been charting the changing seasons and deciding when to begin the planting cycle. Farmers used the slash-and-burn method of agriculture (and the Maya still do today). When the time was propitious (before the rains began in the spring), Maya farmers cut the trees on a section of land, leaving stumps about a foot above ground. Downed trees were spread evenly across the landscape in order to burn uniformly; residual ash was left to nourish the soil. At the proper time, holes were made with a pointed stick, and precious maize kernels were dropped into the earth, one by one. At each corner (the cardinal points) of the cornfield, offerings of *pozole* (maize stew) were left to encourage the gods to give forth great rains. With abundant moisture, crops were bountiful and rich enough to provide food even into the following year.

The Maya knew the value of allowing the land to lay fallow after two seasons of growth, and each family's *milpa* (cornfield) was moved from place to place around the villages scattered through the jungle. Often, squash and tomatoes were planted in the shade of towering cornstalks to make double use of the land. With the coming of electricity to the outlying areas, pumps are being used to bring water from rivers and lakes to irrigate crops. Outside of irrigation methods, today's Maya follow the same ancient pattern of farming as their ancestors. The government is suggesting more efficient management of the land with less destruction to the rainforest;

this "alternate" farming method reuses a plot of ground, with the help of fertilizers, after it's been left fallow for a short time. Education, intended to teach the indigenous people alternatives to slash-and-burn, is beginning to take hold.

Maize

Corn was the heart of Maya nutrition, eaten at each meal. From it they made tortillas, stew, and both alcoholic and nonalcoholic beverages. Because growing corn was such a vital part of Maya life, it is represented in drawings and carvings along with other social and religious symbols. Corn tortillas are still a main staple of the Maya people. Grinding the corn into tortilla dough has been done by hand for centuries (and still is in isolated places). Others pay a few more cents and buy their tortillas by the kilo hot off the *tomal* (griddle). It's amazing that the Maya came up with the combination of corn and beans without a dietitian telling them it was a complete protein; they did not raise cattle, sheep, or pigs before Spanish times. They did include in their diets turtle, manatee, iguana, fresh seafood, and many small animals that roam the jungle.

GASTRONOMICAL ADVENTURE

Taste as many different dishes as possible! You'll be introduced to spices that add a new dimension to your diet. Naturally, you won't be wild about everything—it takes a while to become accustomed to squid served in its own black ink, for instance! A hamburger might not taste like one from your favorite "fast foodery" back home. Be prepared to come into contact with many new and different tastes—you're in *Belize,* after all, a land of myriad cultures and cuisines. You will easily find Chinese, Mexican, Creole, and European. Look for such delicacies as conch, conch soup, fried lobster, iguana, armadillo, shark, black beans and rice, great fried chicken, fried plantain, papaya, and don't turn your nose up if someone invites you to a "boil up" (seafood stew). Though turtle is an endangered species, a government law allows fishermen to take them at certain times of the year, so you may also see turtle offered on a menu—but perhaps if no one buys them the fishermen will quit catching them in their nets!

Seafood

You won't travel far before realizing that one of the favorite Belize specialties is fresh fish. All along the Caribbean and Gulf coasts are opportunities to indulge in piscine delicacies: lobster, shrimp, red snapper, sea bass, halibut, barracuda, conch, and lots more prepared in a variety of ways. Even the tiniest cafe will prepare sweet fresh fish.

Try the unusual conch *kaahnk,* which has been a staple in the diet of the Mayan and Central American along the Caribbean coast for centuries. It's often used in ceviche. Some consider this raw fish; actually, it's marinated in lime juice with onions, peppers, and a host of spices—no longer raw, and very tasty! Another favorite conch is pounded, dipped in egg and then cracker crumbs, and sautéed quickly (like

cleaning conch, still an important staple along the Caribbean coast

---

SAVE THE LOBSTER

Since the influx of tourists into the small country of Belize, a very big concern has been the safety of the lobster beds off the coast, which have provided food and support for the locals for many years. Because the price of a lobster dinner in Caye Caulker, for instance, is so much cheaper than in the U.S., the demand has increased rapidly. In order to keep happy tourists, a few fishermen supply the restaurants open season or closed, legal size or not! The population of lobster cannot continue to flourish with these illegal activities, and the collapse of the Belizean fishing industry will follow.

As a responsible traveler, you are urged *not* to order lobster during the closed season, which is from 15 March-14 July. Also, if (during the open season) a restaurant is offering a lobster dinner for BZE$7-8, it is most likely a "short," which means it is under legal size. Minimum size for a lobster tail is four ounces. Ask around town for restaurants that sell legal-size tails, and then patronize them with a positive comment about saving the lobster.

All of the above advice goes for the conch as well. Closed season for conch is 1 July-30 September, and the minimum size is three ounces of meat.

---

abalone steak in California) with a squirt of fresh lime. Caution: If it's cooked too long it becomes tough and rubbery. Conch fritters are minced pieces of conch mixed into a flour batter and fried—tasty.

If you happen to be on a boat trip the crew will probably catch a fish and prepare it for lunch, maybe cooked over an open fire, or in a "boil up," seasoned with onions, peppers, and *achiote,* a fragrant red spice grown locally since the time of the early Maya.

Garifuna Style

A very ethnic way to prepare fish is to cook it in coconut milk and local spices; it's called *seri.* In many dishes plantain or green bananas are grated into various recipes, and seaweed is used now and then. All contribute to new and unique flavors.

Wild Game

Many ethnic groups in Belize are hunters, and if you explore the jungle paths very much, you'll see men and boys on foot or on bicycles with rifles slung over their shoulders and full game bags tied behind them. Jungle game varies. Wild duck is served during certain times of the year and is prepared in several ways that *must* be tried. Iguana is common, gibnut (a rabbit-like rodent) is said to be very tasty (I haven't tried it yet, but Queen Elizabeth has!), and the Maya eat a wide variety of wild game cooked in a spicy red sauce. If you're invited for dinner by a local Maya, don't be surprised to find the likes of crested guan, tinamou, brocket deer, peccary, armadillo, agouti, paca, turtle, iguana, and iguana eggs. This is the norm for people who live in and around the forest, although I didn't say it was all legal.

Restaurants

Most small cafes that cater to Belizeans are open all day until about 10 p.m. Hotels with foreign tourists offer dinner early in the evening to cater to British, Canadian, and American tastes. Most hotels and restaurants add tax and a 20% service charge onto the bill. It's still gracious to leave a few coins for the waiter. If the tip isn't added to the bill, leaving 10% is customary.

Fried chicken is found on almost every menu in Belize, along with black beans and rice, which is considered a "typical" dinner. Some of the more local restaurants offer gibnut, a rabbit-like rodent that was served to Queen Elizabeth when she visited some years back, causing British newspapers to print half-page headlines stating the queen was served rat in Belize. Oh, well; newspapers go to any lengths to be noticed.

A ploy used by many seasoned adventurers when they're tired of eating cold food from their backpacks: in a village where no cafes exist go to the local pub, grocery store, church, or city hall and ask if there's a housewife in town who, for a fee, would be willing to include you at her dinner table. Almost always you'll find someone, usually at a fair price (determine price when you make your deal). With any luck you'll find a woman renowned for her cooking. You'll gain a lot more than food in this arrangement; the cultural swap is priceless.

Food Safety

When preparing your own food in the backcountry, a few possible sources of bacteria are fresh fruit and vegetables, especially those with thin, unpeeled skin, like lettuce or tomatoes. When washing these foods in local water (and they should definitely be washed thoroughly before consuming), add either bleach or iodine (8-10 drops per quart) to the water, unless of course you carry your own portable filtering system. Soaking vegetables together in a container or plastic bag for about 20 minutes is easy; carrying along zipper-lock plastic bags is essential. If you're at the beach and short of water, substitute sea water (for everything but drinking). Remember not to rinse the bleached food with contaminated water; just pat dry, and if they have a distasteful lingering flavor, a squirt of lime juice tastes great and is very healthy. Some foods nature has packaged hygienically; a banana has its own protective seal so is considered safe (luckily, since they're so abundant in Belize). Foods that are cooked well are also considered safe if eaten immediately.

HEALTH CARE

TRAVELER'S DISEASE

Some travelers to foreign countries worry about getting sick the moment they leave their own country. But with a few simple precautions, it's not a foregone conclusion that you'll come down with something. The most common illness to strike visitors is **traveler's disease,** known by many names but, in plain Latin, it's diarrhea. No fun, it can cause uncomfortable cramping, fever, dehydration, and the need to stay close to a toilet for a few days. It's caused by, among other things, various strains of bacteria managing to find your innards, so it's important to be very careful about what goes into your mouth.

Studies show that the majority of tourists who get sick do so on the third day of their visit, and that traveler's illness is common in every country. They say that in addition to bacteria, a change in diet is equally to blame and suggest that the visitor slip slowly into the eating habits of the country, especially if the food tends to be spicy. In other words, don't blast your tummy with the *habanero* or jalapeño pepper right off the bat. Work into the fried food, drinks, local specialties, and new spices gradually; take your time changing over to foods you may never eat while at home, including the large quantities of wonderful tropical fruits that you'll want to eat in some tropical countries. Blame is also shared by mixing alcohol with longer-than-usual periods of time in the tropical sun. The body chemistry is changed with alcohol and it becomes very difficult to handle excessive heat.

It's The Water

While the above theories are often valid, water is probably the worst culprit. According to locals, the water from the faucet in Belize City is said to be safe, but smaller villages and more isolated areas are still "iffy"—you'd be wise to take special precautions. A good rule of thumb: if you're not sure about the water, ask the locals or the desk clerk at your hotel; they'll let you know the status. Hotels prefer healthy guests—they'll return.

In the backcountry, hikers may want to carry their own water and then, whether the source is out of the tap or a crystal-clear pond, boil it or purify it with chemicals. That goes for brushing your teeth as well. If you have nothing else, a bottle of beer will make a safe (though maybe not sane) mouth rinse. If using ice, ask where it was made and if it's pure. Think about the water you're swimming in; you might want to avoid some small local pools.

The easiest way to purify the water is with purification tablets; **Hidroclonozone** and **Halazone** are two, but many safe brands are available at drugstores in all countries. Or carry a small plastic bottle of liquid bleach (use 8-10 drops per quart of water) or iodine (use five to seven drops per quart) to purify the water. Whichever you use, let the water stand for 20 minutes to improve the flavor. Boiling the water for 20-30 minutes will purify it as well. Even though it takes a heck of a lot of fuel that you'll probably have to carry on your back, don't get lazy in this department. You can get very sick drinking contaminated water, which you can't identify by looking at—unless you travel with a microscope!

Giardiasis

Giardia is a parasite that can be present in streams and ponds almost anyplace in the world. It can be destroyed by boiling the water. However, if fuel is a problem, the water can be treated with iodine. The amount and most efficient form of iodine (crystals or liquid?) to use are up for debate, so check with your doctor. An inexpensive water treatment kit that uses crystalline iodine is available from Recreational Equipment Incorporated. Write for more information (Box 88125, Seattle, Washington 98138-0125; tel. 800-426-4840). The company also offers the more expensive Swiss-made Katadyn PF Pocket Water Filter for those who cannot tolerate iodine for either taste or thyroid reasons. Outdoor supply shops are a good place to check for the latest in portable water purifiers.

Camping

When camping on the beach where fresh water is

scarce, use sea water to wash dishes and even yourself. Before leaving home, check at a sporting goods or marine shop for **Sea Saver Soap.** (A rub of bar soap on the bottom of pots and pans before setting them over an open fire makes for easy cleaning after cooking.)

Other Sources Of Bacteria
Money can be a source of germs. Wash your hands frequently, don't put your fingers in your mouth, and carry individual foil packets of disinfectant cleaners, like Wash Up, that are handy and refreshing in the tropic heat. Hepatitis is another bug that can be contracted easily if you're around it.

When in backcountry cafes, remember that fruit and vegetables, especially those with a thin edible skin (like tomatoes), are a possible source of bacteria. If you like to eat food purchased from street vendors (and some shouldn't be missed), use common sense. If you see the food being cooked (killing all the grubby little bacteria) before your eyes, have at it. If it's hanging there already cooked and is being nibbled on by small flying creatures, pass it by. It may have been there all day, and what was once a nice sterile morsel could easily have gone bad in the heat, or been contaminated by flies. Be cautious of hotel buffets; their shellfish may have been sitting out for hours—a potential bacteria source unless they are well iced. When buying food at the marketplace to cook for yourself, use the hints given in "Food Safety," p. 51.

Treatment
Remember, it's not just the visitor who gets sick from bacteria. Each year locals die from the same germs, and the government is working hard to remedy their sanitation problems. Tremendous improvements have taken place that ultimately will be accomplished all over Belize, but it's a slow process. In the meantime, many careful visitors come and go each year with nary a touch of the trots. If after all your precautions you still come down with traveler's illness, many medications are available for relief. Most can be bought over the counter, but in the U.S. you may need a prescription from your doctor. **Lomotil** and **Immodium** are common, and certainly turn off the faucet after a few hours of dosing; how-

ever, they have the side effect of becoming a plug. These medications do not cure the problem, only the symptoms; if you quit taking it too soon your symptoms reappear and you're back to square one. In their favor, Lòmotil and Immodium work faster than **Pepto Bismol** or **Kaopectate,** and if you're about to embark on a seven-hour bus ride to Placencia you might consider either one of those "quick-stop" drugs a lifesaver. **Note:** Immodium no longer requires a prescription; Lomotil, however, does.

If you're concerned, check with your doctor before leaving home. Also ask him about some new formulas called Septra and Bactrim that attack the "bug" that's causing the problem. Something else to be aware of; Pepto Bismol can turn the tongue a dark brownish color— nothing to be alarmed about.

For those who prefer natural remedies, lime juice and garlic are both considered good when taken as preventatives. They need to be taken in large quantities. Douse everything with the readily available lime juice (it's delicious on salads, fresh fruit, and in drinks). You'll have to figure your own ways of using garlic (some believers carry garlic capsules, available in most health-food stores in the U.S.). Fresh coconut juice is said to help (don't eat the oily flesh; it makes your problem worse!). Plain boiled white rice soothes the tummy. While letting the ailment run its course, stay away from spicy and oily foods, and fresh fruits. Drink plenty of pure water. Don't be surprised if you have chills, nausea, vomiting, stomach cramps, and run a fever. This could go on for about three days. But if the problem persists, see a doctor.

SUNBURN

Sunburn can spoil a vacation quicker than anything else, so approach the sun cautiously. Expose yourself for short periods the first few days; wear a hat and sunglasses. Apply a good sunscreen to all exposed areas of the body (don't forget your feet, hands, nose, ears, back of knees, and top of forehead—especially if you have a receding hairline). Remember that after every time you go into the water, sunscreen lotion must be reapplied. Even after a few days of desensitizing the skin, wear a T-shirt

QWITCHER ITCHIN'

It's no fun to have a mosquito bite or two or a dozen. But if you're planning a trip to the tropics you say it's almost inevitable?—well not necessarily! Beware: a mosquito bite can be more than an annoyance; it can be the introduction to a particularly nasty ailment, malaria. But you can fight back against these flying, buzzing critters.

First of all, check with the Centers for Disease Control and Prevention, tel. (404) 639-1610, or with a physician who specializes in tropical diseases. They can advise you about the area you're going to visit. If it happens that you're going into a malaria-infected zone, there are precautions you can take. It used to be a simple matter of popping a quinine pill once a week and not to worry. But in *some* areas mosquitoes have developed a resistance to the common medications. Medication is still important. However, if you can avoid getting bitten in the first place that's the way to go.

A few suggestions and a few facts to keep in mind about the mosquito:

✓ Wear shoes and high socks when trekking through jungle terrain. Sandals and bare feet invite trouble.

✓ Wear clothing with high necks and long sleeves, dark rather than light colors, and remember: the mosquito can bite right through sheer fabric.

✓ Leave the shiny, sparkly jewelry back at the hotel, as well as cologne, after-shave, and aromatic lotions.

✓ When you plan your day, remember that the worst time to be out among the beasties is at dusk and in the evening. In *most* cases, daytime trekking avoids the pests.

✓ Don't leave your clothes on the ground, but if you do, give them a good shake before putting them back on. Same goes for shoes.

in the water to protect your exposed back, especially if spending the day snorkeling, and thoroughly douse the back of your neck with sunscreen lotion. PABA—para-aminobenzoic acid—solutions offer good protection and condition the skin. PABA is found in many brand names and strengths, and is much cheaper in the U.S. than in Belize. **Note:** Some people are allergic to PABA and it is said to cause cancer in isolated cases; check with your doctor before using. The higher the number on sunscreen bottles the more protection.

If, despite precautions, you still get a painful sunburn, do not return to the sun. Cover up with clothes if it's impossible to find protective deep shade (like in the depths of a dark, thick forest). Keep in mind that even in partial shade (such as under a beach umbrella), the reflection of the sun off the sand or water will burn your skin. Reburning the skin can result in painful blisters that easily become infected. Soothing suntan lotions, coconut oil, vinegar, cool tea, and preparations like Solarcaine will help relieve the pain. Usually a couple of days out of the sun will cure it. Drink plenty of liquids (especially water) and take tepid showers (see "Simple First-aid Guide," pp. 58-60).

HEALING

Most cities in Belize have a medical clinic. More than likely someone there speaks English. In the bigger cities you can usually find a doctor who will make a house call. When staying in a hotel, get a doctor quickly by asking the hotel manager; in the larger resorts, an English-speaking doctor is on call 24 hours a day. A taxi driver can be your quickest way to get to a clinic when you're a stranger in town. In small rural villages, if you have a serious problem and no doctor is around, you can usually find a *curandero*. These healers deal with the old natural methods (and maybe just a few chants thrown in for good measure). This person could be helpful in a desperate situation away from modern technology. Locals who live in the dense, jungle areas inhabited by poisonous snakes go to the local "snake doctor." Again, this might be a possibility in a remote emergency situation where help is needed quickly, and yet, medical people say every time, *no matter what,* don't go to a snake doctor. A **Cutter's Snake Bite Kit** can be helpful if used immediately after a bite, though its use is controversial in medical circles.

INSECT REPELLENT

There are many insect repellents around, some better than others. Read the labels and ask questions. Some formulas were designed to spray the outdoors, some a room, others your clothes—none of these are for the skin. Some repellents are harmful to plants and animals, some can dissolve watch crystals, and others can damage plastic eyeglass lenses. This can be a particular problem if labels are written in a foreign language that you cannot read. It's best to bring your repellent from home.

Many of the most efficient repellents contain di-ethyl-toluamide (DEET). Test it out before you leave home; the more concentrated solutions can cause an allergic reaction in some people, and for children a milder mix is recommended. Avoid use on skin with sores and abrasions.

Long Road Travel Supplies has come up with the **Indoor Travel Tent**. This lightweight, portable, net housing is made of ultra-fine mesh netting and fits right on top of the bed. A nylon floor and lightweight poles provide you with a roomy rectangular shape and free-standing protection from both flying and crawling insects that can make sleeping impossible. Convenient with a zipper door, folding flap for extra footroom, and an inside pocket for keeping valuables close at hand. Packed in its own carrying bag, and weighing just 2.3 pounds (for single bed), the price is US$79, double weighs 2.8 pounds and the price is US$99. Ask about the budget priced Indoor Tent II, with a drawstring door; single size is US$49 and weighs 1.25 pounds. For more info call (800) 359-6040 or (510) 540-4763, Box 9497, Berkeley, California 94709.

When using repellents remember:

✓ If redness and itching begin, wash off with soap and water.

✓ Apply repellent by pouring into the palms of your hands, then rubbing together and applying evenly to the skin. If you're sweating reapply every two hours. Use caution if perspiration mixed with repellent runs down your forehead and into your eyes—an absorbent headband helps.

✓ If you swim, reapply after coming out of the water.

✓ It's helpful to either dip your socks, or spray them heavily, or (as suggested by the World Health Organization) dip strips of cotton cloth, two or three inches wide and wrap around your lower legs. One strip is effective for several weeks. Mosquitoes hover close to the ground in many areas.

✓ Apply liberally around the edges of your sleeves, pants cuffs, or shorts cuffs.

✓ Sleeping in an air-conditioned room with tight-fitting windows is one good way to avoid nighttime buzzing attacks; in other situations use a mosquito net over the bed. It helps if the netting has been dipped in repellent, and make sure it's large enough to tuck well under the mattress. A rectangular shape is more efficient than the usual conical, giving you more room to sit up so you'll avoid contact with the critters that might bite through the net.

Ancient Healing

A delightful lady from Chicago, Rosita Arvigo, and her husband, Greg Shropshire, have been practicing the ancient Maya art of healing for some years. Both graduates of Chicago National College of Naprapathy, Rosita is a professor of botanical studies and has been a practicing herbalist for more than 20 years. She continues to be intrigued with the study and exploration of nature's healing herbs. For some years

OZ MALLAN

Rosita Arvigo with Don Eligio Panti, a revered Belizean bush doctor who perpetuates Maya healing methods

in Belize's Cayo District, Rosita was a student of Don Eligio Panti, a 96-year-old Maya bush doctor who has spent most of his life healing people using only the ancient Maya method plus added techniques learned from a Carib Indian during the chicle days of the 1930s. Today Rosita is his assistant. She and Don Eligio are trying very hard to keep the ancient ways alive, especially valuable as only a few remaining Maya remember the old ways. In most cases only one or two people in each group knew these ancient secrets and often they were handed down within the family. This part of the culture has dimmed over the years by the intrusion of modern medicine, which often isn't available to most of the Maya either by choice, or by circumstances.

Rosita has been recording Don Eligio's therapies, treatments, and remedies so that future generations of his people (and the world) will always have access to their effectiveness. Rosita offers her services to anyone who is willing to travel to her home, **Ix Chel Farm,** in Cayo. She is also well known for nature walks through her forest property (for a fee), where she introduces many of the plants used in Maya treatment; strolling lectures bring the old ways into the modern world with a knowledgeable, humorous, humanitarian outlook on life. With her contagious enthusiasm, Rosita brings to life information that otherwise might be pedestrian.

While walking the **Panti Trail,** a lovely path through the woods at Ix Chel Farm, visitors learn about the medicinal or healing value of various roots, vines, plants, and trees; each has a sign with its name. A booklet explains the use of each one. Here visitors will see the **grapevine** provides pure water to cleanse the navel of a newborn infant; the bark of the negrito tree, also called **dysentery bark,** that treats severe dysentery (and was sold for high prices by druggists in Europe when discovered by pirates many years past). Tea made from the **China root** is used for blood building after an attack from parasites. Another tea made from **ki bix** acts as birth control by coating the lining of the uterus.

With Rosita, her assistant, or with just the small guidebook, you will discover fruit and food sources that made it possible for the Maya of old to glean a good part of daily subsistence from the jungle. The breadnut (also known as the Ramon Tree), tasting something like a cross between a potato and a chestnut, served the Maya well for centuries when the corn crop was minimal. It can be stored up to a year, roasted over coals and eaten plain, or ground up and used to make tortillas.

This is just a tiny sampling of the information Rosita shares with her guests, plus folksy anecdotes about her experiences as a bush healer. The most recent excitement is working with scientists who come from the U.S. and other countries to Ix Chel, and together with Rosita and Greg spend weeks gathering bushels of certain barks and leaves for experimentation to find a cure for cancer and the AIDS virus. If you have a problem with mosquito or other bug bites that drive you crazy with itching, buy a vial of Rosita's **Jungle Salve;** it works! For more information about Ix Chel Farm and Rosita (see p. 196), write to Rosita Arvigo (General Delivery, San Ignacio, Cayo District, Belize, C.A.; tel. in Cayo 92-2267).

(previous page) Maya site at Copan, Honduras;
(this page, top) Copan, Honduras;
(bottom left) Caracol, Belize; (bottom right) Tikal, Guatemala (photos by Oz Mallan)

ROSIE'S ORIGINAL MAYAN HERB COMPANY

All herbs are wild-crafted, hand-chopped, and sun-dried. They contain no pesticides or poisons of any kind. Each packet contains complete instructions for use.

Blood Tonic Tea
For anemia, rheumatism, arthritis, toxicity, and fatigue. High in iron and minerals. Mild tasting. Contains wild yam and China root.

Balsam Bark Tea
For conditions of the kidneys, bladder, and liver. Suitable for children, the weak, and the aged.

Party Punch
A delightful, pleasant-tasting beverage—hot or cold. Contents: lemon grass, rose petals, mint, and orange peel.

Smoking Tobacco
An alternative to toxic and addictive nicotine. Mild and pleasant. Contents: wild trumpet tree leaves.

Bellyache Tea
For chronic indigestion, gastritis. Mild sedative. Contents: man vine.

For a one-ounce package, prices range from US$5.75 to US$11.50 including postage and packing. For more information write to Rosita Arvigo, D.N., Ix Chel Farm, San Ignacio, Cayo District, Belize, C.A.

Self Help
The smart traveler carries a first-aid kit of some kind with him. If backpacking, at least carry a minimal first-aid kit:

adhesive tape	insect repellent
alcohol	Lomotil
antibiotic ointment	aspirin
pain killer	baking soda
sterile, adhesive strips	sunscreen
cornstarch	tweezers
gauze	water-purification
hydrogen peroxide	tablets
iodine	needle

Many first-aid products are widely available, but certain items, like aspirin and Band-Aids, are sold individually in small shops and are much cheaper if bought in your hometown. Even if not out in the wilderness you should carry at least a few sterile strips, aspirin, and an antibiotic ointment or powder or both. Travelers should be aware that in the tropics, with its heavy humidity, a simple scrape can become infected more easily than in a dry climate. So keep cuts and scratches as clean and as dry as possible.

Another great addition to your first-aid kit is David Werner's book, *Where There Is No Doctor*. It can be ordered from the Hesperian Foundation (Box 1692, Palo Alto, California 94302). David Werner drew on his experiences living in Mexico's backcountry to create this practical, informative book.

Centers For Disease Control
Check on your tetanus shot before you leave home. If you anticipate backpacking in jungle regions, call the **International Traveler's Hotline** at the **Centers For Disease Control and Prevention,** tel. (404) 332-4559. This hotline advises callers of the conditions abroad, what areas are experiencing an outbreak of disease and will make suggestions for immunizations. It is updated as conditions warrant. A booklet also is available, *Health Information for International Travelers,* from the U.S. Government Printing Office. To obtain a copy, send US$5 to the Superintendent of Documents (U.S. Government Printing Office, Washington, DC 20402).

SIMPLE FIRST-AID GUIDE

Acute Allergic Reaction
This, the most serious complication of insect bites, can be fatal. Common symptoms are hives, rash, pallor, nausea, tightness in the chest or throat, and trouble speaking or breathing. Be alert for symptoms. If they appear, get prompt medical help. Start CPR if needed and continue until medical help is available.

Animal Bites
Bites, especially on the face and neck, need immediate medical attention. If possible, catch and hold the animal for observation, taking care not to be bitten again. Wash the wound with soap and water (hold under running water for two to three minutes unless bleeding heavily). Do not use iodine or other antiseptic. Bandage. This also applies to bites by human beings. In case of human bites the danger of infection is high. (See also "Rabies" and "Snakebites.")

Bee Stings
Apply cold compresses quickly. If possible, remove the stinger by gentle scraping with a clean fingernail and continue cold applications till pain is gone. Be alert for symptoms of acute allergic reaction or infection requiring medical aid.

Bleeding
For severe bleeding apply direct pressure to the wound with a bandage or the heel of the hand. Do not remove cloths when blood-soaked; just add others on top and continue pressure until bleeding stops. Elevate bleeding part above heart level. If bleeding continues, apply a pressure bandage to arterial points. Do not put on tourniquet unless advised by a physician. Do not use iodine or other disinfectant. Get medical aid.

Blister On Heel
It is better not to open a blister if you can rest the foot. If you can't, wash the foot with soap and water; make a small hole at the base of the blister with a needle sterilized in 70% alcohol or by holding the needle in the flame of a match; drain fluid and cover with strip bandage or moleskin. If a blister breaks on its own, wash with soap and water, bandage, and be alert for signs of infection (redness, festering) that call for medical attention.

Burns
Minor burns (redness, swelling, pain): apply cold water or immerse burned part in cold water immediately. Use burn medication if necessary. Deeper burns (blisters develop): immerse in cold water (not ice water) or apply cold compresses for one to two hours. Blot dry and protect with a sterile bandage. Do not use antiseptic, ointment, or home remedies. Consult a doctor. For deep burns (skin layers destroyed, skin may be charred), cover with sterile cloth; be alert for breathing difficulties and treat for shock if necessary. Do not remove clothing stuck to burn. Do not apply ice. Do not use burn remedies. Get medical help quickly.

Cuts
Wash small cuts with clean water and soap. Hold wound under running water. Bandage. Use hydrogen peroxide or other antiseptic. For large wounds see "Bleeding." If a finger or toe has been cut off, treat severed end to control bleeding. Put severed part in a clean cloth for the doctor (it may be possible to reattach it by surgery). Treat for shock if necessary. Get medical help at once.

Diving Accident
There may be injury to the cervical spine (such as a broken neck). Call for medical help. (See also "Drowning.")

Drowning
Clear airway and start CPR even before trying to get water out of lungs. Continue CPR till medical help arrives. In case of vomiting, turn victim's head to one side to prevent inhaling vomitus.

Food Poisoning
Symptoms appear a varying number of hours after eating and are generally like those of the flu—headache, diarrhea, vomiting, abdominal cramps, fever, and a general sick feeling. See a doctor. A rare form, botulism, has a high fatality rate. Symptoms are double vision, inability to swallow, difficulty in speaking, and respiratory paralysis. Get to an emergency facility at once.

Fractures
Until medical help arrives, do not move the victim unless absolutely necessary. Suspected victims of back, neck, or hip injuries should not be moved.

Suspected breaks of arms or legs should be splinted to avoid further damage before victim is moved, if moving is necessary.

Heat Exhaustion

Symptoms are cool, moist skin, profuse sweating, headache, fatigue, and drowsiness with essentially normal body temperature. Remove the victim to cool surroundings, raise the feet and legs, loosen clothing and apply cool cloths. Give sips of salt water—one teaspoon of salt to a glass of water—for rehydration. If the victim vomits, stop fluids and take the victim to an emergency facility as soon as possible.

Heat Stroke

Rush the victim to a hospital. Heat stroke can be fatal. The victim may be unconscious or severely confused. The skin feels hot and is red and dry with no perspiration. Body temperature is high. Pulse is rapid. Remove the victim to cool area and sponge with cool water or rubbing alcohol: use fans or a/c and wrap in wet sheets, but do not over chill. Massage arms and legs to increase circulation. *Do not* give large amounts of liquids. *Do not* give liquids if victim is unconscious.

Insect Bites

Be alert for an acute allergic reaction that requires quick medical aid. Otherwise, apply cold compresses and soothing lotions. If bites are scratched and infection starts (fever, swelling, redness), see a doctor. (See also "Spider Bites," "Bee Stings," and "Ticks.")

Jellyfish Stings

The symptom is acute pain and may include a feeling of paralysis. Immerse in ice water for 5-10 minutes or apply aromatic spirits of ammonia to remove venom from skin. Be alert for symptoms of acute allergic reaction and/or shock. If this happens, get the victim to a hospital as soon as possible.

Mosquito Bites

See "Insect Bites."

Motion Sickness

Get a prescription from your doctor if boat traveling is anticipated and this illness is a problem. Many over-the-counter remedies are sold in the United States: Bonine and Dramamine are examples. If you prefer not to take chemicals or if these make you drowsy, then something new, the Sea Band, might

work for you. It's a cloth band that you place around the pressure point of the wrists. For more information write:

Sea Band
1645 Palm Beach Lake Blvd.
Ste. 220
W. Palm Beach, Florida 33401

Medication is also available by prescription from your doctor that's administered in adhesive patches behind the ear.

Muscle Cramps

Usually a result of unaccustomed exertion, "working" the muscle or kneading it with the hand relieves cramp. If in water, head for shore (you can swim even with a muscle cramp), or knead the muscle with your hand. Call for help if needed. *Do not* panic.

Mushroom Poisoning

Even a small ingestion may be serious. Induce vomiting immediately if there is any question of mushroom poisoning. Symptoms—vomiting, diarrhea, difficulty breathing—may begin in one to two hours or up to 24 hours. Convulsions and delirium may develop. Go to a doctor or emergency facility at once.

Nosebleed

Press bleeding nostril closed, pinch nostrils together, or pack with sterile cotton or gauze. Apply cold cloth or ice to nose and face. The victim should sit up, leaning forward, or lie down with head and shoulders raised. If bleeding does not stop in 10 minutes, get medical help.

Obstructed Airway

Find out if the victim can talk by asking "Can you talk?" If so, encourage the victim to try to cough up the obstruction. If the victim cannot speak, a trained person must apply the Heimlich maneuver. If you are alone and choking, try to forcefully cough object out. Or press your fist into your upper abdomen with a quick upward thrust, or lean forward and quickly press your upper abdomen over any firm object with a rounded edge (the back of a chair, the edge of a sink, or a porch railing). Keep trying until the object comes out.

Plant Poisoning

Many plants are poisonous if eaten or chewed. Induce vomiting immediately. Take the victim to emergency facility for treatment. If the leaves of the diffenbachia (common in the Yucatán jungle) are chewed, one of the first symptoms is swelling of the throat. (See also "Mushroom Poisoning.")

Poison Ivy, Poison Oak, Or Poison Sumac
After contact, wash affected area with alkali-base laundry soap, lathering well. Have a poison-ivy remedy available in case itching and blisters develop.

Puncture Wounds
Usually caused by stepping on a tack or a nail, puncture wounds often do not bleed, so try to squeeze out some blood. Wash thoroughly with soap and water and apply a sterile bandage. Check with a doctor about tetanus. If pain, heat, throbbing, or redness develops, get medical attention at once.

Rabies
Bites from bats, raccoons, rats, or other wild animals are the most common threat of rabies today. Try to capture the animal, avoiding being bitten, so it can be observed; do not kill the animal unless necessary and try not to injure the head so the brain can be examined. If the animal can't be found, see a doctor who may decide to use antirabies immunization. In any case, flush bite with water and apply a dry dressing; keep victim quiet and see a doctor as soon as possible. See also "Animal Bites."

Scrapes
Sponge scrapes with soap and water; dry. Apply antibiotic ointment or powder and cover with a non-stick dressing (or tape on a piece of cellophane). When healing starts, stop ointment and use antiseptic powder to help scab form. Ask a doctor about tetanus.

Shock
Shock can result from any kind of injury. Get immediate medical help. Symptoms may be pallor, a clammy feeling to the skin, shallow breathing, a fast pulse, weakness, or thirst. Loosen clothing, cover the victim with a blanket but do not apply other heat, and lay the person on the back with feet raised. If necessary, start CPR. *Do not* give water or other fluids.

Snakebite
If the snake is not poisonous, toothmarks usually appear in an even row (an exception, the poisonous gila monster, shows even tooth marks). Wash the bite with soap and water and apply a sterile bandage. See a doctor. If the snake is poisonous, puncture marks (one to six) can usually be seen. Kill the snake for identification if possible, taking care not to be bitten. Keep the victim quiet, and immobilize the bitten arm or leg, keeping it on a lower level than the heart. If possible, phone ahead to be sure antivenin is available and get medical treatment as soon as possible. *Do not* give alcohol in any form. If treatment must be delayed and a snakebite kit is available, use as directed.

Spider Bites
The black widow bite may produce only a light reaction at the place of the bite, but severe pain, a general sick feeling, sweating, abdominal cramps, and breathing and speaking difficulty may develop. The more dangerous brown recluse spider's venom produces a severe reaction at the bite, generally in two to eight hours, plus chills, fever, joint pain, nausea, and vomiting. Apply a cold compress to the bite in either case. Get medical aid quickly.

Sprain
Treat a sprain as a fracture until the injured part has been X-rayed. Raise the sprained ankle or other joint and apply cold compresses or immerse in cold water. If swelling is pronounced, try not to use the injured part till it has been X-rayed. Get prompt medical help.

Sunburn
For skin that is moderately red and slightly swollen, apply wet dressings of gauze dipped in a solution of one tablespoon baking soda and one tablespoon cornstarch to two quarts of cool water. Or take a cool bath with a cup of baking soda to a tub of water. Sunburn remedies are helpful in relieving pain. See a doctor if the burn is severe.

Sunstroke
This is a severe emergency. See "Heat Stroke." Skin is hot and dry; body temperature is high. The victim may be delirious or unconscious. Get medical help immediately.

Ticks
Cover ticks with mineral oil or kerosene to exclude air and they will usually drop off or can be lifted off with tweezers in 30 minutes. To avoid infection, take care to remove the whole tick. Wash area with soap and water. Check with a doctor or the health department to see if deadly ticks are in the area.

Wasp Stings
See "Bee Stings."

WHAT TO TAKE

Whatever time of year you travel to Belize you can expect warm to hot weather. Most airlines allow you to check two suitcases, and you can bring another carry-on bag that fits either under your seat or in the overhead rack; this is fine if you're planning a one-destination trip to a self-contained resort and want a couple of changes of clothes each day. But if you plan on moving around a lot, you'll be happy if you keep it light—one bag and one carry-on.

Experienced women travelers pack a small foldable purse into their carry-on, leaving them with only one thing to carry while en route. And be sure to include a few overnight necessities in your carry-on in the event your luggage doesn't arrive when you do. Valuables are safest in your carry-on stowed under the seat in front of you rather than in the overhead rack, whether you're on a plane, boat, or bus.

Security

It's smart to keep passports, traveler's checks, money, and important papers in a hotel safe or on your person at all times. (It's always a good idea to keep a separate list of document numbers in your luggage and leave a copy with a friend back home. This expedites replacement in case of loss.) The do-it-yourselfer can sew inside pockets into clothes; buy extra-long pants, turn up the hem, and sew three-fourths of the way around, closing the last section with a piece of Velcro. Separate shoulder-holster pockets, moneybelts, and pockets around the neck inside clothing—all made of cotton—are available commercially. If you're going to be backpacking and sloshing in jungle streams, etc., put everything in zipper-lock plastic bags before placing them in pockets. Waterproof plastic tubes are available that will hold a limited number of items around your neck while swimming.

Clothing

A swimsuit is a must, and if you're not staying at one of the larger hotels, bring a beach towel. In today's Belize you'll see a wide variety of clothing. **Women:** Unless you want to attract a lot of attention, do not wear bikinis, short shorts, or revealing tight clothes while strolling the streets of Belize City. Save that for the beach areas or the pool at your hotel. If traveling during Nov.-Jan., bring along a light wrap since it can cool off in the evening. The rest of the year you'll probably carry the wrap in your suitcase. For women, a wraparound skirt is a useful item that can quickly cover up shorts when traveling through the villages and some cities (many small-village residents really gawk at women wearing shorts; whatever you do, don't enter a church wearing them). The wraparound skirt also makes a good shawl when it cools off. Cotton underwear is the coolest in the tropics, but nylon is less bulky and dries overnight, cutting down on the number needed. Be sure that you bring broken-in, comfortable walking shoes; blisters can wreck a vacation almost as much as a sunburn. For those planning on long treks through the jungle, lightweight hiking boots give protection from scratching brush, flying biting insects that hover near the ground, and, yes, snakes.

Necessities

If you wear glasses and are planning an extended trip it's a good idea to bring an extra pair or carry the lens prescription; the same goes for medication (make sure the prescription is written in generic terms). Bring your favorite toiletries and cosmetics as the selection here is small. American cigarettes are available but are pricey. If you smoke a pipe bring plenty of tobacco since it's almost impossible to find.

Reading Material

Avid readers from the U.S. and Canada are in luck in Belize. Because the official language is English, you'll seldom have a hard time finding English-language books; however, don't expect a huge selection of best-sellers. Both small and large hotels have book-trading shelves. If they aren't obvious, ask at the desk. Most travelers are delighted to trade books. Many travelers come prepared with an "itty bitty" Book Light for rooms where there's either no electricity or dim bulbs. For books on Belize, see "Booklist."

Backpackers

If you plan on hitchhiking or using public transportation, don't use a large external-frame pack; crowded buses have very little room and it won't fit in most small cars or public lockers. Smaller packs with zippered compartments that will accommodate mini-padlocks are most practical. A strong bike cable and lock secures the pack to a YH bed or a bus or train rack. None of the above will deter the real criminal but might make it difficult enough to discourage everyone else.

Experienced backpackers travel light with a pack, an additional canvas bag, a small water- and mosquito-proof tent, a hammock, and mosquito netting.

Sensible Planning

Leave expensive jewelry at home. Don't flaunt cameras and video equipment or leave them in sight in cars when sightseeing, especially in some parts of Belize City. Remember, this is a poor country and petty theft is their number-one crime—don't tempt fate. (As in London, the police don't carry guns.) It is also wise not to wander around alone on foot late at night in Belize City—for the same reasons. Go out, but take a taxi. Most of the Belizeans are friendly decent people but, as in every community, a small percentage will steal anything—given the opportunity. Expect to be hustled, whether in the market, a cafe, or a bar. To the Belizeans,

BEWARE THE
RASTAFARIAN SALESMEN!

This may never happen to you—or most travelers to Belize—but beware the Rastafarians! They'll hound you to buy dope and can get ugly when refused. Tell the persistent dealers that one of the Rasta brothers has already sold you what you need. Usually that's all it takes and with a smile they're off—satisfied you're okay. It's mostly young adults who are harrassed this way.

Americans and Canadians come off as "rich" whether they are or not. The local hustlers are quite creative when it comes to thinking of ways to con you out of some cash. Keep your wits about you, pull out of conversations that appear headed in that direction, and remember—you're in their country. Don't give out your hotel or room number freely or where they can be overheard by strangers. Don't be surprised if someone tries to sell you a controlled substance on the street; if you buy, don't be surprised if the same guy turns you in to the local authorities and earns a payoff. The police come down heavily on substance users in Belize. All of this advice is valid in Paris, downtown Los Angeles, Jakarta, and many other large cities throughout the world.

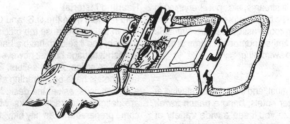

LOUISE FOOTE

INFORMATION

See "General Tourist Information," p. 104, for addresses of the Belize Tourist Board and other associations.

MONEY

The currency unit is the Belize Dollar (BZE$), which has been steady at BZE$2 to US$1 for some years. While prices are given in US$ in this book, travelers should be prepared to pay in Belizean currency on the street, boats, in cafes, and at other smaller establishments; however, carry both just in case. Of course, the larger hotels accept U.S. dollars. When you buy or sell currency at a bank, be sure to retain proof of sale. The following places are authorized to buy or sell foreign currency; all are located close together near the plaza in Belize City. Hours are Mon.-Fri. till 1 p.m., Sat. till 11 a.m.

Atlantic Bank Ltd.
Bank of Nova Scotia
Barclays Bank
Belize Bank of Commerce and Industry
Belize Global Travel Services Ltd.

At the Mexican-Belize border you'll be approached by moneychangers (and you can bet they don't represent the banks). Many travelers buy just enough Belize dollars to get them into the city and to the banks. Depending on your mode of transport and destination, these moneychangers can be helpful. Strictly speaking, though, this is illegal—so suit yourself. The exchange rate is the same but you'll have no receipt of sale. If selling a large quantity of Belize dollars back to the bank, you might be asked for that proof.

Airport departure tax is US$11.25 (including security tax) when leaving the country, except for in-transit passengers spending fewer than 24 hours in the country. When entering the country and flying to any other in-country destination, a US75 cents charge is required to clear security.

Credit Cards And Traveler's Checks
Credit cards are taken only at the larger business establishments, so bring traveler's checks and cash as well. You will find representatives of Visa, MasterCard, and American Express at the four commercial banks in Belize City.

TIPS TO KNOW BEFORE YOU GO

The electricity is 110/220 volt, 60 cycles. Removal of archaeological artifacts will get you

BELIZE TELEPHONE SERVICE AND USE

Belize has a fine, modern telephone system that enables visitors to make contact with the rest of the world quickly and efficiently with direct dial service. Belize's country code is 501 and the area codes follow. The number of digits varies from city to city.

AREA CODES	
2	Belize City
8	Belmopan
93	Benque Viejo
3	Blue Creek
28	Burrell Boom
22	Caye Caulker
4	Corozal
5	Dangriga
6	Independence
25	Ladyville
3	Orange Walk Town
6	Placencia
7	Punta Gorda
92	San Ignacio
4	San Joaquin
26	San Pedro
8	Spanish Lookout

thrown in jail. Religious services available are Protestant, Roman Catholic, and Anglican; ask for church locations at your hotel. While the water is said to be good from the tap in Belize City, experienced travelers still drink only bottled water. If you're looking for a water substitute, Coke signs are everywhere, and rum and **Belikin beer** are plentiful (both are made in Belize). Some travelers take advantage of the privilege and bring in one bottle of their own personal favorite liquor. Most restaurants and hotels include the tip on the check; if the tip isn't added to the bill, then 10% is the norm. It is not customary to tip taxi drivers unless they help you with your luggage. The local time is Greenwich Mean Time minus six, the same as U.S. Central Time, year-round (no daylight saving time). Shops are generally open daily 8 a.m.-12 p.m. and 1-4 p.m., closed Sundays and public holidays.

CAMERAS AND PICTURE TAKING

Bring a camera to Belize! Nature and people combine to provide unforgettable panoramas, well worth taking home with you on film to savor again at your leisure. Many people bring simple cameras such as instants that are easy to carry and uncomplicated. Others prefer 35mm cameras that offer higher-quality pictures, are easier than ever to use, and are available in a variety of price ranges. They can come equipped with built-in light meter, automatic exposure, self-focus, and self-advance—with little more to do than aim and click.

Film
Two reasons to bring film with you: it's cheaper and more readily available in the U.S. Two reasons *not* to bring quantities of film: space may be a problem and heat can affect film quality, both before and after exposure. If you're traveling for more than two weeks in a car or bus a good part of the time, carry film in an insulated case. You can buy a soft-sided insulated bag in most camera shops or order one out of a professional photography magazine. For the average vacation, if your film is kept in your room there should be no problem. Many varieties of Kodak film are found in camera shops and hotel gift shops in Belize. In the smaller towns you may not be able to find slide film.

X-ray Protection
If you carry film with you when traveling by plane remember to take precautions. Each time film is passed through the security X-ray machine, a little damage is done. It's cumulative, and perhaps one time won't make much difference, but most photographers won't take the chance. Request hand inspection. With today's tight security at airports, some guards insist on passing your film and camera through the X-ray machine. If packed in your checked luggage, it's wise to keep film in protective lead-lined bags, available at camera shops in two sizes: the larger size holds up to 22 rolls of 35mm film, the smaller holds eight rolls. If you use fast film, ASA 400 or higher, buy the double lead-lined bag designed to protect more sensitive film. Carry an extra lead-lined bag for your film-loaded camera if you want to drop it into a piece of carry-on luggage. (These bags also protect medications from X-ray damage.)

If you decide to request hand examination (rarely, if ever, refused at the Belize airport), make it simple for the security guard. Have the film out of boxes and canisters placed together in one clear plastic bag that you can hand him for quick examination both coming and going. He'll also want to look at the camera; load it with film *after* crossing the border.

Film Processing
For processing film the traveler has several options. Most people take their film home and have it processed at a familiar lab. Again, if the trip is lengthy and you are shooting many photos, it's impractical to carry used rolls around for more than a couple of weeks. Larger cities have one-hour photo labs, but they only handle color prints; color slides must be processed at a lab out of the city, which usually takes a week or two. Kodak mailers are another option but most photographers won't let their film out of sight until they reach their own favorite lab.

Camera Protection

Take a few precautions with your camera while traveling. At the beach remember that a combination of wind and sand can really gum up the works and scratch the lens. On 35mm cameras keep a clear skylight filter on the lens instead of a lens cap so the camera can hang around your neck or in a fanny pack always at the ready for the spectacular shot that comes when least expected. If something is going to get scratched, better a $15 filter than a $300 lens. It also helps to carry as little equipment as possible. If you want more than candids and you carry a 35mm camera, basic equipment can be simple. Padded camera cases are good and come in all sizes. A canvas bag is lighter and less conspicuous than a heavy photo bag, but doesn't have the extra protection the padding provides.

Safety Tips

Keep your camera dry; carrying a couple of big zipper-lock bags affords instant protection. Don't *store* cameras in plastic bags for any length of time because the moisture that builds up in the bag can damage a camera as much as leaving it in the rain.

It's always wise to keep cameras out of sight in a car or when camping out. Put your name and address on the camera. Chances are if it gets left behind or stolen it won't matter whether your name is there or not, and don't expect to see it again; however, miracles do happen. (You *can* put a rider on most homeowner's insurance policies for a nominal sum that will cover the cost if a camera is lost or stolen.) It's a nuisance to carry cameras every second when traveling—especially for a long period. During an evening out, we always leave our cameras and equipment (out of sight) in the hotel room; so far everything has been intact when we return. However, if this makes you crazy with worry, some hotel safes are large enough to accommodate your equipment.

Cameras can be a help or a hindrance when trying to get to know the people. When traveling in the backcountry you'll run into folks who don't want their pictures taken. Keep your camera put away until the right moment. The main thing to remember is to ask permission first and then if someone doesn't want his/her picture taken, accept the refusal with a gracious smile and move on.

Underwater Photography

One of the newer delights for the amateur photographer is shooting the denizens of the deep in living color. If you're fortunate enough to have one of the upscale 35mm cameras put out by Nikonos or Hanimex you've got it made. Even the simple cameras, such as Weathermatic put out by Minolta, will give you a lot of pleasure and good souvenirs to take home. The simpler inexpensive cameras are generally usable only to a depth of 15 feet. The Nikonos and Hanimex are waterproof up to 150 feet.

Some hotels, resorts, and shops in Belize have underwater cameras for rent. Don't expect a large selection. Remember, when buying film the best for underwater is natural-, red-, or yellow-tint film; film like Ektachrome with a bluish cast does not give the best results. A strobe or flash is a big help if shooting in deep water or into caves. Natural-light pictures are great if you're shooting in fairly shallow water. It's best to shoot on an eye-to-eye level when photographing fish. Be careful of stirring up silt from the bottom with your fins. Try to hold very still when depressing the shutter, and if you must stabilize yourself, *don't* grab onto any bright-colored coral—you will kill it. If it's colored it's alive, so grab only the drab grayish, tannish coral; grabbing live coral can cut your hands and often cause infection. Enjoy the reef and make sure the reef enjoys you—this is a natural haven for fragile life that must be preserved and cared for.

Other Photo Information

Belize has some mighty fine local photographers. If you're not a camera carrier and decide you'd like to take home some great pictures, including underwater shots, here are a few people to check out. On Caye Caulker stop by the photo gallery and gift shop of **James Beveridge**—look for the sign that says **Sea-ing is Belizing**. Another super place on Caye Caulker to see good photos, including underwater shots, is **Ellen MacRae's Galeria Hicaco**.

GETTING THERE

Many travelers are under the misguided notion that a passport is not needed to travel to Belize—wrong. You *must* have a current passport, and you may be asked at the border to show a return ticket and ample money. You do not need a visa if you are a British Commonwealth subject or a citizen of Belgium, Denmark, Finland, Greece, Iceland, Italy, Liechtenstein, Luxembourg, Mexico, Spain, Switzerland, Tunisia, Turkey, the United States, or Uraguay, provided you have valid documents. Remember to save US$11.25 for **departure tax** when going home. Mostly the officials are suspicious of people who appear scruffy and are traveling with little luggage. They're trying to discourage hippie-type "substance"-oriented squatters.

Charles Lindbergh
Belize is a small country that, without a national airline, is dependent on foreign airlines to bring visitors from the U.S., Mexico, and the rest of Central America. However, this may change in the future given the history of the commuter airlines within the country and how they have grown. To Belizeans, flying in and out of Belize was a farfetched idea when American hero Charles Lindbergh paid a dramatic visit to the small Caribbean nation. At the time, 1927, Lindbergh was the world's most famous pilot, having completed his flight across the Atlantic nonstop from New York to Paris. It was shortly after his famous "Lindy Hop" that he paid a visit to Latin America in his ongoing effort to promote and develop commercial aviation. On his visit to Belize, the **Barracks Green** in Belize City served as his runway and the sound of his well-known little craft, The *Spirit of St. Louis*, overhead attracted hundreds of curious spectators. This

was an exciting event for Belizeans, the beginning of an idea that would develop into the important aviation industry that has since linked the isolated parts of Belize.

By Air
Most travelers planning a visit to Belize arrive at Philip Goldson International Airport nine miles from Belize City in Ladyville. (Taxi fare to and from the international airport is about US$15.) Transport to Belize is getting easier every year. The international airport recently extended a runway and added a modern new terminal building. Further studies are planned for future development.

Board direct flights from **Louisiana, Texas, Florida, Cancun,** and several points in **Latin America** daily. Airlines serving Belize include **American, Continental, Taca International,** and **Tan Sahsa,** plus a new service to and from Mexico (Cancun via Chetumal) aboard Mexicana Airlines.

As you fly into the international airport you'll notice camouflaged hangars that house British Harriers. Don't be alarmed—the British still maintain an active military presence at the request of the Belizean government, giving the young country a chance to establish their own defense forces.

AIRLINE PASSENGERS

Remember to reconfirm your airline reservations 48 hours before your arrival and departure date whether it's a national or international flight; not all airline offices have a computerized reservation service.

New Airstrips

A current study is being made to prepare a master plan for the safe and orderly development of domestic air traffic within Belize. Plans are being discussed to move and enlarge the present airport in San Pedro away from the center of town.

Two new airstrips are in operation in the country, one at **Caye Caulker** and one in **Cayo District** at **Central Farms** about eight miles from San Ignacio. Both are serviced by Tropic and Island airlines. At Caulker you will be dropped off and picked up during regularly scheduled flights to Belize City *upon request* (just as they do for

Caye Chapel). At this time, regular routing has not been established for the Cayo District airstrip, but charters are available.

Approximate price when filling *all* seats on a charter is about US$50 pp. For more information and prices, call the airlines (see the chart "Airlines Serving Belize").

From Mexico

Traveling to Belize via Mexico's state of Quintana Roo on the Yucatán Peninsula is an efficient way to arrive. Combining a vacation in both countries is economical and a way to see a little more than usual. Shop around for budget

AIRLINES SERVING BELIZE

NAME	TELEPHONE	SERVICE
American Airlines	(800) 433-7300	from the U.S.; Dallas, Ft. Worth, Miami
Continental Airlines	(800) 525-0280	from the U.S.; nonstop from Houston
Sahsa	(800) 327-1225 (800) 238-4043 (in Florida)	from Houston, New Orleans, Miami (special baggage allowance for diving equipment)
Taca Airlines	(800) 535-8780	from Houston, New Orleans, Miami, Los Angeles, New York Kennedy, and Washington Dulles
Tropic Airlines	(800) 422-3435 (2) 26-2012/45-671 fax: 26-2338	scheduled: Belize Municipal, San Pedro, Belize International, charters
Maya Airlines	(800) 422-3435 (713) 440-1867 (in Texas) (2) 72-312/(2) 77-215	scheduled: Belize Municipal, San Pedro, Belize International, Corozal, Caye Caulker, Dangriga, Big Creek, Punta Gorda, charters, ambulance
Cari-Bee Air Service	(2) 44-253	charters, domestic, international, ambulance
Javier Flying Service	(2) 33-140 fax: (2)62-192	charters, domestic, international
Su-Bec Air Service	(2) 44-027	charters, domestic, international
Island Air	(501) 26-2484 fax: (501) 26-292	regular service: International, Municipal, San Pedro. Charters available (including Tikal)

flights from the U.S. into Cancun or even Isla Cozumel (just a short ferry ride to Playa del Carmen and its efficient bus depot, then continue by bus). From Cancun it's immensely cheap and easy to travel the 218 miles by bus to Chetumal and then across the Rio Hondo.

The Rio Hondo forms a natural border between Quintana Roo and Belize. Chetumal is the only land link between the two countries and a departure point for Batty and Venus bus lines traveling to many points in Belize. If traveling to the **Adventure Inn** in Corozal, the cost is about US$7 by bus or about US$15 by taxi.

Henry Menzies Travel and Tours (Box 210, Corozal Town, Corozal District, Belize, C.A.; tel. 4-22-725/23-414), runs a taxi service and has the run between Chetumal and Corozal down to a science. Henry guides first-timers across the border with great ease. Call a day or two in advance (if in Mexico). If possible don't wait to call from Chetumal; for some reason telephoning from here can be very difficult at times. And the problem is not the phone service in Belize, which is modern. Even with short notice, Henry will usually pick you up within the hour. The trip between Chetumal and Corozal takes about 20 minutes, including the border crossing. (No matter what your travel mode, don't go at peak times like 8 a.m. or 5 p.m.—opening and closing hours—without expecting a long wait.) He will take you any place you'd like in Belize. Make fare arrangements before you climb in the cab. Henry is a good, helpful driver and an excellent guide with a comfortable a/c van.

By Boat
An on-again/off-again ferry operates two or three times a week from Punta Gorda to Livingston and Puerto Barrios, Guatemala (about US$10). However, operations were recently suspended when a large amount of cocaine was seized and the captain arrested. It may be back in business by the time you get there, but don't make your plans around the ferry. Usually other "on and off" small boats also make that trip. For information call (7) 22-495.

By Car
If your own vehicle is a low-slung sports car—leave it home. Off the three main highways

---

SEAPORTS OF ENTRY INTO BELIZE

If you plan on traveling aboard your own vessel, these are the towns of entry:

> Belize City
> Punta Gorda Town
> San Pedro on Ambergris Caye

In San Pedro on Ambergris Caye, you can obtain clearance, but you must pay for a custom agent to fly from the mainland.

Boats are required to have:

> The vessel's official documentation.
> Clearance from the last port of call.
> Three copies of the crew and passenger manifesto.
> Three copies of stores used or list of cargo on board; if none, an imballast manifesto.

For more information contact the Belize Embassy in Washington D.C., 2535 Massachusetts Ave. NW, Washington, DC 20008; tel. (202) 332-9636, fax (202) 332-6741 or Belize Gov't. Tourism Office, tel. (800) 624-0686.

---

roads are rough and potholed. When it rains, you'll heave through thick mud where tires have cut deep ridges. The hot tropical sun appears and dries it into cement mounds. The higher the car the better; 4WD is best. If traveling by car you'll need Belizean insurance bought on the Belize side of the border with Belizean dollars (a couple of insurance offices are close to the border and in Corozal). Moneychangers are readily available at the border crossing, and, as discussed under "Money," it seems that the standard rate of exchange is BZE$2 to US$1 whether from the moneychangers or the banks in the city (the banks may charge a few-cents conversion fee). Visas for ongoing travel to Guatemala can be obtained at the Guatemalan Embassy at Mile 6.5, New Northern Highway, tel. 25-2614 in Belize City. **Note:** See the "Travel Advisory" in the "Guatemala" chapter, p. 250.

Note for the RV buff or hardy driver: the route between Brownsville, Texas, and the border of Belize is just under 1,400 miles. If you don't stop to smell the flowers along the way, the drive can be made in a few days. The all-weather roads are paved, and the shortest route is through Mexico by way of Tampico, Veracruz, Villahermosa, Escarcega, and Chetumal.

However, the Mexican government has recently made changes in their rules for travelers who are passing through Mexico to another destination. Travelers must purchase a bond to insure that they will not sell their car in Mexico (often done by U.S. car thieves). The bond is bought at the border *only* with a credit card when entering Mexico, and it is required to exit at the same border crossing when leaving Mexico (which sounds simple, but isn't). I suggest you call a Mexico Government Tourism Office near you for more precise information.

GETTING AROUND

By Bus

Probably the cheapest way to get around the country is the bus system, which, in most cases, is surprisingly good. Most buses offer regular schedules and run frequently; for longer trips it's best to reserve your seat the day before you wish to travel. Expect lively music in fairly modern vehicles where all the passengers have seats. In most cases, standing is not allowed and the driver will pack passengers three to a seat if necessary. The exceptions are the afternoon buses to Punta Gorda.

Batty and **Venus** lines serve Belize and go into Mexico and Guatemala. Get information from Batty (54 E. Collet Canal, Belize City, Belize, C.A.; tel. 2-74-924, in Corozal 4-23-034). Get Venus bus line information on Magazine Rd. in Belize City, tel. (2) 73-354, 77-390, or on 7th Ave. in Corozal, tel. (4) 22-132. Both companies offer upscale charter tours as well. **Urbina** buses travel from Belize City to Orange Walk departing from Cinderella Plaza. Catch the **Z-Line** to go south to Dangriga and Punta Gorda, departing from the Venus Terminal on Magazine Rd., tel. (2) 73-937.

James' Bus service travels to the southern part of the country, leaving Belize City from the Pound Yard Bridge. To go west to Belmopan, San Ignacio, and on to the Guatemalan border, depart from the Batty depot on E. Collet Canal or from **Novelo's** on W. Collet Canal. Novelo's buses travel to the Cayo District, tel. (2) 77-372. **Carmen** buses also travel to the Cayo District leaving from the Pound Yard Bridge.

Travel time from Belize City to Corozal or San Ignacio is about two hours, to Dangriga about four hours, and to Punta Gorda 8-10 hours (this can be a bumpy ride). Fares average about US$2-4 to most destinations, about US$7-9 for the longer routes. Remember that these are not luxury buses, but they are the cheapest way to travel. And for anyone who wants to meet the Belizean people, this is the way to go. Most of these buses make frequent stops and will pick up anyone on the side of the road anywhere—as long as space permits. The drivers will also drop you off wherever you wish if you holler when you want off.

Note: Travel aboard a newish bus line, **Caribe Express** that operates between Mexico (Cancun, Mérida, Campeche, Chetumal), and several cities in Belize. You must get off the bus at the border and will be helped through the process when arrangements are made with **Belize Transfer Service** (BTS). The bus is modern, with a/c, movies, bathroom, an attendant, and snacks. For more information and reservations, call or write BTS (Box 1722, Palo Alto, California 94302; tel. 415-641-9145).

Car Rentals

Some rental companies offer only small, mid-size, and large 4WD Jeeps. Vans and passenger cars are also available, some with a/c—they cost more, though prices have come down somewhat from a few years ago. Insurance is mandatory. Driving rules are U.S.-style and it's wise to obtain an international driver's license before you leave home (about US$5 at most auto clubs). Gasoline also is quite costly, about US$3 a gallon. Tour guides, package trips, and drivers are available—pricey (though maybe not compared with the cost of a car and gas), but it just might be the best way for you to see the country.

Renting a car in Belize is usually a simple matter but is always subject to Murphy's Law. High deposits can be put on credit cards. If you

CAR RENTALS

Avis	Radisson Fort George Hotel	(2) 31-987, fax (2) 30-225
Crystal	Belize City	(2) 31-600, fax (2) 31-900
National	Belize City	(2) 31-586, (25) 22-94
Budget	Belize City	(2) 32-435, fax (2) 30-237

know exactly when you want the car and where, it's helpful to make reservations in advance.

Insurance
Mandatory car insurance from rental car agencies runs US$10-15 per day and covers only 80% of damages (which many travelers are unaware of). In most cases in Belize, when an accident occurs the police take action first and ask questions later. With an insurance policy, most of the problems are eased over. Rental agencies also offer medical insurance for US$4-6 p/d. Your private medical insurance should cover this (check).

Getting The Car
Check out the car *carefully* before you take it far. Drive it around the block and go over the following:
✓ Make sure there's a spare tire and working jack.

✓ Make sure all doors lock.
✓ Make sure the seats move forward, have no sprung backs, etc.
✓ All windows should lock, unlock, roll up and down properly.
✓ Trunk should lock and unlock.
✓ Check for proper legal papers for the car, with addresses and phone numbers of associate car rental agencies in towns you plan to visit in case of an unexpected car problem.
✓ Make sure horn, emergency brake, and foot brakes work properly.
✓ Make sure clutch, gear shift, and all gears work properly (don't forget reverse).
✓ Get directions to the nearest gas station; the gas tank may be empty. If it's full it's wise to return it full, as you'll be charged top dollar per gallon of gas.
✓ Ask to have any damage, even a small dent, missing door knob, etc., noted on your contract, if it hasn't been already.
✓ Note the hour you pick up the car and try to return it before that time: a few minutes over will get you another *full* day's rental fee.

Payoff Time
When you pick up your rental car, the company makes an imprint of your credit card on a blank bill, one copy of which is attached to the papers you give the agent when you return the car. Keep in mind that the car agency has a limit of how much you can charge on one credit card at one time (ask the maximum when you pick up the car). If you go over the limit be prepared to pay the balance in cash or with another credit card.

BATTY BROS. BUS TIMETABLE Western Schedule 1.2

GOING WEST — BELIZE CITY TO GUATEMALA (READ DOWN)

DAILY (EXCEPT SUNDAY)

LV Belize City	6:00 a.m.	6:30 a.m.*	7:30 a.m.**	8:00 a.m.	9:00 a.m.	10:15 a.m.
AR The Place/Belize Zoo	7:00 a.m.	—	8:30 am.	9:00 a.m.	10:00 a.m.	11:15 a.m.
LV Belmopan	7:30 a.m.	8:30 a.m.	9:00 a.m.	10:00 a.m.	11:00 a.m.	12:00 p.m.
LV San Ignacio/Benque	9:00 a.m.	9:30 a.m.	10:30 a.m.	11:00 a.m.	12:00 p.m.	1:15 p.m.
AR Melchor de Mancos	9:45 a.m.	10:15 a.m.	—	—	—	2:00 p.m.

SUNDAY

LV Belize City	6:00 a.m.	7:00 a.m.	8:30 a.m.	9:30 a.m.	10:30 a.m.
AR The Place/Belize Zoo	7:00 a.m.	8:00 a.m.	9:30 a.m.	10:30 a.m.	11:30 a.m.
LV Belmopan	7:30 a.m.	8:30 a.m.	10:00 a.m.	11:00 a.m.	12:00 p.m.
LV San Ignacio	9:00 a.m.	9:30 a.m.	11:00 a.m.	12:30 p.m.	1:30 p.m.
AR Melchor de Mancos	9:45 a.m.	10:15 a.m.	12:15 p.m.	—	2:15 p.m.

GOING EAST — GUATEMALA TO BELIZE CITY (READ DOWN)

DAILY (EXCEPT SUNDAY)

LV Melchor de Mancos	12:00 p.m.**	1:00 p.m.	2:00 p.m.	—	3:30 p.m.	—
LV San Ignacio	1:00 p.m.	2:00 p.m.	3:00 p.m.	4:00 p.m.	5:00 p.m.	5:45 p.m.
LV Belmopan	1:30 p.m.	2:30 p.m.	3:30 p.m.	4:30 p.m.	5:30 p.m.	6:30 p.m.
AR The Place/Belize Zoo	2:00 p.m.	3:00 p.m.	4:45 p.m.	—	6:15 p.m.	—
AR Belize City	3:00 p.m.	4:00 p.m.	5:45 p.m.	5:45 p.m.	7:15 p.m.	7:15 p.m.

SUNDAY

LV Melchor de Mancos	1:00 p.m.	2:00 p.m.	—	3:30 p.m.	—	—
LV San Ignacio	1:00 p.m.	2:30 p.m.	3:00 p.m.	4:30 p.m.	5:00 p.m.	—
LV Belmopan	2:30 p.m.	3:30 p.m.	4:00 p.m.	5:00 p.m.	5:30 p.m.	6:30 p.m.
AR The Place/Belize Zoo	3:00 p.m.	3:45 p.m.	4:45 p.m.	5:30 p.m.	6:00 p.m.	7:00 p.m.
AR Belize City	4:00 p.m.	4:45 p.m.	5:45 p.m.	6:30 p.m.	7:00 p.m.	8:00 p.m.

*Express to/from Belmopan
**Friday, Saturday, and Monday only

BATTY BROS. AND VENUS BUS LINES Northern Schedule 1.2

(Both lines travel between Belize City and Mexico)

GOING NORTH—BELIZE CITY TO CHETUMAL, MEXICO (READ ACROSS)

LV BELIZE CITY	LV ORANGE WALK TOWN	LV COROZAL	AR CHETUMAL
Batty Bus	*Batty Bus*	*Batty Bus*	*Batty Bus*
4:00 a.m.	6:00 a.m.	7:00 a.m.	8:00 a.m.
5:00 a.m.	7:00 a.m.	8:00 a.m.	9:00 a.m.
6:00 a.m. Express	*7:30 a.m. Express*	*8:15 a.m. Express*	*9:30 a.m.*
6:00 a.m.	8:00 a.m.	9:00 a.m.	10:00 a.m.
7:00 a.m.	9:00 a.m.	10:00 a.m.	11:00 a.m.
8:00 a.m.	10:00 a.m.	11:00 a.m.	12:00 p.m.
9:00 a.m.	11:00 a.m.	12:00 p.m.	1:00 p.m.
10:00 a.m.	12:00 p.m.	1:00 p.m.	2:00 p.m.
11:00 a.m.	1:00 p.m.	2:00 p.m.	3:00 p.m.
Venus Bus	*Venus Bus*	*Venus Bus*	*Venus Bus*
11:45 a.m.	1:45 p.m.	2:45 p.m.	3:45 p.m.
1:00 p.m.	3:00 p.m.	4:00 p.m.	5:00 p.m.
1:30 p.m.	3:30 p.m.	4:30 p.m.	5:30 p.m.
2:00 p.m.	4:00 p.m.	5:00 p.m.	6:00 p.m.
2:30 p.m.	4:30 p.m.	5:30 p.m.	6:30 p.m.
3:00 p.m.	5:00 p.m.	6:00 p.m.	7:00 p.m.
3:30 p.m.	5:30 p.m.	6:30 p.m.	7:30 p.m.
4:00 p.m.	6:00 p.m.	7:00 p.m.	8:00 p.m.
4:30 p.m.	6:30 p.m.	7:30 p.m.	8:30 p.m.
5:00 p.m.	7:00 p.m.	8:00 p.m.	9:00 p.m.
5:30 p.m.	7:30 p.m.	8:30 p.m.	9:30 p.m.
6:00 p.m.	8:00 p.m.	9:00 p.m.	10:00 p.m.
7:00 p.m.	9:00 p.m.	10:00 p.m.	11:00 p.m.

BATTY BROS. AND VENUS BUS LINES Northern Schedule 1.2 (cont.)

(Both lines travel between Belize City and Mexico)

GOING SOUTH—CHETUMAL, MEXICO TO BELIZE CITY (READ ACROSS)

LV CHETUMAL	LV BORDER	LV COROZAL	LV ORANGE WALK TOWN	AR BELIZE CITY
Venus Bus	Venus Bus	Venus Bus	Venus Bus	Venus Bus
5:00 am	6:00 a.m.	6:15 a.m.	7:30 a.m.	9:00 a.m.
5:30 a.m.	6:30 a.m.	6:45 a.m.	8:00 a.m.	9:30 a.m.
6:00 a.m.	7:00 a.m.	7:15 a.m.	8:30 a.m.	10:00 a.m.
6:30 a.m.	7:30 a.m.	7:45 a.m.	9:00 a.m.	10:30 a.m.
7:00 a.m.	8:00 a.m.	8:15 a.m.	9:30 a.m.	11:00 a.m.
7:30 a.m.	8:30 a.m.	8:45 a.m.	10:00 a.m.	11:30 a.m.
8:00 a.m.	9:00 a.m.	9:15 a.m.	10:30 a.m.	12:00 p.m.
8:30 a.m.	9:30 a.m.	9:45 a.m.	11:00 a.m.	12:30 p.m.
9:00 a.m.	10:00 a.m.	10:15 a.m.	11:30 a.m.	1:00 p.m.
9:30 a.m.	10:30 a.m.	10:45 a.m.	12:00 p.m.	1:30 p.m.
10:00 a.m.	11:00 a.m.	11:15 a.m.	12:30 p.m.	2:00 p.m.
10:30 a.m.	11:30 a.m.	11:45 a.m.	1:00 p.m.	2:30 p.m.
11:00 a.m.	12:00 p.m.	12:15 p.m.	1:30 p.m.	3:00 p.m.
Batty Bus	**Batty Bus**	**Batty Bus**	**Batty Bus**	**Batty Bus**
11:00 a.m.	12:00 p.m.	12:15 p.m.	1:30 p.m.	3:00 p.m.
12:00 p.m.	1:00 p.m.	1:15 p.m.	2:30 p.m.	4:00 p.m.
1:00 p.m.	2:00 p.m.	2:15 p.m.	3:30 p.m.	5:00 p.m.
2:00 p.m. Express	3:00 p.m. Express	3:15 p.m. Express	4:15 p.m. Express	5:30 p.m.
2:15 p.m.	3:00 p.m.	3:30 p.m.	4:30 p.m.	6:00 p.m.
3:00 p.m.	4:00 p.m.	4:15 p.m.	5:30 p.m.	7:00 p.m.
4:00 p.m.	5:00 p.m.	5:15 p.m.	6:30 p.m.	8:00 p.m.
5:00 p.m.	6:00 p.m.	6:15 p.m.	7:30 p.m.	9:00 p.m.
6:30 p.m.	7:15 p.m. to Corozal Only			

Batty Bros. Phones: Corozal (4) 23-034, Belize City (2) 74-924
Belize Transfer Service: Box 1722, Palo Alto, California 94302; tel. (415) 641-9145

KATHY ESCOVEDO SANDERS

MUNDO MAYA

For several years five Latin American nations (Mexico, Belize, Guatemala, Honduras, and El Salvador) have discussed the need to preserve the remaining culture of the Maya, one of the greatest civilizations of all time. The Maya were dynamic engineers who created architecturally flamboyant buildings, massive reservoirs, more cities than were in ancient Egypt, and innovative farmlands. They developed a written language, tracked and recorded movements of the universe, and at its zenith the society numbered more than five million people. Present-day descendants of the Maya, along with thousands of structures hidden in thick tropical jungles, continue to tell the story of the past.

An ambitious project, tagged **Mundo Maya** ("World of the Maya"), has been designed to both exhibit and preserve, to see that the rapid growth of population—and tourism—will not destroy what has been quietly enduring nature and her elements for hundreds and in some cases as long as three thousand years. Many factors are involved in project decisions that will affect millions of people; not only the Maya who have lived in isolated pockets and out-of-the-

way villages for centuries, but also the people of each country involved, plus thousands of visitors who are discovering this culture for the first time. La Ruta Maya ("the Maya route") will encompass the entire area that was once inhabited by the Maya, where they have left their footprints in the form of amazing stone structures all over the landscape.

The project will require the cooperation of five countries, concentrating on the preservation of natural resources and rainforests, including the birds and animals that live within their boundaries (already extinct in other parts of the world). Perhaps the most important challenge the countries face is to come up with a way to encourage the development that tourism dollars can bring without infringing upon the cultural, historical, and environmental heritage of the Maya people.

A way must be found to induce the population to stop cutting the rainforest to create pastureland for raising crops and grazing cattle. Several plans are being studied. Those who have been supporting themselves in traditional ways for centuries must be taught ways to make a living without destroying the surrounding rainforest. Options include harvesting and selling such rainforest products as coffee, cacao, medicines, and fruits, and raising water buffalo (which survive nicely in the wet rainforest) rather than cattle—the meat is a viable substitute for beef. And maybe the biggest money-maker for the people of the future is tourism—rather, ecotourism.

A first step was taken when the five governments involved met in Oct. 1988 in Guatemala City, an event hosted by President Vinicio Cerezo Arevalo. One of the most innovative suggestions was to build monorail-type transportation that would travel the 1,500-mile route throughout the environmentally precarious landscape, to avoid bringing roads into these areas. Road development invariably brings uncontrolled settlement and destruction. There was talk of a regional Mundo Maya tourist visa and a Eurail-type pass that would allow visitors to move freely across the borders of the five countries.

No doubt it will take years of planning and agreements before these ideas come to pass, but Mexico and Guatemala have made one of the first moves by creating two adjoining biosphere reserves totaling 4.7 million acres of wildlands. In May 1989 Mexico's President Salinas Gortari and Guatemala's then-president Cerezo signed an agreement to cooperate and conserve natural areas of the border zones and to protect endangered species. This is a hopeful sign for the future; in the recent past, the only things these two countries shared at the border were animosity and military patrols pointing guns at each other.

Belize has been chosen as the site for the headquarters for Mundo Maya. A plot of ground just outside of Belize City is being readied as we go to press. This is a feather in Belize's cap, and perhaps an indication that the other countries do indeed respect Belize's conservation programs and ideals.

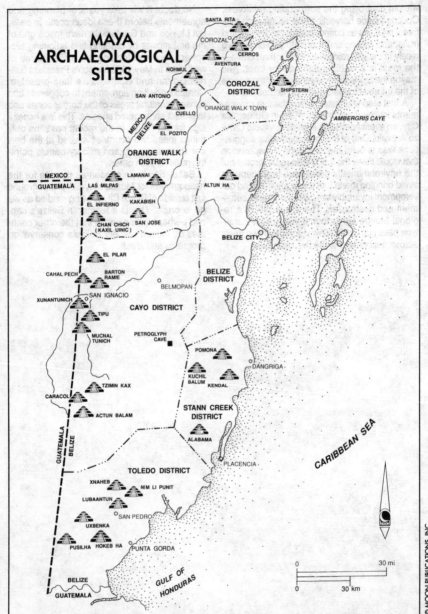

MAYA
ARCHAEOLOGICAL
SITES

SANTA RITA
COROZAL
CERROS
AVENTURA
NOHMUL
COROZAL
DISTRICT
SHIPSTERN

SAN ANTONIO
CUELLO
ORANGE WALK TOWN
AMBERGRIS CAYE

EL POZITO

ORANGE WALK
DISTRICT

MEXICO
BELIZE

LAMANAI
LAS MILPAS
ALTUN HA
EL INFIERNO   KAKABISH
CHAN CHICH
(KAXIL UINIC)   SAN JOSE

MEXICO
GUATEMALA

EL PILAR

BELIZE CITY

CAHAL PECH   BARTON
RAMIE

BELIZE
DISTRICT

XUNANTUNICH   SAN IGNACIO
TIPU

BELMOPAN

CAYO DISTRICT

MUCNAL
TUNICH

PETROGLYPH
CAVE

POMONA
DANGRIGA
TZIMIN KAX   KUCHIL
BALUM   KENDAL
CARACOL
ACTUN BALAM

STANN CREEK
DISTRICT

ALABAMA
PLACENCIA

TOLEDO DISTRICT

CARIBBEAN SEA

XNAHEB   NIM LI PUNIT
LUBAANTUN
SAN PEDRO
UXBENKA
PUSILHA   HOKEB HA   PUNTA GORDA

GUATEMALA
BELIZE

BELIZE
GUATEMALA

GULF OF
HONDURAS

0   30 mi
0   30 km

© MOON PUBLICATIONS, INC.

MAYA ARCHAEOLOGICAL SITES OF BELIZE

A thousand years before modern seafarers came along, the Maya inhabited Belize. They are believed to be the first *Homo sapiens* that peopled the country. At one time archaeologists estimate at least one million Maya lived in the area that is now called Belize. More Maya sites are discovered each year and it's quite common for Belizean families to have ruins in their back yards without official archaeological knowledge. These are often small oratorio-style buildings or caves with artifacts that date back hundreds of years. As money becomes available, whether from the government or outside universities, more discoveries are made and it becomes apparent that Belize is a veritable treasure chest of Maya culture.

Hints For Touring The Archaeological Sites

Seven of the archaeological sites described below are open to the public. Four are visited widely and soon will be official reserves with supporting facilities. Right now visitors will find no bathrooms, snack bars, or even water in any of them. In some areas it's necessary to trek through tall grasses and jungle terrain, so dress accordingly; wearing long pants and sturdy walking shoes with socks pulled over your pants cuffs (that have been previously sprayed with the type of insect repellent that can be applied to the skin) is one efficient way to approach these areas. Flying and crawling insects thrive in the jungle terrain. Of course the other usual mom-given tips apply: sun block, a loose floppy hat, and a canteen of water all help to protect the body inside and out against the hot sun and its effects.

Know the locations and distances of the sites you wish to visit. Some are lengthy treks from the closest town. Other sites are located on private property and can only be visited if prior permission is obtained. For more information write or visit the **Department of Archaeology** in Belmopan or the **Association for Belizean Archaeology** at the **Center of Environmental Studies** on Eve St. in Belize City.

Santa Rita

Santa Rita was still a populated community of Maya when the Spanish arrived. One mile northeast of Corozal, the largest Santa Rita structure was explored at the turn of the century by Thomas Gann. Sculptured friezes and stucco murals were found along with a burial site indicating flourishing occupation in the early Classic period (about A.D. 300), as well as during the late post-Classic period (A.D. 1350-1530). Two significant burials were found from distant periods in the history of Santa Rita; one from A.D. 300 was a female, and the other was a king from a period 200 hundred years later. In 1985 archaeologists Diane and Arlen Chase discovered a tomb with a skeleton covered in jade and mica ornaments. Some believe that Santa Rita was part of a series of coastal lookouts. It has been excavated and somewhat reconstructed under the Chases' jurisdiction; only one structure is accessible to the public. Post-Classic murals, mostly destroyed over the years, combined Maya and Mexican styles, depicting the ecumenical flavor of the period. Santa Rita is probably more appealing to an archaeologist than to the average tourist.

Cerros

Cerros was an important coastal trading center during the late pre-Classic period (350 B.C. to A.D. 250). It's situated on a peninsula in the Bay of Chetumal, across from the town of Corozal. Magnificent frescoes and heads were uncovered by archaeologist David Friedel, signifying that elite rule was firmly fixed by the end of the pre-Classic period. The tallest of its temples rises to 70 feet, and because of the rise in the sea level the one-time stone residences of the elite Maya are partially flooded. It would appear that Cerros not only provisioned the oceangoing canoes, but was in an ideal location to control ancient trade routes that traced the Rio Hondo and New River from the Yucatán to Peten and the Usumacinta basin. A plaster-lined canal for the sturdy oversized

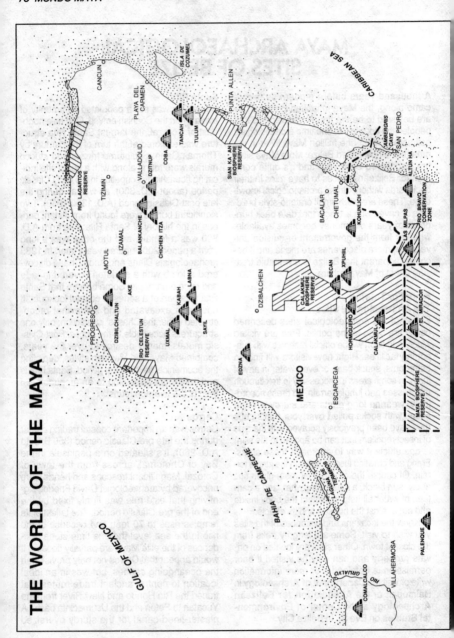

THE WORLD OF THE MAYA

GULF OF MEXICO

CARIBBEAN SEA

CANCUN

ISLA DE COZUMEL

PLAYA DEL CARMEN

PUNTA ALLEN

TANCAH

TULUM

SIAN KA'AN BIOSPHERE RESERVE

RIO LAGARTOS RESERVE

TIZIMIN

VALLADOLID

DZITNUP

COBA

AMBERGRIS CAYE

SAN PEDRO

ALTUN HA

MOTUL

IZAMAL

DZIBILCHALTUN

BALANKANCHE

CHICHEN ITZA

BACALAR

CHETUMAL

KOHUNLICH

RIO BRAVO CONSERVATION ZONE

PROGRESO

AKE

LABNA

LAS MILPAS

KABAH

UXMAL

SAVIL

RIO CELESTUN RESERVE

DZIBALCHEN

XPUHIL

BECAN

CALAKMUL BIOSPHERE RESERVE

EL MIRADOR

EDZNA

HORMIGUERO

CALAKMUL

MEXICO

MAYA BIOSPHERE RESERVE

ESCARCEGA

BAHIA DE CAMPECHE

LAGUNA DE TERMINOS

GRIJALVO

COMALCALCO

VILLAHERMOSA

PALENQUE

RIO HONDO

RIO USUMACINTA

© MOON PUBLICATIONS, INC.

ocean canoes was constructed around Cerros. Archeaologists have determined that extensive fishing and farming on raised fields took place, probably to outfit the traders. But always the question remains, why did progress suddenly stop? Cerros can be reached by boat (hired in Corozal or from the **Adventure Inn** at Consejo Shores or **Tony's Inn** at Corozal). If you travel during the dry season (Jan.-April) you can get to Cerros by car. Along the way you'll pass the picturesque towns of **Chunox, Progresso,** and **Copper Bank,** as well as lovely lagoons.

Nohmul

Nohmul was a major ceremonial site. It is the tallest structure in the Orange Walk/Corozal districts. Twin ceremonial groups are connected by a *sacbe* (raised causeway). The center shows it once catered to a thriving occupation in the late-pre-Classic and late-Classic periods (350 B.C.-A.D. 250 and A.D. 600-900) and controlled an area of about 12 square miles. Nohmul ("Big Hill") was named by the people living in the vicinity of the site.

Located in the sugarcane fields behind the village of San Pablo, the entrance is one mile down the road going west from the center of the village. Public transportation from Belize City, Orange Walk Town, and Corozal passes through the village of San Pablo several times daily. Simple accommodations can be found in Orange Walk Town eight miles away.

Cuello

The ruins of Cuello were studied by a Cambridge University archaeology team in the 1970s, led by Dr. Norman Hammond. A small ceremonial center, a proto-Classic temple, has been excavated. Lying directly in front is a large excavation trench, partially backfilled, where the archaeologists gathered this historical information that revolutionized previous concepts of the antiquity of the ancient Maya. Artifacts indicate that trade was carried on with people hundreds of miles away. Among the archaeologists' out-of-the-ordinary findings were bits of wood that proved, after carbon testing, that Cuello had been occupied as early as 2600 B.C., much earlier than ever believed; however, archaeologists now find that these tests may have been incorrect. Also found was an unusual style of pottery—apparently in some burials clay urns were placed over the heads of the deceased. It's also speculated that it was here over a long period that the primitive strain of corn seen in early years was refined and developed into the higher-producing plant of the Classic period. Continuous occupation for approximately 4,000 years was surmised with repeated layers of structures all the way into the Classic period. However, archaeologists are still debating the accuracy of this back dating.

These structures (as in Cahal Pech) have a different look than at most of the Maya sites. They are covered with a layer of white stucco as they were in the days of the Maya.

At Cuello, archaeologists have renovated the Maya ruins in the ancient manner by covering them with a white stucco coating.

OZ MALLAN

OZ MALLAN

Lamanai site

The ruins of Cuello are situated on the same property as the rum distillery of the same name. It's about four miles west of Orange Walk Town on Yo Creek; taxis are available. This site isn't developed, cleared, restored, or ready for the average tourist, but if you're interested in more information, contact the **Department of Archaeology** at Belmopan, or if you're in the area ask at the distillery for permission to enter.

Chan Chich

In the northwestern corner of Belize in Orange Walk District, near the Guatemala border, an old overgrown logging road blazed originally by the Belize Estate And Produce Co. (logging operators) was reopened. Here, the Maya site of Chan Chich (Kaxil Uinich) was rediscovered. As recently as four years ago the only way in (for rare adventurers, pot farmers, or grave robbers) was with machete in hand and a canoe to cross the swiftly flowing river. After sweating and cutting into dense jungle to the end of the barely visible track the adventurer's sudden reward was a 100-foot-tall rock-strewn hill—an introduction to another Maya ceremonial site! This complex has two levels of plazas, each with its own temples, all surrounded by unexcavated mounds.

When found, three of the temples showed obvious signs of looting with vertical slit trenches—open—just as the looters had left them. No one will ever know what valuable artifacts were removed and easily sold to private collectors all over the world. The large main temple on

the upper plaza had been violated to the heart of what appears to be one or more burial chambers. A painted frieze runs around the low ceiling. Today the only temple inhabitants greeting outsiders are small bats.

Chan Chich has a unique new guard: Belizean-born Barry Bowen, owner of the property, who has built a group of simple thatch cabañas in one of the plazas of the Maya site. Though deplored by some archaeology buffs, these cabañas are very popular with birdwatchers and Mayaphiles who agree with Bowen that they will serve as a deterrent to temple looters who think nothing of defiling the ancient stone cities, and marijuana growers who find these isolated spots a perfect hiding place for their illegal crops. For more information about Chan Chich Lodge see p. 171.

Lamanai

Set on the edge of a forested broad lagoon are the temples of Lamanai. One of the largest ceremonial centers in Belize, it was described as an imperial port city encompassing ball courts, pyramids, and the more exotic Maya features. Hundreds of buildings have been identified in the two-square-mile area. A few sites to look for:

The Mask Temple N9-56: Here two significant tombs were found, as well as two early classic stone masks.

The High Temple N10-43: At 33-meters tall, this is the tallest securely dated pre-Classic structure in the Maya area. Among many findings was a dish containing the skeleton of a bird, and pre-Classic vessels dating back to 100 B.C.

Temple N10-9: Dated to the sixth century A.D., this temple had structural modifications in the 8th and 13th centuries. Jade jewelry and a jade mask were discoved here as well as an animal-motif dish.

The Ball court: The game played in this area held great ritual significance for the Maya. In 1980, archaeologists raised the huge ball court marker stone disc and found lidded vessels containing miniature vessels with small jade and shell objects on top of a mercury puddle.

Archaeologist David Pendergast headed a team from the Royal Ontario Museum that, after finding a number of children's bones buried under a stela, presumed that human sacrifice was a part of the religion of these people. Large masks depicting a ruler wearing a crocodile headdress were found in several locations, hence the name Lamanai ("Submerged Crocodile") originated. Another unique find under a plain stone marker was a pottery container with a pool of mercury. Excavations reveal continuous occupation and a high standard of living into the post-Classic period, unlike other colonies in the region.

It's believed to have been occupied from 1500 B.C. to the 19th century, as evidenced by the remains of two Christian churches and a sugar mill. This site has not been cleared or reconstructed; the landscape is overgrown, and the trees and thick vines grow from the tops of buildings—the only sounds are bird calls echoing off the stone temple. To see above the thick jungle canopy you can climb to the top of the temple on ancient steps that are still pretty much in place, and don't be surprised if you find Indiana Jones's hat at the top—it's that kind of a place.

Located in Orange Walk District, on the high banks of New River Lagoon about 50 miles northwest of Belize City, the trip alone is worth the visit. Most people travel by boat through tropical flora and fauna, and on the way you may see such exotics as black orchids, old tree trunks covered with sprays of tiny golden orchids, a multitude of birdlife, and even the jabiru stork (the largest flying bird in the New World with a wing span of 10-12 feet).

This area is a reserve so look for some wildlife you may not see in other, more inhabited areas. On the paths you'll see numbered trees that

correspond to a pamphlet of information available from the caretakers at the entrance of Lamanai Reserve. Look for these trees:

1. Santa Maria
2. cohune palm
3. trumpet tree
4. tubroos
5. cotton tree
6. allspice
7. red gombolimbo
8. pimenta palm
9. bucut
10. cedar
11. rubber tree
12. breadnut tree
13. copal tree
14. cordoncia

Birds Seen in the Reserve: Around the Mask and High temples, look for the **black oropendola.** The **black vulture** is often spotted slowly gliding over the entire area. A woodpecker with a distinct double tap rhythm and a red cap is the male **Guatemalan ivorybill.** Near the High Temple, the **collared *aracari*** sits on the highest trees and chirps like an insect; this is a variety of toucan. The **citreoline trogon** is covered with color: a yellow chest, black-and-white tail, and a back of blue and green. Though it looks like the **northern jacana** is walking on water, it's the delicate floating vegetation that holds the long-toed bird above the water as it searches along the water's edge for edible delicacies.

Other fauna spotted by those who live there are jaguarundi, agouti, armadillos, hikatee turtles, and the roaring howler monkey.

Altun Ha
Travel north on the New Northern Highway from Belize City until it intersects with the Old Northern Highway. Take the Old Northern Highway about 12 miles; a sign marks the Altun Ha access road. It's about one and a half miles to the archaeological site (see map p. 111) from here. It wasn't until the archaeologists came in 1964 that the name Rockstone Pond was translated into the Maya words Altun Ha. The site covers an area of about 25 square miles, most of which is covered by trees, vines, and jungle. Altun Ha, a trading center as well as a religious ceremonial

center, is believed to have accommodated a population of about 10,000 people. Archaeologists, working in the midst of a community of Maya families that have been living there for several centuries, have dated construction about 1,500-2,000 years ago.

A team led by Dr. David Pendergast from the Royal Ontario Museum began work in 1965 on the central part of the ancient city, where upward of 250 structures have been found in an area of about 1,000 square yards. So far, this is the most extensively excavated of all the Maya sites in Belize. For a trading center Altun Ha was strategically located—a few miles from **Little Rocky Point** on the Caribbean and a few miles from **Moho Caye** at the mouth of the Belize River, both believed to have been major centers for the large trading canoes that worked up and down the coasts of Guatemala, Honduras, Belize, the Yucatán, and all the way to Panama.

Near Plaza B, the **Reservoir,** also known as **Rockstone Pond,** is fed by springs and rain runoff. It demonstrates the advanced knowledge of the Maya in just one of their many fields: engineering. Archaeologists say that for centuries an insignificant little stream ran through the

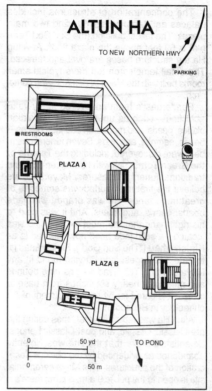

jungle. No doubt it had been a source of fresh water for the Maya—but maybe not enough. The Maya diverted the creek and then began a major engineering project, digging and enlarging a deep, round hole that was then plastered with limestone cement. Once the cement dried and hardened, the stream was rerouted to its original course and the newly built reservoir filled and overflowed at the east end, allowing the stream to continue on its age-old track. This made the area liveable. Was all of this done before or after the temple structures were built? Is the completion of this reservoir what made the Maya elite choose to locate in this area? We may never know for sure. Today Rockstone Pond is surrounded by thick brush and the pond is alive with jungle creatures, including tarpon, small fish, and turtles and other reptiles.

OZ MALLAN

Altun Ha

The concentration of structures includes palaces and temples surrounding two main plazas. The tallest building (the Sun God Temple) is 59 feet above the plaza floor. At Altun Ha the structure bases are oval and terraced. The small temples on top have typical small rooms built with the Maya trademark—the corbel arch.

Pendergast's team uncovered many valuable finds, such as unusual green obsidian blades, pearls, and more than 300 jade pieces—beads, earrings, and rings. Seven funeral chambers were discovered, including the **Temple of the Green Tomb,** rich with human remains and traditional funerary treasures. Maya scholars believe the first man buried was someone of great importance. He was draped with jade beads, pearls, and shells. And it was next to his right hand that the most exciting find was located—a solid jade head now referred to as **Kinich Ahau** ("The Sun God"). Kinich Ahau is, to date, the largest jade carving found in any Maya country. The head weighs nine pounds and measures nearly six inches from base to crown. It is cared for by the Department of Archaeology in Belmopan.

Altun Ha was rebuilt several times during the pre-Classic, Classic, and post-Classic periods. Scientists believe that the site was violently abandoned as evidenced by the obvious desecration of the structures. This Maya ceremonial site is open to the public 9 a.m.-5 p.m.; there's a small entrance fee, less than US$2.

Xunantunich

The word Xunantunich (pronounced zoo-nahn-too-NEECH, "stone lady") is derived from local legend. A thousand years ago, Xunantunich was already a ruin. It's believed to have been built some time during A.D. 150-900, the golden age of the Maya. Though certainly not the biggest of Maya structures, at 135 feet high **El Castillo** is one of the taller structures (Maya or otherwise) in the country of Belize. El Castillo has been partially excavated and explored. The eastern side of the structure displays a unique stucco frieze (looks new and fresh, like it hasn't been too long since its reconstruction), and three carved stelae can be seen in the plaza. Xunantunich contains three ceremonial plazas surrounded by house mounds. It was first

Xunantunich

opened by noted archaeologist Sir J. Eric Thompson in 1938 after centuries of neglect. As the first Maya ruin to be opened in the country, it has attracted the attention and exploration of many other archaeologists over the years.

In 1950, the University of Pennsylvania (noted for its years of outstanding work across the Guatemala border in Tikal) built a facility in Xunantunich for more study. In 1954 visitors were invited to explore the site after a road was opened and a small ferry was built. In 1959, archaeologist Evan Mackie made news in the Maya world when he discovered evidence that Xunantunich had been partially destroyed by an earthquake in the late-Classic period. Some believe it was then that the people began to lose faith in their leaders—an unearthly sign from the gods. But for whatever reason, Xunantunich ceased to be a religious center long before the end of the Classic period.

This impressive Maya ceremonial site is well worth a visit and a climb—from the top the panorama encompasses the thick green Guatemalan Peten District, the Maya Mountains, and a grand view of the entire Cayo District and Belize jungle stretching for miles to the horizon. To get to the top follow a path that meanders across the front and side of the structure. At the top is a typical small Maya temple; watch out for the large step over a hole in the cement. On one of our last visits, the site was empty except for one lone believer meditating on the very top of the temple in a perfect lotus position. He appeared to be in complete harmony with the blue sky and puffy white clouds above, the jungle below—and perhaps with the Maya gods of Xunantunich within.

To find Xunantunich, travel about eight miles south of San Ignacio on the Western Highway toward Benque Viejo and the Guatemala border (look for a small wooden sign on the side of the road that reads "Xunantunich"). At the river's edge hop on the free, hand-cranked cable ferry. If driving, either park here or drive onto the ferry (it can handle two cars), and from the bank it's less than a mile farther up gentle hills to the site. The short, leathery-faced aged man that cranked the ferry for years and years has been replaced by a young robust fellow said to be a relative of the stern-faced old Mayan. There's a small fee to enter the grounds, and Elfego Panti, a very knowledgeable guide, will explain the site: the history, what's been restored, and what's in the future. This major center is located on a natural limestone ridge. The funky ferry operates daily 8 a.m.-5 p.m.

Caracol

Perhaps the largest site in Belize, Caracol ("Snail") is an enormous ceremonial center covering more than five square miles. On a low plateau deep in the **Chiquibul Forest Reserve**, evidence remains of primary rainforest. The tallest temple structure stands 136 feet above the plaza floor (just slightly higher than El Castillo at Xunantunich) with a base broad enough to rival any of the ruins at Tikal (in Guatemala). This Classic site is noted for the rare use of giant date glyphs on circular stone altars. Again the Maya exhibited their engineering skills, building extensive reservoirs and agricultural terraces. More of Caracol continues to be discovered by archaeologists Diane and Arlen Chase and their energetic assistants—student interns from Tulane University and University of Central Florida. According to John Morris, archaeological commissioner of Belize, a lifetime of exploration remains to be done within six to nine miles in every direction from today's discoveries. It's proving to have been a powerful site that controlled a very large area.

Many carvings are dated A.D. 300-600 indicating Caracol was settled about A.D. 300 and continued to flourish when other Maya sites were in decline. Carvings on the site also indicate that Caracol and Tikal engaged in ongoing conflicts, each defeating the other on various occasions. Following a war in A.D. 562, however, Caracol dominated the area for more than a century. The name Caracol was given to the site by a former archaeological commissioner because of the numerous snail shells found at the site.

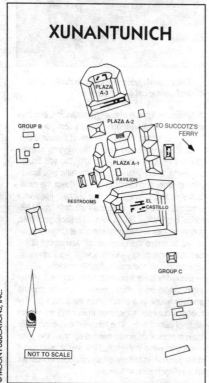

XUNANTUNICH

PLAZA A-3

GROUP B

PLAZA A-2

TO SUCCOTZ'S FERRY

PLAZA A-1

PAVILION

RESTROOMS

EL CASTILLO

GROUP C

NOT TO SCALE

© MOON PUBLICATIONS, INC.

(CONTINUED ON PAGE 88)

LIFE ON AN ARCHAEOLOGICAL DIG

In March 1992 when the new road into Caracol had barely begun, we were delighted to be invited to the archaeological site at an exciting time. On 17 March, a new tomb was opened and the remains of at least two people were found (one a woman) as well as 17 unbroken vessels. What a time to visit! Everyone was on a natural "high," and deservedly so: Day-by-day work on an archaeological dig can be tedious, and these marvelous finds don't happen on a daily basis. Archaeologists Diane and Arlen Chase and the *tomb* were the stars, with *National Geographic* cameras and crew, as well as Belizean Archeological Commissioner John Morris, American Consul Eugene Scassa and his wife, "Voice of America" broadcasters, and several Belize City reporters. Three young British hikers were also present.

We barely made it to the site by bouncing, slipping, and slidding on the muddy mire of a road; we only hit one tree and afterward had to tie the right passenger door shut with a rope. But it was all worth it.

Archaeologists are very different kinds of human beings. They come with an insatiable curiosity and an

Solar panels bring electricity to the isolated archaeological site of Caracol.

auto-wind wellspring of energy, motivation, and love for their work. Interestingly, these scientists always manage to attract student workers of the same ilk.

Students generally spend the digging season (the dry season) carefully prodding the soil, brushing away 1,000-year-old dirt, washing and scrubbing shards, and climbing up and down the multitudes of steps, often carrying buckets filled with precious soil that might contain valuable bits of historical information. Unlike many archaeological sites, a crew of four armed men remain at Caracol year-round to guard the site, and all equipment is left behind to discourage looters who regularly damage structures and steal valuable artifacts.

Everyday life adapts to the environment. Housing is simple *palapa* huts, separate latrines, and the shower house is a small mazelike affair with tiny roofless cubicles separated from each other with walls of palm fronds. The "shower" is nothing more than a bucket of water hauled up from the river and left to warm in the sun. However, a solar panel does provide limited electricity for such necessities as a refrigerator and freezer.

a student archaeologist washing shards dug up around Caracol

OZ MALLAN / 2

one (very) young archaeologist enjoying Mickey Mouse in the middle of the jungle, with the help of solar panels

Food, as usual, is an important part of daily life. Supplies, including frozen chicken and beef, are brought in on the weekend. Meats are served about three times a week; the rest of the time the menu is supplemented with canned foods and beans. At each meal the *fogon* (stone grill) is fired up and covered with handmade tortillas; birthdays are always celebrated with a homemade cake.

Our first surprise at Caracol occured soon after we climbed out of the mud-covered Land Rover and wandered over to a group of thatched, pole houses clustered just beyond the entrance. We discovered a kitchen, a dining room, and experienced a mild shock when we walked into another room to find Mickey Mouse on the small screen in living and talking color! And what's more, a tiny little three-year-old boy sat on his trike mesmerized by the TV. At first I thought this was just a weird dream. However, looking around it was obvious that this was a gathering place for the "community," with its bleacherlike arrangement of boards and logs.

The average city dweller would readily admit that life is not easy here. The weather is very hot and humid. In the past it's been necessary to regrade the road each year after the damaging rains (the new all-weather road should make a big difference). The bug problem never quits; mosquitoes are the bane of the tropics. And, yet, many archaeologists quickly admit they have it a lot easier today than the earliest scientists—*long* before solar panels.

OZ MALLAN / 2

Caracol can be reached by forestry road through Douglas DeSilva (formerly called Augustine) in the Mountain Pine Ridge. However, although the site is only 30 miles farther on, visitors are advised to travel with 4WD vehicles as the road is extremely rough. **Note:** The new road should be completed by now, making the trip easier, but until I travel over it, I won't suggest you drive your sports car! The closest accommodations are near the Douglas DeSilva Forestry Station and in and around the Cayo District (see p. 177). At this time gas is not available along this road, so it behooves visitors to make all arrangements necessary to carry ample fuel. Camping is not allowed in the area without permission from the Forestry Department in Belmopan. The **Department of Archaeology** and/or the **Forestry Department, Western Division** must be informed, prior to any visits, for permission and advice on ac-

cessibility. Once the road is complete, groups of visitors will be brought into the area by tour bus.

Cahal Pech

Cahal Pech ("Place of the Ticks") is in San Ignacio in the Cayo District near **Tipu.** This medium-sized Maya site was discovered in the early 1950s, but scientific research did not begin until 1988 when a team from the University of San Diego began excavation. Thirty-four structures were compacted into a two- to three-acre area. Excavation is ongoing and visitors are welcome. Watching the archaeological team in action gives visitors an opportunity to see how ruins look before restoration and how painstaking the work can be. There's a small fee at Cahal Pech, and a new, small museum where you will see artifacts found at the site. This site is within walking distance of San Ignacio.

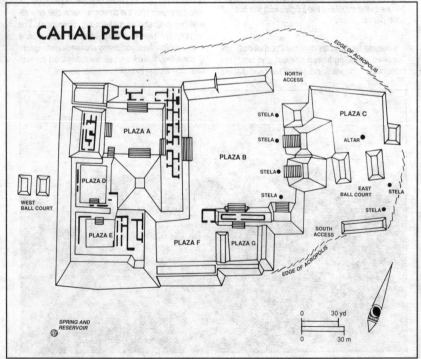

CAHAL PECH

(top left) celebrating Garifuna Settlement Day, Dangriga;
(top right) Kulcha Shack kids, Seine Bight;
(bottom) Kulcha Shack drummers (photos by Oz Mallan)

(top left) Belize City street market;
(top right) conch shells after the harvest, Laughing Bird Caye;
(bottom) Hand-cranked ferries are common in the Belize countryside. (photos by Oz Mallan)

Cahal Pech

Lubaantun

Northwest of Punta Gorda, north of the Columbia River and one mile beyond San Pedro is the Maya ruin of Lubaantun ("Place of the Fallen Stones"). It was built and occupied during the late-Classic period (A.D. 730-890) and first noticed in 1875 by refugees from the southern U.S. that left the States during and after the Civil War. Its ridge location gives it a commanding view of the entire countryside. Eleven major structures are grouped around five main plazas, in addition to smaller plazas, for a total of 18 plazas and three ball courts. Most of the structures are terraced and the tallest structure rises 50 feet above the plaza, from which you can see the Caribbean Sea, 20 miles distant. Notice that some corners of structures are rounded. Lubaantun's distinct style of architecture sets it apart from Maya construction in some parts of Latin America. This large late-Classic site has been studied and surveyed several times by familiar names, such as Thomas Gann and, more recently, by Norman Hammond in 1970. Distinctive clay whistle figurines (similar to those found in Mexico's Isla Jaina) illustrate lifestyles and occupations of the era. Other artifacts include a unique carved glasslike skull, obsidian blades, grinding stones (much like those still used today to grind corn), beads, shells, turquoise, and shards of pottery. From all of this archaeologists have determined that the city flourished until the 8th century A.D. Until then it was a farming community that traded with the highland areas of

today's Guatemala, and the people worked the sea and maybe the nearby cayes just offshore. To get to Lubaantun from Punta Gorda, go 1.5 miles west past the gas station to the Southern Highway, then take a right. Two miles farther you'll come to the village of San Pedro. From here go left around the church to the concrete bridge; cross and go almost a mile—the road is passable during the dry season. Park before you reach the aged wooden bridge. This site has not been made into a park, so it's largely overgrown with brush and jungle; wear your hiking boots and long pants.

Nim Li Punit

Right off the Southern Highway before the San Antonio turnoff, 25 miles north of Punta Gorda town, you'll find Nim Li Punit (a 15-minute walk from the highway along a trail marked by a small sign). The site has enjoyed only preliminary excavations (1970), and is believed to have held a close relationship with nearby Lubaantun. One of the memorable finds was a 30-foot-tall carved stela, the tallest ever found in Belize—and in most of the rest of the Maya world. About 25 stelae have been found on the site dated A.D. 700-800. Rediscovered in 1974, it was looted almost immediately. However, the looters missed a tomb later uncovered by archaeologist Richard Leventhal in 1986. If you're not driving a car it's best to make arrangements to see these ruins and the villages with a guide prior to your arrival to Punta Gorda (see p. 231).

Uxbenka

Found only recently (1984), Uxbenka has revealed more than 20 stelae, seven of which are carved. One dates back to the early Classic period, an otherwise nonexistent period in southern Belize and a rare date for stelae in the entire Maya area. The site is perched on a ridge overlooking the traditional Maya village of Santa Cruz and provides a grand view of the foothills and valley of the Maya Mountains. Here you'll see hillsides lined with cut stones resembling massive structures. This method is unique to the Toledo District. Uxbenka ("Old Place") was named by the people of nearby Santa Cruz. It's located just outside the village, about three miles west of San Antonio Village. The most convenient way to see the site is with a rental car. However, if staying in San Antonio or Punta Gorda ask around town; a local may be willing to take you and act as a guide. Arrange your price in advance.

Other Sites

There are hundreds of unexcavated and probably undiscovered Maya sites hidden in the shadows of Belize's forests. Because of the attraction of big bucks on the black market attached to Maya art, a partially excavated site is an open invitation to looters. The government is willing to leave these unknown sites undisturbed hoping that looters will not find them first. A few other sites that have been documented are in various stages of excavation:

Actun Balam, near Caracol in the Cayo District.
Tzimin Kax ("Mountain Cow"), in the Cayo District.
Pusilha, on the Moho River near Lubaantun.

This is far from a complete list. As growth in the country continues and money becomes available, the mysterious Mundo Maya will continue to reveal itself.

Rio Azul

Beyond Blue Creek and across the border into Guatemala, one of the newest and most exciting archaeological sites, Rio Azul, was rediscovered a couple of years ago. Without roads, it is not yet accessible from the Belizean side, but has already produced new and exciting artifacts, such as a screw-on-lid pottery jar—a few more pieces to fit into the puzzle of the advanced Maya civilization.

LOUISE FOOTE

KATHY ESCOVEDO SANDERS

BELIZE DISTRICT

BELIZE CITY

Belize City straddles the estuaries of Haulover Creek, part of the Belize River that empties into the Caribbean Sea. In this bustling harbor city of about 50,000 (mostly Afro-Creoles), small businesses abound. With Belize's new independence, changes are being implemented slowly but surely. However, if you want to get a taste of what colonial life was like "back when," don't wait. Come before the town is spiffed up, painted, and highrises line the coast. Visit before the old Swing Bridge is replaced—nothing is quite like watching the traffic jams at 5:30 a.m. and 5:30 p.m. each day when the low-lying bridge across Haulover Creek closes to cars while it pivots to allow tall-masted boats to pass through. (If you happen to drive across the Swing Bridge after dark, be sure to turn your headlights down as there's a hump in the bridge—car headlights blind oncoming traffic!) Haulover Creek is a left-over name from the time when the cattle were attached to each other by a rope wrapped around their horns and "hauled" across the river.

Visitors, Note:
Most travelers planning a visit to Belize arrive at Belize's Philip Goldson International Airport, fresh and new. However, you should know that Belize City is not a Caribbean "paradise" in terms of a Cancun or Cozumel. The city is old, run down, and, though perched on the edge of the gorgeous Caribbean, has no beaches. Antiquated clapboard buildings on stilts—unpainted, weathered, tilted, and streaked with age—line the narrow streets but are slowly being replaced by concrete structures. The banks of the Belize River, meandering through the middle of the city, are often dirty and smelly—face it, the country is not only old, but also poor; that's the *down* side. The *up* side is that you'll find, tucked here and there, almost-white sedate public structures—and very few modern glitzy buildings. The people are friendly and their future is glowing. Schools are everywhere, a few trendy shops are popping up, and some of the simplest bars are gathering places for the most interesting people. It's Som-

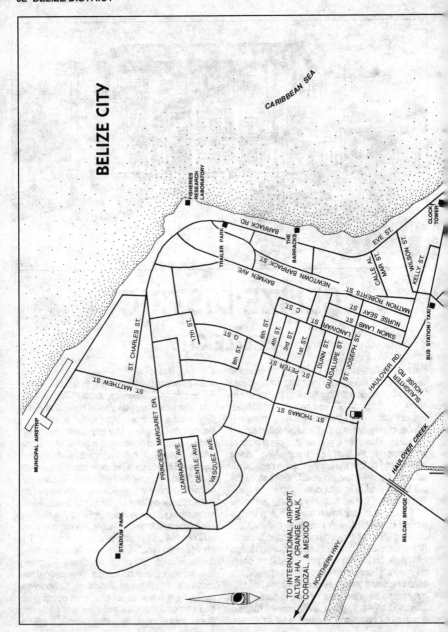

BELIZE CITY

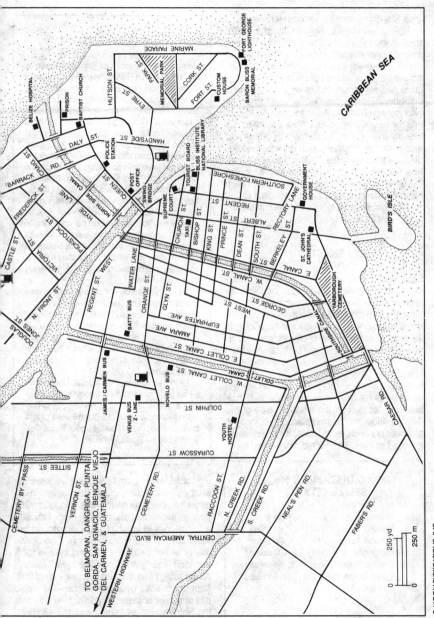

CARIBBEAN SEA

BIRD'S ISLE

MARINE PARADE

FORT GEORGE LIGHTHOUSE
BARON BLISS MEMORIAL
CUSTOM HOUSE
CORK ST.
FORT ST.
PARK ST.
MEMORIAL PARK
HUTSON ST.
EYRE ST.

BELIZE HOSPITAL
PRISON
BAPTIST CHURCH

HANDYSIDE ST.

DALY ST.
CRAIG RD.
POLICE STATION
CANAL ST.
NORTH SIDE
QUEEN ST.
POST OFFICE
SWING BRIDGE

BARRACK RD.
HYDE LANE
FREDERICK ST.
PICKSTOCK ST.
VICTORIA ST.
CASTLE ST.

TOURIST BOARD
BLISS INSTITUTE
NATIONAL LIBRARY
SOUTHERN FORESHORE

GOVERNMENT HOUSE

SUPREME COURT
CHURCH ST.
TAXI
BISHOP ST.
KING ST.
PRINCE ST.
DEAN ST.
SOUTH ST.
BERKELEY ST.
RECTORY LANE
REGENT ST.
ALBERT ST.

ST. JOHN'S CATHEDRAL

N. FRONT ST.
DOUGLAS JONES ST.

REGENT ST. WEST
WATER LANE
ORANGE ST.
GLYN ST.
WEST ST.
W. CANAL ST.
GEORGE ST.
E. CANAL ST.
YARBOROUGH CEMETERY

BATTY BUS

AMARA AVE.
EUPHRATES AVE.
E. COLLET CANAL ST.
W. COLLET CANAL ST.
COLLET CANAL
SOUTHSIDE CANAL

JAMES / CARMEN BUS
NOVELO BUS
VENUS BUS
Z - LINE

DOLPHIN ST.

YOUTH HOSTEL

CURASSOW ST.
CEMETERY BY - PASS
SITTEE ST.
VERNON ST.
CEMETERY RD.
RACCOON ST.
N. CREEK RD.
S. CREEK RD.
NEAL'S PEN RD.
CAESAR RD.
FABERS RD.
CENTRAL AMERICAN BLVD.

TO BELMOPAN, DANGRIGA, PUNTA
GORDA, SAN IGNACIO, BENQUE VIEJO
DEL CARMEN, & GUATEMALA
WESTERN HIGHWAY

250 yd
250 m
0

erset Maugham country—at least for a while.

After a few days in Belize City (if a visitor stays that long), you'll get over the culture shock and no longer notice the "run-down" condition of the city. Instead, you'll begin to feel comfortable while the sensation of living in an era past takes over (ever been to Disney's Pirates of the Caribbean?). If pirate-Captain Lafitte came swaggering down the street today, he'd fit right into the neighborhood. But there's more to this friendly city—it's an excitement in the air, an electricity that's buzzing with growth, dreams, plans—it's history in the making. Ten years from now Captain Lafitte probably won't recognize the city—however, he still might have to watch his wallet. And we know he'd be shocked to find a traffic light, Belize City's first, at the intersection of N. Front St. and Hyde Lane.

SIGHTS

Bliss Promenade meanders along the waterfront and eventually brings you to the **Bliss Institute;** social functions and seminars are held here. It is also the location of a theater, museum, and library, as well as the National Arts Council. Take a look at the display of Maya stelae and altars retrieved from the Cayo District.

Market
Saturday-morning market in Belize City will never be the same. The seedy old colonial marketplace, located on the southern side of the Swing Bridge, has been replaced by a modern three-story concrete structure. It's not quite as crowded as the old, tin-roofed, open-sided build-

BARON BLISS

Henry Edward Ernest Victor Bliss, also known as the "Fourth Baron Bliss of the former Kingdom of Portugal," was born in the County of Buckingham, England. He first sailed into the harbor of Belize in 1926, though he was too ill to go ashore because of food poisoning he had contracted while visiting Trinidad. Bliss spent several months aboard his yacht, the *Sea King,* in the harbor, fishing in Belizean waters. Although he never became well enough to go ashore, Bliss learned to love the country from the sea and its habitués—the fishermen and officials in the harbor all treated him with great respect and friendliness. On the days that he was only able to languish on deck, he made every effort to learn about the small country. He was apparently so impressed with what he learned and the people he met that before his death he drew up a will that established a trust of nearly two million dollars for projects to benefit the people of Belize.

So far, over a million dollars in interest from the trust has been used ,for the erection of the Bliss Institute, Bliss School of Nursing, Bliss Promenade, and In-transit Lounge at the Belize International Airport, plus contributions to the Belize City water supply, the Corozal Town Board and Health Clinic, and land purchased for the building of Belmopan.

An avid yachtsman, Bliss stipulated that money be set aside for a regatta to be held in Belize waters, a focal point of the gala Baron Bliss Day celebrations each year. The Baron's white granite tomb is at the point of Fort George in Belize City, guarded by the Bliss Lighthouse.

ROAD DISTANCES FROM BELIZE CITY TO:

Belmopan	55 miles
Benque Viejo	81 miles
Corozal Town	96 miles
Dangriga	105 miles
Orange Walk Town	58 miles
Punta Gorda	210 miles
San Ignacio	72 miles

ing, but friendly people still sell vegetables, skinned iguana, fish, meats, and exotic fruits, as well as Belizean handicrafts. When strolling through the market and a lovely black lady with a bright-colored kerchief wrapped around her head says, "Try a tamarind darlin'," go ahead (peel it and enjoy the flesh around the seeds)! A tamarind is tasty and looks like a dark reddish brown string bean; it tastes like tangy dried fruit. Man doesn't live by apples alone—the tropic has many exotic fruits to try. Whoever said that the historical Belize market was the seediest,

OZ MALLAN

Admiral Burnaby's Coffee Shop

darkest, most run-down market in the country will be in for a big surprise when next he visits.

From here walk across the Swing Bridge over the Belize River. Meander through the Fort George area. From the **Fort George Radisson Hotel** dock you'll get a good view of the harbor. Originally this was Fort George Island; until the 1850s it was the location of the army barracks. The strait separating the island from the mainland was filled in during the early 1920s and dedicated as a memorial park for the dead of WW I. Today it is the site of the **Baron Bliss Memorial** and the Fort George Hotel. After WW II visiting dignitaries from England surveyed the country with plans for various agricultural projects; they also could find no place to stay. Accommodations went to the top of their priority list and became one of the first postwar projects in the colony. An easygoing, low-key charmer with excellent service and tasty meals, Fort George was the best hotel in town. Today, the hotel is part of the Radisson chain and a partner of the Villa hotel. It is the most noticeable structure in the area, especially since the addition of the new, modern, six-story-tall glass wing.

Several other nice hotels occupy the area, and, in general, the Fort George neighborhood is one of the most pleasant in Belize City.

Downtown

An early morning stroll through the weathered old clapboard buildings of Belize City gives you a taste of the community. The downtown area offers office buildings, small shops (many operated by East Indian and Chinese merchants), banks, a post office, and lots of traffic. **Brodies Department Store** is a modern emporium that sells clothes, groceries, and hardware, with a modern boutique upstairs. The large store has a deli case with luscious-looking cold cuts and sandwiches. **Bennett's Rexall Drug Store** has a prominent sign that tells all that they are licensed—to sell poison, that is!

Here in the main business section of Regent and Albert streets (originally called Front and Back streets—the only streets in 18th-century Belize City) you'll see old brick slave houses, with timber-and-shingle second floors. Slaves were kept in chains in the brick basements when not working in the fields. Feel like sipping a tropical fruit drink? Stop in at **Bluebird** on Albert Street. Want a cup of coffee and some lively conversation? Go to **Admiral Burnaby's** and ask for Emory (9 Regent St.; tel. 2-77-453); it's a combination bookstore, art gallery, and coffee shop, run by transplanted U.S. writer and sometimes actor, real-estate salesman, travel guide, and comedian Emory King. How did he get to Belize? He says he bumped into a reef of staghorn coral at English Caye (literally) one moonlit night aboard the yacht *Vagabond,* bound for a world cruise out of Florida. Even though the boat was eventually repaired, he never left—that was in 1953. A well-known character in Be-

BOB RACE

clock tower

as though everyone is selling the same "attic treasures." This is the location of the original courthouse built in 1818. It has since been twice rebuilt (once after a demolition in 1878, and again after a fatal fire in 1918 that took the life of then-governor William Hart Bennett).

Church And State
Belize has the oldest Protestant church in Central America, **St. John's Anglican Cathedral.** This lovely old building is the only typically British structure in the city, surrounded by well-kept green lawns. The slaves in Belize (in 1812) helped to erect this graceful piece of architecture using bricks brought as ballast on sailing ships from Europe. Several Mosquito Coast kings (from the Waiki tribe) were crowned in this cathedral with ultimate pomp and grandeur; the last was crowned in 1815. Located behind the cathedral (at the southern end of Regent St. and also on Southern Foreshore) is **Government House,** which before Hurricane Hattie and the ensuing construction of Belmopan, was the home and office of the governor general, the official Belizean representative of the Queen of England. The Prime Minister still keeps an office here. (Today the governor general can be found in Belmopan at Belize House.) Mostly the lovely old structure now serves as a guesthouse for visiting VIPs and a place for social functions. Queen Elizabeth was a houseguest here on her last visit in 1985, and Prince Philip stayed on his last visit in May 1988. The old wooden buildings (built 1812-14) are said to have been designed by acclaimed British architect Christopher Wren, and until recently were described "as elegant as it gets," surrounded by sprawling lawns and wind-brushed palms facing the sea along Southern Foreshore.

Note the colonial house at the corner of Hutson St. and 20 Gabourel Lane. It was built in New England, dismantled, and transported to Belize as ship's ballast. It was reconstructed 120 years ago and houses the entire **U.S. Embassy,** which has been in Belize since 1840.

lize, with his pen and a flare for drama, he fought for Belize's independence over the years, and even played a bit part with Harrison Ford in the 1986 film *Mosquito Coast*. Today Emory describes the country as "a little bit south of Paradise, a little bit north of frustration."

The **Supreme Court building** is across from Belize City's **Central Park.** The antiquated town clock is located atop the white clapboard building and shows a different time from all four sides—each wrong since it stopped running a while back (like most clock towers in Belize), but who's keeping time anyway? (Actually a recent visitor wrote to say that one side of the clock was showing the correct time. So noted!) The structure is decorated with a graceful white-metal filigree stairway that leads to the long veranda overlooking the square.

The public square offers frequent flea-market activity with a mishmash of gewgaws set out on small blankets, park benches, or the ground. On close examination this colorful scene, with owners huddling close together holding brilliant-hued umbrellas to screen out the hot sun, looks

ACCOMMODATIONS

Most hotels all over the country add about 20% to listed prices (service charge and tax). And if

BELIZE CITY HOTELS

BUDGET HOTELS

Belcove Hotel, 9 Regent St.
(2) 73-054
US$20 d

Golden Dragon, 29 Queen St.
(2) 72-817
US$17 s, US$25 d

Hotel Las Palmeras, 39 George St.
(2) 73-345
US$16 s, US$21 d private bath; US$8-11 s, US$13 d, US$20 t shared bath

Mira Rio Hotel, 59 N. Front St.
(2) 44-970
US$8 s, US$16 d

North Front Street Guest House
124 N. Front St.
(2) 77-595
US$15 s, US$25 d

Seaside Guest House, 3 Prince St.
(2) 78-339
US$13 s, US$18 d, US$7.50 dorm

Venus Hotel, 2371 Magazine Rd.
(2) 73-354/73-390
US$13 s, US$19, US$38 t

MODERATE HOTELS

Bakadeer Inn, 74 Cleghorn St.
(2) 31-286/31-400, fax (2) 31-963
US$42 s, US$63 d, includes breakfast

Belize Guest House, 2 Hutson St.
(2) 77-569
US$33 s, US$44 d

Bliss Hotel, 1 Water Lane
(2) 72-552
US$27.50 s, US$27.50 d; US$37.50 s, US$40 d a/c

Colton House, 9 Cork St.
(2) 44-666
shared bath are US$30 s, US$35 d; private bath, US$35 s, US$40 d

El Centro Hotel, 4 Bishop St.
(2) 77-739, fax (2) 74-553
US$52 d

Fort Street Guest House, 4 Fort St.
(2) 30-116, fax (2) 78-808, in the U.S. (800) 538-6802, fax (303) 674-8735
US$44 s, US$58, breakfast included

Mom's Triangle Inn & Restaurant
11 Handyside St.
(2) 45-523, (2) 45-073, fax (2) 78-163
US$25 s, US$30 d; US$35 s, US$40 d a/c

Mopan Hotel, 55 Regent St.
(2) 77-351, (2) 73-356, fax (2) 75-383
US$21 s, US$32 d fan; US$32 s, US$37 d a/c

UPSCALE HOTELS

Bellevue Hotel, 5 S. Foreshore
(2) 77-051/77-052, fax (2) 73-253, (800) 223-9815
US$79 s, US$83 d

Biltmore Plaza, Mile 3, Northern Highway
(2) 32-302
US$100 s or d

Chateau Caribbean, 6 Marine Parade
(2) 72-813/72-826/30-800, fax (2) 30-900
US$69 s, US$79 d, US$95 d deluxe

Radisson Fort George Hotel, 2 Marine Parade
(2) 77-400, fax (2) 73-820, (800) 333-3333, (800) 633-4734
US$64 -159

Radisson Villa Wing, 13 Cork St.
(2) 32-800, (2) 30-276, (800) 465-4329
US$110, US$120 d, US$130 t

Ramada Reef Resort Hotel, Newton Barracks
(2) 32-670, fax (2) 32-660, (800) 228-9898
US$132 s, US$149 d

the business accepts a credit card (many don't), be prepared for maybe three to five percent more. One of the publications put out by the Belize Tourist Authority says you can find rooms from US$12 and up. Well, the "and up" rooms are easy to find, but you'll have to look a little harder to find the cheapies! And then you should study them carefully. Expect community bathrooms and only cold water in some. Ample economy-types are around for those willing to search them out. Upscale hotels are growing in size (literally)—many have added rooms in the past year in response to the keen interest in Belize. Two newer hotels are the **Ramada Reef** and the **Biltmore Plaza.**

Budget
One little gem is the **Seaside Guest House.** The rooms are clean, though small, and have only cold water and a community bathroom. But it has a sea view, and it's kept cool by the trade winds. It's quiet, only six blocks from the bus station, and three blocks from the central square. Breakfast and dinner are available (fresh fish, rice, salad—about US$5 and US$7). Manager Philip Remare is willing to help with ongoing hotel, sightseeing, and transportation arrangements. Rates are about US$13 s and US$18 d; a dorm room is available with four beds for US$7.50 pp; five rooms in all. Write for more information (3 Prince St., Belize City, Belize, C.A.; tel. 2-78-339).

Another budget hostelry is the **North Front Street Guest House.** This small simple hotel offers eight rooms with shared bath; breakfast is available as well as laundry service. Near the center of town, it's just one block from the Caye Caulker boat dock. Room rates are US$15 s, US$25 d. Write or call for more information (124 N. Front St., Belize City, Belize, C.A.; tel. 2-77-595).

The **Mira Rio Hotel** is ultra simplicity downtown. With communal bathroom facilities and clean small rooms, rates are US$8 s, US$16 d; check out the new penthouse (59 N. Front St., Belize City, Belize, C.A.; tel. 2-44-970). The restaurant on the premises, **Bistro Caribe,** serves a great barbecue and an unusual seaweed drink. A liquor store is also on-site. This is the pickup location for travelers going to **Ricardo's Beach Huts and Lobster Camp** (59 N. Front St., Belize City, Belize, C.A.; tel. 2-44-970).

A small hotel called **Hotel Las Palmeras,** located on the corner of George and Bishop streets, offers small economical rooms, some with private bathroom; a boutique and a cafeteria are on the premises. Rates with private bathroom are US$16 s, US$21 d; with community bathroom US$8-11 s, US$13 d, US$20 t; no credit cards. Write for more information (39 George St., Belize City, Belize, C.A.; tel. 2-73-345).

Moderate
Colton House is a charming old house owned and operated by Alan and Ondina Colton. It's obvious from the sparkling hardwood floors that a lot of love (and labor) went into renovating the 60-year-old house. Some of its appeal lies in the white wooden hanging swings on the front porch, the green plants scattered about, and the sheer white curtains on the windows. Bedrooms are fan cooled. Both of the Coltons are usually on hand to give good information about Belize; they actually live downstairs. The Coltons offer four rooms, two with private bathrooms; the other two share a bathroom. The Colton House doesn't offer food, but it's near quite a few cafes, including (just around the corner) the **Fort Street Dining Room.** Rates with shared bath are US$30 s, US$35 d, with private bathroom, US$35 s, and US$40 d (9 Cork St.; tel. 2-44-666). Colton House is catty-corner to the Radisson Hotel.

Another popular guesthouse is **Mom's Triangle Inn & Restaurant.** This oldie but goodie has been around for many years and is still a meeting place for Belizean regulars. Some rooms have a/c (US$35 s, US$40 d), others have just a fan (US$25 s, US$30 d). The guesthouse is clean with a homey atmosphere and typically old; some rooms have private baths, others share a community bathroom (all with hot water). Color TV is available in the living room. Mom's also offers a bar, gift shop, and restaurant downstairs that serves American and Creole food (11 Handyside St.; for reservations write to Box 332, Belize City, Belize, C.A.; tel. 2-45-523/45-073, fax 2-78-163). Ask about special fishing, diving, and adventure-tour packages.

In the Fort George area, a charming old colonial house, the **Belize Guest House,** has seven rooms with private bath and a/c, US$33 s, US$44 d. These comfortable, clean rooms are unusually large for Belize, with full kitchen facilities available. They also have a sea view and fresh sea breeze. The guesthouse is run by Charles Hope (2 Hutson St.; tel. 2-77-569). He also rents Suzuki Samurais for around US$80 p/d, including insurance; credit cards okay.

A little more money but very delightful is a small guesthouse in a charming old Victorian building simply called **Fort Street Guest House,** 4 Fort Street. The relaxing Casablanca-style decor with wooden shutters, wicker furniture, slow-moving ceiling fans, and clean community bathrooms is special! Energetic American Rachel Emmer owns and operates it; she's full of good info about the city and sightseeing on the cayes and in the countryside. Put your order out the night before and fresh coffee is delivered to your room at 7 a.m. The cooking here is outstanding and a favorite with local Belizeans when they want a special evening out. By night the simple tropical Victorian decor takes on a crystal, linen, and candlelight sparkle, and—most important—the food is excellent! Head cook Yolanda makes elegant Belizean or continental dinners (US$10-12) with lobster or melt-in-your-mouth steaks (splurge and try one of the special desserts such as "death-by-chocolate cake" or "rum-time pie"), and mouth-watering breakfasts (US$6-7), such as "mosquito toast" (a sinfully rich french toast filled with cream cheese and fruit). She also packs a mean box lunch that can include steak sandwiches or cold chicken, chocolate cake (from scratch), and fresh fruit—perfect to take for a day sightseeing in the country. Room rates are US$44 s, US$58 d, including breakfast. Write or call Rachel Emmer for more information and reservations (Box 3, Belize City, Belize, C.A.; tel. 2-30-116, fax 2-78-808). In the U.S. contact **Turquoise Reef Group,** tel. (800) 538-6802; in Colorado tel. (303) 674-8735, fax (303) 674-8735.

The **Bakadeer Inn** receives raves from clients for its good food, friendly staff, and comfy rooms. It is located in Belize City, with a lush tropical patio, a/c, carpeting, accommodations for parking cars and trailers, and a full American breakfast (included in the price) US$42 s, US$63 d. Write for more information (74 Cleghorn St., Belize City, Belize, C.A.; tel. 2-31-286/31-400, fax 2-31-963).

The **Mopan Hotel** is another simple but friendly hotel with reasonable rates. The bar is known far and wide as a meeting place for regular Belizean travelers, interesting people, or just those who want to watch a Super Bowl game (hijacked from the U.S. via satellite) while sipping Belikin beer and enjoying friendly kibitzing. The roomy, elderly house has eight rooms, a/c in some, private bathrooms. Rates for fan-cooled rooms are US$21 s, US$32 d; for a/c US$32 s, US$37 d. Write or call for more information and reservations (55 Regent St., Belize City, Belize, C.A.; tel. 2-77-351/73-356, fax 2-75-383).

More Expensive

One of the most upscale hotels in Belize City is the **Radisson Fort George Hotel** at 2 Marine Parade on the waterfront. Rooms are nicely appointed, with private bath, a/c, TV, and a minibar; some ocean views. It has a swimming pool and its own boat dock. Rates start at US$64 s, US$75 d for the motel wing, garden level is US$129 d, upper level is US$139 d, and a superior room in the new section with a water view US$159 d. The Fort George recently opened the new deluxe wing with 30 luxury a/c rooms; it's six stories tall and very impressive for Belize. The hotel dining room serves a full buffet breakfast daily and offers a different special each day; on Thanksgiving count on a turkey dinner. You'll also find the **Seventh Heaven Guest Deck,** a bookstand, gift shop, and Avis car rental desk with 4WD vehicles available. And if you see a big bowl of bananas in the lobby, help yourself! Write or call for more information and reservations (Box 321, Belize City, Belize, C.A.; tel. in Belize 2-77-400/77-242, fax 2-73-820). In the U.S. call (800) 333-3333, (800) 633-4734, from Canada (402) 967-3442, telex (310) 220.

The **Chateau Caribbean** has all the amenities of a fine hotel, including a restaurant and bar. The Chateau is located on the waterfront at 6 Marine Parade. Rates are US$69 s, US$ 79 d, and US$95 d deluxe. Write or call for reservations and more information (Box 947, Belize City, Belize, C.A.; tel. 2-72-813/72-826/30-800, fax 2-30-900).

Nearby is the **Radisson Villa Wing,** now a part of the Radisson Fort George Hotel. The Villa also overlooks the sea (13 Cork St.). All rooms have a/c and TV. The Villa has a bar and a restaurant. The 30 new rooms are really quite nice. The service charge is *not* added to your bill, US$110 s, US$120 d, US$130 t; credit cards okay. Write or call for reservations (Box 1240, Belize City, Belize, C.A.; tel. 2-32-800/30-276, 800-465-4329, fax 2-30-276).

The **Bellevue,** located at 5 S. Foreshore, is a charming elderly hotel that was built as a private home in the early 1900s. The same family that built this hotel still owns and operates it. Most of the rooms are spacious with private bathrooms, a/c, and telephones. The hotel features a pool, restaurant, bar, and a lively disco that makes music into the wee hours of the morning. The Bellevue Bar is a good meeting place for the locals. The restaurant has a very tranquil atmosphere and serves excellent food with a great wine list from the vineyards of Europe, personally chosen by owner Roger Dinger. Rates are US$79 s, US$83 d. The in-house tour company, **Maya Circuit Tours,** offers a variety of trips to the Maya ruins, as well as fishing, diving, birdwatching, and nature tours. Write or call for more information and reservations (Box 428, Belize City, Belize, C.A.; tel. 2-77-051/77-052, fax 2-73-253; in the U.S. call 800-223-9815).

The **Biltmore Plaza** is one of the newer Belize City hotels and is really very comfortable and attractive once inside. They really need a landscape architect to get the outside looking as nice. Nothing rustic about these 92 rooms; mid-size, with good beds, TV, direct-dial phones, tile bathrooms and showers, and the upper story opens onto cool verandas. All the rooms surround a green garden with a pool in the middle that has a swim-up bar. The **Victorian Room** is an upscale dining room open daily from 7 a.m.-11 p.m. The **Squires Lounge** is adjacent to the restaurant and opens at 4:30 p.m. for pre-dinner drinks or a handy game of darts. This really gives the feeling of an English Pub; you might find a group of British soldiers having an ale and tossing darts! It's located three miles from downtown Belize and seven miles from the international airport in the Bella Vista area. Prices are US$100 s or d (Mile 3, New Northern Highway, Belize C.A.; tel. 2-32-302, 800-327-3573, fax 2-32-301).

Another new hotel is the **Ramada Reef Resort Hotel** in Belize City on the waterfront, 20 minutes from the international airport and just a few minutes from downtown. The 114 rooms offer fine accommodations with a/c, ceiling fans, direct-dial phones, tile bathrooms and showers, and room service—rooms facing the sea have a fine view. Non-smoking rooms are available. The Reef offers oceanfront dining, and the **Toucan** is a casual poolside dining area for light meals and drinks. The **Blue Hole** is a lobby bar with terrace seating and live entertainment. Room rates start at US$132 s, and US$149 d (Box 1248, Newtown Barracks, Belize City, Belize, C.A.; tel. 2-32-670, 800-228-9898, fax 2-32-660).

Trailers

North of Haulover Creek toward the airport on Barrack Rd. is a trailer park that's little more than a parking lot with full hookups for trailers. Located across the street from the sea, rates are US$4-9 depending on the electricity you use.

Out-of-the-City Accommodations

On the New Northern Highway near the international airport find the **Belize International Airport Hotel.** Not fancy, but 60 rooms all have a/c and a tennis court on-site; rates are US$46 s, US$97 d, apartments available; call (2) 52-049. The **Belize River Lodge** is a laid-back guesthouse. The lodge, run by Margarite Miles, is not too far from the international airport. When you reach the sign, ring the bell on the tree and someone will come across the river and pick you up. Write or call for more information (Box 459, Belize City, Belize, C.A.; tel. 2-52-002, fax 2-52-298). Call for package prices only.

The **Bluefield Range** is a group of cayes a short distance south of Belize City. **Ricardo's Beach Huts and Lobster Camp,** the ultimate of funky, is situated on one of the islands, 21 miles south of the city. Originally two shacks on stilts built over a sand spit of shallow water leading out from a mangrove island, they now have four very basic huts built on cleared land. A path has been built up and leads to the swimming and snorkeling beach on the west side of the island. Units face east, overlooking a lagoon surrounded by more mangrove islands. Ricardo's father cooks fresh seafood and local dishes. Fish and snorkel the nearby reefs and cayes. That's where dinner comes from.

OUT-OF-THE-CITY RESORTS

Belize International Airport Hotel,
Northern Highway
(2) 52-049
US$46 s, US$97 d

Belize River Lodge, Box 459, Belize City
(2) 52-002, fax (2) 52-298
call for prices—packages only

Gallows Point Resort, 9 Regent St. W
(2) 73-054
US$87 s, US$120 d, meals included

Manatee Lodge, Gales Point
Box 1242, Belize City
(800) 334-7942, (8) 23-320
US$1265 pp per week

Maruba Lodge, Mile 40.5 Northern Highway
(3) 22-199, (800) 552-3419, (713) 799-2031
US$142 s, US$212 d, meals included

Ricardo's Beach Huts and Lobster Camp
Bluefield Range, Box 55, Belize City
(2) 44-970
US$120 pp, for two nights/three days,
meals included

Spanish Bay Resort, Box 35, Belize City
(2) 77-288/72-725, fax (2) 72-797,
in the U.S. (800) 359-0747
three-night packages start at US$341 pp double
occupancy

Expect camp-out conditions: outhouse, bucket shower, bugs. Bring mosquito coils, repellent, and a mosquito-net bed/tent. On the up side, this is one of the few chances to experience outer-island living just as it has been for the natives who spend their lives fishing these waters—a chance to meet, talk to, and know this special group of people, sort of a *National Geographic* experience. Some manatees live in the lagoon and may be sighted at sunrise and sunset.

Ricardo and his father appreciate the conservation value of mangroves and have underbrushed just enough so guests can watch the birdlife of the area. It's one of the best anchorages for any weather (even a recent tropical wave with 30-40-knot winds caused nary a problem). Ricardo's is "bloody ethnic with some really genuine people running it" observed a recent visitor. A trip here is a package deal, a fish and lobster camp. Because the island has no bar, feel free to bring your favorite bottle; Cokes and ice are provided. Bring your own fishing and snorkeling gear. For two to four people the rate is US$120 pp; for five or more it drops to US$100. Price includes two nights and three days at Ricardo's, including accommodations, meals, and RT boat transfers from and to Belize City. Visitors are picked up at the **Mira Rio Hotel** (59 N. Front St., Belize City). For more information contact Ricardo Castillo or Anna Lara (Box 55, Belize City, Belize, C.A.; tel. 2-44-970).

Gallows Point Resort is on its own island at the doorstep of the Belize Reef, only seven miles from Belize City. Here vacationers enjoy snorkeling, scuba diving, fishing, and glass-bottom-boat trips. At the **Wave Hotel** rates include three meals, room, reception at the airport, and transport to the island; US$87 s, US$120 d. Ask about **Elder Hostel,** designed with persons 50 and older in mind. Contact your travel agent for rates. Write or call Gallows Point Resort for more information (9 Regent St. West, Belize City, Belize, C.A.; tel. 2-73-054). **Note:** Boaters will find on the island **Weir Dow Marina,** a landlocked yacht anchorage with chandler and a shuttle service to Belize City.

Maruba Lodge is a small retreat that could be described as an oasis of charm and grace—or a jungle spa. Located in Maskall Village in the heart of the rainforest, visitors will find an emphasis on health and rejuvenation of the body and mind. Guests are pampered with exotic drinks, a Japanese tub, swimming pool, excellent food, jungle expeditions, river rides, caving and—for those interested—a weight-control program, body massage, tropical herbal wrap, seaweed body wrap, mineral baths, African honeybee pat, and exercise classes. Each thatch room is decorated in a different flamboyant style; the jungle suite has its own jacuzzi and balcony. Prices begin at US$142 s, US$212 d, less in the summer, and all prices include breakfast and dinner. Contact Maruba Resort (Box 300703, Houston, Texas 77230; tel. 713-799-2031, 800-552-3419, 3-22-199).

When you approach the **Spanish Bay Resort** from the sea on a sunny day, the simple white cabañas built over the blue-green water are quite spectacular. It's located on Spanish Lookout Caye, 10 miles east-southeast of Belize City, about a 30-minute boat ride. Five cabañas with 10 rooms, hot showers, and private baths are connected to the island by a dock. The rooms are furnished with two double beds, and a circular bar/dining room overlooks the sea. Power is solar, with backup generators. Diving is one of the favorite activities here with a PADI dive master and instructor on-staff. A number of boats are available for divers and snorkelers to get to and from the nearby reefs, including the 57-foot live-aboard, *Reef Maiden*. The resort is only one mile west of the main barrier reef and about eight miles west of central Turneffe Island. Most dives are done in front of Shag Caye to Rendezvous Caye. The resort offers weeklong packages that include seven nights, all meals, airport transfers, two day-trips with lunch on neighboring cayes, hotel tax, and 12 dives for dive-package guests. Nightlife is good conversation, though in late afternoon guests enjoy climbing up to the Crow's Nest to watch the sinking sun—if you stay long enough you'll see nature's sparkling light show in the sky. A three-night package for nondivers is US$341 pp double occupancy, US$479 for divers, US$395 for snorkelers, with many other options. Write or call for more information (Box 35, Belize City, Belize, C.A.; tel. 800-359-0747, 2-77-288/72-725, fax 2-72-797). Departure point for Spanish Bay Resort is from N. Front St., Belize City.

FOOD AND NIGHTTIME ENTERTAINMENT

While in Belize be sure to try the country favorites: Creole-style beans, rice, and stewed chicken. They're often served with coleslaw and fried plantain (large cooking bananas). Fried chicken and fresh fish are also popular. For years it was the custom for international travelers to eat in their hotel, where simple food was prepared. Few restaurants were available, and even those were really nothing to speak of. However, more and more travelers are opting to try the cuisine of the country. As a result a few more restaurants are opening each year. Hotels are beginning to discover good chefs, and a few outstanding restaurants (such as Fort Street) are becoming known outside the country. Belize City is not a gourmet delight *yet*, but things are looking up.

If staying at a guesthouse, ask if the cook makes "fried bread" for breakfast. (Yolanda at the Fort Street guesthouse does—it's *good!*) **Fort Street Restaurant** is also a popular spot

Belize Street

INTERNATIONAL EXPEDITIONS

for a candlelight dinner. Try the tender beef fillet, and sweets lovers should ask for the scrumptious "death-by-chocolate-cake"—you'll just die! (See p. 99.) **Macy's,** at 18 Bishop St., is a small cafe that serves excellent Creole food for reasonable prices. If you see conch fritters on the menu give them a try (but please don't order them out of season—1 July-30 Sept.). The adventurous can try armadillo, gibnut, or other game. Stop by **Pearl's,** located on Handyside St. next to Mom's Triangle Inn, for great Italian meals and sandwiches—you'll also meet Pearl and Budda Bill. Ice-cream lovers go to **Scoops** on Gaol Ln. at Eve St. for ice-cream cones and sundaes, and for pizza try the **Pizza House,** 11 King St., west of Albert Street. All of the luxury-class hotels offer **continental** cuisine in lovely surroundings, though the food is apt to be a little pricey. You'll find many **Chinese restaurants** to choose from, such as **Jane's Ping Woo, Ocean, Shen's Peking Panda, China Town** (across from Shen's), **Golden Dragon** (just off Queen St.), and **China Village** (Regent and Dean streets)—by the time you're there, maybe even more will have opened. **Mom's Triangle Cafe** is known for good American-style home cooking. The **Fort George Hotel** serves a beautiful buffet with a multitude of delicious seafood delicacies. For a special evening try **The Grill:** good food and a fine lounge bar, located at 164 Newtown Barracks, a short walk from the Ramada Reef Hotel (tel. 2-45-020).

Nightlife
Anyone looking for nightlife in Belize City will find it at hotels such as the **Bellevue** where music goes on often until the wee hours of the morning. Wanna dance? Try the **Pub** behind the commerce building at 91 N. Front St., just east of the Swing Bridge (small cover charge). Check out the **Hard Rock Cafe** (not the one you're thinking of) located at 35 Queen St., and the **Riverview,** run by Allie Nuñez. Look around, ask at your hotel, take a taxi; something's always going on at night in Belize.

Performing Arts
The **Belize Performing and Visual Arts Consortium** is a nonprofit arts-umbrella formed to showcase the multicultural artistic talents of the Belizean people. All celebrate the life and culture of a people dedicated to peaceful coexistence: dance and song groups that document Creole, Maya, or Garifuna culture; story-telling and interpretive drama; artists whose styles remind one of ancient times or that record the new independence.

Recent shows included Peter's Boom and Chime Band, the Leomar Dancers, Myrna Manzanaras, UCB Folk Ensemble, and the Aranda Brothers. Weekly exhibitions, art shows, and other events are scheduled in Belize City and, occasionally, throughout the country. Visitors have the opportunity to see local talent that is not only great entertainment, but gives visitors a look into the real traditions of the country. Eventually the top performers will tour other countries similar to Mexico's *folklórico* dancers. Until now it's been a well-kept secret that Belize has a **national dance company.** Ask at your hotel for a schedule. Currently dinner shows (US$25) and cocktail shows (US$15) are presented at the Radisson Villa Hotel. The program is made possible by a grant from International Expeditions of the United States. In the U.S., call (205) 428-1700 or (805) 969-0818 for a brochure.

OFFSHORE ACTIVITIES

Water Transport
If you want to take a trip to the cayes, you can get scheduled trips to several spots. For Caye Caulker go to the Shell station near the Swing Bridge on N. Front St. (the better side of the river in Belize City); it takes about 45 minutes, and the fare is US$6 OW. The *Soledad,* with Captain Chocolate, takes either U.S. or Belizean dollars. A light wrap is handy for windy or rainy trips. Chocolate will stop at **Caye Chapel** on his way to Caulker; ask before you board.

Talk to Chocolate if you're interested in a charter trip to **Goff's Caye,** a tiny island southeast of Belize City on the reef. He'll make a stop to see the manatees on the way. For the adventurers who enjoy watching the birds and animals of the jungle along the river shores, he's also available for river trips. Write or call Chocolate for more information (Box 332, Belize City, Belize, C.A.; tel. 2-22-151).

Pegasus is another boat available for passenger service to Caye Caulker. It leaves from the

Captain Chocolate provides dependable transport aboard his SS Soledad to and from Caye Caulker.

Shell station on N. Front St. near the Swing Bridge. The boat is also available for group charters to outlying cayes and the reef, and for river cruises. Write or call for prices and more information (Box 743, Belize City, Belize, C.A.; tel. 2-22-122).

For Ambergris Caye, the **Andrea I and II** fast outboard motorboat makes the run from Belize City daily at 4 p.m. (from the Belvedere Hotel dock) to San Pedro (departs San Pedro at 7 a.m.); the fare is about US$10 OW, US$17.50 RT. Buy your tickets at the **Universal Travel Agency** in Belize City next to Mom's or at their San Pedro office in the Alijua building on Front Street. The trip between Belize City and Ambergris takes about 75 minutes. **Miss Belize** leaves from the dock behind the Supreme Court building. The **Hustler** leaves San Pedro daily at 7 a.m. and returns from Belize City at 4 p.m. from the new dock near the courthouse and new market; US$10 OW, US$17.50 RT. The **Thunderbolt** docks at the Swing Bridge in Belize City and has the same schedule as the Hustler. Also check with the chamber of commerce regarding who might direct you to one of the

freight boats that make occasional trips to the island, or ask around the dock near the Swing Bridge. A few regularly scheduled trips run between the cayes.

The Shell station is a good place to pick up a boat if you're interested in hitching a boat ride anyplace. This is where the boats come to fill up—if you're not fussy you might catch a ride to any one of the many coastal communities along the Caribbean coast. It's a great way to meet the locals and to get a glimpse of out-of-the-way canals, rivers, and coastal towns; of course, establish the cost before you climb aboard.

Black Line Marina
The **Black Line Marina** offers full marina facilities, marine ways, hookups, and supplies including fuel, water, and ice. The dive shop offers NAUI open-water scuba certification courses (US$300 pp) and dive packages. Full-day fishing trips with experienced guides can be exciting light-tackle excursions on either the rivers, at shallow saltwater flats, or on the barrier reef. Overnight charter trips are available. For radio contact from boats use VHF Channel 70 (143.500 MHz). Black Line Marina is located at Mile 2.5 on the New Northern Highway. For more information call (2) 44-155, or write (Box 332, Belize City, Belize, C.A.). **Boat owners note:** Vessels traveling to the area must have permission before entering Belize.

GENERAL TOURIST INFORMATION

Belize Tourist Board: 83 N. Front St., Box 325, Belize City, Belize, C.A.; tel. (2) 77-490/77-213. Or in the U.S. write to 15 Penn Plaza, 415 Seventh Ave., 18th floor, New York, New York 10001; tel. (212) 268-8798, (800) 624-0686.

Belize Tourist Industry Association: 99 Albert St., Belize City, Belize, C.A.; tel. (2) 75-717.

Belize Consulate: 611 S. Wilton Pl., Los Angeles, California 90005: tel. (213) 385-6499.

Belize Embassy: 2535 Massachusetts Dr. NW, Washington, DC 20008; tel. (202) 332-9636, fax (202) 332-6741.

Florida Belize Consul General: 4343 W. Flagler St., Ste. 400, Miami, Florida 33134; tel. (305) 442-2114.

(CONTINUED ON PAGE 108)

THE BELIZE ZOO

The Belize Zoo, established in 1983, has brought together some of the country's fascinating animals. For now they live in thatch-roof cages, and the environment is fairly simple and small. However, money is being raised with pledges, contributions, and fund-raisers sponsored by the private sector to build new modern housing for the animals. The financial goal has not yet been reached and the galas continue. One yearly event is April's birthday party, vegetarian birthday cake and all. April is a Baird's tapir (the national animal)—also known as a mountain cow—and spends much of her time happily submerged in her own pond. She's the hands-on favorite attraction. Besides April, another animal of special interest is the jaguar. The zoo is located at Mile 30 on the Western Highway, open from 10-5. US$5 admission charged.

Note: The local buses will only drop you off on the highway at the entrance road (you must ask the driver to stop at the zoo road). From there it's about a mile walk to the zoo. Taxis can also be taken from Belmopan for under US$10, depending on how many people are going.

Sharon Matola, the founding director of the Belize Zoo, tells the story of the zoo with affection and love: "Some people call it funky; others say that it's the best zoo they have ever seen, and everyone tells us that the animals who live at the Belize Zoo seem . . . well, they seem so happy. Welcome to the Belize Zoo!" As the founding director she thrives on the unique opportunity to work among rare species of tropical animals, and to work with a local staff of employees who proudly share their natural heritage—the dramatic wildlife of Belize—with visitors to the zoo.

April

Everyone who comes through the gates receives a tour of the zoo by one of the Belizean zookeepers, including a visit with April. An old superstition says that the tapir can skin a person alive with its nose, but of course, as a guide explains, this is not true. And as April, the five-hundred-pound tapir, trundles over to get a closer look at the curious visitor, it can be seen that the personal touch of animal care and wildlife education has intermingled to produce a unique zoo experience.

Education

Hand-painted, homespun signs provide simple educational messages that cause visitors to laugh as well as learn. A glance at the sign in front of the peccary enclosure tells visitors, "We are warries, and we like the way we smell." Warries are members of the piglike peccary family. Peccaries do smell funny, but a sign explains the purpose of this odd scent in a way that helps observers to appreciate this animal's unusual natural history.

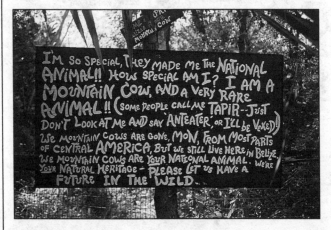

The "back-yard" feeling is promoted by these clever signs at each exhibit.

OZ MALLAN

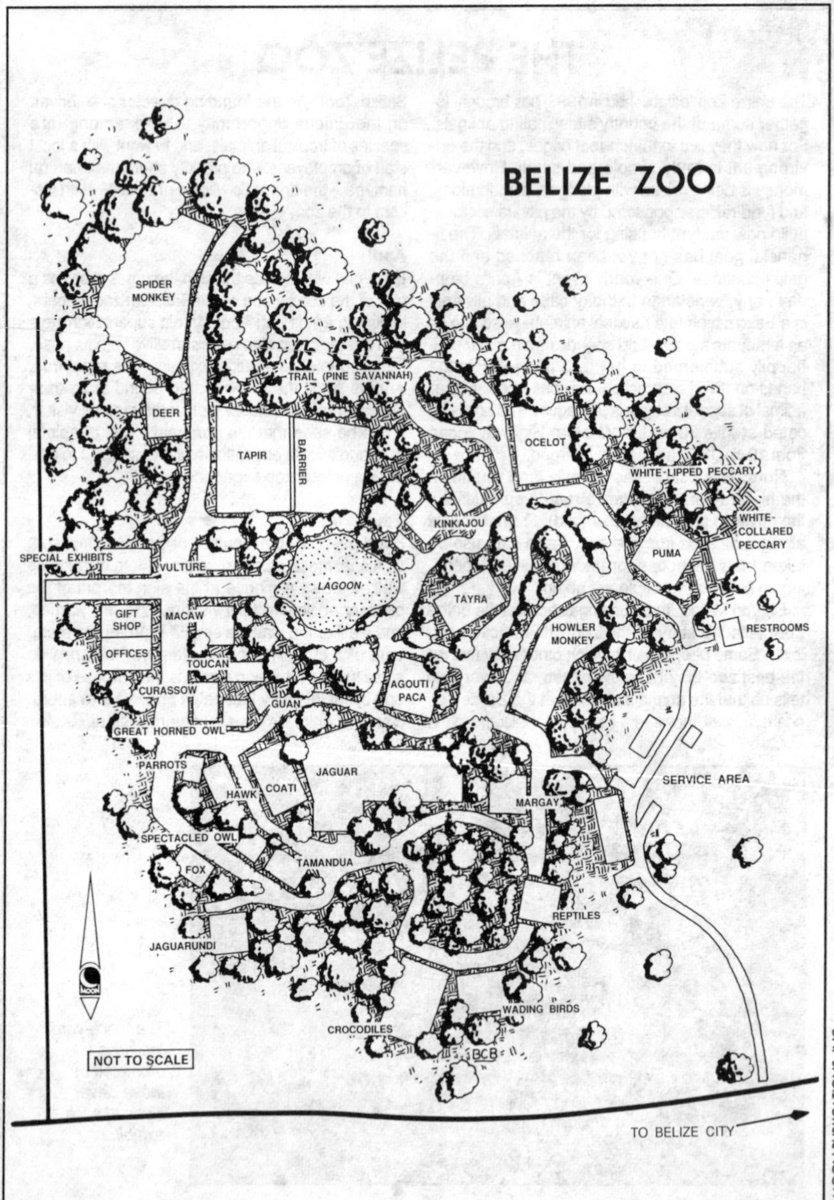

BELIZE ZOO

SPIDER MONKEY

TRAIL (PINE SAVANNAH)

DEER

TAPIR

BARRIER

KINKAJOU

OCELOT

WHITE-LIPPED PECCARY

WHITE-COLLARED PECCARY

PUMA

SPECIAL EXHIBITS

VULTURE

LAGOON

TAYRA

HOWLER MONKEY

RESTROOMS

GIFT SHOP

OFFICES

MACAW

TOUCAN

CURASSOW

GUAN

AGOUTI/PACA

GREAT HORNED OWL

PARROTS

HAWK

COATI

JAGUAR

MARGAY

SERVICE AREA

SPECTACLED OWL

FOX

TAMANDUA

JAGUARUNDI

REPTILES

WADING BIRDS

CROCODILES

BCB

NOT TO SCALE

TO BELIZE CITY

© MOON PUBLICATIONS, INC.

OZ MAILAN

April, the national animal, loves the attention and TLC she gets at the Belize Zoo.

Beginnings

Sharon Matola started the Belize Zoo in January 1983. Coming to Belize to begin a zoo and build a wildlife education program was not what she considered part of her destiny at that time. She had arrived in Belize to manage a small collection of local animals for a natural film company. However, after only five months of working on the project, funds were severely reduced, and it became evident that the group of animal "film stars" would have to be disbanded.

Get Rid Of The Animals?

Sharon says that besides the fact that these wild cats, birds, anteaters, and snakes had become her friends and companions, there were other reasons that made getting rid of them difficult. Once a wild animal has become semi-tamed and dependent on people for care, returning to a life in the wild is impossible.

So, as an alternative she told herself, "This country has never had a zoo. Perhaps if I offered the chance for Belizeans to see these unique animals, their existence here could be permanently established."

And so a zoo was born. From the very beginning the amount of local interest shown in the zoo was incredible. The majority of the people in Belize live in urban areas, and their knowledge of the local fauna is minimal. The Belize Zoo offered many Belizeans the opportunity to see the animals that share their country. It was touching to see the looks on the faces of small children who were experiencing for the first time the animals of their homeland. The modest be-

ginnings of the zoo were based upon the simple idea that children deserved the chance to grow up knowing animals, especially those living in the thick forests and jungles not too many miles from their city homes.

School Programs

This initial interest was exciting and prompted Sharon to begin a country-wide education program. She took colorful slides of the animals to schools along with invitations for the teachers to bring their children—free of charge—to the new zoo. Those modest beginnings have evolved into a major wildlife awareness program that has touched the hearts of thousands of children and adults throughout Belize. The zoo now has a collection of Belizean fauna that numbers well over one hundred species. The zoo staff is a dedicated crew of Belizean zookeepers who not only provide excellent care for the animals, but who travel around the nation with wildlife education programs.

Special events at the zoo further enhance wildlife awareness efforts. Every child in the nation is invited to come to the zoo and join in the celebration. Besides singing "Happy Birthday" to a tapir, eating cake, and being entertained by Rose Tattoo, the famous clown of Belize, the children learn more about their special natural heritage.

Learning about their country's animals is important. Today, throughout Central America, much of the wildlife is standing on the brink of extinction. To lose, forever, the roaring call of the howler monkey, or the dramatic flashes of red that belong to the scarlet macaw, or the discreet presence of the mighty jaguar, would be a tragedy.

One of the important messages provided by the Belize Zoo is to let zoo visitors know where they can view the animals of Belize in the wild. When watching the howler monkeys playing in the trees at the zoo, a nearby sign informs zoo guests that they can see these monkeys at the **Bermudian Landing Community Baboon Sanctuary.** A walk by the jaguar exhibit will not only provide an impressive look at these beautiful big cats, but will also encourage visitors to visit the **Cockscomb Basin Jaguar Preserve**—"the only place in the world where the big cat can roam protected and forever free."

A Success Story
This type of progressive wildlife education has helped to bring about a growing pride among the people of Belize for the animals of their country. This sense of pride will lead to a feeling of propriety that will ultimately help to ensure the animals' future in the Belizean wild. The zoo's success story will develop further, and the future is an exciting one. The little zoo will be moving to an underdeveloped piece of land where both animals and zoo visitors will have more room to roam about. Using a master plan for development that was donated by zoo architects from Seattle, Washington, the goal is to display each Belizean animal in a natural wild setting.

Raising money to implement this master plan has been a local as well as an international effort. It has not been easy, but slow and steady progress is being made. A visit to the Belize Zoo is fun, inspiring, and educational for the local as well as foreign visitors. The funky, "down home" approach puts people from all walks of life in touch with the magic of the animals of Belize—animals that are the natural heritage of this unspoiled, tropical country, and are also the natural treasures of the entire world.

Role Model
The Belize Zoo is becoming increasingly well known throughout the world. The unique educational programs and the conservation efforts of the zoo have consistently made international environmental news. The publishers of the *Belize Handbook* believe that the efforts of the Belize Zoo should be encouraged and supported by all. If you wish to help, it's easy! All you have to do is make the appropriate donation to become a member of the Belize Zoo. Join today by sending your name and mailing address to:

The Belize Zoo
P.O. Box 474
Belize City, Belize, C.A.
Membership categories are (in U.S. dollars):
Individual, $25
Family, $35
Patron, $65
Participating, $130
Sustaining, $250
Supporting, $500
Benefactor, $1,000
Every single dollar helps! Whatever your contribution, you will receive the zoo's informative newsletter and other benefits, depending on your level of participation. Plus, you'll have the personal satisfaction of knowing you're helping to educate the world around you and protect the unique wildlife of Belize.

Caribbean Tourism Association; 20 E. 46th St., New York, New York 10017; tel. (212) 682-0435.

Belize Audubon Society
The **Belize Audubon Society** has offices and representatives all over the country. They are a splendid source of information for travelers who wish to investigate any of the wildlife reserves in Belize. In each case they are involved in managing the reserves. They have the most up-to-date information about current seasonal conditions and when and if you can use the facilities. Ask about **Bermudian Landing Baboon Sanctuary, Cockscomb Basin Jaguar Sanctuary, Crooked Tree Sanctuary,** and **Half Moon Caye Natural Sanctuary.** Although you will see many offices, the one located at 12 Fort St., tel. (02) 35-004, (02) 34-987; fax (02) 34-985, is probably the best equipped to answer tourists' questions.

CONSULS AND VISAS

You'll find resident diplomatic and consular representatives from 20 countries in Belize including:

British High Commission
Embassy Square, Belmopan
(8) 2146/2147
Canadian Consulate
83 N. Front Street, Belize City
(2) 31-060
Costa Rican Embassy
34/36 Half Moon Ave., Belmopan
(8) 22-725
El Salvador
13 Eve St., Belize City
(2) 73-166
Guatemala Embassy
Mile 6½, Northern Hwy.
Belize City
(2) 25-2614
Honduras
6 Gabourel Lane, Belize City
(2) 72475.
Mexican Embassy
20 N. Park St., Belize City
(2) 30-193/30-194
Panamanian Embassy
3 Orchid Garden, Belmopan
(2) 30-193/30-194
U.S. Embassy
29 Gabourel Lane, Belize City
(2) 77-161
Venezuelan Consulate
18/20 Unity Blvd., Belmopan
(8) 2384.

Visitors to Belize must be in possession of passports and certain categories will require visas as well. British subjects (Commonwealth citizens) and citizens of the U.S. who have return or ongoing tickets issued in their country do not need visas. Check with your embassy before taking off.

Belize Consulates in the U.S.:

CALIFORNIA:	611 S. Wilton Place Los Angeles 90005 (213) 385-6499
FLORIDA:	4343 W. Flagler St. Ste. 400 Miami 33134 (305) 442-2114
MICHIGAN:	27166 Selkirk Southfield 48076 (313) 559-7407
LOUISIANA:	1500 W. Esplanade Ave., #8B Kenner 70065 (504) 465-9904
TEXAS:	1415 Louisiana, Ste. 3100 Houston 77002 (713) 658-0207

Belize Embassy in the U.S.:

2535 Massachusetts Dr. NW
Washington, DC 20008
(202) 332-9636
fax (202) 332-6741

Local Tour Operators

Belize offers much for the visitor to see and many ways to do it: travel independently with a rental car or by bus, hire a taxi, or travel with a tour operator who provides transportation as well as guidance. For those interested in letting someone else do the driving, various tour operators are reliable. In Belize City, for example, Sarita and Lascelle Tillet of **S & L Guided Tours** operate as a husband/wife team. They drive late-model a/c sedans or vans and travel throughout the country with airport pickup available. The Tillets have designed several great **special interest vaca-** tions and will custom design to your interests whether they be the Maya archaeological zones (including Guatemala's Tikal), or the cayes—or the caves and the countryside. Lascelle is a great birdwatcher; he always seems to spot the unique before anyone else and knows the names and living habits of each winged creature; it was he who pointed out our first jabiru stork in Belize (Box 700, 91 N. Front St., Belize City, Belize, C.A.; tel. 2-73-062, fax 2-45-211).

Belize Mesoamerica is another excellent Belizean tour agency. Tell them what you want and they will make it easy for you. They have an office

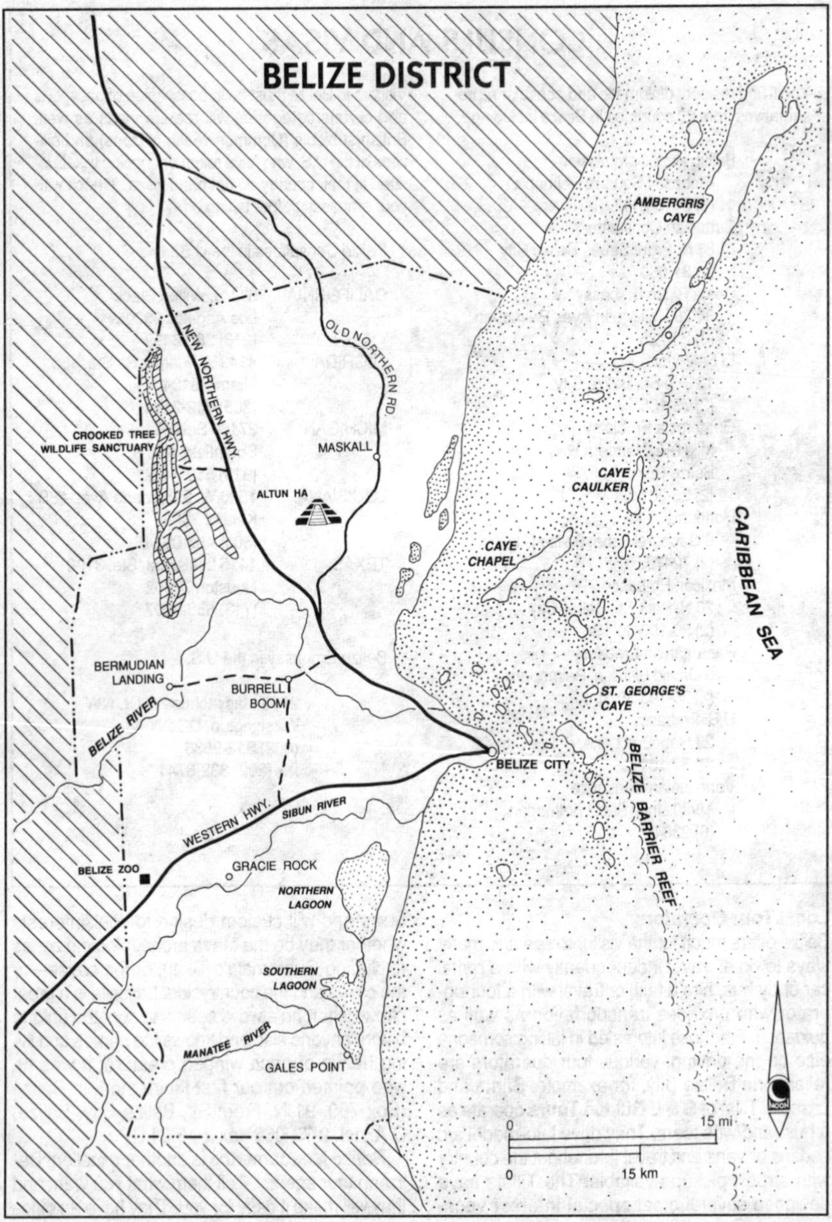

BELIZE DISTRICT

AMBERGRIS CAYE

OLD NORTHERN RD.

NEW NORTHERN HWY.

CROOKED TREE
WILDLIFE SANCTUARY

MASKALL

ALTUN HA

CAYE
CAULKER

CAYE
CHAPEL

CARIBBEAN SEA

BERMUDIAN
LANDING

BURRELL
BOOM

BELIZE RIVER

ST. GEORGE'S
CAYE

BELIZE CITY

WESTERN HWY.   SIBUN RIVER

BELIZE ZOO

GRACIE ROCK

NORTHERN
LAGOON

BELIZE BARRIER REEF

SOUTHERN
LAGOON

MANATEE RIVER

GALES POINT

0   15 mi

0   15 km

© MOON PUBLICATIONS, INC.

at the Belize International Airport and offer tours to all the attractions in the country, whether natural history, archaeology, or adventure. Contact them for more information (4 S. Park St., Box 1217, Belize City, Belize, C.A.; tel. 2-73-383, fax 2-30-750).

Drinking Water In Belize City
Use your common sense as far as food and water are concerned. The water in Belize is commonly runoff from rooftops; it is then stored in cisterns or tanks. In some cases it's perfectly safe; in others it's *iffy!* If you're concerned, ask for bottled water. In case it's not available, carry a small bottle of laundry bleach as a backup. Add a couple of drops per quart of water, shake, and let stand 30 minutes before drinking. Another option is to travel with a small portable water purifier. (See "Health Care.")

Local Doctors
If you should need a doctor, the U.S. Embassy recommends **Dr. Manuel Lizama,** (13 Handyside St., Belize City, Belize, C.A.; tel. 2-45-138). **Belize City Hospital** is a public government facility; **St. Francis Hospital** (28 Albert St., Belize City, Belize, C.A.; tel. 2-77-068) is a small private hospital.

Taxis
Taxi fares are controlled by the government. Even so, they should be determined before getting in the cab. From the international airport to Belize City the fare is usually US$15, from the municipal airstrip, US$4. The fare for one passenger carried between any two points within Belize City (or any other district town) is US$1.50. For two or more passengers it is US$1

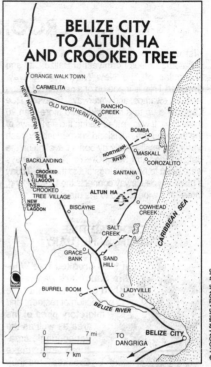

per person. If you plan on making several stops, tell the cabbie in advance and ask what the total will be. This eliminates lots of misunderstandings. Generally speaking, most of the city is accessible on foot, even the bus stations. Taxis can be hired by the hour (US$12.50) or for long trips out of town.

CROOKED TREE

History

Located 33 miles northwest of Belize City and two miles off the New Northern Highway, **Crooked Tree** is made up of a network of inland lagoons, swamps, and waterways. **Crooked Tree Lagoon** is up to a mile wide and more than 20 miles long. It was settled during the early days of the logwood era, an island surrounded by fresh water, accessible only by boats traveling up the Belize River and Black Creek. The waterways were used to float the logs out to the sea. Today a mile-long causeway connects the six-mile-long, three-mile-wide island to the mainland.

CROOKED TREE WILDLIFE SANCTUARY

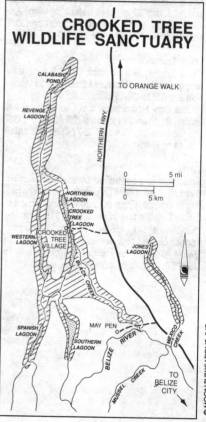

In 1984 **Crooked Tree Wildlife Sanctuary** was established on the island for the protection of resident and migratory birds of the area as well as the varied jungle creatures that make Crooked Tree their home. The wildlife sanctuary is divided into two sections. The largest is a series of six connected lagoons open to visitors and accessible by boat and road. A smaller water area, Mexico/ Jones Lagoon, is not open to tourists.

BOB RACE

Audubon Society

Although several organizations have had a hand in founding the park with financial aid, ongoing credit for supervision goes to Belize Audubon Society. The Society, with the continued help of devoted volunteers, maintains a small business center/museum located in a small building on your right just after you cross the causeway. Do sign in; this validates the sanctuary and gives the Society a reason to sponsor it. For now there is no admission fee, but that will be changing in the future. You will always find a knowledgeable curator willing to answer questions about the birds and flora encountered at the sanctuary. By the way, they have an outhouse-type toilet in the back yard.

Flora And Fauna

Multitudes of birds find the sanctuary a safe resting spot during the dry season, with enormous food resources along the shorelines and in the

CROOKED TREE WILDLIFE SANCTUARY

CALABASH POND

TO ORANGE WALK

REVENGE LAGOON

NORTHERN HWY

0   5 mi

0   5 km

NORTHERN LAGOON

CROOKED TREE LAGOON

WESTERN LAGOON

CROOKED TREE VILLAGE

JONES LAGOON

BLACK CREEK

SPANISH LAGOON

MAY PEN

SOUTHERN LAGOON

BELIZE RIVER

MEXICO CREEK

MUSSEL CREEK

TO BELIZE CITY

© MOON PUBLICATIONS, INC.

Local canoes are
carved from one
large log.

trees. After a rain, thousands of miniscule frogs (no more than an inch long) seem to drop from the sky. They're fair game for the **snowy egret** and **great egret**—quick hunters with their long beaks. A fairly large bird, the **snail kite** picks up the **apple snail** all around the lake, then returns to its nesting tree and gorges—a dead giveaway with piles of empty snail shells underneath. Two varieties of ducks, the **black-bellied whistling duck** and the **Muscovy**, nest in trees along the swamp. All five species of **kingfishers** are represented in the sanctuary, and **ospreys** and **black-collared hawks** are seen diving for their morning catch. Black Creek, with its forests of large trees, provides home to **black howler monkeys, Morelet's crocodiles, coatimundi, turtles,** and **iguana.** On a recent trip, we watched from our dory as a **peregrine falcon** quietly circled high above the lake until the time was right to make a jetlike dive after a small **American coot.** The falcon did this several times, but with each attempt the flock of floating coots spotted him first and dove beneath the water, eluding the airborne predator!

The Village

The village is divided into three neighborhoods: **Crooked Tree, Pine Ridge,** and **Stain,** with a total population of 800. Villagers operate farms and raise livestock, and have a small fishery. Visitors will find the village spread out on the island, consisting of a cricket field, two churches, and neat wooden houses (many on stilts) in the middle of large, well-kept plots of land, each with its own tank to catch rainwater—a tranquil community.

Accommodations

This is not a tourist area—yet. It does, however, have a few places to have a cold drink, and a couple of small hostels (cabaña resort/restaurant/bar combinations.) **Crooked Tree Resort** faces the lagoon on the northern edge of the village. So far it has seven cabañas (three singles and four doubles), a separate dining room, and the bar sits on a dock over the water where you can watch the birds at play. Ask about guided tours of the region. Sam Tillett, one of the owners, is hard to beat for knowledge of the locale.

Visitors have a choice of roaming around Crooked Tree on horseback or on foot. The cabañas have thatch roofs, constructed of native hardwoods, and are simple and comfortable with both hot and cold water. Price for a room only is US$52 s, US$65 d; with three meals it's US$75 s, US$95 d. Ask about guided tours and prices to Altun Ha and the Baboon Sanctuary. For more information contact Crooked Tree Resort (Box 1453, Belize City, Belize, C.A.; tel. 2-77-745).

This one we haven't seen, but check out **Crooked Tree Bird's Eye View Resort.** All rooms have hot water and private baths. For campers, ask about an area set aside for tents. Rates are: room only, US$52 s, US$65 d; with breakfast and dinner US$68 s, US$85 d; bed-

THE DEVELOPMENT OF A LIVING ANIMAL SANCTUARY

THE BERMUDIAN LANDING HOWLER MONKEY SANCTUARY

When zoologist Robert Horwich from the University of Wisconsin at Milwaukee began a population survey thoughout the range of the **howler monkey**, it was the beginning of what would become the first viable animal sanctuary. The scientist spent time in the howler's range, which covered southern Mexico, northeast Guatemala, and Belize. Until then, no one had formally studied the primate and its rainforest habitat.

The results were disturbing. In Mexico the monkeys were hunted by the locals for food and their living habitat was fast being eliminated with the destruction of the rainforest. Conditions in Guatemala were only slightly better. Here, too, the monkeys were hunted by locals in the forests around Tikal, and as the forest habitat shrunk in the country, so too did the numbers of howler monkeys.

It was the last survey that was surprising. In Belize, at Bermudian Landing, the communities of monkeys were strong and healthy, the forest was intact, and the locals seemed genuinely fond of the noisy creatures. This was definitely a place to start talking *wildlife reserve*.

With the help of Jon Lyon, a botanist from the State University of New York, the two scientists began a survey of the village. After many meetings with the town fathers, there was actually an excitement about the idea of saving the "baboon" (the local name for the monkey). Homeowners agreed to leave the monkey's food trees, hogplums and sapodillas, and small strips of forest between cleared fields as aerial pathways for the primates, as well as 60 feet of forest along both sides of waterways.

The landowners signed voluntary pledges promising to follow the management plans set forth by Horwich and Lyon—a sanctuary was born. At last count there were more than 70 landowners (in seven villages covering eighteen square miles along a stretch of the Belize River that measures 20 miles) who were taking part. Villages include **Double Head Cabbage** and **Flowers Bank.**

The monkeys are happy and the population has grown to a whopping 1,000. By now sanctuary management may have acted on the plan to move some of the troops south into the Cockscomb Basin Wildlife Sanctuary. One of only six species of howler monkeys in the world, the black howlers are the largest monkeys in the Americas.

One of the outgrowths of this innovative plan in Belize is the knowledge that educating the people about conservation and arousing in them a basic fondness for all of nature has been much more successful than enacting a stringent hunting law. The

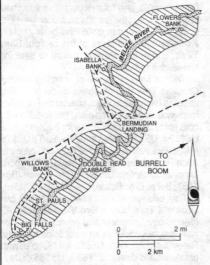

BERMUDIAN LANDING COMMUNITY BABOON SANCTUARY

FLOWERS BANK

BELIZE RIVER

ISABELLA BANK

BERMUDIAN LANDING

WILLOWS BANK

DOUBLE HEAD CABBAGE

TO BURRELL BOOM

ST. PAULS

BIG FALLS

0   2 mi

0   2 km

BOB RACE

© MOON PUBLICATIONS, INC.

managers of the sanctuary are local villagers who understand their neighbors and much of their time is spent first at schools and then with the adults in interested villages. Part of their education includes basic farming techniques and sustained land use that eliminates the constant need to cut forest for new corn *milpas;* this might be the most important feature of learning for the forest inhabitants.

A museum at **Bermudian Landing** has been opened that gives visitors an overview of rainforest ecology along with specific information and lore about the black howler monkey and other animals living within the sanctuary. From the museum, visitors can explore three miles of forest trails that surround Bermudian Landing. The tourist brings in a few extra dollars for the subsistence economy of the area. Future plans include building guest cabañas, selling wood

carvings created by locals, and offering visitors a trip down the river into monkey country.

If it all sounds perfect, it isn't! There are still those people from the more urban areas who come to the sanctuary to kidnap baby monkeys to sell for pets. The only way anyone can kidnap a baby howler is by killing the mother, since she will never relinquish her young without a fight. A lively debate continues among traditional conservationists about allowing the people to live within a wildlife preserve. However, Belize's grass roots conservation is proving that it can succeed. Other countries such as Australia and Sierra Leone are watching carefully to see how this same concept can be adapted to the needs of their own endangered species without kicking out the people who have lived on the land in some cases for many generations.

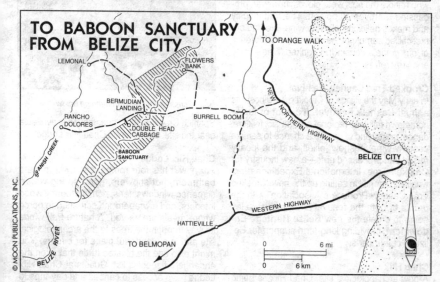

and-breakfast rates, US$58 s, US$72 d; with three meals US$75 s, US$95 d. Write or call for more information (Box 1976, Belize City, Belize, C.A.; tel. 2-44-101, or fax 2-77-594).

Crooked Tree mainly attracts nature lovers. But visitors will find barefoot boys going home for lunch with fishing poles over their shoulders and, maybe, a string of healthy-looking

fish. Ladies with floppy hats gabbing over back fences always flash a friendly smile with a gracious hello. And if you indulge in conversation you'll have a chance to hear the lovely soft Creole patois that is common throughout the country. While strolling through the village you might see the local boys having a hard workout on the cricket field.

The Cashew Seed/Nut

The village is also known for its thick stand of cashew trees. In the past this was a mild infusion into the budgets of the local women. Once a year they picked, processed, and sold about 400-500 quarts of bulk cashew nuts to a distributor in Belize City, who then packaged and sold them to the consumer. A new business is about to be born. The town will be doing what they did before, only now they will go on to package the nuts for visitors and local consumers in shops and hotels around the country.

The cashew is very unusual—the only plant that grows its seed on the outside of the fruit (see p. 24). One bean-shaped pod hangs from the bottom of each fruit—one fruit, one cashew nut. (No wonder they're expensive!) The shell contains a highly irritating poison that for most people causes blisters and inflammation. Those who handle the nuts wear gloves; however, processing removes all poison. The fruit is juicy and makes delicious jelly and wine. We had our first chilled sample of the wine at the back fence of our guide's cousin in Crooked Tree—tasty and very refreshing!

Crooked Tree Cashew Festival

In early May the village of Crooked Tree hosts its annual **Cashew Festival**. It's a lot of fun, a hometown fair, with regional arts, music, folklore, dance, crafts, and of course a chance to sample cashew wine, cashew jellies, and the locally raised and processed nuts—a new industry for Crooked Tree. International Expeditions Inc. was instrumental in setting up the new "Crooked Tree Cashew Producers Association" with the profits of both the festival and product sales going to create the new **Belize Heritage Endowment,** providing long-term support for Belizean cultural arts.

Chau Hiix

A new archaeological site, Chau Hiix, is being studied nearby. Under the auspices of the University of Indiana at Indianapolis, Dr. Kay Anne Pyburn is leading the dig. They have already made some startling discoveries that include a ball court and ball-court marker, along with small artifacts. Preliminary studies indicate the site was occupied from 1200 B.C.-A.D. 1500. **Sapodilla Lagoon** is located south of Crooked Tree on

cashew fruit with nut hanging below

Spanish Creek. A small guesthouse is available near the site, aptly named Chau Hiix Lodge.

Chau Hiix Lodge

For now it has four rooms, each with private bathroom, hot showers, good spring water, screened windows, fans, rich mahogany wood interiors, and a wraparound screened-in porch where meals are served. A nature trail winds its way through the trees to the archaeological site and is a wonderful place for birders. You might also see the hicatee turtle that is on the endangered-species list. Guests at Chau Hiix Lodge have access to canoes and day-trips to the Community Baboon Sanctuary, or they might choose to just wander the trails on the 4,000-acre grounds of the lodge. Although drop-ins are welcome, most stays are packaged, including airport pickup, arrival by boat through beautiful lagoons, all meals, guided trips, and other lodge activities. Rates are listed for pp double occupancy; three-night packages US$525, four nights US$635, seven nights US$935. For more information call (800) 765-2611, fax (304) 765-2148; in Belize City (2) 73-787.

Getting There And Around

If you're a nature lover, this is a don't-miss trip. However, getting there is another thing. At the present time you have a choice of hiring a taxi (a little pricey), or taking a local bus (check with Batty Bus in Belize City), or check with a travel agent or tour operator in Belize City or at any of the hotels around the country that offer day-trips.

Another great way to see Crooked Tree Sanctuary as well as a waterway with banks lined with jungle vines and plants is a tour that originates in the United States. **International Expeditions** (offices in Alabama) offers a naturalist tour appropriately called the **Naturalist Quest.** Crooked Tree is just one of the stops made and travelers approach the sanctuary by boat from just outside Belize City. From here they travel a short distance up the wide Belize River over gentle rapids to a narrow, winding jungle stream. Keep your eyes open and you'll see (and undoubtedly hear) black howler monkeys, giant iguanas sunning on tall tree limbs, as well as a huge variety of birds, including squawking species of parrots and maybe even the elusive and almost-extinct jabiru stork. The photographer will have several miles of jungle stream to catch exotic flora and fauna on film before reaching Crooked Tree Lagoon and its concentration of trees, plants, and myriad birds. The boat stops at **Crooked Tree Village** where travelers are given a chance to explore the scenic settlement.

The Naturalist Quest gives Belize visitors a look into the heart of the country accompanied by a knowledgeable guide who will explain birds, animals, plants, growth patterns, seasonal curiosities, the weather, and a lot more. For more information contact International Expeditions (One Environs Park, Helena, Alabama 35080; tel. 800-633-4734, 205-428-1700).

Local Guides

One recommended way to visit Crooked Tree is to hire a local guide who really knows his digs. Locals take you in boats in order to really experience the lagoon. Sam Tillett (one of the Crooked Tree Resort owners) was a local guide. Ask him if he's available to paddle you around the lagoon in his dugout canoe (a dory); this silent transport enables you to get very close to the shoreline without a motor that might tangle with thick plants, such as water lilies (called "tum tum") that grow on the surface of the lagoon. This is Sam's country, and after years of practice he knows what he's doing; he silently glides across the water to the birds without a swish. Sam, like most Belizeans, speaks a wonderful Creole (as well as good English) and will tell you, in English and Spanish, the names of unique birds, unusual plants, and animals. A profusion of wild ocher pokes up from the water covered with millions of pale pink snail eggs. Grazing cows wade into the shallows of the lagoon to munch on the tum tum, a delicacy that keeps them fat and fit when the grasses turn brown in the dry season.

From Belize City, if you want to be sure you'll have a guide and transportation once in Crooked Tree, check at the Belize Audubon Society office in Belize City and they will be happy to have a guide and boat waiting for you when you arrive.

KATHY ESCOVEDO SANDERS

THE CAYES

INTRODUCTION

Along the coast of Belize, more than 200 cayes (pronounced "kees" and derived from the Spanish word *cayo*) lie off the mainland. They range in size from no more than a half-block-long patch of mangrove forest to the largest, **Ambergris Caye,** which is 25 miles long and nearly 4.5 miles at its widest point. Some of these islands are inhabited by people, others only by wildlife. Most of the cayes lie within the protection of the Belize Reef (almost 200 miles long), which parallels the mainland. Without the protection of the reef—in essence a breakwater—the islands would be washed away by the constantly pounding surf. Within the reef the sea is calm, shallow, and inviting; in some areas with a white sandy bottom, the color of the water is a rich aqua—even more inviting! Mangroves provide wonderful breeding grounds for the magnificent sealife that attracts divers worldwide.

The cayes first opened the doors of tourism with the influx of divers. One of these islands (Ambergris) is the most popular diving destination in the entire country—with simple to elaborate accommodations available. However, almost everything must be brought over by boat, including food, furniture, fuels, everyday living essentials, and building materials. Expect the prices to be a little higher than on the mainland for similar lodging and meals.

Fauna

The uninhabited islands are alive with all manner of exotic wildlife, though fewer animals and birds are seen on the larger cayes as more people visit them. However, you will see the common **iguana,** which can grow to more than six feet (a local food source), along with its smaller cousin, the **wishwilly** or **spiny-tailed iguana** (note the lethal-looking jagged spines that run down its back); both avowed vegetarians and usually harmless, they can devastate a garden in no time. Also lurking in the underbrush are **opossum, armadillo, raccoon, peccary, deer, paca (gibnut),** and maybe even an **ocelot.** The **giant blue land crab** is an unusual critter, as is the **hermit crab** that moves

DIANA LASICH-HARPER

into the closest vacant shell and often leaves it behind—sometimes in the crook of a tall tree.

Two snakes make their home on the islands: the **boa constrictor** and the **black-tailed indigo.** Both are good rat catchers and supposedly harmless to adults (too big to be crushed). These snakes will bite if cornered; do guard small pets and children. A variety of frogs and lizards are fun to search out, especially the **Central American basilisk.** This small lizard often streaks past upright on its hind legs—even along the surface of the water. It's often referred to by the natives as the **Jesus Christ lizard.** The black **anole** has a colorful habit of spreading a bright, salmon pink throat pouch when claiming territory or looking for a female.

Birds

The most impressive members of this wild kingdom, however, are the birds that thrive on the multitude of cayes, whether a tiny mangrove patch or busy tourist destination. Colorful land birds count up in the hundreds, including 27 different varieties of migrant warblers. Birdwatchers will also find the **magnificent frigate, brown pelican, cormorant, royal tern, laughing gull,** and **brown-** and **red-footed boobies.** The best time to be a watcher on the cayes is September and October when thousands of birds are migrating south. Many go no farther and spend the winter right here. Wading birds have found the islands the perfect place to live year-round. Look for the **snowy egret, green heron, great egret, cattle egret, little blue heron,** and **great blue heron,** along with many, many others.

Travelers, Note:

Make reservations as soon as you decide to travel to the cayes—especially if you are planning your trip Dec.-March. In most cases there are limited accommodations, and even on the largest island, Ambergris, reserve in advance.

POPULAR CAYES

ENGLISH CAYE

Though this is just a small collection of palm trees, sand, and coral, an important lighthouse is located here at the entrance to the Belize City harbor from the Caribbean Sea. Large ships stop at English Caye to pick up one of the two pilots who navigate the 10 miles in and out of the busy harbor. Nearby is **Goff Caye,** a favorite little island for picnics and day-trips thanks to a beautiful sandy beach and its proximity to Belize City.

THE MANGROVES AND TURTLE GRASS

Two eco-systems lie within the country, and both are frowned upon by developers and certain segments of the tourism industry: mangroves and the accompanying grass flats.

Many people see mangroves as an eyesore, a breeding place of mosquitoes and sandflies. As beachfront property becomes more desirable, mangroves and turtle grass are apt to be removed to make way for a white beach, clear swimming areas, and hotels for visitors.

Fortunately, biologists and lovers of nature are informing the public that without the mangroves and the turtle grass, the cayes will erode and lose many feet of land mass.

Caye Caulker has a good example of this at the Split, which originally was a shallow ditch dug across the island for easy dory transport. However, in 1961 Hurricane Hattie blasted through the small ditch making a much larger cut. That was made worse in the early 1980s when a small resort cut down the protecting mangroves to make a beach. Since then, the erosion continues and the buttonwood mangrove along the edge have fallen one by one into the swiftly flowing waters of the channel.

As the mangroves and grasses are uprooted, cayes lose their "anchors." And what makes turtle grass important? Lobster, conch, and stone crab proliferate in the protection of the wispy grass. And it's an important food source for Belize's manatees and sea turtles. These marine creatures, globally endangered, are just two who have managed to survive in Belize's waters.

Turtle grass, along with a variety of mangroves, is a natural hatchery for many fish species, which in turn provide the fry to feed larger fish, pelicans, cormorants and other sea birds.

Mangroves are salt resistant, growing where most other plantlife find it impossible. In Belize, two species (of the four known in the country)—the red mangrove and the black mangrove shield large areas of the Belizean coastline and hundreds of cayes. Red mangrove in excess of 30 feet is found in tidal areas, inland lagoons, and river mouths, but always close to the sea. Its signature is its arching prop roots. Black mangrove grows almost double that height. Its roots are slender, upright projectiles that grow to about 12 inches, protuding all around the mother tree. Both types of roots provide air to the tree. Another species, white mangrove, is found inland along riverbanks. The buttonwood mangrove thrives in drier areas of the cayes and mainland.

Mangroves are amazingly resilient, second only to the barrier reef in providing hurricane protection. When wiped out, they immediately begin to regrow. They propogate by their prop roots, and by seeds that germinate on the tree. As soon as the seeds hit the mud they begin their growth cycle. If the seeds fall into the water, they can survive for six months floating and bobbing until they happen upon the right conditions to set down roots in.

Mangrove cayes nurture invertebrates and reptiles, including boa constrictors, iguanas and saltwater crocodiles. Sea turtles, including loggerhead and hawksbill, thrive on encrusted sponges and crustaceans clustered at the roots. Spoonbill, ibis, and heron feed around the roots; frigates, pelicans, and cormorants roost and nest in the rich, green foliage.

Mangroves and turtle grass are Belize's most important eco-systems. Again, Belizeans are becoming role models to other developing countries with their choice of priorities. And though the tourist dollar is *very* important to the economy, the people are making decisions now that will protect their natural assets; they are choosing now the type of tourist that they prefer to visit the country in the future.

(top) fishermen on the New River;
(bottom) wash day on the Mopan River (photos by Oz Mallan)

(top left) lobster claws growing at Chaa Creek; (top right) jungle vulture;
(bottom left) Rambo the Toucan is the free-wheeling pet at the Belize Zoo.
(bottom right) Black orchids are the national flower of Belize. (photos by Oz Mallan)

CAYE CHAPEL

Just one by three miles long, this privately owned caye is about 25 minutes by boat from Belize City (15 miles)—and has its own 3,600-foot-long landing strip. Caye Chapel, with its waving palms, beautiful wide beach, and coral heads at the reef a mile offshore, pampers visitors at its only hotel, **Pyramid Island Resort and Marina,** run by the owners of the caye. The hotel offers 32 large, a/c, comfortable rooms, good food, a golf driving range, tennis and basketball courts, a dive shop, fishing and diving boats, sailboards, and a marina for those who wish to cruise in on their own boats. The caye is set up to provide excellent diving services for the most experienced divers. Prices (depending on the season) include use of the tennis and volleyball courts and Sunfish sailboats; US$40-60 s, US$60-96 d, beach house US$150-175. For a complete meal plan add US$30 pp p/d (the resort raises all of its own vegetables, will cook your catch, and provides barbecues if you choose to grill it yourself). Ask about good-value, all-inclusive dive packages. Write or call for reservations and information (Box 192, Belize City, Belize, C.A.; tel. 2-44-409, fax 2-32-405).

ST. GEORGE'S CAYE

This small caye, nine miles from Belize City, is steeped in history. It was the first capital of the British settlement (1650-1784) and the scene of the great sea battle between Spaniards and British settlers. Today the small cemetery gives evidence of the heroic battle.

St. George's Caye is far from commercialized—on the contrary, it's very quiet with mostly residential homes and their docks. The British army has a rest center here, and often the only sounds heard are the whoops and hollers of young soldiers playing volleyball in the sand. However, two small resorts attract divers and people searching for total peace and relaxation near the sea, both with great diving and snorkeling facilities available.

Cottage Colony is a marvelous little resort of small colonial-like white- and pastel-painted cottages surrounding a large sandy courtyard with hammocks slung between shady palms (for a leisurely nap or a good read). The attractive second-floor dining room/bar overlooks the sea, has classy marine decor, and the food is tasty. Individual cottages accommodate as many as 25 people. The suites have a sitting room, a kitchen, and a/c. The rooms are fan-cooled, simply but comfortably furnished, and have private bathrooms. They are located 20 minutes from the **Bellevue Hotel** dock in Belize City. Both the Bellevue Hotel and the Cottage Colony are owned by the Dinger family, so it's easy to make a smooth trip/connection to Belize City and St. George's Caye. Cottage Colony has a good diving program with several boats capable of handling large dive groups. PADI certification classes are available. Room rates are from US$79 s, US$83 d. Meals range from about US$7 for breakfast to US$17.50 for dinner. Ask about dive packages; reservations can be made at either the Bellevue Hotel, tel. (2) 77-051, or at Cottage Colony tel. (3) 33-571, fax (2) 73-253.

TURTLE PENS TURNED SWIMMING POOLS

In the days when pirates roamed the high seas for months at a time, they had regular stopping places; islands with abundant supplies of water were probably the most important. St. George's Caye was a favorite spot to pick up giant sea turtles. The seamen built large square pens (called *kraals*) at the end of wooden docks and would keep the captured turtles here until they left for the bounding main. Several turtles were taken on board and fed, kept mostly on their backs and out of the way (they would live that way for a month or two), until they were slaughtered for their meat. Often, turtle was the only meat the crews would eat for many months. No doubt animal-rights groups would have plenty to say about that today!

Over the years the pirates dwindled and St. George's Caye became the unofficial capital of Belize. Many more homes were built along the waterfron, and *kraals* became "crawls," swimming pens for people. Today many of the bright-white wooden houses still have the small "pools" at the end of their docks.

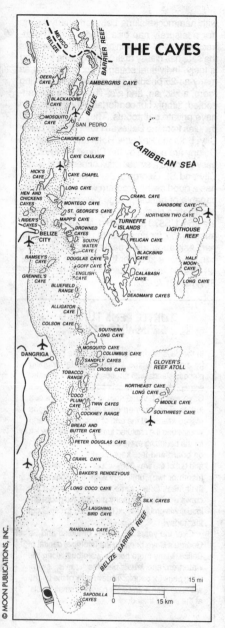

THE CAYES

MEXICO
BELIZE

BARRIER REEF

DEER CAYE

AMBERGRIS CAYE

BLACKADORE CAYE

MOSQUITO CAYE

SAN PEDRO

CANGREJO CAYE

CAYE CAULKER

CARIBBEAN SEA

HICK'S CAYE

CAYE CHAPEL

LONG CAYE

HEN AND CHICKENS CAYES

MONTEGO CAYE

CRAWL CAYE

RIDER'S CAYES

MAPPS CAYE

ST. GEORGE'S CAYE

SANDBORE CAYE

NORTHERN TWO CAYE

TURNEFFE ISLANDS

LIGHTHOUSE REEF

BELIZE CITY

DROWNED CAYES

SOUTH WATER CAYE

PELICAN CAYE

BLACKBIRD CAYE

RAMSEY'S CAYE

DOUGLAS CAYE

GOFF CAYE

HALF MOON CAYE

GRENNEL'S CAYE

ENGLISH CAYE

CALABASH CAYE

LONG CAYE

BLUEFIELD RANGE

DEADMAN'S CAYES

ALLIGATOR CAYE

COLSON CAYE

SOUTHERN LONG CAYE

DANGRIGA

MOSQUITO CAYE

SANDFLY CAYES

COLUMBUS CAYE

CROSS CAYE

GLOVER'S REEF ATOLL

TOBACCO RANGE

NORTHEAST LONG CAYE

COCO PLUM CAYE

TWIN CAYES

MIDDLE CAYE

COCKNEY RANGE

SOUTHWEST CAYE

BREAD AND BUTTER CAYE

PETER DOUGLAS CAYE

CRAWL CAYE

BAKER'S RENDEZVOUS

LONG COCO CAYE

SILK CAYES

LAUGHING BIRD CAYE

RANGUANA CAYE

BELIZE BARRIER REEF

0   15 mi

0   15 km

SAPODILLA CAYES

© MOON PUBLICATIONS, INC.

At the southern end of the caye visitors are invited to stay at the delightful **St. George's Lodge,** less than a mile from the reef. Divers are regulars here, but it's a quiet and relaxing spot for anyone who takes pleasure in the beauty of the sea, sky, and lovely surroundings. Don't expect a nightlife other than the good fellowship of other travelers, either in the comfortable bar/lounge or outdoors under the palms watching the stars over the sea. The main building consists of 12 rooms with private bathrooms, dining room, secluded sun deck, and rosewood bar—all constructed of beautiful Belizean hardwoods. Four thatch cottages sit on a dock over the water. Electricity is provided by the lodge's own windmills, and a solar-heated hot tub is always available for the guests. Good home cooking is provided—lots of fresh fish, fresh breads, and great lobster pizza. Rates are: lodge rooms US$252 s diver, US$226 pp, d, divers; cottages US$282 s diver, US$246 pp, d, divers. Prices are slightly less for nondivers; cottages are US$180 s, US$300 d,

Brit soldiers on sailboards

OZ MALLAN

THE GRAY LADY

As in all good myths and legends, details are sketchy, but facts are usually delicious. It is said that Henry Morgan often roamed the waters of the Caribbean, frequently off the coast of Belize City. In his wanderings, Henry brought his lady-fair with him, a very independent miss. It's easy to imagine that life occasionally got testy living in such close quarters aboard a caravel. And though Henry and his lady-fair usually kissed and made up, one lightning-slashed night, just off the coast of St. George's Caye, they were unable to settle a nasty argument—something to do with the seaman standing watch the night before? He was the captain after all; his word was law! The lady ended up walking the plank into the stormy sea, gray gossamer gown whipping around her legs in the angry wind. Since that fateful night the lady in gray has been roaming the small caye of St. George trying to find her blackguard lover—they say. Don't scoff; some islanders will speak no ill of the Gray Lady, and on stormy nights they stay safely behind closed doors.

plus 20% tax and service charge. This includes all roundtrip ground transportation from Belize International Airport to the lodge, three meals daily, tanks, weights, and full diving privileges with boats and guides (two boat dives daily). Write or call for more information and reservations (Box 625, Belize City, Belize, C.A.; tel. 2-44-190, 800-633-4734, 813-488-3788, fax 2-31-460).

Another commercial endeavor on the island is **Bela Carib.** Karl, originally from Austria, has a workshop on the beach where he constructs glass aquariums, collects tropical fish (which he breeds and exports), and now makes personalized St. George T-shirts for the few tourists that stop by. Ask around and you'll find him; his sales room is about the size of a closet, with a few gift items for sale. Another small gift shop along the waterfront between Cottage Colony and St. George's Lodge has a small collection of Belizean artwork and souvenirs. Hours are pretty sporadic, probably any time a client climbs up the stairs to the front door.

TURNEFFE ISLANDS

Fishing And Diving

This is a great fishing destination 25 miles east of Belize City. The islands, part of the Turneffe chain, are small dots of sand, mangrove clusters, and swampy land. Many are home only to birds and coconut palms; a few support a small colony of fishermen and divers. If you're into bonefish and permit, miles of crystal "flats" are alive with the hard-fighting fish. Tarpon are abundant late March-June within the protected creeks and channels throughout the islands. For those who seek larger trophies you'll find a grand choice of marlin, sailfish, wahoo, grouper, blackfin tuna, and many more. Divers will find a different dive spot everyday and any type of diving they want—be it wall dives, shallows for photography, fish life, creek dives, coral heads, or drift dives. And of course most divers wish to dive the **Elbow** (just 15 minutes from Turneffe Island Lodge). This now-famous dive spot offers both a steep sloping drop-off (covered with tube sponges and deep-water gorgonians) as well as shallow reef, multitudes of colorful fish, and a wrecked ship to explore.

At the northern end of the atoll, divers especially enjoy the walls and reefs around **Rendezvous Point.** Others investigate the colorful tube sponges and black coral at **Vincent's Lagoon.** Live-aboards frequently visit this northern end of Turneffe Islands and **Mauger Caye.**

Accommodations

Accommodations are limited. The **Turneffe Island Lodge,** with eight rooms accommodating 16 people on 12 acres of beautiful palm-lined beaches is one option. It's on Caye Bokel, the southernmost island in the Turneffe Chain. A one-week package includes meals, sports facilities, and transfers from Belize International Airport, with emphasis on either diving or fishing. Rooms are next to the sea, have private bathrooms with showers, hot and cold water, and 24-hour electricity. The lodge has good food, a bar, a gift shop, and planned evening activities so the guests won't get bored on their desert island. Hosts/owners are Americans Dave and Jill Bennett. The dive package is US$1195 per week, pp; the fishing package is US$1495 per week, pp. Write or call for more information and

ACCOMMODATIONS ON POPULAR CAYES

Blackbird Caye Resort, in the Turneffe Islands Group, 1415 Louisiana St., Ste. 3100, Houston, Texas 77002
(713) 658-1142
seven-day packages start at US$1100 pp

Blue Marlin Lodge, on South Water Cay
Box 942, Belize City
(5) 22-296, (800) 790-1550
weekly package from US$1125 d pp, meals included

Cottage Colony, on St. George's Caye
(2) 77-051, (3) 33-571, fax (2) 73-253
US$79 s, US$83 d

Glovers Atoll Guest House
in Sittee River Village (Middle Bank)
(8) 22-149, (92) 3310
US$5 pp per night, US$2 pp to camp

Glovers Atoll Resort, on Glover's Reef,
Box 563, Belize City
rooms US$85 pp d per week, camping US$48 pp per week

Leslie Cottages, on South Water Caye,
210 Washington St., Sherborn,
Massachussets 01770
(508) 655-1461, fax (508) 655-4445
call for prices

Lighthouse Reef Resort, on Northern Two Caye,
Box 1435, Dundee, Florida 33838
(2) 31-205, (800) 423-3114, (813) 439-6660
weekly packages from US$900, includes meals and airfare from Belize City

Manta Resort, on Southwest Caye, Glovers Reef,
(2) 31-895, (800) 342-0053, fax (305) 388-5842
from US$1150 pp per week, meals included

Pyramid Island Resort and Marina, on Caye Chapel, Box 192, Belize City
(2) 44-409, fax (2) 32-405
from US$40-60 s, US$60-96 d, beach house
US$150-175

Slickrock Kayak Adventures, on Glover's Reef,
Box 1400, Moab, Utah 84532
(801) 259-6996, fax (801) 259-8698
US$1195 for nine-day package, meals included

St. George's Lodge, on St. George's Caye,
Box 625, Belize City
(2) 44-190, (800) 633-4734, (813) 488-3788,
fax (2) 31-460
from US$252 s pp, US$226 d pp, includes three meals; prices are slightly less for nondivers

Turneffe Island Lodge, on Caye Bokel,
Box 480, Belize City, (2) 72-155/30-276,
11904 Hidden Hills Dr.,
Jacksonville, Florida 32225
(800) 338-8149, (904) 641-4468
from US$1195 pp per week

reservations (Box 480, Belize City, Belize, C.A.; 2-72-155/30-276; in the U.S. 11904 Hidden Hills Dr., Jacksonville, Florida 32225; tel. 800-338-8149, 904-641-4468).

On the eastern side of Turneffe Islands, **Blackbird Caye Resort** is 4,000 acres of a planned environmentally responsible resort. Presently it offers 10 thatch cabañas, with cold-water showers, private baths, and single and double beds. **Note:** For several months of the year, Blackbird Resort exclusively caters **Oceanic Society Expeditions** to the fondly nicknamed **Dolphin Embassy** on Blackbird Caye. A favorite of the Oceanic Society, the Dolphin Embassy is a modern research center created to study communications between humans and dolphins. Groups are taken out with a resident researcher to spot and count dolphins, and sometimes have the opportunity to swim with them. Plan on a 1.5-hour boat ride from Belize City. The reef is a stone's throw from their beach; prepare to snorkel in an untouched area. Seven-day packages start at US$1100 pp; US$1350 pp (diving); US$1550 pp (fishing); US$1450 pp (combination). Packages (land only) begin with your pickup at the Belize International Airport and include all meals; no alchoholic drinks are available on the island—feel free to bring your own. Write or call for information and reservations (1415 Louisiana St., Ste. 3100, Houston, Texas 77002; tel. 713-658-1142). For prices and information about the Oceanic Society Expeditions to Blackbird Caye, call (800) 326-7491.

Cottage Colony is a relaxing spot between diving or snorkeling.

OZ MALLAN

GLOVER'S REEF ATOLL

Seventy miles and a five-hour trip southeast of Belize City brings you to **Glover's Reef,** said by some to be a dream-come-true of island fantasy—white sand, blue sea, and coconut palms with a fringe of white water breaking over the nearby reef. It was named for pirate John Glover who, in his own way, also loved this offshore reef. The atoll is a circular necklace of almost continuous coral reef around an 80-square-mile lagoon with depths to 50 feet; the various colors of blue in the water are so intense they seem phony. Within the lagoon divers will find 700 shallow coral patches. And for the adventurer looking for sunken ships, the sea on the north and northeastern sides of the reef embraces the bones of at least four ships. This is a favorite destination for boaters large and small, including live-aboard dive boats that come from the U.S. and Belize City.

Fishermen will have a chance at bonefish and permit, as well as the big trophies including sailfish, marlin, wahoo, snapper, and grouper.

Accommodations

Manta Resort is located on the southern tip of **Southwest Caye,** Glover's Reef, a 13-acre speck of sand that is pure fantasy. Available arrangements for fishing and diving include equipment and scuba instruction. Each cabaña has a private bath, warm-water showers, and daily maid service. The mahogany cabañas each have a private porch, a hammock close by, and are cooled by the trades. The rooms are simple but comfortable. A spacious restaurant/bar is built on a pier that extends over the water under an enormous thatch umbrella; good food is enjoyed by all, even homemade chocolate-chip cookies when the chef is feeling especially good! Ask about her "five-alarm garlic hot sauce"—a remarkable potion. When you're sitting around in the late evening, ask the staff about the ghosts that still wander the cayes off the Belize coast—tingling stories for late at night. Only eight-day, seven-night packages are available; the diving package (high season) is US$1600 s; US$1195 pp double occupancy, US$1150 pp triple occupancy; the seven-night fishing package is US$1595 pp double occupancy. Ask about prices for nondivers and fishermen. These prices are all inclusive from the moment you land in Belize City (airfare to Belize City not included). It is a four-hour boat ride to Manta Resort. For more information contact **Manta Resort,** tel. (2) 31-895, (800) 342-0053, fax (305) 388-5842.

Glover's Reef now has a couple more options for accommodations. **Glover's Atoll Resort** is located right on top of Long Caye, a striking reef surrounded by crystalline water. It's especially popular with the backpacker, adventurer, and anyone who's looking for a budget paradise and enjoys going camping. The members of the Lamont family are born hosts and invite all to come and experience their lifestyle of 24 years. Guests have a choice of camping or of a simple but delightful beach cabin on stilts overlooking the reef. The cabin has two beds, a cooking corner equipped with everything (except food), shower, private outhouse, candlelight, and rainwater for drinking. Basic groceries and simple meals are available, or you are welcome to carry all of your own groceries and beverages with you from the mainland. Prices for cabins are US$85 pp d per week, US$132 pp d per two weeks; camping is US$48 pp per week and US$69 pp per two weeks (Box 563, Glover's Reef, Belize City, Belize, C.A.).

Transportation to the atoll is provided from the **Sittee River Village** (also called Middle Bank) aboard a 50-foot diesel sailer, included in the price; one departure weekly—Sun. 8 a.m. A smaller boat is used if the numbers warrant. Probably the most difficult part of the adventure to get to the Atoll Resort (unless you're traveling in a car) is getting to Sittee River Village from Belize City in time to catch the a.m. boat to the resort. If you have no other way but by bus and must spend a night waiting for transport, there is a *very* primitive, no-privacy, overcrowded dorm accommodation in Sittee River Village, **Glover's Atoll Guest House,** for US$5 pp, per night or US$2 pp to camp. If you should decide to stay, be sure to bring bug repellent; mosquito nets are provided on the beds. Limited groceries, fresh fruit, meals, and a car park are available. It's really best to shop for groceries in Dangriga if you decide to stay at Hopkins Sandy Beach at the Women's Co-op; you might be able to hire someone to drive you to Sittee Village in time to connect with the Sun. 8 a.m. boat departure. **Note:** This is an adventure for the hardy; but once there, everyone loves it!

Tents are for rent. To book, call Belize Communications (8) 22-149 or (92) 3310 for information at Hopkins Sandy Beach.

Slickrock Base Camp
Slickrock Adventures is a must for those interested in ocean kayaking (see p. 235). The cabins here are simple but comfortable, meals include lots of fresh fish, and kayakers can easily explore other cayes. The rate for a nine-day package is US$1195 pp. Write or call for information (Box 1400, Moab, Utah 84532; tel./fax 801-259-6996).

Island For Rent
Want to rent an island? Sounds magical, huh? This one is Northeast Caye at Glover's Reef—available part of the year only. For more information, contact Slickrock Adventures, Inc.; tel./fax (801) 259-6996.

LIGHTHOUSE REEF

The most easterly of Belize's three atolls, **Lighthouse Reef** lies 50 miles southeast of Belize City. The 30-mile-long, eight-mile-wide lagoon is the location of the **Blue Hole,** a favorite destination for divers that was made famous by Jacques Cousteau. The underwater cave is a karst-eroded sinkhole with depths that exceed 400 feet. In the early '70s Cousteau and his crew explored the tunnels, caverns, and the listing stalactites that were angled by past earthquakes. This is a rich habitat for shrimp and jewfish. If flying over the coast you'll easily recognize the landmark by its magnificent blue hues in a large circular pattern along the coast.

REEF FISH

Atlantic spadefish	green moray	spanish grunt
banded butterfly fish	honey damselfish	spotfin butterfly fish
bar jack	nurse shark	spotted drum
bluestriped grunt	queen triggerfish	trunkfish
blue tang	schoolmaster	white grunt
dog snapper	sergeant major	yellow jack
foureye butterfly fish	smallmouth grunt	yellowtail damselfish
French grunt	southern stingray	yellowtail snapper

ISLAND VIEWS

Lighthouse Reef
Resort

HALF MOON CAYE

Dedicated as a monument in 1982, crescent-shaped **Half Moon Caye Natural Monument** was the first reserve created within the new climate of protecting Belize's natural beauty. Measuring 45 acres, the caye is located at the southeast corner of Lighthouse Reef. Boaters use the rusted hull of the wreck, once known as the *Elksund*, as a landmark in these waters. The caye, eight feet above sea level, was formed by the accretion of coral bits, shells, and calcareous algae. It's divided into two different ecosystems. The section on the western side has dense vegetation with rich fertile soil. The eastern section is primarily coconut palms and little vegetation.

The waters off the caye are supposedly the clearest in Belize (with visibility as far as 200 feet), and the beaches are among the best. You must climb the eight-foot-high central ridge that divides the island and gaze south before you see the striking half-moon beach with its unrelenting surf erupting against limestone rocks.

Half Moon Caye's first lighthouse, built in 1820, is situated on the eastern side of the caye. Another was built in 1848 and modernized and enlarged in 1931; today the lighthouse has entered the age of high tech with solar power.

Fauna
The **red-footed boobies** are the principal inhab-

itant of Half Moon Caye (and the main reason for its status as a monument). Ninety-eight percent of the 4,000 adult breeding birds on the caye are white, a very rare occurrence. Naturalists must travel to an island near Tobago in the West Indies to find a similar booby colony as most adult red-footed boobies are dull brown. Along with the boobies 98 other species of birds have been recorded on the caye, including the **magnificent frigate, white-crowned pigeons, mangrove warblers,** and **ospreys.** A couple of varieties of iguana skitter through the underbrush, and in the summer the **hawksbill** and **loggerhead turtles** return by instinct to lay their eggs on the beaches.

Flora
The variety of vegetation is not large, but you will see the **ziricote** forest along with the **red-barked gumbo limbo, ficus fig, coconut palms,** and the **spider-lily plant.** Everyone should go to the observation tower in the ziricote forest and climb above the canopy for an unbelievable view. Every tree is covered with perched booby birds in some stage of growth. The air is filled with them coming and going, attempting to make their usually clumsy landings (those webbed feet weren't designed for landing in trees).

Getting There
Only chartered or privately owned boats and seaplanes travel to Half Moon Caye Monument; so far no regular public transportation is avail-

lighthouse

able. **Note:** Anyone traveling to Belize on their own vessel must clear with the authorities before entering Belizean waters. Check with the Belize Embassy in Washington D.C., tel. (202) 332-9636, fax (202) 332-6741. On the leeward side of the island, sailors will find a dock with a pierhead depth of about six feet. Large ships must anchor in designated areas *only*. Hopefully this will help to protect the reef from further (irreversible) damage such as that caused by large anchors in the past. Amphibious planes are also welcome to land here.

Camping

Guests must register at the park warden's office, located near the lighthouse, where you'll be directed to maps, camping and sanitation facilities, and given other general information about the caye. The biggest concern is the preservation of Half Moon Caye and its plants and animals. Please observe the rules of the house: bring your own water (island water is very scarce); no pets allowed; when camping use only designated sites and firepits; stay on trails to avoid damage to fragile plantlife and to avoid disturbing nesting birds; no hunting or fishing; carry everything out with you; don't litter; and, finally, do not collect *anything*—eggs, coral, shells, fish, plants—even sand!

NORTHERN TWO CAYE

Diving is great at **Northern Two Caye,** the location of a resort called **Lighthouse Reef Resort.** The island covers 1,200 acres, though almost half is mangrove lagoon. A 3,000-foot paved runway accommodates arriving guests from Belize City via **Tropic Air.** The resort has 16 acres of tropical beauty and nature has provided wonderful diving along tremendous walls and shallow reefs.

Three villas (one two bedroom with kitchen, and two with one bedroom for two people) with colonial-style architecture and solid wooden roofs are located along three miles of pristine beach facing the sea catching the northeasterly trade winds. Rooms have mahogany interior accents and Mexican-tile floors, Persian rugs, "antique"-type furnishings, bath and shower, hot water, a/c, space for diving equipment, an immeasurable supply of fresh water from four wells, and a dining room/bar where family-style meals are served. Unsurpassed bonefishing and diving.

The one-week package price is US$1200 pp, double occupancy; the nondive package is US$900 pp; the fishing package is US$1499 pp. Rates include three meals, snacks, three dives daily, guide and boat, and transport from the international airport to Northern Two Caye by way of **Tropic Air.** Special fishing packages or combination fishing/diving packages are available. Divers must have certification cards with them. More cabañas and two-bedroom villas are in the planning stage. Write or call for more information and reservations (Box 1435, Dundee, Florida 33838; tel. 2-31-205, 800-423-3114, 813-439-6660).

SOUTH WATER CAYE

South Water Caye is another scenic, postcard-pretty, privately owned island 35 miles south/southeast of Belize City and 14 miles offshore Dangriga. The **Blue Marlin Lodge** offers 15 double rooms and six cabañas just steps away from the sea, each with private bath, hot water, and electric fans; the bar/dining room over the sea serves meals, snacks (included), and drinks. Diving equipment, dive master, fishing boats, and guides are available—and best of all South Water Caye is only 120 feet from the reef. Daytrips to Glover's Reef, the Blue Hole, and other wonderful dive spots are nearby. Prices begin at US$500 pp for nondivers in a/c dorm units (two to three per room), all meals included; a seven-night vacation package is US$1300 s, US$1125 d pp; for a seven-night dive package, US$1400 s, US$1125 d pp. Ask about the fish package. Prices include transport from Belize City. Write, call, or fax for reservations (Box 942, Belize City, Belize, C.A.; fax to Belize 5-22-296; in the U.S. call 800-790-1550).

Nearby find **Leslie Cottages** (elevation three feet) right on the beach, each with a kitchen and bathroom. Cottages are rented by the week with boat transportation from the mainland. Contact IZE for prices and information (210 Washington St., Sherborn, Massachusetts, 01770; tel. 508-655-1461, fax 508-655-4445).

LITTLE-KNOWN CAYES

Along with the better-known cayes are hundreds with interesting names that most visitors never get to. Some of the tinier cayes that were around during the days when pirates roamed the Caribbean have been blown away by hurri-canes over the years. And undoubtedly new mangrove-bits of cayes are here now that were not hundreds of years ago. If cayes could only talk, they'd probably all have an exciting story to tell—tales of the ancient ceremonies of the mysterious Maya and later the shenanigans of rip-roaring pirates. Today, in many cases we can get a hint of the past (or not) by the names that have lasted over the years: **Baker's Rendezvous, Deer, Drowned, Frenchman's, Hunting, Long, Middle Long, Montego, Negro, Pajaros, Paunch, Ramsey's, Rider's, Romero, Rosario, Sapodilla, Simmonds, Spanish, Spanish Lookout, Swallo, Tobacco, Tostado,** and **Water** cayes.

LIVE-ABOARD DIVE BOATS

Several excellent live-aboard vessels based in Belize City take their guests cruising around the cayes, up and down the coast. These boats were really designed for skin divers, but this is a very relaxing kind of a vacation whether you're a fisherman, diver, or just a sea lover and explorer. Your hotel and chef travel with you to some of the most scenic spots in the tropical world. Tariff includes all meals, diving, fishing, cruising, guides, and equipment. Alcohol and tips are extra.

Aggressor Fleet
In the luxury category and accommodating 14-18 people, the *Aggressor* offers carpeted, a/c

Iguanas love the sun.

OZ MALLAN

staterooms with single and double berths, hot water, a desalination water maker, a self-service bar, a stereo, and a VCR, as well as a spacious dining room for buffets and barbecues on the sundeck, and plenty of good food.

Divers enjoy unlimited diving (twin compressors for an unlimited air supply, tank, backpack, weightbelt, and weights are provided). A personal dive locker is available right on the dive deck with a wide dive platform plus two ladders. Camera buffs will find a complete video and photo center with daily E-6 processing (camera rentals available). You'll also find certification courses, photo and wildlife seminars, and lots of TLC, including airport transfers. Live the good life from Saturday to Saturday. Contact Aggressor Fleet Limited for more information (P.O. Drawer K, Morgan City, Louisiana 70381; tel. 800-348-2628, fax 504-384-0817). Rates for a one-week diving vacation are US$1395 pp based on double occupancy.

Manta IV

For some real excitement, take a dive trip on the *Manta IV.* Eye to eye, fish to man, you can be the director of your own video, take still photos, or just watch the activity of the classic denizens of the deep. The *Manta IV* also provides dive trips leaving from the shores of Ambergris Caye (now operating out of **Belize Yacht Club** in San Pedro) to magnificent locations that all divers yearn to visit: **Blue Hole, Half Moon Caye, Long Caye,** and **Turneffe Islands.**

You have your choice of day-trips or overnight excursions. The *Manta IV* is a 54-foot diesel, fiberglass V-hull, with freshwater showers. It was used in the film *Cocoon II.* For more information about prices and reservations, in Belize call (26) 2130; in the U.S., call (904) 620-0774, fax (904) 620-0684.

Reef Roamer I And II

Out Island Divers has been taking divers to Lighthouse Reef and the Blue Hole for 10 years. The crew and owner explain to the uninitiated that Belize got its great reputation for the diving from the atolls, not the barrier reef. And the Blue Hole is only part of the excitement; the walls and sealife are fantastic too! *Reef Roamer I,* 38 feet with a wide beam, is used for day-trips; *Reef Roamer II,* 50 feet with two main decks, makes customized one- to three-night trips; it leaves from Caye Caulker, Ambergris Caye, and sometimes Belize City. For more information write or call (Box 3455, Estes Park, Colorado 80517; 800-Blue-Hol, 303-586-6020, fax 303-586-0870; in Belize, 26-2151, fax 26-2810).

Other Live-aboards

Excellent dive trips are available from a few other live-aboards that cruise the water:

Belize Aggressor II: call (800) 348-2628, (504) 385-2628.

Wave Dancer: Peter Hughes Diving, call (800) 932-6237, (305) 669-9391.

KATHY ESCOVEDO SANDERS

AMBERGRIS CAYE

The largest caye along the Belizean coast is Ambergris, and if it weren't for a very small canal separating the island from the Yucatán mainland, Ambergris could easily have been part of Mexico. In fact, Mexico has occasionally staked its claim over the years. As for its name, Ambergris is a waxy substance occasionally found floating in or on the shores of tropical seas. Believed to originate in the intestines of the sperm whale, it is rare and, at great cost, is used in the manufacture of perfume. San Pedro is the only town on Ambergris and for years has been the main tourist attraction of Belize. This may change in the future with the development of hotels and guesthouses all over the country. But despite its many new hotels and golf carts, this small island still offers the "feeling" of old Belize and hopefully it will never change. Activities are pretty low key, but if you're looking you will find a couple of discos and bars with a lively nightlife.

Enjoy a Belikin beer at one of the waterfront hangouts and watch the sometimes hectic but mostly quiet traffic in the harbor. It's not unusual to see a small sailboat balancing a car on wooden planks across its bow (the only way to get a car to the island) and locals say one or

two have been lost over the side! At one time cars were really a rarity, but more are showing up on the sandy roads. The government has recently eliminated the duty on electric golf carts, which should bring more of the quiet vehicles to the island—instead of cars. In harbor traffic you may also see a small boat hanging heavy in the sea, loaded to the waterline with a tall mound of sand brought from the mainland or another caye for construction—and then watch the men shovel it out onto the shore (San Pedro sand has too much salt).

Don't be surprised if a local Creole comes into the bar or cafe where you're having a Belikin and offers to sell you an old beer bottle filled with a potion made in his kitchen from seaweed; it is said to ease hangovers, cure ulcers, and is frequently given to colicky babies. No hard sell here; just offering a needed service. The waitress or potion-peddlars will be happy to talk to you, tell you about their families, their island, their lives. For a special holiday celebration, visit San Pedro during the Dia de San Pedro holiday, 26-29 June. These are friendly, sociable people, and many can trace their family roots back to the beginnings of Ambergris, even before Blake bought the island. Enjoy Belize for

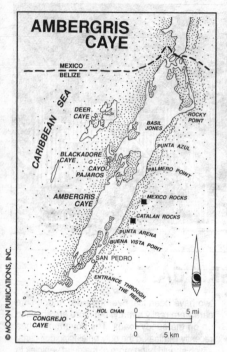

AMBERGRIS CAYE

MEXICO
BELIZE

CARIBBEAN SEA

DEER CAYE

BASIL JONES

ROCKY POINT

PUNTA AZUL

BLACKADORE CAYE

CAYO PAJAROS

PALMERO POINT

AMBERGRIS CAYE

MEXICO ROCKS

CATALAN ROCKS

PUNTA ARENA

BUENA VISTA POINT

SAN PEDRO

ENTRANCE THROUGH THE REEF

CONGREJO CAYE

HOL CHAN

0   5 mi

0   5 km

© MOON PUBLICATIONS, INC.

dug it deeper and wider to allow their warships easy access to the other side of the peninsula.

Ambergris Caye was formed by an accumulation of coral fragments. That, along with the silt emptied nearby from the Rio Hondo River, has created a lovely bit of terra firma where people have been making a living since pre-Hispanic times as fishermen. The caye is made up of mangrove swamps, 12 lagoons, a plateau, and sand ridges. The largest lagoon, fed by 15 creeks, is 2.5-mile-long **Laguna de San Pedro** on the western side of the village. San Pedro is located on a sand ridge at the southern end of the island. Over the years the constant wind, rain, and tide have reduced the shoreline and beachfront of the village by 30 feet. The water surrounding the caye offers rich fishing grounds and has supported fishermen for more than 300 years. At the southern end of Ambergris, navigable channels (often only big enough for a skiff) meander in and out of mangrove swamps and small and large lagoons. The backside is a haven for myriad varieties of birds, including the rare spoonbill.

HISTORY

The Maya

As with the rest of Belize, the first people on the caye were the Maya. They managed to rout the invading Spaniards as early as 1508. Very little is known about these Maya. However, a small post-Classic site located in the Basil Jones area and a few jade and carved ornaments have been found along with obsidian flakes and fragments of pottery. At the southern end of the caye the ruins of Marco Gonzalez are also considered of strategic importance. It is presumed that because of the location of Ambergris Caye (in the center of the sea-lane) it was a stopover for Maya traders traveling up and down the coast. And because of its close proximity to Mexico, no doubt it had great military value as well.

Pirates

By the 17th century, pirates found the cayes around the Belizean mainland perfect for resting, drinking, refurbishing their ships, and replenishing water and food supplies. Small treasures

what it is and don't expect something it isn't, a luxury resort—à la Cancun. A BZE$19.2 million contract has been signed for the San Pedro Water and Sewer Project—soon the town will have 200,000 gallons of fresh water daily.

THE LAND

Twenty-five-mile-long Ambergris is three-quarters of a mile off the Belize Reef and 35 miles from Belize City. Its beach runs parallel to the reef except at Rocky Point where they briefly come together. Four and a half miles north of Rocky Point, at Boca Bacalar Chico, a narrow channel separates Belize and Mexico. The scant strait is said to have been dug by hand by the ancient Maya so that they could bring their canoes through, rather than going all the way around the peninsula. In dry years when the water receded it was impossible to get a boat through, so in 1899 the Mexican government

downtown Ambergris

OZ MALLAN

of gold coins and antiquated bottles dating from the era indicate the pirates used these islands regularly. In the past, outsiders were "strenuously" discouraged by locals from using metal detectors for fear they'd find one of the "gold treasures" buried on the island by pirates according to legendary stories handed down over the years.

The Blakes

Between 1848-49, during the Caste War on the Yucatán Peninsula, Yucatecan mestizos migrated to Belize, and four families were the first permanent residents of what has developed into present-day San Pedro on Ambergris Caye. Before long there was a population of 50 self-sufficient fishermen—also growing corn and vegetables. Life was idyllic for these simple people—until 1874 and the coming of the Blake family.

James Blake paid the Belize government BZE$650 for Ambergris Caye (taking over every parcel of land except one parcel set aside for the Catholic Church) and began collecting rent from people who had been there for many years. After this, the history of the island was tied up with the fortunes of the Blakes and their in-laws, the Parhams and Alamillas. Their story reads like a script from a soap opera—including illicit love affairs, illegitimate children, unlikely marriages, and (some say) oppression of the poor. The Blakes controlled everybody and everything on the island, including the coconut and fishing industries, though in the end (after

almost 100 years) the good guys won out—or so it seems today. After many years of complaints, the tyrannical rule of the Blake family came to a close when the Belizean government stepped in and made a "forced purchase" of San Pedro. It redistributed the land, selling lots and parcels to the same islanders who had been living on the land for generations.

The Fishing Industry

The caye saw industry change according to the political climate: from logwood to chicle to coconuts, and then to lobsters. Before 1920, the spiny lobster was thrown away and considered a nuisance, constantly getting caught in fishing nets. That all changed in 1921 when the lobster became a valuable export item. Though the fisherman was only getting a penny a pound, it became lucrative when freezer vessels and freezer-equipped seaplanes began flying between the cayes and Florida. After struggling long and hard, fishing cooperatives were established. Once the fishermen shook off the human "sharks," the fishing industry on the cayes became successful, with the benefits finally going to the fishermen.

TODAY'S AMBERGRIS

The island is rich in lore, some of which still reaches out and taps the modern islander on the shoulder. The establishment of the fisher-

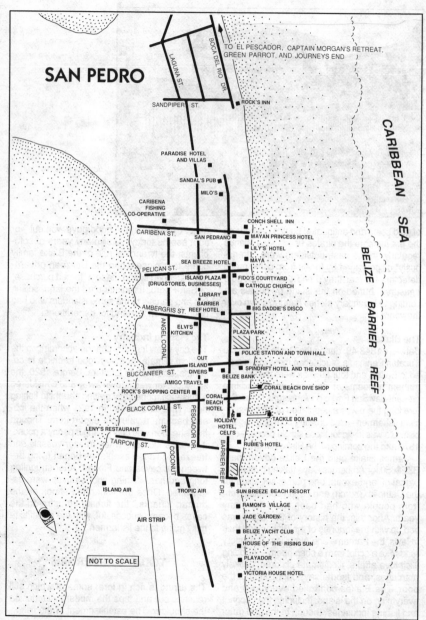

SAN PEDRO

CARIBBEAN SEA

BELIZE BARRIER REEF

LAGUNA ST.

BOCA DEL RIO DR.

TO EL PESCADOR, CAPTAIN MORGAN'S RETREAT, GREEN PARROT, AND JOURNEYS END

SANDPIPER ST.

ROCK'S INN

PARADISE HOTEL AND VILLAS

SANDAL'S PUB

MILO'S

CARIBENA FISHING CO-OPERATIVE

CONCH SHELL INN

CARIBENA ST.

SAN PEDRANO

MAYAN PRINCESS HOTEL

LILY'S HOTEL

SEA BREEZE HOTEL

MAYA

PELICAN ST.

ISLAND PLAZA [DRUGSTORES, BUSINESSES]

FIDO'S COURTYARD

CATHOLIC CHURCH

LIBRARY

BARRIER REEF HOTEL

AMBERGRIS ST.

BIG DADDIE'S DISCO

ELVI'S KITCHEN

PLAZA/PARK

OUT ISLAND DIVERS

POLICE STATION AND TOWN HALL

BUCCANEER ST.

SPINDRIFT HOTEL AND THE PIER LOUNGE

AMIGO TRAVEL

BELIZE BANK

ROCK'S SHOPPING CENTER

CORAL BEACH DIVE SHOP

CORAL BEACH HOTEL

BLACK CORAL ST.

TACKLE BOX BAR

LENY'S RESTAURANT

HOLIDAY HOTEL, CELI'S

TARPON ST.

RUBIE'S HOTEL

ANGEL CORAL

PESCADOR DR.

COCONUT ST.

BARRIER REEF DR.

ISLAND AIR

TROPIC AIR

SUN BREEZE BEACH RESORT

RAMON'S VILLAGE

JADE GARDEN

AIR STRIP

BELIZE YACHT CLUB

HOUSE OF THE RISING SUN

PLAYADOR

VICTORIA HOUSE HOTEL

NOT TO SCALE

© MOON PUBLICATIONS, INC.

men's co-op enabled the population of Ambergris to develop a good middle-class economy over the years. The financial upswing has allowed the town to improve the infrastructure of the island, which in turn has created a good atmosphere for tourists.

Tourism

The earliest tourists came to Ambergris Caye aboard the boat *Pamelayne* in the 1920s. By 1965 the first real hotel was established, and the industry has been growing ever since. The caye is considered the most developed and successful tourism area of Belize. San Pedro boasts a new water system in the works, 24-hour-a-day electricity, and modern telephone communication to anywhere in the world. The Lion's Club runs a clinic with a nurse and two doctors. You can buy the beautiful Belizean stamps and mail letters from the caye. On the down side, who knows how this influx of outsiders will affect the culture, values, and traditions of the tiny island? The ecology is threatened, but scientists in the country are on the alert and taking precautions to preserve the flora and fauna. Ambergris Caye is a laid-back combination of tropical paradise (with accommodations from simple to upscale, but not glitzy) and old-flavor fishing village: the best of both worlds, which must be seen and experienced.

THE REEF WORLD

Probably the main reason that people first started traveling to Belize is its pristine dive areas. Get together with a group of serious divers and at least one will rave about the underwater adventure encountered in Belizean waters. Since dive stories can be even more remarkable than fish stories, neophytes normally should take it all with a grain of sand—except in Belize. Divers tell of swimming with wild dolphins, swarms of horse-eye jacks, and more than two dozen eagle rays at one time. Some divers go strictly to photograph the eerie underwater beauty and color. Others enjoy the excitement of coming head to head with pelagic creatures that are carrying on with life as though the two-legged outsider was invisible, such as during the January full moon when hundreds of groupers gather at their primeval mating grounds on the reef. These stories tell of so many groupers (hundreds!) that the reef face is covered with these thick-lipped, ugly fish releasing sperm and eggs in such a fury and quantity that you cannot see two feet in front of you.

Belizean waters are universally clear except where, during heavy rains, the river outlets gush silt-clouded water into the sea. Particularly pristine areas are around the atolls, the reef, and certain cayes. In some cases visibility is extraordinary; more than 200 feet. Coral heads are magical with unique shapes reaching, floating, and quivering, interspersed with minute to immense fish all with personalities of their own. Garish-colored sponges decorate steep vertical walls that drop into black nothing. Bright red and yellow tube sponges grow tall, providing habitat for similarly colored fish.

Some divers prefer searching for sunken ships; all have heard the stories of magnificent sunken treasure never found—but then who would tell if they did find it? For more than 300 years the Belize Reef has served as a watery grave for ships thrown into the destructive limestone wall during forceful unexpected storms, including hurricanes. **CEDAM,** a group of divers allied in the early 1950s, has salvaged several old vessels along the reef. The booty from these old ships wasn't gold treasure but other practical items such as equipment, kitchen implements, tools, arms, beads, and an occasional coin, all contributing to our understanding of another era. CEDAM is an acronym for Conservation, Exploration, Diving, Archaeology, and Museums. The first ship discovered and explored was **Mantanceros.** It was named for Punta Mantanceros, the point off the Quintana Roo beach close to where it's believed the ship went down. On 22 Feb. 1742, the Spanish ship ended up in a skirmish with a British ship—part of the Admiral's fleet engaged in blockading any ships along the coast. The Spanish galleon was loaded with 270 tons of mixed cargo bound for New World ports. Many years after CEDAM salvaged the ship, the information about it was discovered in the Archives of the Indies in Seville, Spain. The real name of the ill-fated ship was *Nuestra Señora de los Milagros* ("Our Lady of the Miracles"). Again, no gold, but many fascinating artifacts from 18th-century Spain.

San Pedro docks

OZ MALLAN

Another doomed ship was **La Nicolasa,** believed to be the Montejo fleet flagship. Montejo was one of the conquerors of the Maya. And at Chinchorro Banks a forty-cannon mystery wreck has defied, for years, efforts to make a definitive identification. According to some divers, the bottom of the sea along the Belize Reef between Isla Mujeres and Honduras Bay is littered with wrecks both ancient and modern.

Diving And Snorkeling

When flying over the reef and as you approach Ambergris Caye, study the seascape around the island. The Belize Reef is clearly visible, located about a half mile in front of the island. If the plane is low enough you can see marinelife suspended in the sea, coral heads, large fish, and, of course, the inviting multicolors of blue that lure even the nonscuba diver to learn how to snorkel. You can also see the layout of the reef, how shallow the water is, and how close to the surface the corals rise, making it impossible for even the most shallow-draft craft to cross over. The cuts (or channels) are also clearly seen; these seven channels are the areas where most day boats bring their divers to explore, both on the seaward side and at the cut itself. This part of the Caribbean attracts divers for many reasons, one of which is the location of three of the only four atolls in the entire Caribbean Sea: **Turneffe Island Atoll, Lighthouse Reef Atoll,** and **Glover's Reef Atoll.**

Almost every hotel on Ambergris employs the services of local divers, and some have on-site dive shops and dive masters. Local guides for the most part have lived on the island most of their lives and operate island-built skiffs 20-30 feet long and generally powered by two outboards. Other options for the visiting diver are live-aboard dive boats that travel farther and stay out at sea longer, from overnight excursions to seven-day cruises that originate from a variety of ports in the U.S., Belize City, or San Pedro. This is a world meant for divers.

Dive Locations

There probably isn't a "secret" dive spot left along the Belizean mainland or island coasts. But if you talk to divers who continue the search, some go away with a curious smile on their face—do you suppose they know something they aren't sharing? **Hol Chan Marine Reserve** is probably the most popular dive destination of the cuts or channels. The words *hol chan* mean "little channel" in the Maya language. The

---

DIVE EMERGENCIES

Divers, Note:
A decompression chamber, manned by volunteers, is now available in San Pedro, on Ambergris Caye. Divers are urged to donate US$1 per tank to help support this important system.

reserve covers about five square miles and is located four miles southeast of San Pedro in the northern section of the Belize Reef. The channel is about 30 feet deep, and since no fishing is permitted in the reserve, it is rich with sealife of every description. Divers can expect to see abundant angelfish, blue-striped grunts, and schoolmaster snapper, as well as hundreds of other varieties. It's also well known for its green moray eels residing in tiny caves along the wall. The areas for recreation are marked with buoys. The usual rule: take only photos! It is clearly spelled out; do not collect coral or fish whether with spear or handlines. Mooring buoys are in place to help protect against anchor damage.

Warning: The current at Hol Chan is very strong. Snorkelers should take note. At least one drowning has resulted from the current.

Another dramatic dive site for the experienced diver is Palmetto Reef. Divers will see flamboyant blue vase and purple tube sponges along with other reaching and twisting corals. Coral shelves plunge from 50-150 feet into dark chasms. **Mexico Rocks** offers a variety of coral heads and clouds of tiny fish. **Caverns** offers swim-through caves filled with colorful fish and sponge-covered walls. At **Sandy Point Reef** also find myriad caverns and deep canyons that provide dramatic diving.

Diving Instructions

Several dive shops on Ambergris give diving lessons, either a brief resort course or full NAUI and PADI courses. Check out **Bottom Time Dive Shop** and **Ramon's Village Hotel Dive School.**

OTHER ACTIVITIES

Boating

Take a boat ride. Explore the Caribbean Sea in and around the many cayes of the area. Some boats have glass bottoms so the nonswimmer can enjoy the beauty of the sea. Snorkeling is also part of the activity on these boats—gear is readily available. Ask at your hotel for the *Coral Jungle,* which makes half-day trips to Hol Chan Marine Reserve; their rum-punch drinks are good! Another day-boat is the *Rum Punch II.* Run by brothers Tony and George, a snorkeling stop at the **Coral Garden,** lunch at

Caye Caulker, and captivating stories make a pleasant day. True to the boat's name, rum punch is served throughout the trip.

Water Toys

Ambergris has joined the high-tech tourist community, and most of the upscale hotels have the fun toys for rent. Along with the latest in diving equipment and dive boats, fun-seekers will find sailboards, jet skis, catamarans, and waterskis. If you've never done any of these things, there are schools and instructors available. Ask at the Sun Breeze Beach Resort for sailboarding instruction. The *Winnie Estelle* is a converted freight boat offering comfortable day-trips to the reef and Caye Caulker for snorkeling. The boat docks at the Paradise Hotel. For more options check at your hotel or at one of the larger hotels on the island.

Birdwatching

The birdlife in Belize is renowned. On Ambergris you need only travel a short distance out of town to see an enormous variety, including the **white egret, white heron,** and **roseate spoonbill.** The best places on Ambergris to watch for these birds is in the mangrove bays.

Fishing

Most dive shops and hotels will make arrangements for fishing, including boat and guide. The area within the reef is a favorite for such fish as tarpon and bonefish. Outside the reef the choice of big game is endless. Local fishing guides include **Freddie Waight** through the **Belize Yacht Club; Jose Gonzales,** (26) 2344; and **Nestor Gomez** (26) 2063. For a trip on a large sportfishing boat, contact him at the dock of the **Journey's End Hotel.** They offer reef and deep-sea fishing, as well as tarpon and bonefish angling.

ACCOMMODATIONS

For such a tiny island you'll find a wide variety of accommodations. Don't expect a lot of luxury; most rooms downtown are very simple, with several upscale exceptions. A few have a/c; most have fans. The majority of the hotels are located downtown, in some cases in a cluster

AMBERGRIS CAYE ACCOMMODATIONS

Belize Yacht Club, Box 1, San Pedro
(26) 2777
US$125 s and d

Captain Morgan's Retreat, 3 miles north of
San Pedro Town
(800) 447-2931, (26) 2567, fax (26) 2616
US$115 s, US$155 d, US$200 t

Caribbean Villas
(800) 345-9786, (26) 2715, fax (26) 2885
US$85-180

Conch Shell Inn, on the beach
(26) 2062
US$50 d, US$60 t

Coral Beach Hotel and Dive Club
Box 16, San Pedro
(26) 2013/2001
US$30 s, US$46, call for package prices

Corona Del Mar Apartments, San Pedro
(26) 2055, fax (26) 2461
from US$85 d

El Pescador, Box 793, Belize City
3 miles north of town
(800) 245-1950
US$110 s, US$175 d, includes meals

Green Parrot Resort, 6 miles north of town
Box 36, San Pedro
(26) 2175, fax (26) 2270
US$90 s pp, US$65 d pp, includes meals (MAP)

House of the Rising Sun, San Pedro Town
(800) 451-8017, fax (26) 2349
US$55-75 s, US$65-85 d

Journey's End Caribbean Club
Box 13, San Pedro, 4 miles north of town
(26) 2173, (800) 541-6796/447-0474
fax (26) 2028
from US$240 d

Mayan Princess, downtown
Box 1, San Pedro
(800) 345-9786, (26) 2778, fax (26) 2784
US$110 s, US$125 d

Paradise Resort Hotel, Box 888, Belize City
(26) 2083, (800) 223-9832, fax (212) 599-1755
US$30 s, US$50 d to US$140 d

Playador, on the beach
US$85 d, with a/c US$50 d to US$140

Ramon's Village, P.O. Drawer 4407
Laurel, Mississippi 39441
(26) 2071/2077, (800) 624-4215, (601) 649-1990
US$115-235

---

separated by narrow walkways in between and along San Pedro's narrow beachfront. In the center of town most of the "beach" is little more than a narrow strip of sand to pull up boats, and a pedestrian walkway. Many of the hotels on Front St. (located on the eastern side of the island and running north and south) provide porches that look out over the sea and reef just offshore. The downtown hotels are right in the middle of things, close to the restaurants, bars, gift shops, dive shops, and all other commerce. For something a little more deluxe check out the hotels on the edges of town where you'll find more traditional beach resorts—and where you'll pay considerably more as well.

Please note that a 5% government tax is added to your room rate, and in many hotels a 10-15% service charge is also tacked on. In some cases an extra 4-5% is charged for the use of a credit card. This raises the quoted rate considerably! Prices also change frequently; traveler's checks accepted.

Budget

Take a look at **Rubie's** on Front St., one of the less expensive hotels on the caye, tel. (26) 2063, fax (26) 2434, from US$15.75 s. On the waterfront, **Lily's Hotel** offers 10 basic clean rooms with private bathrooms; six rooms have a seafront view. The food is excellent with plentiful family-style servings—let Felipe know in the morning if you plan to eat dinner that evening. The simple hotel is run by the Felipe Paz family, friendly long-time residents of San Pedro. Ask for a room that overlooks the harbor. Rates in winter are about US$30 s, US$35 d; summer rates are slightly less—US$25 s, US$30 d; Visa and MasterCard okay. Write to

AMBERGRIS CAYE ACCOMMODATIONS

Rock's Inn, San Pedro Town
(800) 331-2458, (26) 2326, fax (26) 2358
US$85 d

Royal Palm, Box 18, San Pedro
(26) 2148
write for prices

San Pedro Holiday Hotel, Box 1140, Belize City
(2) 44-632, in San Pedro, (26) 2014
(800) 633-4734
US$74 s and d

Seven Seas Resort, on the beach
(26) 2382, (800) 633-4734
US$85 s, US$95 d

Spindrift Hotel, in town
(26) 2174, (800) 633-4784
US$72.50 s and d

Sun Breeze Beach Resort, south end of town
(26) 2191
US$80 s, US$90 d

Victoria House, south end of town
Box 20785, Houston, Texas 77225
in Texas (713) 662-8000
(800) 247-5159,
fax (713) 661-4025
from US$110 s, US$130 d

BUDGET ACCOMMODATIONS

Barrier Reef Hotel, San Pedro Town
(26) 2075
US$31.50 s and d

Lily's Hotel, on the waterfront
(26) 2059
US$25 s summer, US$30 s winter

Martha's, Box 27, San Pedro
(26) 2053, fax (26) 2589
US$15 s

Rubie's Hotel, Barrier Reef Dr.
(26) 2063, fax (26) 2434
US$15.75 s, US$26-37 d

San Pedrano, Barrier Reef Dr.
(26) 2054
US$25 s, US$30 d, a/c + US$10

Thomas' Hotel, Barrier Reef Dr.
(26) 2061
US$25 d

Lily's Hotel, attn. Felipe Paz (San Pedro, Ambergris Caye, Belize, C.A.; tel. 26-2059). **Martha's Hotel And Cafe,** two blocks from the waterfront and originally someone's home, is unpretentious, laid-back, and the least expensive at about US$15 s, US$27.50 d (Box 27, San Pedro, Ambergris Caye, Belize, C.A.; tel. 26-2053, fax 26-2589).

Moderate
The **Coral Beach Hotel and Dive Club** offers 11 clean rooms, each with private bathroom, hot water, a/c, and fan. The building is across the road from the sea. Rates are without meals US$30 s, US$46 d, and with meals US$55 s, US$90 d. The Coral Beach offers several package prices as well. A diving tour, four days/three nights based on double occupancy, is US$295 pp; seven days/six nights

is US$475 pp. A fishing tour, four days/three nights based on double occupancy, is US$320 pp. A beachcomber tour, four days/three nights based on double occupancy, is US$250 pp. Dive and fishing packages include a boat, guide, equipment, room, meals, transportation to and from Belize International Airport, tackle, etc. All packages include tax. For info contact Coral Beach Hotel (Box 16, San Pedro, Ambergris Caye, Belize, C.A.; tel. 26-2013/2001) or Coral Beach Travel (172 N. Front St., Box 614, Belize City, Belize, C.A.; tel. 02-7036).

More Expensive
More and more "resort" types are taking hold on the island. **Sun Breeze Beach Resort** is at the southern end of San Pedro—on the beach amidst lovely surroundings; American plan (all

meals included) US$117 s, US$164 d; European plan (no meals) US$80 s, US$90 d. For dive-package information and room reservations write to the Sun Breeze Beach Resort (San Pedro, Ambergris Caye, Belize, C.A.; tel. 26-2191).

San Pedro Holiday Hotel offers a charming ambience—the wooden structure faces the sea with wide verandas open to the cooling trade winds of the tropics. On the waterfront, a unique fenced-in piece of the Caribbean is the Holiday's "open salt-water pool." Other services include a dive shop. Room only is about US$74 s or d; with all meals add US$15 pp. On the premises, **Celi's Restaurant** serves delicious food; dinner is by reservation only. Write or call for more information and reservations (Box 1140, Belize City, Belize, C.A.; tel. 2-44-632, in San Pedro 26-2014; in the U.S. 800-633-4734).

Ramon's Village is a delightful full-service resort with 500 feet of beachfront, located just south of San Pedro. Warning: if you stayed at Ramon's five or six years back you'll be in for a surprise; they've added a lot more cabañas so the space on the beach is really quite crowded. However, it's a favorite for divers and non-divers alike. Airport pickup is just one of the courtesies provided to guests. Sixty well-appointed palm-thatched beachfront cabañas are cooled by fans, five have a/c, and a saltwater pool is steps away from the cabañas. Simple and charming, each has private bathroom, hot water, and daily maid service, with laundry service and child care on request. Though convenient to town, there's a great restaurant on the premises, as well as a recreational pier with a dive, photo, and video shop; boats, guides, and all diving equipment are available for reef trips. Room rates are US$115 d; during Christmas holidays US$120; suites US$235. Meals are a set price; breakfast US$8, lunch US$9, box lunch US$7, dinner US$16. Recreational rentals include sailboards, aqua cycles, speed boats, bicycles, and motorscooters. Scuba instruction given (in the U.S., P.O. Drawer 4407, Laurel, Mississippi 39441; tel. 800-624-4215, 601-649-1990, fax 601-425-2411; in Belize tel. 26-2071/2077).

Another charmer is the **Mayan Princess,** located in the center of town. In one big room guests have a bed, a small kitchen with a microwave oven and eating counter, a/c, a hide-a-bed, and a lovely tropical ambience. Luxury honeymoon suites are also available. Balconies overlook the sea. Rates are US$110 s, US$125 d, Ask about special deals in off-season. Write or call for more information (Box 1, San Pedro, Ambergris Caye, Belize, C.A.; tel. 800-345-9786, 26-2778, fax 26-2784.

Victoria House two miles south of town offers delightful (though pricey) oceanfront casitas or deluxe rooms. The facilities include stucco and thatch casitas with tile floors; rooms have ocean views, private bathrooms, and ceiling fans. Excellent meals are included, and diving and fishing equipment is available; a bar and a gift shop are

Victoria House Resort

OZ MALLAN

*snorkeling off
Ambergris Caye*

OZ MALLAN

on the premises. Rates for casitas are US$170 d, for rooms US$110 s, US$130 d. Rates for rooms without meals are available. Packages are the best deals; seven-night packages for rooms are US$989 pp double occupancy, for casitas US$1079 pp, including RT airfare from Houston, New Orleans, or Miami to Belize, RT airfare from Belize to San Pedro, transfer to hotel, three meals a day, four days of diving or four half days of fishing, plus one night dive, boat, guide, and equipment. Write or call for more information and reservations (Box 20785, Houston, Texas 77225; tel. in Texas 713-662-8000, outside Texas 800-247-5159, fax 713-661-4025).

North Of Town
The **Green Parrot Resort** is a small, intimate resort six miles north of San Pedro, but just a stone's throw (quarter mile) from famous Mexico Rocks, which offers spectacular snorkeling. The Green Parrot has four double cabañas and two triple cabañas set on the beach, and a dining room and bar are available for guests and locals. Full American Plan (FAP, three meals) and Modified American Plan (MAP, two meals) are available. All cabañas have ceiling fans and hot showers. Snorkeling and fishing are provided by the resort at a minimum fee. Diving, deep-sea fishing and numerous tours are also available. Rates are MAP, US$90 s, US$65 d pp; FAP US$95 s, US$70 d pp. Write or call for more information (Box 36, San Pedro, Ambergris Caye, Belize, C.A.; tel. 26-2175, fax 26-2270).

The **Paradise Resort Hotel** is on a sandy beach at the northern edge of San Pedro and offers a relaxed and casual "barefoot" feeling with its own dock. The hotel has a restaurant and bar, and an outstanding reputation for good food. You'll find gift and dive shops, and all fishing arrangements are conveniently made on the premises. You'll have your choice of a room, a thatch cabaña, villa, or a minisuite with a/c. Room rates vary according to season, location, and type: Cabañas start at US$50 s, US$70 d; rooms start at US$30 s, US$50 d; villas are available starting at US$60 s, US$80 d. Those are minimum rates (they go up from there), and expect a US$10 surcharge for a/c; meal plans are available. Paradise Hotel charges only five percent service charge. Write or call for information and reservations (Box 888, Belize City, Belize, C.A.; tel. 800-223-9832, 26-2083, fax 212-599-1755).

Take a look at the deluxe resort suites next door to the Paradise Hotel at **Paradise Villas Condominiums,** with all the amenities of a hotel plus a fully equipped kitchen and a spacious living room. The one-bedroom units (only one two-bedroom unit is available) feature daily maid service and each unit accommodates up to four adults. Rates for high season are US$125 for one-bedroom units, US$150 for two-bedroom units, (no service charge). These prices will come down during the off-season. For more information call from the U.S., (800) 626-DIVE, or in Belize, (26) 2531.

Journey's End Resort, San Pedro

JOURNEY'S END CARIBBEAN CLUB

El Pescador has 10 rooms and one suite, all with private bathrooms. The hotel is located three miles north of San Pedro. Rooms are in a large colonial building, with a long veranda facing the sea and the reef just 200 yards offshore. This small resort specializes in tarpon fishing, much of which is catch-and-release. Fishermen go outside the reef for sailfish or wahoo and cast the lagoons for ladyfish or snook. They troll the reef for kingfish and barracuda and jig the bottoms with bait for snapper and grouper—something for every fisherman. Rates include all meals, US$110 s, US$175 d (Box 793, Belize City, Belize, C.A.; tel. 800-245-1950).

Captain Morgan's Retreat is special—a real tropical paradise where life is easy. The palms really sway, and the staff is to love! Guests will find 21 clean, attractive beachfront casitas with a freshwater pool and excellent food. Fishing, diving, snorkeling, and sailing trips are available. Prices per cabaña rise and fall with the season. High season rates—1 Nov.-30 April—are US$115 s, US$155 d, US$200 t, a little more during holidays, considerably less during the summer months. A meal plan is available for US$35 per day (three meals) and US$25 (two meals). Ask about a couple of great package plans (including airfare from the U.S.). Captain Morgan's is located a couple miles north of San Pedro, and it's almost impossible to walk to. Boat transport is available; call (800) 447-2931, (26) 2567, fax (26) 2616.

Journey's End Caribbean Club is a pricey (some say *too* pricey for what you get), laid-back, casual kind of a resort that makes a vacation memorable. This is the place to go for isolation! Located four miles north of San Pedro, all the usual swimming, snorkeling, tennis, sailing, Hobiecatting, sailboarding, canoeing, beachcombing, sun worshipping, and eating come for about US$240 d; service charge, tax, and credit-card surcharge *not* included. One recent visitor was disappointed that it was necessary to take a boat to go snorkeling; she added, though, that the food was outstanding. To get in and out of town you must go on the hotel boat, and, according to one recent visitor, you'll have a choice of four trips daily. Diving equipment is available (extra fee). For more information about special package prices and reservations contact Journey's End Caribbean Club (Box 13, Ambergris Caye, Belize, C.A.; tel. 26-2173, fax 26-2028; in the U.S. call 800-447-0474).

South Of Town
The **Royal Palm,** south of San Pedro, is in the process of a reformation into condos and should be opened in 1993. It features a swimming pool

and a white sandy beach shaded by swaying palms and edged by the clear blue Caribbean—perfect for snorkeling, scuba diving, fishing, with the reef just offshore. Contact Jim or Jamila for more information (Box 18, San Pedro, Ambergris Caye, Belize, C.A.; tel. 26-2148).

The lovely **Caribbean Villas** is located in a two-story building close enough to town to bike in and out at your leisure (bikes compliments of the hotel). The rooms are spacious and come with cooking facilities, a/c, and fans. Relax in a hot tub, go horseback riding, fishing, diving, or snorkeling. Climb up to the people perch and watch the birds or the stars. Rooms come in all sizes from a double room to a deluxe suite with a loft. Prices start at US$85-180. Rates are lower May-15 Nov. and higher 15 Dec.-15 Jan. For more information call in the U.S. (800) 345-9786; in Belize (26) 2715, fax (26) 2885.

Apartments

More apartments and condos are becoming available. Check out the **House of the Rising Sun** and **Rock's Inn;** each advertises nine luxury beachfront apartments with fully equipped kitchens. The manager will make diving arrangements for guests. For prices and reservation information call House of the Rising Sun, (800) 451-8017, fax (26) 2349 or Rock's Inn, tel. (800) 331-2458, fax (26) 2358. **Corona Del Mar Apartments** are three-quarters of a mile south of San Pedro on the beach. Prices are US$85 d, with a/c US$95 d, US$10 per extra person; it's a little less in the low season, and during the holidays the prices rise to US$125. Call (26) 2055, fax (26) 2461.

Buying Property

Many people fall in love with the easygoing, water-oriented lifestyle of Ambergris Caye. For all those who just can't tear themselves away, take a look at the newish **Belize Yacht Club** with villas, swimming pool, health club, marina, restaurant, and bar. The marina will accommodate small crafts in the 50-60 foot class. The **Mayan Princess** continues to build condominiums in the center of town (on the site of the old Ambergris Lodge). For more information contact John Edwards of **Southwind Properties** (Box 1, San Pedro, Ambergris Caye, Belize, C.A.; fax 26-2331).

FOOD

You will find plenty of restaurants in San Pedro. At one time the only place to have a good meal was at your hotel. Most of the hotels still serve good food, in fact some are outstanding, but today the visitor also has a choice of other cafes springing up around town. The selection grows each year; you will find seafood (especially), Asian, Italian, Mexican, American, and typical Belizean fare. For the hungry diver who's yearning for a pizza, try the **Pizza Place.** You can buy a slice for US$1.40, up to a deluxe large combination for about US$18 and enough to feed you and your whole diving crowd (well, *almost*). Eat it there or carry it away. And if the pizza just whet your appetite for further Italian dishes, try **Little Italy** at the Spindrift Hotel. At **Elvi's Kitchen** customers enjoy a thatch-roofed, fan-cooled, tropical cafe—a little pricey, but with a good selection of fish and hamburgers. Want

San Pedro Beach

OZ MALLAN

a good Chinese meal? Try the **Jade Garden** just south of Ramon's Village. For a choice that ranges from sweet-and-sour shrimp to chop suey and chow mein, expect to pay from US$3.50-7; the service is great. Check out **Fido's** for breakfast and lunch. **The Hut** is another little spot that serves good food.

SERVICES

Shopping in San Pedro is much the same as in Belize City—no outstanding crafts typical of Belize, but several **gift shops** around town. If you want T-shirts you'll have a choice, and the few souvenir-type books you'll find on the shelves will give historical information about the country. **Grocery stores** are limited. Remember: This is an island and everything must cross the sea, so the choice is limited and pricey. You'll find snacky canned and packaged foods on the shelves along with Belikin beer and Belizean rum.

The **post office** is open Mon.-Friday. It's always fun to look at their beautiful, artistic, and often very large postage stamps; they make great gifts for the folks back home and are perfect for framing or for the traditional stamp collector. The **Atlantic Bank** is located in the **Spindrift Hotel.** Two travel agencies, **Amigo Travel** on Front St., and **Universal Travel** in the new Alijua Building on Barrier Reef Dr., can handle all of your travel needs, whether airline tickets or a tour into the countryside of Belize (tel. 26-2031, fax 26-2185. Camera enthusiasts should look for **Island Photo,** which will process normal and underwater film (E-6 film). The shop also rents underwater cameras and videos. And, yes, San Pedro *does* have a **gas station** a short distance south of town.

ENTERTAINMENT

If you collect statistics of this sort, in the small town of San Pedro you can count 22 bars. I'd love to hear from readers with a rating list. For lively nightlife check out **Big Daddie's Disco.** A daytime favorite is the **Tackle Box Bar**—friendly people on a waterfront pier with a tank filled with sharks and giant sea turtles. This is the place to meet "who's who" in Belize. Now for

some really funky entertainment drop into the **Pier Lounge** (in the Spindrift Hotel) on Monday afternoons for crab races and the "World Famous" **Chicken Drop** on Wednesday afternoons.

GETTING THERE

A 2,600-foot-long runway accommodates both private and commercial small planes on Ambergris, and from the strip it's just a few minutes' walk to downtown San Pedro (although there's talk of moving this strip to a 550-acre spot south of town). Two airlines (Maya Airways and Tropic Air) run regular and frequent flights to San Pedro. From Belize City it's 15 minutes to the caye; flights to Ambergris are available from other towns in Belize as well. For schedules and prices contact U.S. travel agents, or **Maya Airways** (6 Fort St., Box 458, Belize City, Belize, C.A.; tel. 2-77-215/72-312). **Tropic Air** offers the same service (Box 20, San Pedro, Ambergris Caye, Belize, C.A.; tel. 800-422-3435 in the U.S., except in Texas 713-440-1867; in Belize 26-2012). Tickets are available at the **Universal Travel Agency** next to Mom's in Belize City. Several charter planes make custom flights: **Belize Aero Co.,** St. Matthew and St. Charles streets, Belize City, tel. (02) 44-021/44-102; **Cari-bee Air Service,** Municipal Airstrip, Belize City, 24-hour tel. (02) 73-210, for local and international charters; **Su-Bec Air Service,** Box 182, Belize City, tel. (02) 44-027/44-734. The flight from Belize City to San Pedro takes about 15 minutes and fare is about US$60 RT.

By Boat

To travel by boat, the ***Andrea I and II*** fast outboard motorboat makes the run from Belize City at 4 p.m. (from the Belvedere Hotel dock) to San Pedro daily (departs San Pedro at 7 a.m.); the fare is about US$10 OW, US$17.50 RT. Buy your tickets at the **Universal Travel Agency** in Belize City next to Mom's or at their San Pedro office in the Alijua Building on Barrier Reef Drive. The trip between Belize City and Ambergris takes about 75 minutes. *Miss Belize* leaves from the dock behind the Supreme Court Building. The *Hustler* leaves San Pedro daily at 7 a.m. and returns from Belize City at 4 p.m. from the new dock near the courthouse and new market; US$10 OW, US$17.50 RT. The **Thunderbolt** docks at the Swing Bridge in Belize City and has the same schedule as above. Also check with the Chamber of Commerce as to who might direct you to one of the freight boats that make occasional trips to the is-

land, or ask around the dock near the Swing Bridge. Do *not* pay in advance; wait until you're safely at your destination. No regularly scheduled trips are available between the cayes; ask around the docks at Caulker and San Pedro and you'll probably find a private boat willing to take you for a fee.

CAYE CAULKER

This tiny island offers its own special brand of laid-back tourism. Though the major industry traditionally has been fishing, tourism is beginning to edge up as a close second. Only a few cars mar the tropical scenery and disrupt the two main sandy roads running north to south, cut by a number of cross roads. Caulker is a place to recover from "burnout"—no traffic, no smog, no high-tech "anything," no business meetings (for anyone), no lawn mowers (no lawns), no Burger Kings, no cake mixes (yet?), and no frozen orange juice. To rejuvenate the psyche, Caulker does have swimming, snorkeling, diving, and a chance to study the sea and sky and all of God's creatures above and below. There's little else to do besides "experiencing" the small "desert island." And the best part? It's *cheap!*

THE LAND

Caulker lies 21 miles northeast of Belize City, 11 miles south of Ambergris Caye, and one mile west of the Belize Reef. The island is four miles long; however, the inhabited part is an area less than a mile long, measuring south from the Split at the northern end. The land north of the Split is uninhabitable, consisting mostly of mangrove swamps with a narrow strip of land along the east coast. The dry season is Dec.-February. Because the island is on a limestone escarpment, most houses have wells. The water, though drinkable, is used mostly for utility purposes because of its slight saline flavor. Drinking water is collected in rain gutters from the aluminum roofs and then channeled into tanks kept by the side of most houses. In the dry season drinking water becomes scarce.

Island Ecology

No doubt the ecology of the island will be an ongoing debate as long as there are those who *want* and those who *don't want* to further develop the small island. The most recent issues of disagreement are the sewage treatment plant, and the recently built airport. Seventeen acres of crocodile and bird nesting lands were destroyed with the construction; 120 species of birds nest on the southern end of Caye Caulker. As is, the infrastructure of the island can ill afford much more development.

FLORA

Caulker is a sandy island that does not support general agricultural production, although coconut, papaya, lime, breadfruit, banana, plantain, and cacao flourish. Colorful flowering trees and plants such as hibiscus, ginger, *flamboyanes,* crotons, succulents, spider lilies, bougainvillea, and periwinkle add an exotic touch to the otherwise stark white (sandy) landscape. The ziricote tree does nicely and locals candy the fruit, as well as use it in salads. Jungle weeds and

Is this sign for the two or three cars on the island—or the pedestrians?

vines thrive in the sandy soil, and no matter how often they are cut back (by hand with machetes), they soon reappear.

FAUNA

Pelicans and frigate birds decorate the sky as they soar along the coast hunting for fish. A few creatures are endemic to the island, such as a variety of lizards, a few snakes (including the boa constrictor), and two types of crabs. During the rainy season, May-Sept., sand flies and mosquitoes are on the attack and drive all human life indoors. On rare occasions malaria and dengue fever have shown up on the island, but not in recent history.

HISTORY

Caye Caulker (on some maps spelled Corker) is another former playground of the pirates—at least they played in the general vicinity. Most historians agree that the island was not permanently inhabited in that era by anyone. However, an anchor dating back to the 19th century was found in the channel on the southern end of the island; a wreck equally as old was discovered off the southern end of Caye Chapel. The island was known to be visited by Mexican fishermen during those centuries because for generations they handed down stories of putting ashore at Caye Caulker for fresh water from a "big hole" on the caye. The island was uninhabited as late as the 1830s. It wasn't until the outbreak of the Yucatán Caste War in 1848, when refugees fled across the border into Belize by the thousands (both Spanish and mestizos), that many permanently settled on Ambergris Caye, with a few finding their way onto Caye Caulker. Many of today's **Jicauqueños** (Caulker Islanders) can trace their family history back as far as the Caste War and even know from which region in Mexico their ancestors originated.

Exact dates of settlement on Caye Caulker are uncertain, but one of the remaining families on the island, the Reyes family, tells of their great-grandfather, Luciano, who arrived in Mexico from Spain and worked as a logwood cutter along the coast of Yucatán and later fled south to avoid the bloodletting in Mexico. He first settled in San Pedro on Ambergris Caye and decided it was going to be his permanent home. Then when land fever erupted he competed in the intense bidding for Ambergris Caye, only to lose out to James Blake, who became the owner with the a bid of BZE$650. It was then that Reyes decided to buy Caye Caulker instead and, with BZE$300, became the owner of the small caye. Over the years land was sold to various people; many descendents of the original landholders are still prominent on Caye Caulker.

Early Economy

Though the town developed into a fishing village, *cocales* (coconut plantations) were planted from one end of the caye to the other. Though no written records have been found, it is believed the original trees were planted in the 1880s and 1890s at about the same time as

local girls selling powder buns, lemon crusts, and other homemade pastries

OZ MALLAN

enjoying the clear water from Caye Caulker docks

OZ MALLAN

those planted on Ambergris Caye. It took a lot of capital to plant a *cocal*. The land had to be cleared of jungle growth, holes dug, seaweed gathered and placed in the holes for fertilizer, and then seedlings planted. After that it took many man-hours to keep the *cocales* clear of brush, pick the coconuts, husk them, and then deliver the harvest to Belize City. Reyes was one of the original planters. His workers would begin at the northern end and stack the coconuts all along the shore where they were picked up by boats. It was time-consuming, laborious work. When the workers finished their sweep of the island, it was time to begin again—the trees produced continually. Slavery was never a part of the Caulker economy, which prevented the development of the stereotypical plantation hierarchy based on race and class that was so common in the Caribbean. Laborers earned a cash wage (albeit small) enabling them to use their income to buy the necessities to supplement their subsistence fishing. The people were very poor. Some of the older folks remember their grandparents and great-grandparents working long days and making only pennies.

Maybe because of the economic conditions, the families on the caye began helping each other out early on. When one man got a large catch of fish, his family and neighbors helped him with it and, in turn, always went home with some. When one man's fruit trees were bearing, he would share the fruit, knowing that he would benefit later on. This created very strong ties, especially between families and extended families. Today's long-time fishing families on Caulker make an above-average living, and many of them add to it by providing some type of service to the tourists that are coming more regularly every year.

THE PEOPLE

In the early days fish brought in very little cash. However, fishing was still preferred to working on the *cocal*. It was less strenuous and less time-consuming and the fishermen enjoyed greater independence. Eventually fishing began to pay off for the people and co-ops were established. Lobster was an important part of their success as it was on Ambergris. Fishermen liked being their own boss and, as a result, to this day Jicauqueños (in Spanish the island name is Cayo Jicaco, which has degenerated into Caye Caulker) are independent thinkers with a lot of self assurance. They take pride in their early roots on the island, and while color-class social thinking is seen in other parts of Belize, the distinction between peoples in Caulker is whether they are *islanders* or *nonislanders!* Along with the title "Jicauqueños" you usually know an islander from such comments as "I belong to Caye Caulker." Most of the original island families were mestizo (commonly referred to in Belize as Spanish). But today the mixture also includes Creoles and a few immigrant Anglos. The Caulker community has been fairly successful in keeping the ownership of land among the locals. Every once in a while someone talks of bigger and better tourist accommodations, but face it: The locals are happy with their small island, small guesthouses, small home-style cafes and want to keep it just the way it is. It appears they don't really *want* more outsiders!

EARLY TOURISM

Until the 1960s few visitors reached the shores of Caye Caulker. But once the hippie backpacker discovered the small relaxed island, more and more travelers began arriving. This was becoming the hushed-secret among adventurers making their way south along the Central American trail. Although most people had never heard of Belize in the 1970s, they did recognize the name of British Honduras with a rough idea of location. The usual description was that Belize was the next country past Mexico. Such people as Jacques Cousteau and *National Geographic* writers began spreading the word that Caulker was the place for the young or the young at heart. It soon became apparent to islanders that incoming visitors *needed* food and lodging, and this was a new way for the women to earn extra money. The men's lives changed little with the influx as they continued their fishing. Houses on Caulker were generally wooden structures built on stilts with a separate cooking shack. The first accommodations, like **Edith's Hotel,** were simple cubicles created by enclosing the space under the house. Others followed and soon simple hotels were built next to their homes. Most offered only the barest of necessities with shared toilet, no hot water, and were often dormitory style, but they served the purpose and were satisfactory for the young adventurers that came. The first cafes were women selling food out of their windows on the sandy lanes. Some women would place a chalkboard in front of their houses announcing that they were cooking boilup, or fish, or *whatever,* that evening and the price. If you wanted to come for dinner, all you had to do was knock on the door early in the day and tell her. It was wonderfully casual, unbelievably cheap, and a marvelous opportunity to get to know the warm friendly people of Caulker. Probably the only black mark during this era was the substance users that became obnoxious and insulting. The people didn't approve of having "stoned" or drunk folks wandering around the small community. In the Caulker of the 1990s, a close watch is kept on anyone who looks the part—that's not to say that the islanders themselves have never indulged in growing a little pot.

TOURISM TODAY

Today's Caulker is changing—a little. The population has grown from 500 to 1,000 in the last 8-10 years. The islanders don't want to "lose" their island as they believe the San Pedranos have

FISHING TIPS
Best fishing times for local fish:

Barracuda, Bonefish, Bonito, Jack, Mackerel, Permit, Snapper, Tuna, Wahoo	Year-round
Grouper	December
Marlin	March-May
Sailfish	March-June
Snook	January-May, November, December
Tarpon	March-July, November

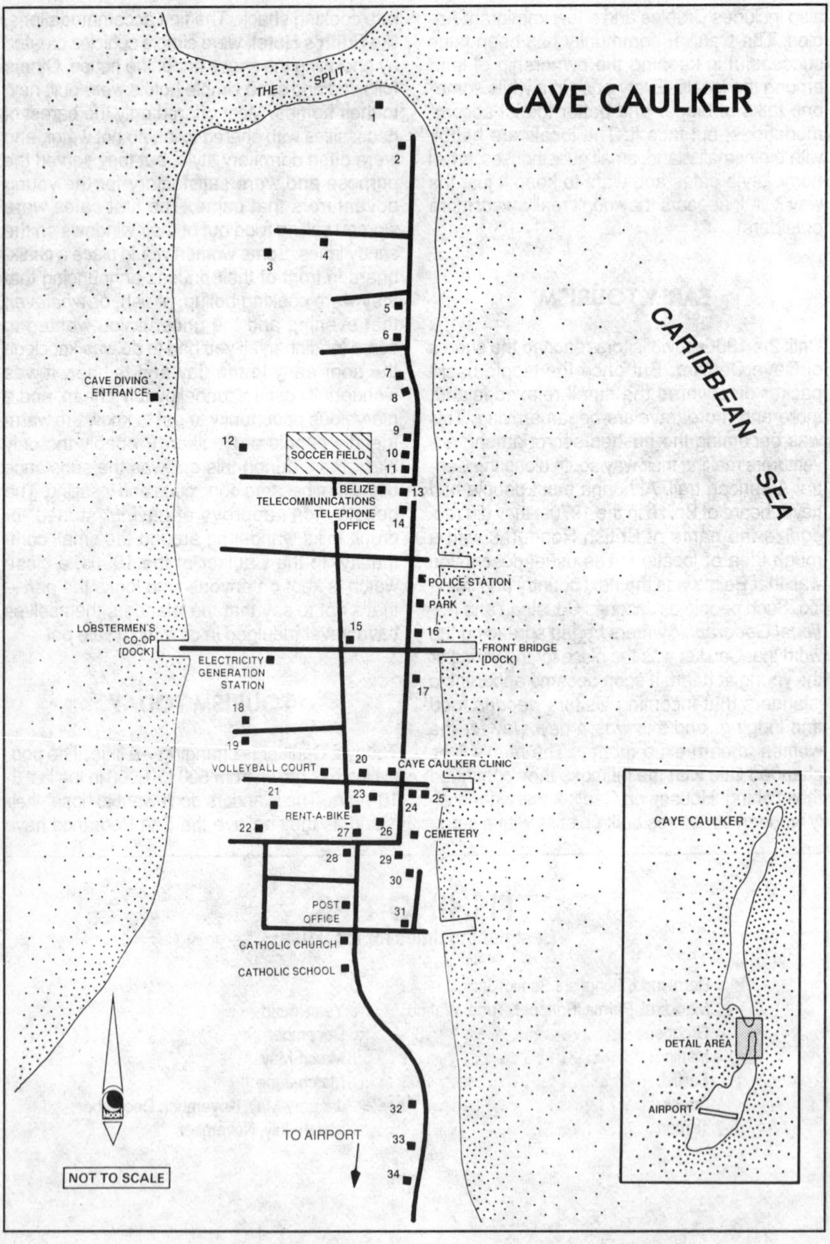

CAYE CAULKER

THE SPLIT

1
2

3   4

5
6
7
8
9
10
11

CAVE DIVING
ENTRANCE

12   SOCCER FIELD

13
BELIZE
TELECOMMUNICATIONS
TELEPHONE
OFFICE   14

POLICE STATION

PARK

LOBSTERMEN'S
CO-OP
[DOCK]   15   16   FRONT BRIDGE
[DOCK]

ELECTRICITY
GENERATION
STATION   17

18
19

20   CAYE CAULKER CLINIC
VOLLEYBALL COURT   21   23   24   25
RENT-A-BIKE   27   26
22   CEMETERY

28   29
30
POST
OFFICE   31

CATHOLIC CHURCH
CATHOLIC SCHOOL

CARIBBEAN SEA

NOT TO SCALE

TO AIRPORT

32
33
34

CAYE CAULKER

DETAIL AREA

AIRPORT

© MOON PUBLICATIONS, INC.

CAYE CAULKER

1. The Split Beach Village [restaurant]
2. The Split Beach Village [cabins]
3. Frenchie's Dive Shop
4. Island Yogurt
5. Jan's Deli and Trips
6. Cabañas Restaurant and Bar
7. Chocolate's Gift Shop and
   Bed & Breakfast
8. Rainbow Hotel
9. Reef Hotel
10. Reef Bar
11. Martinez Caribbean Inn,
    Restaurant and Bar
12. Belize Diving Services
13. Hotel Miramar
14. Aberdeen's Chinese Restaurant
15. The Corner Restaurant
16. Toucan Gifts
17. Vega Inn and Gardens
18. Glenda's Bakery
19. Syd's Restaurant and Bar
20. Hotel Marin
21. Miss Petty's Bakery
22. Jimenez Huts
23. Templo Evangelico
    Asambleas de Dios Church
24. Daisy's Hotel
25. Lena's Hotel
26. Hideway Hotel
27. Marin's Restaurant
28. Edith's Hotel
29. Tropical Paradise Hotel and Restaurant
30. Sea Beezz Hotel
31. Tom's Hotel
32. The Anchorage
33. Ignacio's Huts
34. Shirley's Guest House

lost San Pedro on Ambergris Caye. The islanders have adamantly kept out foreign investors, and they keep the prime pieces of land for their homes. Newer hotel cabañas now provide private bathrooms and some even have hot water and dining rooms, but they still maintain the wonderful low-key Caribbean ambience. Many are just simple thatch huts.

Visitors are not just backpackers. Though the island still attracts many young adults, it also finds whole families visiting who thrive on the low-key, unhurried, uncrowded atmosphere. Visitors can expect nice people, productive fishing, exotic snorkeling and diving, a laid-back atmosphere—and reasonable prices! More small hotels are springing up around the island each year. In January and February you'll run into the largest number of tourists, during the summer the least. And, according to some readers, at any particular time "hustlers" from Belize City can pester visitors to the point of wanting to leave. Hope the city fathers do something about that in a hurry!

The caye has sandy streets and very few are marked with street signs; just ask anyone for directions. You can walk from one end of the island to the other, and backside to frontside on a lazy morning, including a stop at **Tropical Paradise Restaurant** for a cold fresh glass of orange juice or a tasty ice cream. Or follow the aroma of baking pastries up a flight of stairs into the spotless big kitchen at **Daisy's Hotel** (watch your step going up—don't walk on the family's pet spider monkey). Try a powder bun or coconut crust and sweet fresh orange juice (served all day), and then continue on your tour of the island. Look around and you'll find plenty of these Caulker "fast-food" outlets with some of the best home-cooked snacks, whether it's fruit yogurt, lobster pies, pastries, or fresh-squeezed orange juice.

If you want to take a little rest first, flake out on one of many wooden docks (locals call them "bridges") that jut out over the clear turquoise sea along the waterfront. In case you didn't know, that's what Caye Caulker is all about—being lazy, lying on your back, and studying the sky and all the unique winged creatures that prefer flying just *above* Caulker. You might see the graceful and magnificent frigate (fish bandit extraordinaire that never gets his feathers wet), always on the lookout for a handout from any *real* fishing bird flapping away with its loaded beak—whamo! The frigate steals the fishing bird's catch and it doesn't know what hit it. In spring you might see the black frigate's brilliant red gular pouch inflated like a balloon under its beak, which means it's courting. When you get tired of that, flip onto your stomach and look over the side of the dock—you can spend the rest of the day studying the constantly changing underwater scene through crystal-clear water, no glass needed.

OFFICIALDOM

The pace here is very slow and the cost is low. The townsfolk do not happily entertain bums or hippie-types, and they're doing their best to keep the small village from being overrun by substance and alcohol users. (Apparently, Caulker has enough over-imbibing locals that it doesn't need to import any more.) The mayor says they love the low-budget travelers—as long as they don't sleep on the docks or wander around nude (both against the law). However, the town has two problems: too few police to do the enforcing and a frequently "broken" jail—prisoners come and go at will. Fortunately, the crimes on Caye Caulker are small transgressions. Also, keep in mind the law does not allow camping on public or private property without permission. The only "official" camping now is at Vega Inn and Gardens (see "Accommodations") and like many places in Belize, the price is almost as much as a cheap room.

OZ MALLAN

This wooden cistern catches precious water.

ACCOMMODATIONS

Visitors planning to visit Caye Caulker should be aware that none of the hotels on the island are luxurious; some just offer more than others. Most of the budget hotels on Caulker have shared bathrooms and are very basic. The newer ones offer electricity, private baths, and ceiling fans—a taste of tropical island life without the frills. The following is not a complete list of hotels; more accommodations are available. Remember, prices are negotiable depending on the time of the year, the number of tourists on the island, and how persuasive you are. You're never too far from the sea on Caulker, but a few places are located right on the water's edge. **Note:** Don't expect long white beaches in Caulker; for the most part the shore is lined with sea grass. One of the best sandy beaches is at the Split. During the high season, most rooms are taken as soon as the tourists from Belize City arrive. Make reservations if possible.

One of the originals, **Vega Inn and Gardens,** offers simple rooms in an old two-story building on the sand. Owned by the Vega family, long-time island residents, the atmosphere is warm and friendly. Tony, 77-year-old patriarch of the group, is a font of information about the island—past and present; he'll talk for hours about establishing the fishing cooperatives, struggling against the big money-and-power folks who controlled the cayes—and winning out. With only seven rooms, reservations are a must, especially during the holiday seasons (Christmas and Easter). Rates for a room with a private bath are US$40 s, US$50 d; with shared bath US$15 and US$10 s, US$20 d; Visa and MasterCard okay.

Campsites can be rented on Vega Inn and Gardens property, but the management doesn't put up with loud or drunken parties! Camping fees are US$6 pp per night. For more information about rooms and camping contact Maria Vega (Box 701, Belize City, Belize, C.A.; tel. 2-22-142, fax 22-31-580). Ask about arrangements for snorkeling and fishing.

Check at Ellen McRae's gift shop, **Galeria Hicaco,** to see her two rooms. Each has a private bath with cold water and solar-heated

(top left) The Blue Hole is a favorite dive site off the Belize coast. (Belize Tourism Office);
top right) sunset sail off Ambergris Caye (Phil Lanier); (bottom left) diving the atolls (International Expeditions);
(bottom right) Clouds of fish swarm the reefs off the Belize shore. (James Beveridge)

Warrie Head Creek waterfall (Oz Mallan)

Vega Inn and Gardens

OZ MALLAN

black-barrel showers. One room has a double and 3/4 bed, US$38; the other has one double bed, US$25, tel. (22) 2178.

Another oldie is **Daisy's Hotel,** which offers one private room with a bathroom (US$15), five dormitory rooms with single beds and shared facilities (US$10 pp), and two others with a double bed in each, US$15 per room, cold water only, and fans.

Tom's Hotel is popular with the young crowd and backpackers: simple bungalows (28 rooms), clean, shared bath, and all have fans and a seaview, US$26 d (five have private baths and hot water), tel. (22) 2102.

A Cut Above The Others

Tropical Paradise Hotel is separated from the colorful village cemetery by a neat white picket fence—both looking out to sea. The wooden cabañas have private ceiling fans, baths, hot and cold water, and a small clean cafe/ice-cream parlor with a friendly staff. Rates for cabañas are US$22.50 s, US$28 d; rooms are US$23 s, US$25 d. The newly completed suites offer a/c, color TV, and a refrigerator, US$65 per night, breakfast included. For more information write to Ramon Reyes (Caye Caulker, Belize, C.A.; tel. 22-2124). From the Tropical Paradise arrangements can be made for snorkeling, fishing, or lobster trapping with guides. You can also hire a guide and boat to take you to neighboring cayes.

For a real touch of Belize hospitality, check out the **Sea Beezz** hotel. You'll find six very clean double units, each with private bath, fresh linoleum, hot water, electricity, and fans, run by a family who can tell you all about the island. The hotel has its own dock and will make arrangements for diving or other water activities. Room rate is US$32, tel. (602) 451-0040, in Belize (22) 2176. The family restaurant (located below the rooms) serves an American breakfast for about US$4, a great shrimp scampi dinner for about US$8, and, as they put it, "freshly cut sandwiches:" cinnamon rolls, coconut crusts, pineapple-upside-down cakes and lots of other homemade goodies.

Just got the word that Captain Chocolate from the *Soledad* has one deluxe room for rent right next to his gift shop, which is next to his home on the walkway to the Split. The double room rate is US$50 and includes continental breakfast; tel. (22) 2151.

The **Rainbow Hotel,** two stories located on the edge of the lane going toward the Split, is a row of eight, clean, motel-style stucco rooms with tile floors, modern (private) bathrooms, electricity, hot and cold water, and fans. Rates are US$25 s, US$30 d. For more information contact Ernesto Marin (Caye Caulker, Belize, C.A.; tel. 22-2123).

The **Reef Hotel,** formerly Hotel Martinez, has been around for a long time. The basic hotel has oceanfront rooms with a grand view of the Belize Reef (US$22 d), private baths, a good restaurant, bar, and friendly staff, tel. (22) 2196.

Sea Beezz Hotel

OZ MALLAN

The Eastern Side

The following accommodations are on the eastern side of Caye Caulker. **The Anchorage** has four, clean, thatch-roof cabañas on a white sandy beach with swaying palms. Each has its own cold-water bathroom and Robinson Crusoe simplicity/tropical ambience. Rates are US$23 d, US$33 for five people.

Shirley's Guest House is clean and comfortable with rooms built with beautiful tropical woods—great wooden floors and walls. The outside is neatly painted white with a green trim. All but the three original rooms have private bathrooms; all are on the beach. This is the farthest hotel on the eastern side. Shirley charges US$18-23 for the original three rooms with shared bath, s or d, about US$40 for double rooms with private bath and fridge. She's been on Caye Caulker for 22 years—a pleasant nononsense lady, tel. (22) 2145.

Jimenez Huts is owned and operated by George Jimenez. The cabañas have private facilities; rates are US$20 s, and US$25 d, tel. (22) 2175. Facing the water, **Ignacio's** offers 13 colorful small wooden huts along the beach, each with a private, cold-water bath, US$15 d. These are very small and may not be everyone's cup of tea.

The Split

The **Split Beach Village** hotel is a group of nine small wooden cabins on short stilts in the sand. Each has a private bath, hot water, fans, and all are clean and tidy. This is where you'll find the nicest sandy beach on the island. It gets very busy during the high season, and tourists come from the rest of the island to soak up the rays and swim in the comparatively grass-free water. There's a snack stand nearby. Rates are US$23-30 per cabin, depending on the season, tel. (22) 2127. The island earned its name after a hurricane "split" it into two pieces. **Beware:** There can be a strong undertow in that split.

FOOD

For such a tiny island, a variety of cafes and food is available; just don't expect lace and linen service. For the most part meals are simple, with fresh seafood and chicken as the featured menu items. **Marin's** has a good selection and always-fresh fish; **Aberdeen's** serves good Chinese food; **Mrs. Rodriguez** makes great home-style Creole dishes right in her home; **Wendy's** (no relation to the U.S. franchise) makes (at home) excellent yogurt with honey and fruit (about US$1.50 for a large jar), and nothing tastes better than her lobster burritos after a hard day of snorkeling. Almost every restaurant on Caye Caulker makes super fried chicken, fried fish, rice, and beans. The **Cabañas Restaurant** toward the Split near Chocolate's Gift Shop offers good seafood at reasonable prices. **Glenda's** serves cheap Mexican food and in the morning try her homemade cinnamon rolls and delicious cheese rolls. **Syd's** makes good burritos, US$1.50. **Martinez Restaurant** offers three meals a day year-round. If you're lucky you'll run into some cute little girls strolling the sandy lanes balancing pans of homemade sweet crusts and wheat bread on their heads—for sale, of course! **Sand Box Restaurant** is open noon-10 p.m., closed on Wednesday, and serves lobster salads, stuffed fish, lasagna and lots more tasty seafood. And do check out **Jan's Deli** for tasty ready-to-go lunches and snacks.

SHOPPING

Island Art
Because of the limited number of visitors to Caulker, most of the business people who make a living from tourism do so through multiple services. For the most part the local men carry on with their fishing; their wives are the backbone of the food businesses and hotels. You'll find that the shops are generally owned by multitalented people who are either artists, photographers, guides, or divers. They all have one thing in common; they're dedicated to saving their natural resources—especially the reef and its rich sealife.

Though you won't find a lot of shops, several sell T-shirts, island art, photos, books, shells, and typical Belizean souvenirs. Just ask anyone—they'll point you to Ellen MacRae's **Galeria Hicaco,** a small gift shop located near

the Tropical Paradise, which sells art, crafts, and clothing made by the Kekchi and Mopan Maya, Garifuna, mestizos, and Creoles. Ellen is a marine biologist/artist who takes outstanding underwater photos of the reef. Ask her about guided trips to the reef or her suggestions for nature lovers. She offers the **Ecology Tour,** where clients are oriented with a one-hour lecture in the morning and then spend an afternoon of guided snorkeling with Ellen. She also offers bird/caye ecology hikes, guided lecture tours to mangrove lagoons, and she takes camping charters to atolls and southern cayes. All tours must be scheduled at least one day in advance, longer for camping charters. Ellen is very involved with the local **Siwa-Ban Preserve.** For more information about rooms available at Ellen's contact CariSearch, Ltd. (Box 47 Caye Caulker, Belize, C.A.; tel. 22-2178).

A fine local artist, **Philip Lewis,** lives on Caulker and produces flamboyantly decorated T-shirts. Philip was co-designer of the national currency and is an earthy primitive artist. His excellent drawings are on display at the Galeria Hicaco, along with his map of Caye Caulker.

Visit the second-floor gift shop operated by Captain Chocolate of the *Soledad.* The shop is located on the waterfront road going toward the Split, in a beautiful natural-wood building. Chocolate's shop offers T-shirts (some of the best on the island), a good selection of Guatemalan/ Mexican handcrafted items, plus hammocks,

*Galeria Hicaco
Gift Shop*

Caulker swimming
area

OZ MALLAN

jewelry, postcards and stamps, and other memorabilia to help you remember the caye. For more information write to Chocolate (Box 332, Belize City, Belize, C.A.; tel. 2-22-151).

Another shop featuring island art is **Sea-ing is Belizing.** Owner James Beveridge is an excellent photographer of underwater and terrestrial wildlife, as well as of outstanding scenics and people pictures. Browse around the shop/gallery (located near the soccer field and Belize Diving Services) and you'll find a **book exchange,** gift items, and invitations to special slide shows on weeknights at 8 p.m., with subjects that include the scenics of Belize, underwater reef shots, and flora and fauna including the jaguar sanctuary. James is a recommended guide as well as a representative of the **Belize Audubon Society,** and very involved with preserving the country's natural resources. (Ask about his underwater photo safaris and sailing trips. Sea-ing is Belizing gives diving lessons.) Write or call for more information (Box 374, Belize City, Belize, C.A.; tel. 2-22-189).

WATER SPORTS

Diving And Snorkeling
Note: It only makes sense that divers and passengers check out the boat they're boarding. Ask questions—does it have two motors? extra gas? how far will you be going? what's the weather outlook both inside the reef and out-

side? In short, take steps to ensure your own safety. Ask a local about the diving reputation of your dive master.

It's easy to find a boatman to take you out to the reef to snorkel. Even the nonswimmer can enjoy the spectacular sights with **Belizario** and son Denis Martinez on trips to the reef, Hol Chan, and San Pedro in their glass-bottom boat; about US$10 to the reef, US$15 to Hol Chan. Inquire at **Martinez Restaurant.**

Although we have not met him, several readers have recommended **Harrison Mark Catle** as a safe, reliable boatman for day-trips to Hol Chan Marine Reserve and San Pedro, Ambergris Caye. He docks his boat at the same dock as Chocolate, or ask Chocolate to put you in touch.

The *Sea Hawk* offers snorkeling and diving trips to the reef, San Pedro, and Half Moon Caye. From Caye Caulker to the reef, divers have three snorkeling/diving stops, US$8 or US$13, including snorkeling gear. From Caye Caulker to San Pedro the captain makes two snorkeling/diving stops, with lunch on San Pedro, US$15. From Caye Caulker to Half Moon Caye (Blue Hole) a six-day trip includes camping and sailing with five to six people maximum. Meals include lots of fresh fruit, catch-of-the-day fish, lobster or conch, US$175 pp. Trips are on a 28-foot Belizean-crafted sailing sloop. For more info contact **Sea Hawk Sailing Trips,** Bobby and Jean Heusner (Caye Caulker, Belize, C.A.)

The **Belize Dive Shop** offers equipment sales and rentals, diver certification, and day and night dives. **Belize Diving Services** offers equipment, certification courses, and guides that take groups diving on the reef as well as at Turneffe. Bring your certification card *and* ask to see your instructor's.

Swimming The Split
While meandering around the island you'll notice the split that was created by Hattie's big blow in 1961. The violent force of the wind and water rammed through the land, blowing away a piece of the mangrove forests—and suddenly the island was cut in two. One of the few Caulker beaches is on this end of the island, but be aware that swimming in the "new" channel can be dangerous; this is a shallow area. The pull of the swift current is very strong and children or weak swimmers should avoid the water here. Around the bend only a few meters out of the channel, the water is calm and safe. Swimming off the "back bridge" on the western side of the caye is even safer.

Cave Diving
Some of the more daring diving sites are the caves that can be reached through the main entry shaft just offshore Caye Caulker. This is an immense cave system, but also dangerous and recommended only for the experienced, trained diver. It has been explored recently by divers under the auspices of the Smithsonian Institute. A few divers have lost their lives over the years in these caves, which should be approached only with an experienced local diver as guide.

Fishing
This is good fishing country; inquire at your hotel about making arrangements with a fisherman (tackle provided) to take you on a hunt for the sweetest seafood in the Caribbean. Or take a walk to the backside of the island, where you'll find fishermen cleaning their fish, working on lobster traps, or mending their nets in the morning, many willing to take you fishing. Main trophies are groupers, barracuda, snapper, and amberjack, all good eating. Small boats are available for rent by the hour; if you want a more organized trip contact **MV *Treasure*,** a 40-foot deep-sea fishing and diving boat that travels to all the cayes and atolls. For more information, in the U.S. call (502) 568-4025.

Fishing And Diving Charters
Rolando "Roly" Rosado offers fishing and diving charters. He'll take you to the reef to dive, or on day-long fishing expeditions. Write or call for more information (Box 743, Belize City, Belize, C.A.; tel. in Belize 2-22-122).

GETTING THERE

By Boat
Outboard skiffs/launches leave from Belize City several times every day. One of the most familiar is the *Soledad,* captained by Caulker local, **Chocolate,** a popular Belize character. His boat takes travelers, groceries, dive equipment, and other small freight to the island daily between 10-11 a.m. Semi-worn cushions give a modicum of padding to the derriere as you bump across the tops of the waves while passing myriad mangrove cayes on your way. Chocolate makes stops if asked (such as at Caye Chapel where there's only one hotel); on Caulker he drops you off at whichever dock you require and leaves Caulker at 6:30-7 a.m. each day to return to Belize City.

Catch Chocolate at the service station near the Swing Bridge, on N. Front St. (the better side of the river in Belize City); the trip between Belize City and Caye Caulker takes about 45 minutes and the fare is US$6 OW. He takes either U.S. or Belizean currency. A light wrap is handy for windy or rainy trips.

Chocolate also takes charter trips to **Goff's Caye,** a tiny island southeast of Belize City on the reef, stopping to see the manatees on the way, and makes river trips for the adventurers who enjoy watching the birds and animals of the jungle. Write or call Chocolate for more information (Box 332, Belize City, Belize, C.A.; tel. 2-22-151).

The *Breeze* speedboat makes the roundtrip between Belize City and Caye Caulker in one day. From A&R's gas station on N. Front St. in Belize, it leaves daily between 9-10 a.m. and departs Caulker in front of the Reef Hotel at 3 p.m. Rates are US$12.50 RT, US$7.50 OW. Charter trips to other cayes and river trips are available. *Pegasus Speedboat* is another boat available for passenger service to Caye Caulker, leaving from the Shell station on N. Front St., near the Swing Bridge. The boat also takes

The controversial Caulker airstrip and one of the commuter planes that make daily stops at Caye Caulker.

OZ MALLAN

group charters to outlying cayes, the reef, and on river cruises. Write or call for prices and more information (P.O. Box 743, Belize City, Belize, C.A.; tel. 2-31-138).

By Air
Skybird Air Service now makes regular flights to Caye Caulker, flying to both the Belize Municipal and International airports. The airstrip

on Caulker is pretty simple—you wait under a tree for your plane. Fares are US$16.50 OW and US$30 RT to the municipal airport (about 10 minutes); or US$26 OW and US$50 RT to International (about 15 minutes).

For more travel information contact **Dolphin Bay Travel;** they will make reservations as well. **Jan's Tours** is another good spot to ask about tours and onward trips.

OZ MALAN

COROZAL DISTRICT

Corozal is the northernmost district in Belize. The ambience is "Spanish," but with a Belizean flavor. If arriving from Mexico the difference between the two countries is apparent immediately. The people of Corozal are a happy bunch, and you'll discover dozens of American expats enjoying the slow pace of Belizean living.

COROZAL TOWN

Just nine miles and 15 minutes from the Rio Hondo (the border separating Belize and Mexico) and 96 miles north of Belize City is the small town of Corozal. The population is about 9,000. While English is the official language, Spanish is just as common since many are descendants of early-day Maya and mestizo refugees from neighboring Quintana Roo. Historically, Corozal was the scene of many attacks by the Maya Indians during the Caste War. What remains of the old fort can be found in the center of town (west of Central Park). Today, it's a quiet little village that lies near the tranquil shores of the Caribbean and close to the Bay of Chetumal.

The town was almost entirely wiped out during Hurricane Janet in 1955 and has since been rebuilt. Strolling through the quiet streets you'll find a library, town hall, government administrative offices, a Catholic church, two secondary schools, five elementary schools, three gas stations, a government hospital, a clinic, a cinema, a couple of small hotels, a couple of funky bars and discos, and several restaurants. Not a whole lot of activity goes on here, unless you happen to be in town during special holidays. The biggest excitement is during the Mexican-style, "Spanish" fiestas of Christmas, Carnaval ("Carnival"), and Columbus Day.

Many houses are clapboard, raised on wooden stilts to avoid possible floods and to catch the wind, creating a cool spot for the family to gather. More of the newer houses are built out of cement block—almost all display TV antennas.

COROZAL TOWN

© MOON PUBLICATIONS, INC.

Be sure to go into the town hall and take a look at the dramatic historical mural painted by **Manuel Villamour.** The flamboyantly colored mural depicts the history of Corozal, including the drama of the downtrodden Maya, their explosive revolt called the Caste War, and the inequities of colonial rule.

The Corozal District economy has for years depended on the sugar industry with its local processing factory. One of the oldest (no longer in operation), the **Aventura Sugar Mill,** began operating in the 1800s. Little is left today, but you can still see the antiquated chimney when driving past the village of Aventura on the New Northern Highway, seven miles from Corozal Town.

ACCOMMODATIONS AND FOOD

Tony's Inn And Resort

On the southern end of Corozal Town take a look at one of Corozal's nicer hotels, **Tony's Inn,** on the sea facing the Maya site of Cerros across the bay. This two-story sparkling-white stucco building is a clean modern hotel with large a/c rooms, private baths, electricity, hot water, a good restaurant, and well-cared-for grounds with a manmade sandy beach and beach bar where you can enjoy the trades off the Caribbean, swimming and other water sports, and pleasant companionship with fellow travelers. Tony's has five single and 12 double rooms. Winter rates for standard rooms are US$35 s, US$45 d, for deluxe rooms, US$60 s, US$70 d, less in the summer; credit cards okay. The restaurant serves a tasty selection, including such dazzlers as curried lobster or a plain filet mignon (à la carte). Tony's is 80 miles from the Philip Goldson International Airport in Belize City, 18 miles from Chetumal, Mexico, and 150 miles from Cancun, Mexico. Owners/managers Dahlia and Tony Castillo are friendly and always ready to assist their guests. Write or call for more information and reservations (Box 12, Corozal Town, Corozal District, Belize, C.A.; tel. 4-22-055, fax 4-22-020). From the U.S. call **International Expeditions**, tel. (800) 633-4734.

Hotels

Hotel Posada Mama is one of the best moderate hotels: very clean, tiny rooms with a toilet and shower tightly placed in separate corners. The eight colorful cement rooms are a/c, have color TV, hot and cold water, and telephones. Rates are US$26 s, US$35 d; on G St. in the southern part of town, tel. (4) 22-107/23-245. **Hotel Maya** is a favorite, though simple, hotel at the south end of town, with hot water, a family atmosphere, and a restaurant that specializes in Mexican and regional dishes. Enjoy a cold beer and ceviche at the bar. Rates are about US$20 s, US$22 d, tel. (4) 22-082; or write to Sylvia and Rosita Mai (Box 112, Corozal Town, Corozal District, Belize, C.A.). A few other basic hotels are worth checking out. Try the **Caribbean Hotel**, southern end, tel. (4) 22-045, rates US$10-20 pp. **Nestor's Hotel** is a real budget hostel that's been around a long time, and probably the best thing about it is its locked parking lot. The rooms are mostly tiny, with fans. If you have chronic ailments and are looking for herbal relief (that may or may not work), check with Mr. Peter, at the hotel, same phone (123 Fifth Ave.; tel. 4-22-354); prices start at US$8 s, $10.50 d. Check out these budget accommodations thoroughly—some look old and gray, but might be just what you're looking for.

Caribbean Motel And Trailer Park
One of the old standards for both RVers and those looking for simple cabins is the Caribbean Motel and Trailer Park. On the bay, under palms that catch the breeze, are Spartan thatch-roof cabañas, and guests are invited to swim from the dock across the street. The restaurant serves great hamburgers, open daily except Tuesday for breakfast, lunch, and dinner. Campsites are about US$5, and cabins rent for about US$22 s or d. At the trailer park, located at the southern end of Corozal, try one of Miss Joe's hamburgers, tel. (4) 22-045.

Food
For local color and good Chinese food try a meal at **Rexo** (okay, they also have pizza, lasagna, and hamburgers—with French fries US$1.75). You'll also find fresh orange juice and a limited selection of groceries in a glass case. Open 11 a.m.-10 p.m. At N. 9th Ave. and 6th St., **Dubie's Bar & Restaurant** is reasonable and good, lots of locals, opens early. Other restaurants in town are small and serve a variety of food. The **Campesino Club** on 4th Ave. is good for a cold drink and lively conversation with the *campesinos* (countrymen). **King Of King's Chinese Restaurant** on 3rd Ave. serves Chinese and barbecue, chicken salad, fried fish, and a variety of soups; liquor also. A separate room is provided for families; open 8:30-1:30 a.m.

Crisis is a neat little place with a lot of atmosphere, good local food, and reasonable prices. It features a lounge, dancing, and live music on the weekends. The rice and beans are good for US$1.75. Check out the shrimp, ceviche, or cheeseburgers, each about US$1.60. Other features include oilcloth tables and fans; open Sun.-Mon. 10 a.m.-10 p.m., closed Sat. morning but open till midnight Sat. night. **The Capital** is still another good Chinese restaurant. Try the brandy lobster, a house specialty, for US$13, or ginger chicken and egg rolls; open 10 a.m.-10 p.m., Santa Elena Rd., tel. (4) 22-487. **Donna's Cafe** at 46 7th Ave. has good economical food and opens early in the morning, tel. (4) 23-065.

SERVICES

Money
If you need to change money, go to **Belize Bank, Nova Scotia Bank**, or **Atlantic Bank** Mon.-Thurs. 8 a.m.-1 p.m., Friday 8 a.m.-1 p.m. and 3-6 p.m.

Getting There

Maya Airways has two flights from Belize City Municipal Airport, with a stop at San Pedro, at 10:30 a.m. and 2:30 p.m. daily except Sunday; from Corozal to San Pedro and Belize City at 8 a.m. and 3:30 p.m. daily except Sunday. Buy your tickets in downtown Corozal—the airstrip is about three miles south of town; taxi service is available.

Local Guides

Two good local guides know the country well, especially the Corozal District, and have well-kept vans: **Henry Menzies Travel & Tours** (Box 210, Corozal Town, Belize, C.A.; tel 4-22-725)

and **Ma-ian's Tours' Manuel Hoare** (13 6th St., South Corozal Town, Belize, C.A.; tel. 4-22-744, fax 4-23-375).

Garage Service

If you're driving your own car and have a mechanical problem, don't fret—**Johnnie's Auto Repair** at 23 8th Ave. S offers 24-hour service.

Bus Service

Both Venus and Batty buses travel between Chetumal and Belize City with stops in Corozal about every two hours until 6 p.m.; Sunday service is more infrequent.

DIANA LASICH-HARPER

OZ MALLAN

CONSEJO SHORES

Going seven miles northeast of Corozal Town brings you to **Consejo Shores,** called the "Miami Beach" of Belize by locals (a wild stretch of the imagination unless you've seen the rest of the country)—rather odd, too, since Corozal has no "real" beach. Walking along the coast it's easy to find a place to enter the lovely blue sea; you'll find good swimming, for example, at Four Mile Lagoon.

Traveling along the ocean road you'll come to the intimate **Adventure Inn** with 20 thatch cottages scattered along the edge of the sea. Run by the Wildman family, accommodations are simple but comfortable with your own shower and private toilet facilities. The sea is perfect for swimming, fishing, sailboarding, and sailing (no snorkeling or diving); for sunning, small pocket beaches have been created with hauled-in sand. You might even get a glimpse of the elusive manatee. On the grounds there's access to tennis courts, bicycle rentals, and fishing and watersport equip-

ment. The Adventure Inn describes itself as "a refreshingly tropical relief from the hustle of the mainstream"—and so it is! Don't expect any more nightlife than what you and fellow guests make for yourselves in the gathering room/dining room/bar called **Tiger Lilly's.** The people who stay at the Adventure Inn are friendly, interesting, relaxed, and usually repeat visitors to Belize. The restaurant serves an à la carte menu with good variety, and outdoor barbecues. However, since the food is exceptional it is also a little pricey. Room rates are US$61 s, and US$71 d; if you want the full board, add US$50 pp p/d. Another service provided is pickup from Belize City (96 miles south), one to six persons for US$110. For hotel reservations and additional information, including escorted sightseeing trips, write or call the Adventure Inn (Consejo Shores, Box 35, Corozal Town, Belize, C.A.; tel. 4-22-187, fax 4-22-243). **Note:** ask about Adventure Inn's housekeeping cabins for longer stays.

SARTENEJA

When you arrive you'd almost think you were in Mexico; but why not? The small fishing village in northern Belize was established by Yucatán settlers from Mexico in the 19th century. The fishermen continue with the skills handed down over the years along with the knowledge of boat building. Obviously the immigrants were not the only people who felt that Sarteneja's location on the Corozal District coast was ideal for the seafaring life; it is apparent that the ancient Maya spent many years here also. To date, only one Maya structure has been partially restored and archaeologists note that the remains of more than 350 structures have been discovered—but not excavated.

The people of nearby villages for generations have robbed the Maya sites for building materials, such as stone blocks and limestone material to make plaster and cement. And, as the scavengers picked and dug around the structures over the years, artifacts made of gold, copper, and shells continued to turn up. Scientists believe Sarteneja was occupied by the Maya from early Classic times into the 1700s.

Agriculture

Today Sarteneja is home not only to fishermen, but also to farmers. Pineapples grow well and for years were transported to Belize City by boat twice a week and sold at the Belize City Wharf. But since the newish all-weather road from Sarteneja opened, the fruit can be delivered more frequently by truck. Other crops are being planted, and with the freedom of coming and going to Belize City more easily, this may develop into a major agriculture community—if tourism doesn't beat it out first! Already there are sport fishermen who prefer Sarteneja's mild climate (with rich catches of fish) to the southern, more humid part of the country.

ACCOMMODATIONS

So far, only one small hotel takes care of visitors at Sarteneja; it is pleasant, clean, budget priced, and recently expanded. Ask around town for Pedro Cruz's **Hotel Diani's;** now that Sarteneja village has electricity, they can use their overhead fans all night. They have a nice little cafe, all family run; tel. (4) 22-154. Dad Pedro Cruz also has a small general store in town.

Blue Heron Lagoon Resort

A reader recently told us of another small bed-and-breakfast type inn that is located at nearby **Catfish Bight** and should be completely opened by now. Run by retired American Anne Lowe from Washington D.C., this is comfortable, low-key, Belizean living—and Anne is a good cook and great company, a real mover and shaker. Stop by if you're in the neighborhood.

Pineapple is a lucrative crop for Sarteneja

OZ MALLAN

The Blue Butterfly Lodge

Though still only in the building stages, the **Blue Butterfly Lodge,** located on Point Alegre at Warrie Bight on the south shore of Chetumal Bay, should be completed by the end of 1993. The California owners have been developing the property for seven years, clearing the land, installing new roads, and providing infrastructure that will protect the bay. For starters, 11 cabañas are going up. Each will have two queen beds, a private bathroom, hot water, and electricity, and a charming dining room will serve local and continental food. The lodge will provide myriad activities: river trips, tours of the ruins, fishing (including tarpon, snook, yellowtail, and grouper), and paths around the area where guests will find beautiful wild orchids and butterflies. We keep watching for this one: the plans sound great.

COROZAL DISTRICT SIGHTS

SANTA RITA

Today's Corozal Town is built on the site of what was once the ancient Maya province of Chetumal. The remaining ruins are today called Santa Rita (see "Maya Archaeological Sites of Belize.") To explore this site either strike out on your own, or go with a guided group from your hotel.

CERROS

Across from the town of Corozal on a peninsula in the Bay of Chetumal you'll find Cerros, an important coastal trading center during the late pre-Classic period (350 B.C.-A.D. 250). For more information about Cerros see "Maya Archaeological Sites of Belize."

Cerros can be reached by boat (hired either in Corozal, at the **Adventure Inn** in Consejo Shores, or **Tony's Inn).** If you travel during the dry season (Jan.-April) you can get to Cerros by car. Along the way you'll pass the picturesque towns of **Chunox, Progreso,** and **Copper Bank,** as well as a number of lovely lagoons.

LAMANAI

Using the **Adventure Inn** or **Tony's Inn** as a base you can travel easily to the outstanding sites of the ancient Maya. One of the favorite trips provided by the Adventure Inn is a boat ride (in a fiberglass dory) up the New River to Lamanai in the Orange Walk District. Travel 30 miles past mestizo, Maya, and Mennonite settlements on a sun-dappled jungle-lined river until you come to a broad lagoon, and on to the temples of Lamanai. One of the largest ceremonial centers in Belize, it was described as an imperial port city encompassing ball courts, pyramids, and the more exotic Maya features. It's believed to have been occupied from 1500 B.C. to the 19th century. Historical Spanish occupation is apparent with the remains of two Christian churches and a sugar mill. The trip is through tropical flora and fauna

Adventure Inn Dock

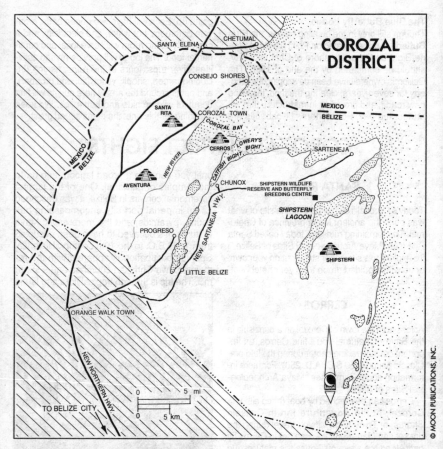

and you might see such exotics as black orchids and the jabiru stork, the largest flying
bird in the New World with a wing span of 10-
12 feet. This is an all-day trip. Price for one to
four persons to Lamanai through the Adventure
Inn is US$250. During the dry season (Jan.-
April) Lamanai can be reached by road from
San Felipe, preferably in a 4WD. See "Maya
Archaeological Sites of Belize.") for more
information.

SHIPSTERN WILDLIFE RESERVE AND BUTTERFLY BREEDING CENTRE

Shipstern is located in the northeastern corner of
the Belize coast. Thirty-two square miles of
moist forest, savanna, and wetlands have been
set aside to preserve as yet unspoiled habitats of
well-known species of birds and mammals associated with the tropics. The reserve encom-

passes the shallow **Shipstern Lagoon,** which, although hardly navigable, creates a wonderful habitat for a huge selection of wading and fish-eating birds. The reserve is home to some 200 different species of birds, 60 species of reptiles and amphibians, and nearly 200 species of butterflies.

The **Audubon Society** and **International Tropical Conservation Foundation** have been extremely generous in their support. Like most reserves, the object is to manage and protect its habitats and wildlife as well as to develop an education program. This entails educating the local community and introducing children to the concept of wildlife conservation in their area. Shipstern, however, goes a step further by conducting an investigation of how tropical countries such as Belize can develop self-supporting conservation areas through the controlled intensive production of natural commodities found within such wildlife settlements. Developing facilities for the scientific study of the reserve area and its wildlife is part of this important program.

Shipstern began the production of live butterfly pupae through intensive breeding. Around the world, tourist attractions (such as Disney World) are providing butterfly habitats, where visitors can wander through an enclosure designed to resemble the deep jungle, with flitting tropical birds and colorful butterflies—all flying free. These butterfly habitats are gaining in popularity and showing up all over the world. Presently there are 60 in Great Britain—ten years ago there were only two. Many of the large animal parks in the U.S., such as Marine World Africa USA in Vallejo, California; San Diego Wild Animal Park; the San Francisco Zoological Society; and many others have either opened a habitat or are in the process of designing one. This is so much more pleasant than a dead collection!

The Butterfly Life Cycle

A butterfly goes through four stages in its life cycle: the egg, caterpillar, pupa, and adult. Shipstern gathers breeding populations of typical Belizeanean species in the pupal stage. Depending on the species, butterflies live anywhere from seven days to six weeks.

In many cities, butterflies have been almost totally depleted for many reasons, including habitat destruction (from logging, for instance) and changing farming practices, particularly the use of pesticides. Shipstern's untouched steamy marshes, swamps, and rainforest have been a natural breeding ground for beautiful butterflies for thousands of years, and hopefully will continue to be so.

For a while the pupae were gathered at Shipstern, carefully packaged in moist cotton inside a cardboard box and then shipped. Once the pupae were unpacked they were carefully "hung" in what is called an emerging cage with a simulated "jungle" atmosphere—hot and humid. A short time later they'd shed their pupal skin, and a tiny bit of Belize fluttered away to the amazement and joy of children and adults who came to visit these popular habitats. However, exporting costs were exceeding benefits, so the export business was stopped. However the butterfly breeding program continues for educational and scientific purposes.

Before starting your trek along the **Botanical Trail,** pick up a book with detailed descriptions of the trail and the trees at the center's headquarters. The trail starts at the parking lot by the office, and meanders through the forest. The walk is lovely and many of the trees are labeled with the Latin and Yucatec Maya name. You will have the opportunity to see three different types of hardwood forests and 100 species of hardwood.

Admission to the Visitor's Center and the Butterfly Breeding Center is free; however, a guided tour of both centers, as well as the Botanical Trail, is US$12 pp, less if more than four people. Hours are daily 9 a.m.-12 p.m., and 1-3 p.m., except for Christmas, New Year's Day, and Easter. It takes about one hour each way driving from Orange Walk to Shipstern Wildlife Reserve. Don't forget a long-sleeved shirt and pants, mosquito repellent, binoculars, and a camera. Write for more information (Box 1694, Belize City, Belize, C.A.; in Switzerland, International Tropical Conservation Foundation, Box 31, CH-2074 Marin-Ne, Switzerland).

BOB RACE

ORANGE WALK DISTRICT

One of the larger towns in Belize, **Orange Walk Town** is located in the **Orange Walk District.** It was settled in the last century by refugees from southern Mexico during the Caste War; you'll still hear more Spanish than English. What's left of two forts, Mundy and Cairns, reminds one that this was the scene of violent battles between Belizean settlers and war-minded Maya trying to rid the area of outsiders. The last battle took place in 1872. Today the most striking people you'll notice on the streets aren't the Maya but the Mennonites who still maintain their simple cotton clothes, horse-drawn buggies, and a stoic countenance.

Logging And Agriculture
For more than 100 years, before settlement by farming-inclined mestizo refugees from Yucatán in 1849, this was timber country. Traveling about two miles north past Orange Walk Town you'll find a reasonably new toll bridge over the **New River.** In years past all the timber logged from the north and middle districts was floated down the New River, on to Corozal Bay, and then to Belize City; from there it was shipped all over the world.

Today's farmers, the Mennonites, have created lovely green pastures and rich gardens; they specialize in the dairy and egg industries. Agriculture is blossoming in many directions in Orange Walk. Sugarcane was the most important crop until recently. Now more and more citrus is grown, and beef producers supply not only the local market but also the export market as well. **Caribbean rum** (a product of sugarcane) is still big business in this area. During the cane harvest the one-lane highway is a parade of trucks stacked high with sugarcane waiting in long lines at the side of the road to get into the sugar mill. Night drivers beware: the trucks aren't new and often have no lights.

ORANGE WALK TOWN

Around Town

Orange Walk Town (population about 10,000) is 66 miles north of Belize City and 30 miles south of Corozal Town. Although Orange Walk Town is one of the larger in Belize, it does not qualify as a tourist destination (at least not yet!). It's another facet of Belize with its own history and style. If passing through, stop and look around. The town has two banks, a cinema, a few hotels, and a choice of many small casual cafes. Close by you'll find several interesting historic sites: **Indian Church** (a 16th-century Spanish mission), the ruins of Belize's original sugar mill built by southern American Civil War refugees, and if you head west and then southwest you'll find **Blue Creek,** a Mennonite development where Belize's only hydroelectric plant is located.

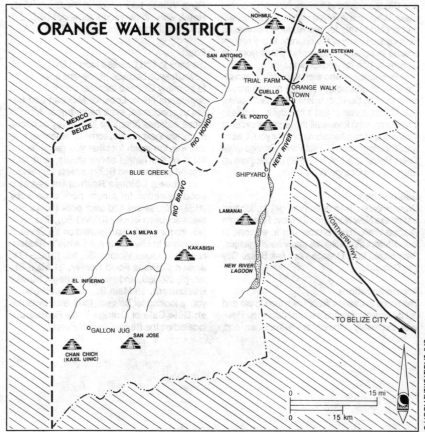

Orchids

The Audubon Society is very involved with the preservation of Belize's wildlife. One of the most important features is 150 species of orchids growing wild throughout the country. **Godoy and Sons** offers a tourist guide service that along with the usual attractions offers orchid tours (4 Trial Farm). Luis Godoy, the eldest son, has developed a unique trek for visitors to the country. From an early age he has been fascinated with orchids. Together with his father's knowledge of the jungle, Godoy offers exciting tours during which visitors will see a variety of tropical blossoms, including the black orchid (the Belizean national flower). Ask about orchid sales. When not involved with touring, they export orchid plants for the Audubon Societies from various parts of the country. Many resorts around the country buy orchid plants from the Godoys to use for landscaping.

Orchid fanciers who wish to buy Belizean orchids must go through special procedures in order to bring the blooms into the United States. Luis Godoy is one of just a handful of people in the country who knows all the legal procedures involved and can handle all of it for you. Call or write for information (4 Trial Farm, Orange Walk Town, Belize, C.A.; tel. 3-22-969) or look them up when visiting Orange Walk Town.

Getting There

Orange Walk Town is easy to get to, located just off the New Northern Highway. Roads from Orange Walk Town enable you to explore, in four different directions, as many as 20 villages. Daily buses from Orange Walk link Belize City and Corozal.

Accommodations

The hotels in Orange Walk Town are simple and not designed for upscale tourist comforts. However, the rooms in the city are basic, clean, and, for the most part, inexpensive. **Baron's Hotel** is the largest with 30 rooms, located on the main road between Belize and Corozal. This is a simple concrete building with a no-frills pool and a disco that often comes to life in the wee hours. Rates are US$25 d, with a/c US$35 (40 Belize Rd., Orange Walk Town, Belize, C.A.; tel. 3-22-518, fax 3-22-847). **Jane's Hotel** at 2 Baker St. offers tiny rooms overlooking the New River. Rooms (singles) are about US$15. **Mi Amor Hotel** offers both private and shared bathrooms, a restaurant, and a bar; 19 Belize/ Corozal Rd., tel. (3) 22-031; rates start about US$15-25. A few miles beyond Orange Walk Town at **Trial Farm Village** take a look at the **Chula Vista Hotel,** with simple rooms for about US$22 d, private bath, restaurant, bar; tel. (3) 22-227.

Food

It's easy to find Chinese food in Orange Walk Town, maybe because at one time it was home to so many Chinese laborers who worked the sugarcane fields. Look for Mexican and Belizean specialties, even hamburgers. Most of these eateries offer little in the way of decor, many are inexpensive, some for whatever reason ask too much for what you get in return. Most of the hotels serve meals, and look around on Main and Baker streets for restaurants. **Lee's Chinese Restaurant** serves a good selection for lunch: pork chop suey (US$4.50), sweet and sour pork (US$5.50), black soybean lobster (US$11.50), and cocktails from a colorful bar, located on Yo Street. A few more to check out are **Camie's Restaurant,** on Queen Victoria St., tel. (3) 22-174; **Jane's Chinese Food Center,** 21 Main St., tel. (3) 22-389; and **Happy Valley Chinese Restaurant,** 38 Main St., tel. (3) 22-554. If you're looking for Belizean food, stop by **Golden Gate Cafe** or **Orange Walk Restaurant** located on the Belize/Corozal Road.

ARCHAEOLOGICAL ZONES

Cuello

Orange Walk District is rich with Maya history, and archaeological sites abound. About five miles west of Orange Walk Town, the archaeology buff will discover **Cuello**. In the 1970s the site was studied by a team from Cambridge University. In the course of their investigations they came up with new and startling data. According to Dr. Norman Hammond, Cuello had been occupied as early as 2600 B.C., much earlier than ever believed! (See "Maya Archaeological Sites of Belize" for more details about Cuello). This site isn't developed, cleared, restored, or ready for the average tourist, but if you're interested in more information, contact the **Department of Archaeology** at Belmopan.

Lamanai

Close by and located on the **New River Lagoon** is Lamanai, another exciting Maya site. One of Belize's largest Maya ceremonial centers, Lamanai can be reached by boat from Shipyard or by road during the dry season from San Felipe. A visit to this unreconstructed ceremonial center, which dates back to 3500 B.C., is an Indiana Jones adventure into the deep shadowed home of the mysterious Maya. (See "Maya Archaeological Sites of Belize" for more details and descriptions of Lamanai.)

Flash! We just got word of a new lodge very close to Lamanai Reserve. The **Lamanai Outpost Lodge** is located along the shore of the New River Lagoon, Belize's largest body of fresh water at 28 miles long. The lodge is just a half mile from the Lamanai Maya site, and guests can either walk or take a quick water-taxi ride to the reserve. The lodge is a comfortable thatch-roof, natural-wood cabaña resort, complete with restaurant/bar. This is a low-key, escape to nature, perfect for the birdwatcher, Mayaphile, naturalist, or just travelers who want to get away from the tourist trail for a while. Overnight rates are US$90 d; packages, including meals, are available. For more information, call or fax (2) 33-578.

Chan Chich

This Maya site is a fairly recent discovery in the northwestern corner of Belize. When flying in, it's apparent that civilization is scarce. Because of its isolation, Chan Chich for years was a favorite spot for marijuana growers and Maya artifact looters. But no more! Owner Barry Bowen did the unimaginable: he built a cottage resort, **Chan Chich Lodge,** in the center of the ancient Maya plaza. A controversy continues in the scientific world, but Bowen has absolutely no qualms about his actions. It is no longer an *easy* task for robbers to dig their trenches and tunnel into the heart of these ancient treasure chests under the constant eye of managers/builders Tom and Josie Harding.

The grounds of Programme Belize, an active conservation organization devoted to preserving Belize's natural resources.

Chan Chich means "little bird." Actually the word has many translations, depending on which Maya dialect you use. It's also the name of the river that runs nearby, as well as the name of the lodge and Maya site. This is a favored resort for archaeology buffs, birdwatchers, naturalists, horseback riders, canoers, or for those who just wish to have an offbeat vacation. Cleared trails wind through the rainforest, green canopy high above. Almost daily you will run into a flock of beautiful oscellated turkeys and hear the roar of the howler monkey, all out for their morning feed. The trekker will discover trenches dug straight into the heart of the Maya structures by looters; the artifacts are now gone.

Chan Chich is located in the middle of **Programme Belize,** 250,000 acres dedicated to scientific exploration, agricultural experimentation, and the protection of indigenous wildlife and archaeological locations of the Maya.

The lodge offers an adventurer's ambience with a jungle location and rustic architecture that blends surreptitiously into the surroundings of mystical Maya and nature. Each of the twelve individual cabañas has a thick thatch roof (good natural insulation against the jungle heat), beautiful hardwood interior, private bathroom with hot-water shower, electricity, ceiling fan, two queen-size beds, veranda, walkways (paved with rounds of cabbage bark logs) that lead to the river, and a charming community dining room/bar/salon with excellent food. Guides are available for horseback riding. Chan Chich is 130 miles from Belize City, a 3.5-hour drive on all-weather roads from the international airport, or (much easier) take a 30-minute charter flight to nearby Gallon Jug. Rates are US$75 s, US$90 d, three-meal packages US$33 adults, US$22 children; all-inclusive prices are US$165 s, US$110 pp, double occupancy, including meals, rooms, Belikin beer, soft drinks, some activities, and tax. Tours and guides to the surrounding areas are easily arranged through Josie. Call or write for more information (Box 37, Belize City, Belize, C.A.; tel. from the U.S. 800-343-8009, fax 508-693-6311, or from Belize 2-75-634, fax 2-75-635).

KATHY ESCOVEDO SANDERS

CAYO DISTRICT

At one time the majority of the people in the Cayo District were mestizo and their families had lived there for generations. Today, while many are descendents of the original settlers, a great many are refugees from unsettled areas in Guatemala and El Salvador. In the past this bustling area depended mostly on the forests to survive, especially at the river port of San Ignacio from which logs and chicle were sent down the river to the sea and then loaded on ships and sent across the world's oceans. But times change and since there is no longer a market for dye woods or chicle,

Cayo District has developed into a booming agricultural center that grows citrus and peanuts and raises cattle. And if the current trend continues, it will one day be a large tourist center. Small cottage resorts are increasing rapidly, attracting travelers from all over the globe who just now are discovering Belize. The newest advance is the dedication of the new Cayo Airport; so far there are no scheduled flights, but charter trips are available on either Maya Air, Island Air, or any of the other airlines currently flying commuters around the countryside.

BELMOPAN

About 50 miles from Belize City, Belmopan is the new capital of the country. The small, unpretentiously planned city was built far away from the coast to be safe from floods after two hurricanes in 30 years rammed their way through the coastal region with amazing destruction. After Hurricane Hattie in 1961, when the relocation was ordained, the government expected large numbers of the population of Belize City to

move along with the government center; it didn't happen. Industry stayed behind and so did the jobs—the masses are still in Belize City, which remains the cultural and industrial hub of the country. Some capital employees continue to commute the 50 miles back and forth each day. However, Belmopan was designed for growth, so when it does happen, the infrastructure is already in place.

FROM BELIZE CITY WEST

Located in the geographical center of the country near the junction of the Western and Hummingbird highways, Belmopan seems more like a quiet suburb rather than the capital of the country. It's worth a visit to see the new government buildings. Though not particularly attractive, they are sturdy with an all-over gray look and built of concrete in a stylistic Maya design. And the new town has a large complex of sporting fields that includes basketball, volleyball, and tennis courts, as well as lots of space for spur-of-the-moment gatherings.

Archaeology Department

If you're interested in antiquities, visit the vaults of the **Department of Archaeology** in the capital. Here the government is preserving finds from the various Maya sites in Belize. The Museum Building Fund is growing and it should not be too much longer before the new museum is begun. Right now, visitors and Mayaphiles can study valuable traces of the last 1,000 years all crammed into a small vault. John Morris, archaeology commissioner of Belize, comments, "Tourists on occasion become irate when they are denied access to the vault. This happens if they come on the wrong day, time, and/or without an appointment." So to anticipate this problem, remember that the vault is open to the public Monday, Wednesday, and Friday, 1:30-4:30 p.m., and an appointment *must* be made two days in advance; tel. (8) 22-106, or fax (8) 23-345, no charge for admittance. Anyone interested in helping out financially should contact the **Association for Belizean Archaeology.**

The most up-to-date projection I have heard is that the museum *should* be open to the public by 1994. The building fund has accumulated about BZE$3 million. The amount needed just to construct the building is about BZE$7 million. The Mexican government is providing a substantial loan; the quid pro quo is that a Mexican construction firm will construct the building.

ACCOMMODATIONS

The **Belmopan Convention Hotel** encourages groups to hold meetings and conventions here, offering 20 comfortable rooms, a swimming pool, bar, restaurant, group facilities, and a communications center—all within walking distance of the government ministries. Expect rates of about US$55 s, US$66 d; write for more information (Box 237, Belmopan, Cayo District, Belize, C.A.; tel. 8-22-130, fax 8-23-066, telex 146 Belcon BZ). Nearby are a few lively spots including the **Bull Frog Inn,** a small hostel with seven a/c or fan-cooled rooms (25 Halfmoon Ave.) with private baths, a unique indoor/outdoor restaurant, and bar. Rates are US$30 s, US$35 d; tel. (8) 22-111, fax (8) 23-155. Close by, the **Circle A Lodge** (35 Halfmoon Ave.) offers 14 clean rooms, US$25-35 s, US$30-45 d, tel. (8) 22-296.

About five miles past the Belmopan turnoff on the Western Highway, stop at JB's for a cold drink, a little local talk, and a sweeping view of the Maya Mountains. This is a favorite stop for the British soldiers stationed close by, as well as travelers and locals.

Right next to JB's (at Mile 31.5 on the Western Highway) look for the sign that leads to **Monkey Bay Wildlife Sanctuary.** Although we haven't been there, we have seen the sign and are told that it's 1,000 acres of diverse vegetation to wander through, with camping facilities that start at US$4. A field research station is available to study the 250 known bird species here; birdwatchers love it. No, there are no monkeys and no bay, but the river does flow through and it is said to be a peaceful sanctuary, a backpacker's delight. Write for more information (Box 187, Belmopan, Belize, C.A.).

All buses from Belize City to San Ignacio and Dangriga stop in Belmopan at Novelo's bus sta-

tion. Also note the small airstrip with air service in and out of the community.

Grove Resort

Between Belmopan and San Ignacio at mile 65.5 on the Western Highway, start looking for a sign that will direct you to the Grove Resort. Set on 50 wooded acres, you'll find an unexpected upscale resort that includes six deluxe villas. Each contains two-room suites with a/c, fans, Italian marble, rattan furniture, refrigerators, and a veranda overlooking the tropical countryside. The concrete buildings are pink and white, with sliding glass doors opening onto private patios. For fun there's a swimming pool, volleyball court, tennis, horseshoes, a nature trail, and touring is made easy with on-premises car rental or escorted day-trips to the cayes or other destinations in the country. Dining is either poolside or in the upstairs clubhouse dining room with a great view. Daily rates are US$100 s, US$125 d; meal plans are pp, US$35 FAP or US$27 MAP. For more information contact Bob or Peg Hufstutler, who have a fine reputation for running resorts after four successful years at Caye Chapel (Box 1, San Ignacio, Cayo, Belize, C.A.; tel./fax 9-22-421).

BOB RACE

SAN IGNACIO

San Ignacio is the largest city in western Belize, with the Macal River separating it from its sister city, Santa Elena. This agricultural community is a peaceful, though busy, hub nestled in rolling hills with clusters of houses scattered in hilly valleys along with the remains of once elegant Maya ceremonial centers. The Maya also appreciated these rich valleys—they were the country's first farmers.

At one time a busy port, now the river is a placid part of both communities, where you'll see women doing their wash, kids splashing around to keep cool (and accomplishing a bath at the same time), and on Sunday there're always car-washing activities in the shallows.

ACTIVITIES

One of the most popular activities in Belize is canoeing along the banks of the many rivers in the country. This is a special kind of sightseeing—a chance to see the wonders of nature. Look for the everchanging flora: plants, trees, vines, and blossoms that thrive along the river banks. Look for the shy animals that live within their own private microcosm, including small underground burrows, sandy river beds, and leafy branches of tall hardwood trees. These rivers were the highways of Belize during the days of the Baymen. Sometimes it's so quiet you can hear a fish jump for a hovering mosquito. Other days you'll hear the dramatic roar of the howler monkey announcing his territory. By all means while traveling along the river keep your eyes and ears open—most will agree this really is the way to see the country.

River Trips

Most of the cottage resorts in Cayo District provide canoes for the use of their guests with or without guides. **Tony's Guided Tours** is probably the most economical independent trip on the river at US$15 pp. Go to **Eva's** and talk to Bob Jones. He will also tell you that river travel is not good during the dry season when the water gets very low. **Belize Whitewater Float** is a firm out of Alaska that brings boaters every season. They provide boats (inflatable kayaks), camping gear and food, and offer a variety of trips. Contact Tom Waite (Box 330, Talkeetna, Alaska 99676; tel. 907-733-2384).

ACCOMMODATIONS

San Ignacio, the busy center of this rural area, offers several hotels. The **San Ignacio Hotel** overlooks the Macal River and the hills of Cayo. The 23 rooms are pleasant and roomy with private bathrooms, hot water, restaurant and bar, swimming pool, various ball courts, disco, gift shop, sightseeing tours, and convention facilities. Rates are US$40 s, US$43 d; credit cards okay. Write or call for more information (Box 33, San Ignacio, Cayo District, Belize, C.A.; tel. 92-2034/2125, fax 92-2134).

Plaza Hotel is the newest hotel in town with hot water, private tile bathrooms in each room, four rooms with a/c, five with a phone, and coffee in the dining room. Rates for a/c rooms are US$30 s, US$38 d; without a/c US$18 s, US$25 d, located at 4A Burns Ave., tel. (92) 3332/3375/3374. The hotel has rather a strange entry from the street; it's next to Beto's Shopping Center, across from a couple of Chinese Restaurants.

Run by local Garifuna Godsman Ellis, the **Piache Hotel** offers 12 clean comfortable rooms and an outdoor bar at 18 Buena Vista St. in San Ignacio. Rooms with fans are US$30 d, with a/c US$40 d. Godsman has a wealth of info on San Ignacio and all of Belize. He offers tours to the surrounding ruins and into Tikal. Transportation to and from the airport is available; he can provide meals and transportation for large groups. The Piache (Garifuna for "doctor") is a small quiet hotel on a hill overlooking town, but close enough to walk to most everything. It's not fancy but, as Godsman says, "It's very Belizean." Peanut butter lovers: Godsman makes some of the best peanut butter anywhere. Write or call for more information (Box 54, San Ignacio, Cayo District, Belize, C.A.; tel. 92-2032, 92-3264, fax 92-2685.

Mayaphiles: the ruins of **Cahal Pech** are about a 15-minute walk from the Piache. This medium-size Maya site was discovered in the early 1950s, but scientific research did not begin until 1988 when a team from San Diego State University's Department of Anthropology began excavation. (For more information see "Maya Archaeological Sites of Belize.") Info and a pamphlet about the site are available at the Piache. Nearby **Tipu** was an important Maya-Christian town during the early years of colonization. Tipu was as far as the Spanish were able to penetrate in the 16th century.

About a quarter mile out of town at Branch Mouth Rd. (ask at Eva's), take a look at **Mida's Resort.** You'll find four circular cottages with thatch roofs, situated on the banks of the Macal River (a 300-yard path from the cottages). Two of the cabins offer private bathrooms and the other two share a bathroom. No electricity is available yet, however oil lamps and hot water are provided. Campers are welcome, US$5 per adult. Rates with bathroom are US$30 s, US$35

Eva's Restaurant

OZ MALLAN

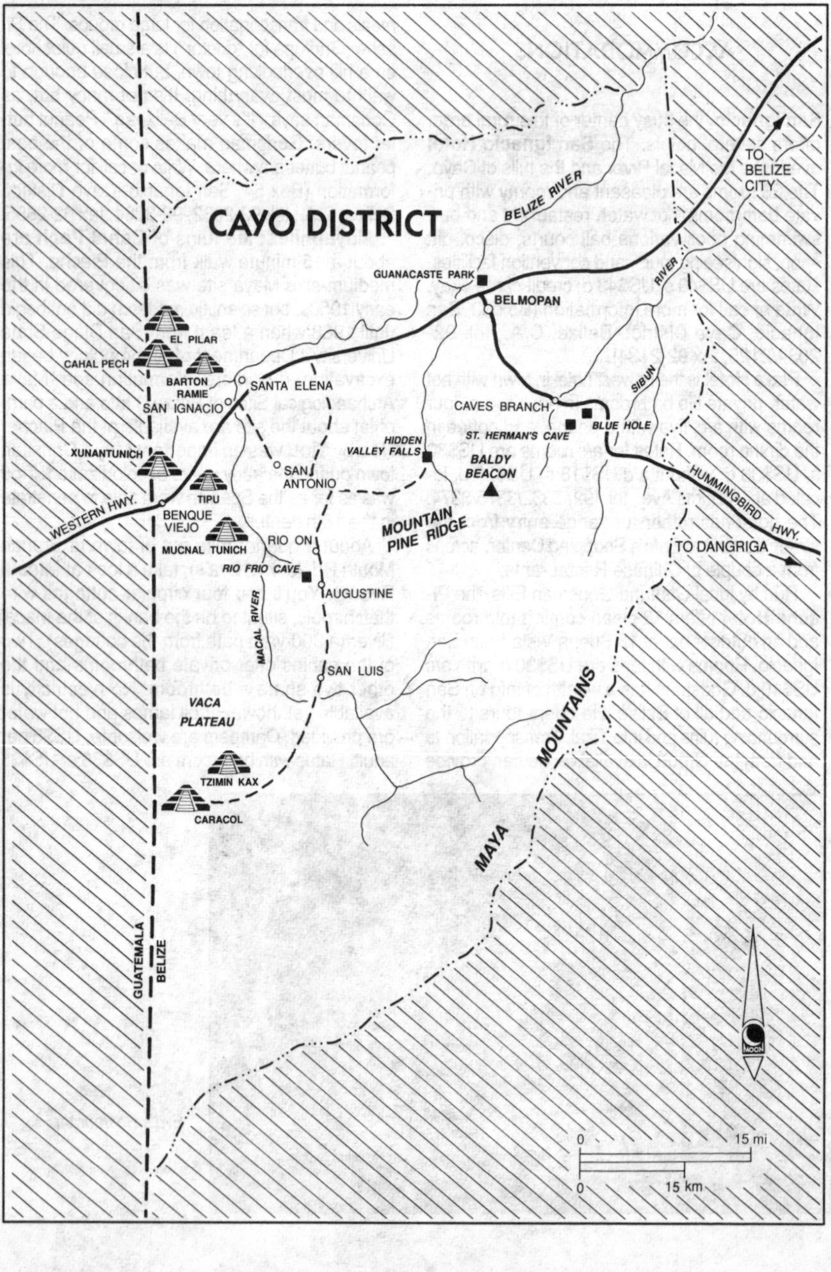

CAYO DISTRICT

TO BELIZE CITY

BELIZE RIVER

GUANACASTE PARK

BELMOPAN

EL PILAR

CAHAL PECH

BARTON RAMIE

SANTA ELENA

SAN IGNACIO

SIBUN

CAVES BRANCH

XUNANTUNICH

HIDDEN VALLEY FALLS

ST. HERMAN'S CAVE

BLUE HOLE

SAN ANTONIO

BALDY BEACON

TIPU

WESTERN HWY.

BENQUE VIEJO

MUCNAL TUNICH

RIO ON

MOUNTAIN PINE RIDGE

HUMMINGBIRD HWY.

TO DANGRIGA

RIO FRIO CAVE

AUGUSTINE

MACAL RIVER

SAN LUIS

VACA PLATEAU

MAYA MOUNTAINS

TZIMIN KAX

CARACOL

GUATEMALA

BELIZE

0   15 mi

0   15 km

© MOON PUBLICATIONS, INC.

d; with shared facilities US$20 s, US$25 d, US$40 for an entire familiy.

Mida's has initiated an **airport service** to and from Belize City (both airports) US$25 pp, US$80 for a group of four. The shuttle departs from Cayo daily at 6:30 a.m. For more information and reservations call (92) 3172/2101. Ask about day-trips to the surrounding areas, including Tikal, Guatemala.

The **Belmoral, Central,** and **Hi-Et** are basic hotels, all budget priced (under US$25); some have a/c, TV, with private or shared baths, but look at the room before you make your decision. These are good places to meet other budget travelers. Don't forget Bob Jones at Eva's; he can usually find a budget spot for you to stay.

FOOD

Try **Eva's Restaurant and Bar.** Eva's is also the **San Ignacio Tourist Information Center,** a clearing house for guides, fellow travelers, and the latest gossip. Owner Bob Jones is a wealth of information for just about anything that's happening in San Ignacio and the river. This is a good place to meet new friends. Bob keeps a list of names to share a ride to "anywhere," cheaper by the group. He has pictures and rates of most of the budget resorts along the river. Plus,

expect good fried chicken for about US$3.25, or peas, rice, and Creole-style chicken for about US$3.50. If you enjoy it, send back a postcard to add to Eva's collection on the walls. Eva's is located at 22 Burns Ave., tel. (92) 2267.

Look for **Serendib Restaurant,** a cafe owned by a Sri Lankan. Along with good hamburgers and chow mein, he serves excellent curries; reasonably priced; located at 27 Burns Ave., tel. (92) 2302.

OTHER SERVICES

While wandering around town you'll find a general store (with fresh-baked goodies and fresh-squeezed orange juice), **Barclays Bank,** a telephone office, police station, and buses **(Novelo** and **Batty)** going to the Guatemala border and to Belize City. The first bus reaches San Ignacio about 9 a.m., continuing through to the Guatemala border; the last one leaves in the opposite direction at about 6 p.m. The buses stop either at the town circle near the police station, at the bridge, or at the parking area off Burns Avenue. Expect only limited service on Sundays. For current schedules between Belize City, San Ignacio, and Benque Viejo (Guatemala border) call the Batty Bus in Belize City, (7) 2025, or the Novelo Bus, (7) 7372.

COTTAGE RESORTS IN THE CAYO COUNTRYSIDE

Small cottages are scattered across the Cayo countryside and attract the visitor interested in exploring rather than diving: long treks through tropical foliage, canoe rides on a choice of rivers, horseback trips to hidden waterfalls, and quiet safaris to search out the shy animals and flamboyant birdlife of the Belizean forest. For a multitude of reasons, these rural resorts are popular and visitors return year after year to their favorite. Each has its own ambience and specialty.

Banana Bank Ranch
One of the older working cattle ranches in the country, **Banana Bank Ranch,** run by artist Carolynn Carr and Montana cowboy-husband

John, offers a change of pace in accommodations. This is a chance to see how a ranch in the tropics operates. Along with a herd of Brahman cattle, guests will discover, while exploring the 75-acre ranch, a respectable-size Maya ruin complete with a lagoon that was handdug by the Maya and today is occupied by several Morlett's crocodiles. Scattered around the property visitors will notice many small "house mounds" as well. As expected, horseback riding is the featured activity of Banana Bank Ranch; however visitors can also take a boating trip down the Belize River, putting you in touch with nature's creatures—with time for a cooling swim. For a lazy ride into the sur-

(CONTINUED ON PAGE 182)

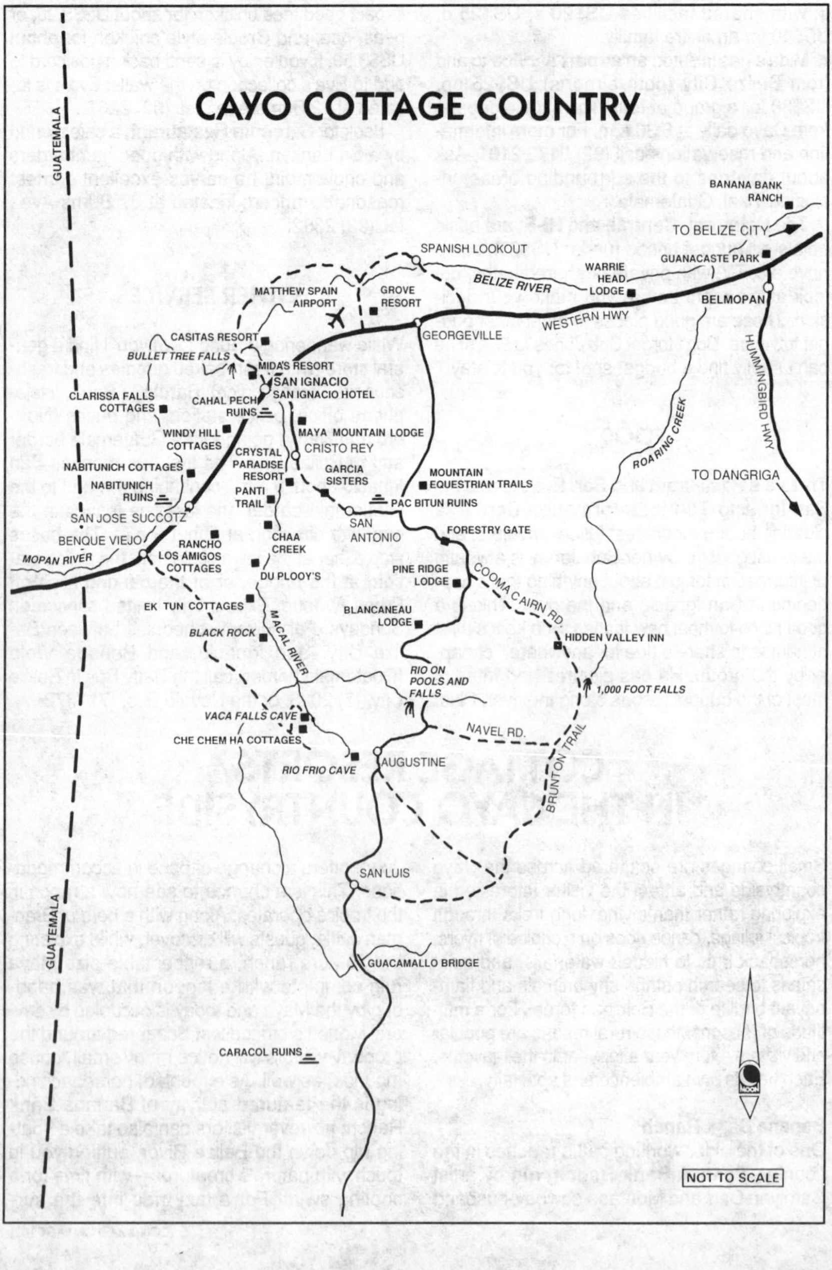

CAYO COTTAGE COUNTRY

GUATEMALA

BANANA BANK RANCH

TO BELIZE CITY

SPANISH LOOKOUT

WARRIE HEAD LODGE

GUANACASTE PARK

BELIZE RIVER

BELMOPAN

MATTHEW SPAIN AIRPORT

GROVE RESORT

GEORGEVILLE

WESTERN HWY

CASITAS RESORT

BULLET TREE FALLS

MIDA'S RESORT

SAN IGNACIO

CLARISSA FALLS COTTAGES

CAHAL PECH RUINS

SAN IGNACIO HOTEL

WINDY HILL COTTAGES

CRYSTAL PARADISE RESORT

MAYA MOUNTAIN LODGE

CRISTO REY

NABITUNICH COTTAGES

GARCIA SISTERS

MOUNTAIN EQUESTRIAN TRAILS

HUMMINGBIRD HWY

ROARING CREEK

TO DANGRIGA

NABITUNICH RUINS

PANTI TRAIL

PAC BITUN RUINS

SAN JOSE SUCCOTZ

BENQUE VIEJO

RANCHO LOS AMIGOS COTTAGES

CHAA CREEK

SAN ANTONIO

FORESTRY GATE

MOPAN RIVER

DU PLOOY'S

PINE RIDGE LODGE

COOMA CAIRN RD.

EK TUN COTTAGES

BLANCANEAU LODGE

HIDDEN VALLEY INN

BLACK ROCK

MACAL RIVER

RIO ON POOLS AND FALLS

1,000 FOOT FALLS

VACA FALLS CAVE

NAVEL RD.

CHE CHEM HA COTTAGES

RIO FRIO CAVE

AUGUSTINE

BRUNTON TRAIL

SAN LUIS

GUACAMALLO BRIDGE

GUATEMALA

CARACOL RUINS

© MOON PUBLICATIONS, INC.

NOT TO SCALE

THE OLD AND NEW WEST OF BELIZE

Cayo District reminds many visitors of America's Old West. San Ignacio Town projects the flavor with narrow streets, old buildings with wooden store fronts and broad overhangs, a general mercantile, an abundance of Chinese restaurants, and country folk coming to town for their weekly supplies.

However, just a short distance out of town, a visit to Mountain Equestrian Trails Ranch (referred to as MET) is a sample of the *new* "West" of Belize. Ranchers Jim and Marguerite Bevis, together with their four children, live the typical ranch life of the 90s in the tropics. They thrive on their way of life. And although living in this isolated area has its problems, it's nothing this family (and many others just like them) haven't adjusted to. School lessons are learned at the dining-room table under Marguerite's supervision, though sometimes a student-teacher from the U.S. comes to live with them for a few months at a time. As the kids get tall enough to climb a horse on their own, they learn the skills to become excellent horsemen under the watchful eye of dad, Jim. And the whole family takes part in running the ranch, one way or another.

Jim moved to Belize with his parents in 1962 when he was 11. By the time he was 13 he had bought his first dory (dug-out canoe), which he traded for one bottle of White Horse whiskey. He speaks fluent Spanish and Creole, knows Belize's rugged bush, the local culture and folklore, and gives a lot of himself to Belize and those interested in Belize. He learned his equestrian skills while growing up and today has a reputation as one of the best expeditionary guides in the country.

Marguerite is a registered nurse from Texas. She's had to use her medical training on more than one occasion in the countryside. To deal with the infrequent emergencies around the ranch, she was taught how to suture (she practiced on a chicken's foot) by a Boston physician. The school desk/dining-room table serves as an examining table. As for children's illnesses, she tells how she has depended on Rosita Arvigo's earthy remedies (see p. 55). She recalls with a shudder one frightening bout with amoebic dysentary; in the end it was Rosie's herbal negrita that cured her daughter.

Though spread out in the hilly district, usually a long distance from a neighbor, this is a close-knit community alive with pioneer spirit—no telephone lines, television stations, supermarkets, or movie theaters.

Communication has been developed using telephone lines in Belmopan and radio frequencies. If you call one of the out-of-the-way jungle cottage resorts in Cayo District, everyone with a radio hears the call come through *and* the conversation—a lot like small town party lines in the Old West. As Marguerite puts it, "we have no secrets." And because of this open community "telephone," neighbors also know when there's an emergency. If help is needed, they give it freely.

Adventurers/guests enjoy visiting MET. Always looking for new challenges, Jim recently took seven people across the Maya Mountain Divide on foot. The group rode horses to Caracol and then on to Las Cuevas, an old sheep campsite deep in the Chiquibul Forest. From here the group began a trek that took 14 days, "some of the most difficult hiking I've done," according to Jim. Although the group was elated by the trek, it had a dramatic ending when the Maya guide slipped on a steep rocky precipice and fractured his pelvis. Fortunately, Jim had a high-frequency radio and was able to get help right away; a military helicopter airlifted the injured man to a hospital in no time. Will the visitors make that trek again? They can't wait, not even the guide!

OZ MALLAN

MET is a working guest ranch and the whole family helps to entertain. Arran, the eldest, started a truck garden. He plants cucumbers, Chinese cabbage, and other vegetables that he then sells to his parents to use in the restaurant. Already learning to be an entrepreneur, he sells the excess at market with the other farmers. Lacy is learning the joys of being a gourmet cook in the dining room. Heather and Trevor, still would rather hang around the stables and the horses, run through the grassy fields, or walk the nature trail.

Marguerite and Jim are very concerned about the preservation of their beautiful countryside, and with other land holders are creating Slate Creek Preserve, a privately owned reserve. Jim and the

kids are establishing a butterfly trail on the ranch for visitors to wander. They've made a study of which plants to leave alone and which they can bring in to attract the beautiful fluttery creatures seen in the jungle throughout Belize.

If you happen along the road, you'll know MET by the beauty and tranquility of the land, healthy horses grazing in green pasture with tall and short trees (covered with brilliant blossoms in March), a lovely house perched on the side of a hill, and a bunch of happy kids who may not know much about the latest Saturday cartoons, but who can tell you which is a gumbo limbo tree, where you can find a Baird's tapir, and who can saddle up a horse in double time (see p. 187).

rounding countryside, try a horse-drawn buggy. And the food at the ranch is great! Banana Bank Ranch is an enigma; we have had glowing letters from readers and then we have had some not-so-glowing letters. Two cabañas each sleep three people, and four more rooms in the main house accommodate guests, three with shared bathroom; one room is furnished with a water bed and has a private bath. Rates are US$35 s, and US$50 d for shared bath; for private bath US$55 s, US$65 d; for the casitas US$65 s, US$75 d, US$85 t, and US$90 q. Food plans are available, MAP US$20, FAP US$26. Write or call for more information (Box 48, Belmopan, Cayo District, Belize, C.A.; tel. 8-22-677, fax 8-22-366; in the U.S., 800-552-3419, fax 218-847-4442).

To get to Banana Bank Ranch follow the Western Highway to Mile 47 across from the Silva airstrip. Follow the signs; from the highway it's 1.25 miles on an all-weather road to the river, and the ranch is just on the other side. If preferred, it just takes a telephone call to the Carrs and they will pick you up at Belmopan for US$10 pp.

duPlooy's

If you received a "challenge" in the mail offering a free weekend in an isolated jungle guesthouse in Central America's Belize to the first couple who brought a gallon of still-frozen Häagen Däaz ice cream to said resort, what would you do? Well, several adventurers *did;* they

packed up their Häagen Däaz and hit the airport on the run. The first couple (from Davis, California) arrived undaunted by jungle heat with a cooler filled with dry ice and not one, but two gallons of their favorite flavors. duPlooys' Cottage Resort had one heck of a party all weekend. And not only did the resort guests enjoy, but also special friends from all over Belize came with a multitude of exotic fruit toppings and lots of chocolate sauce.

This is typical of the feeling you get at duPlooy's, a family-run resort (all daughters) with fun-timers Judy and Ken duPlooy at the helm. The small resort is set on 20 acres of rolling countryside wrapped on the east and north by the Macal River. You can use this as either a place to relax on a sandy beach by the river, or a base from which to explore the caves, the nearby waterfalls, the Maya ruins, or even Guatemala and Tikal. Guests choose their mode of exploring either on horseback, ferry, canoe, or on foot. Don't miss exploring duPlooys' grounds. Ken is a great gardener; take a look at the orchid house and, as Ken says, if a cutting isn't *stolen,* it won't grow well. He is also a great birder and loves to take guests on *night* birding expeditions in the back of his pickup with his powerful beam. It's a new world of birds that play in the dark.

Guests have two choices: the **Jungle Lodge,** with its stucco cabañitas with red-tile roofs, screened porches, private bathrooms, hot showers, ceiling fans, and large rooms with many

At duPlooy's, paths lead around green grassy hills down to the cottages along the riverbank.

windows to bring in the pleasant views; or **du-Plooy's Hotel** with shared bathrooms, hot water, ceiling fans, dining room, lounge, and covered porch on three sides of the building. The rooms are simple, clean, and comfortable. Meals are good and ample. At the Jungle Lodge, breakfast is delivered to your room in a basket filled with homemade breads, fresh fruit, and coffee or tea; lunch can be a voucher in a local restaurant, a packed picnic, or served in the river-view dining room. Dinner consists of four courses served in the dining room. Rates for the Jungle Lodge are US$88 s and US$132 d, including three meals. Hotel prices are US$38 s, US$49 d, US$60 t, and include continental breakfast. Package rates, including sightseeing trips, are available; for more information call duPlooys, tel./fax (92) 3301, or contact International Expeditions, tel. (800) 633-4734, (205) 428-1700, fax (205) 428-1714.

Warrie Head Creek Lodge

Another great Cayo lodge! A stroll down a grassy hillside brings you to bubbling cascades (where the Belize River and Warrie Head Creek meet), a walking trail, and a spring-fed pool that's perfect for swimming. This is a bit of paradise with orchid trails, 189 species of birds, and 40 varieties of fruit trees. Eight comfortable rooms are fan cooled with hot water, showers, bar service, and delicious food. Owners Bia and Johnny Searle offer both river trips and trips to the popular sights in the country, as well as

horseback riding. If you have the chance, take the time to talk to Bia. She was born and raised in Belize and can tell you interesting things about Belize past and Belize today. She has wonderful stories about growing up with a Creole nanny who became her surrogate mother and grandmother to her children for many years before her death. Ask her about "ground" food (giant yams and potatoes), *calalu,* and *ackee* (a Jamaican tree that is a substitute for eggs). Bia is in the process of collecting antique Belizean colonial furniture. Eventually she will have it in all of the rooms; for now the upstairs' lounge is furnished with it. Ask about a canoe trip to Iguana Creek, with or without a paddler, US$10 half day (Box 244, Belize City, Belize, C.A.; tel. 2-77-257, fax 2-75-213; in the U.S. call International Expeditions, 800-633-4734).

Maya Mountain Lodge

At Santa Elena a sign directs you to Maya Mountain Lodge. The jungle hideaway is operated by Susie and Bart Mikler. A meandering trail on the property introduces the neophyte to a variety of plants and trees. The rooms and cottages are campy, and the Miklers serve a menu that includes Belizean, International, and Mexican food, along with homemade breads and buckets of fresh-squeezed orange juice; no liquor is sold (you can, however, bring your own). Electricity, hot water, private bathrooms, and friendly people are provided. Rate for cottages or rooms is US$85 s or d, with meals

CAYO ACCOMMODATIONS

Belmopan Convention Hotel
Box 237, Belmopan
(8) 22-130/22-340, fax (8) 23-066
US$55 s, US$66 d

Banana Bank Ranch, Box 48, Belmopan
(8) 22-677, fax (8) 22-366,
in the U.S. (800) 552-3419
US$35 s, US$50 d shared bath; US$55 s,
US$65 d private bath;
US$65 s, US$75 d casitas

Bull Frog Inn, 25 Halfmoon Ave., Belmopan
(8) 22-111, fax (8) 23-155
US$30 s, US$35 d

Chaa Creek, Box 53, San Ignacio
(92) 2037, fax (92) 2501
US$80 s, US$105 d bed and breakfast

Circle A Lodge, 35 Halfmoon Ave., Belmopan
(8) 22-296, US$25-35 s, US$30-45 d

duPlooy's Riverside Cottages and Hotel
Macal River
tel./fax (92) 3301, in the U.S. (800) 633-4734,
(205) 428-1714
hotel US$38 s US$49 d, US$60 t includes
continental breakfast; jungle lodge US$88 s,
US$132 d includes three meals

Ek Tun, General Delivery, Benque Viejo
(93) 2536
or in the U.S. Box 18748, Boulder
Colorado 80308-8748
(303) 442-6150
US$135 s, US$165 d includes all meals

El Indio Perdido Jungle Lodge, Benque Viejo
(800) 833-9992
US$33 s, US$55 d shared bath; US$44 s,
US$66 d private bath; breakfast included

Grove Resort, Mile 65.5 Western Hwy., Box 1,
San Ignacio
tel./fax (9) 22-421
US$100 s, US$125 d

Hidden Valley Inn, Cooma Carin Rd.,
Mountain Pine Ridge, Box 170 Belmopan
(8) 23-320, fax (8) 23-334, (800) 334-7942
US$77.50 s, US$105 d includes breakfast

Maya Hotel, 11 George St., Benque Viejo
(93) 2116
under US$15

Maya Mountain Lodge, Box 46, San Ignacio
(92) 2164/2029, in the U.S. (800) 344-MAYA,
US$85 s or d

Mida's Resort, Branch Mouth Rd., San Ignacio,
(92) 3172/2101
US$20 s, US$25 d, US$40 family shared bath;
US$30 s, US$35 d private bath. Campers
US$5 per adult

Mountain Equestrian Trails, Central Farm Post
Office, Cayo, or Box 180, Belmopan
(8) 23-180, (8) 22-149, fax (8) 23-235
or (8) 23-505
US$60 s, US$70 d

Nabitunich, San Lorenzo Farm, Cayo
(93) 2309, fax (93) 2096, US$27 s, US$38 d;
US$49 s, US$60 d bed and breakfast; US$66 s,
US$88 d includes all meals

Oki's, 47 George St., Benque Viejo
(93) 2006, under US$15

Piache Hotel, 18 Buena Vista St.,
Box 54, San Ignacio
(92) 2032, (92) 3264, fax (92) 2685
US$30 d with fan, US$40 d with a/c

Pine Ridge Lodge, Box 2079, Belize City
(92) 3310, (216) 781-6888
US$45 d forest view, US$85 d river view

Plaza Hotel, 4A Burns Ave., San Ignacio
(92) 3332/3375/3374
US$18 s, US$25 d without a/c; US$30 s,
US$38 d with a/c

San Ignacio Hotel, Box 33, San Ignacio
(92) 2034/2125, fax (92) 2134
US$40 s, US$43 d

Warrie Head Creek Lodge, Box 244, Belize City
(2) 77-257, fax (2) 75-213, (800) 633-4734
US$60 s, US$70 d

Windy Hill Cottages, Graceland Ranch,
San Ignacio (92) 2055, (92) 2017,
(800) 345-9786, fax (504) 366-9986
US$45 s, US$60 d,
US$75 t, breakfast included

CAYO ACCOMMODATIONS

JUNGLE ADVENTURE CAMPS

Black Rock ECO Jungle Tours,
Box 48, San Ignacio
tel./fax (92) 2341
US$36 s, US$42 d, US$46 t, breakfast US$5,
lunch US$6, dinner US$10

Clarissa Falls Cottages, Mile 5.5 on
Benque Viejo Rd.
(93) 2424
US$8 pp

Cosmos Camping, San Ignacio
US$5 camping; US$5 s, US$7 d cottages

Rancho Los Amigos, San Jose Succotz
(93) 2261
US$15 pp, including 2 meals

SAN IGNACIO BUDGET HOTELS (ALL PRICED UNDER US$25)

Belmoral, 17 Burns Ave.
(92) 2024

Central Hotel, 24 Burns Ave.
(92) 2253

Hi-Et Hotel, 12 West St.
no phone

Venus Hotel, 29 Burns Ave.
(92) 2186

served family style. Ask about less expensive rooms and hammock accommodations; breakfast US$7, lunch US$6, dinner US$12. Write or call for reservations and more information (Box 46, San Ignacio, Cayo District, Belize, C.A.; tel. 92-2164, fax 92-2029, 800-344-MAYA).

Windy Hill Cottages
On the Western Highway after leaving San Ignacio going west, you'll come to a sign that directs you to Windy Hill Cottages at Graceland Ranch, another Belize-style guesthouse. You'll find rustic charm with thatch-roof cottages, green grass, private baths, hot water, ceiling fans, 24-hour electricity, a swimming pool, and recreation hut complete with TV, hammocks, bar, table tennis, and billiards. Arrangements can be made for horseback riding, nature tours, and hiking trails. Ask about escorted tours, including one into the newly opened **Caracol archaeological site.** Cottage rates are US$45 s, US$60 d, US$75 t, breakfast included; credit cards okay. Meals are served in a casual thatch-roof dining room, lunch US$8 and dinner US$13. Write or call Windy Hill Cottages for more information (Graceland Ranch, San Ignacio, Cayo District, Belize, C.A.; tel. 92-2055 or 92-2017; in the U.S. contact Sea & Explore, 1809 Carol Sue Ave., Ste. E, Gretna, Louisiana 70056; tel. 800-345-9786, 504-366-9985, fax 504-366-9986).

El Indio Perdido Jungle Lodge
This lodge (formerly **Indio Suiza**) is a two-mile detour off the Western Highway through a cow pasture. No, you haven't gone on the wrong road if you come to a dead end at the Mopan River; just give a holler or toot the horn and someone will come and fetch you from the other side of the river on a hand-pulled float. Staying at El Indio Perdido is like visiting Aunt Jenny's farm back home—only with a tropical flare set on 75 beautiful acres. You'll see many animals, and if you visit in springtime you'll be greeted by a whole new set of cavorting baby critters. Accommodations are in separate cottages or rooms in the main house. No electricity or hot water is available (so far). Some rooms have a private bathroom; it's not fancy but it's comfortable and clean. The kitchen, dining room, and bar are in the main house. From here there's a trail to Xunantunich, or instead you can rent a raft and paddle down the river. Rates, including breakfast, are US$44 s, US$66 d with private bath; US$33 s, US$55 d with shared bath. Complete meal plans are available; credit cards okay. For information and reservations write to El Indio Perdido Lodge (Benque Viejo, Cayo District, Belize, C.A.; in the U.S. contact Legrand Travel in Monterey, California, tel. 800-833-9992, 408-646-1621.

Chaa Creek Lodge

OZ MALLAN

Chaa Creek

On the Western Highway about five miles west of San Ignacio, look for the Chaa Creek sign and make a left turn onto the dirt road that leads to a secluded hideaway on the edge of the Macal River. This is a favorite to which guests return year after year. If you arrive in the middle of the afternoon and approach from the parking lot in back of the thatch-roof kitchen, you'll see pans of unbaked homemade rolls lining the windowsill and rising in the warm afternoon shade. Check in at the bar/lounge palapa across from the dining palapa, where you'll probably meet owners Mick and Lucy Fleming. This American wife/British husband team are both world travelers who came to visit Belize in the late '70s, fell in love with it, and never left. Chaa Creek was one of the first cottage resorts in Cayo, and if you ask Mick he'll tell you its colorful history, from overgrown farm to Private Nature Reserve of 330 acres where three small Maya plaza groups are located along the resort's Ruta Maya trail system; ask for a map or take one of the daily walks with a Chaa Creek guide.

A bright, flower-lined path brings you to the white stucco cottages with tall peaked *palapa* roofs and wooden shutters that close over bright-colored curtains (you don't need glass—no mosquitoes here!). The 19 double cottages (two rooms in each with two double beds in each room) have private baths and hot water, Mexican-tile floors, decor of rich Guatemalan fabrics, and oil lamps that are lit when the sun sets

(no electricity). The cottages, reminiscent of Africa from the Flemings's earlier years in Kenya and Uganda, are scattered across the brow of a grassy hillside that slopes down to the edge of the Macal River. Guests can swim along the shore, go sightseeing on the trails, or paddle a dory down the river to San Ignacio (takes about two hours). The river meanders through thick trees and tangled growth. Local housewives pound sudsy clothes clean on river rocks under a leafy arbor, while iguanas blink at you in the lazy afternoon sun. It's a great outing and you can relax knowing that someone will pick you up in the van or Land Rover in San Ignacio for the trip back if you wish.

Chaa Creek is an easy gateway to the Guatemala border and the fabulous Tikal ruins. Day-trips to the ruins of Xunantunich (close by) as well as to Tikal can be arranged here. Rooms are available either with breakfast, lunch, or dinner, or all three, but you must decide in advance and are charged accordingly. After dinner, enjoy the art of conversation or enjoy the starry sky; look for the magic light show in tall trees around the grounds—fireflies do their mating dance and cast a sparkling glow on the spreading branches.

Bed and breakfast is US$80 s, US$105 d; a packed lunch is US$6, lunch US$9, dinner US$16.50, plus tax and service charge. Ask about Chaa Creek's **Chiquibul Camp Site**, located four hours away between Mountain Pine Ridge and the Chiquibul Reserve on the banks of the Macal River. This is great for anyone who enjoys camping and trekking in a remote setting—habitat for tapir, Morelet's crocodile, and scarlet macaw. Write or call for canoe rental fees, inland expeditions, reservations, and prices (Box 53, San Ignacio, Cayo District, Belize, C.A.; tel. 92-2037, fax 92-2501).

Nabitunich

Here a group of cottages is run by Rudi and Margaret Juan, friendly people who have the knack of making you feel at home. It's near the river, with rolling grass to the bank—a nice relaxed atmosphere. Guests have access to canoes and horses. Hot and cold water are available, as well as a plug and good lights in the bathroom for shaving; but if you like to read in bed, bring your "itty bitty" Book Light with plenty of batteries. Dinners at Nabitunich are always delicious, multicourse and often served on crystal and linen. Ask for the "stone cottage"; though all are nice, some still have an open common ceiling. Make yourself at home in the comfortable lounge. This a great gathering place for interesting people. When last we were there a group of archaeologists was staying while they worked at nearby Xunantunich. Or, you might meet a group of doctors who, with Margaret's help, come to the **Good Shepherd Clinic** in Benque Viejo area every year to donate free medical assistance. People come from all over the district for this needed service, many from across the Guatemalan border. Nabitunich is walking distance to Xunantunich. Look for the entrance across from the Chaa Creek turnoff. Rates for room only are US$27 s, US$38 d; bed and breakfast is US$49 s, US$60 d; with breakfast and dinner US$60 s, US$77 d; including three meals US$66 s, US$88. For more information call (93) 2309, fax (93) 2096.

Mountain Equestrian Trails

Jim and Marguerite Bevis offer a wonderful change of pace and an opportunity to see areas of Belize that are without roads—this is especially interesting if you're an equestrian. Before the Bevis family took over and built the lovely cabañas, only the "horse people" thought of coming here. No more. This small resort now offers a relaxing alternative to those on the seaside. In order to take advantage of the loca-

tion—close to the Mountain Pine Ridge area, the mountains, Caracol, and the entire Cayo District—it helps to have a car. No matter that the small cantina is a 20-minute drive from San Ignacio, it's still a great gathering place for drinks, dinner, and good conversation with both visitors and locals.

For the horseperson, this is a working ranch, with 20 beautiful quarter horses in peak condition and expertly trained on the 150-acre ranch; you have your choice of a gentle or spirited horse. Trips are designed to suit every taste, from mountain trails that wander past magnificent waterfalls and pools where everyone is lured for a swim, to pine forests that take in creeks, Maya caves, Caracol, exotic butterflies, and more than 150 species of orchids. The equestrian trails are only a few miles from **Rio Frio Caves** and **Hidden Valley Falls,** where the water drops more than 1,000 feet into the jungle below. Programs are designed for both begin-

preparing for a ride into the forest to see dramatic waterfalls, rushing rivers, and unique wildlife

OZ MALLAN

ners and experienced riders—children from age 10 with previous riding experience welcome (kids feel right at home with the Bevis brood—all excellent riders, even down to the youngest, Trevor). Guests will find lovely cabañas of thatch, stucco, and exotic wood interiors with private bathrooms and hot water (no electricity—yet); very comfortable. Meals are served in the cozy cantina/restaurant, which serves a variety of excellent food (breakfast US$5, lunch US$10, dinner US$12). Ask about customized camping trips. Room rates are US$60 s, US$70 d, plus US$5 service charge pp per night; riding fees are extra. Riders are required to carry personal liability insurance to cover themselves while touring. The resort is located at Mile 8, Mountain Pine Ridge Road. For a brochure and more information write to Mountain Equestrian Trails (Central Farm Post Office, Cayo District, or Box 180, Belmopan, Belize, C.A.; tel. 8-23-180, 8-22-149, fax 8-23-235). For a special look at the Bevis family, see pp. 181-182.

Ek Tun

This new and growing resort offers guests a jungle ambience in an isolated area of the Macal River. For now, the luxurious stick-and-thatch hut accommodates up to six people. Food, cooked by Phyllis, the wifely half of the partnership, includes such specialties as chilled papaya soup, jicama salad, Indonesian chicken, green chili, and who knows what tomorrow's surprise might be. Most of the fruits and vegetables served are grown in the Ek Tun gardens. Meals are served in the open dining room overlooking the surrounding mountains and the surging Macal River. Main activities are river trips that explore limestone caves in the nearby Vaca Cave system, and trekking through the trails of Ek Tun. The cabin is charming (a new one should be complete by now), about 500 square feet with two double beds in the loft and another downstairs. It is furnished with antiques and offers hot and cold water, flush toilets, stucco walls in the bathroom, and kerosene lamps; described by former guests as *rustic elegance*. At the present time only one generator is used for electricity, and it usually goes off early. Readers, just ask and you'll receive a mini book light. Prices include all meals; US$135 s, US$165 d; add

US$60 for each additional person up to four, and US$50 up to 6. Take the Chaa Creek turnoff, follow the signs, and within a mile you'll see the parking lot and Ek Tun; a motorized rubber boat will carry you across the 500 feet of water, and then a short walk brings you to the lodge. Pickup from San Ignacio is US$25. For more information contact Ken or Phyllis Dart in the U.S. (Box 18748, Boulder, Colorado 80308-8748; tel. 303-442-6150; in Belize, General Delivery, Benque Viejo, Cayo District, Belize, C.A.; tel. 93-2536).

Jungle Adventure Camps

Black Rock ECO Jungle Tours are not for everyone, but these are great getaways for those who thrill to the outdoors, with vistas that include jungle foliage, wildlife, and the unspoiled Macal River. Be prepared that the last leg to Black Rock is a hike along a small footpath for about 20 minutes; the *only* way in. Guests stay in permanently staked, roomy tents, with two beds, screens, and palapa waterproof roofs overhead. Excellent food is served in an open-air dining pavilion. Though in a primitive setting, Black Rock has used modern technology to provide solar electricity, solar hot water, and solar water pumps. From here guests strike out on their own to hike, explore on horseback or canoe, swim and lounge around the riverside beach, watch birds, or take day-trips to nearby caves and Maya archaeological sites. Rates are US$36 s, US$42 d, US$46 t. Meals are US$5 full breakfast, US$6 lunch, US$10 dinner. For more information contact Caesar Sherrard (Box 48, San Ignacio, Belize, C.A.; tel./fax 92-2341).

If you aren't driving a vehicle, the easiest way to get to Black Rock is to hop the airport bus going to Belize City, get on either Novelo's or Batty's bus on the way to San Ignacio, and asked to be dropped off in front of **Caesar's Place**, at Mile 62 on the Western Highway.

Clarissa Falls Cottages (Mile 5.5 on Benque Viejo Rd.) is laid-back resort where guests stay in simple stick and thatch cottages, with inner paneled walls, two twin beds and a hammock space in each, and room to add a cot; separate toilet and shower building. Activities include horseback riding (US$10 per hour, pp, with guide), and from here it is a nice walk along the

Mopan River to the Maya archaeological site of Xunantunich. You can see the ruins from Clarissa Falls Cottages. The dining room serves mostly Mexican food, including a few specialties that including black mole soup and great Mexican-style tacos. Rooms are moderately priced at US$8 pp. Food can be as inexpensive as US40 cents for an order of tacos, to US$4 for a full meal. This is a food-hangout for locals; tel. Chena Galvez (owner), (93) 2424, or contact Tom Waite at **Belize Whitewater Floats,** tel. (907) 733-2384.

Cosmos Camping is another small settlement for campers. Located a half mile from the center of San Ignacio on Branch Mouth Rd., right along the river. You'll have a choice here of two cottages with beds, one cottage with hammocks, as well as hammock shelters for those traveling with their own hammock. Kitchen facilities are available as well as flush toilets, showers, and a laundry area. Rates are US$4 for camping (with your own equipment), US$5 camping and renting a hammock, US$4 to rent tent, US$1 extra pp. The cottages are US$5 s, US$7 d. For more information contact Tuula Nordling (Cosmos Camping, San Ignacio, Belize, C.A.).

Everyone who stays at the simple **Rancho Los Amigos** has nothing but good things to say about it. The family that runs these budget casitas (Ed and Virginia Jenkins and clan) exemplifies the hospitality of Belize. Here, on 88 acres in San Jose Succotz, one mile from the **Xunantunich ferry,** you won't find electricity or running water; instead on the top of a hill the thatch huts are built on a Maya mound—and whether it's the vibes from the ancient history buried below or otherwise, the sky seems bluer, the spring water purer, and the stars brighter than usual. Virginia is a great cook; don't miss her fettuccini Alfredo and scrumptious home-baked bread. Rooms are US$15 pp, including a full breakfast and dinner (vegetarian available); tel. (93) 2261.

DIANA LASICH-HARPER

BENQUE VIEJO

Eight miles beyond San Ignacio on the Western Highway going toward the Guatemala border is **Benque Viejo,** the last town on the Belize side (the border is about one mile farther). Like the rest of the area the houses are on posts, and the town is scattered across hillsides with lush mountains standing guard. This is a quiet little town with a low-key, peaceful atmosphere. Benque Viejo has been greatly influenced by the Spanish, both from its historical past when Spain ruled Guatemala and later when Spanish-speaking *chicleros* (chicle workers) and loggers worked the forest. The Latin influence persists with today's influx of Guatemalans. Many residents are Mopan Maya Indians, and many more of these descendents live in the nearby Maya village of **San Jose Succotz.** At one time Benque Viejo ("Old Bank"—riverside logging camps were referred to as banks) was a logging camp. This was the gathering place for chicle workers and logs were floated down the river from here to be shipped to England.

SERVICES

If you *must* spend the night, you have but a few choices, and these you should look over very well before committing yourself. The **Maya Hotel** and **Oki's** are both on George Street. Neither charges over US$9 per night. A couple of small restaurants offer simple menus; try the fried chicken at the Maya Hotel. Small general stores sell a little of everything: canned goods, sweets, sundries, and cold drinks. You'll also find a gas station, police department, fire station, and telephone service. This is a good place to fill your gas tank before entering Guatemala.

Note: See the "Travel Advisory" in the "Guatemala" chapter, p. 250.

Buses To And From Guatemala

Both Batty and Novelo buses move through town fairly often starting with a 6:30 a.m. departure from Belize City. Some bus drivers going to the border pick you up and waive the fee since it's so close. Traveling in the other direction (from Benque Viejo to Belize City) buses begin moving through at 4-10 a.m. Remember when traveling on Sundays in Belize, the schedule is much shorter, so check ahead of time.

At The Guatemala Border

The border is open 8 a.m.-12 p.m. and 2-6 p.m. Someone will let you through during off hours, but will charge an extra fee, both for you and your car. If you're trying to get to Tikal, take the 6:30 a.m. Batty bus from Belize City, which passes through Benque Viejo, crosses the bor-

Inside this local gas station in Benque Viejo you can buy cold drinks, cookies, and sundries.

OZ MALLAN

der, and arrives at the first town, Melchor de Mencos, about 10 a.m. Here it meets with the bus to Flores where you'll hope to connect with a bus to Tikal from the El Cruce junction. Occasionally you can hitch a ride, but if you're not a gambler, you may want to go directly to Flores where buses run more frequently to Tikal. (For more detailed information about crossing the border, traveling into Guatemala and Tikal, accommodations, and Maya archaeological sites, see "Guatemala," p. 250.) Those going straight to Tikal should change money at the bank in Melchor de Mencos (or even with the money-changers that hang out at the border station). The bank at Flores closes daily at 2 p.m. Tikal has no banks, and though hotels and restaurants will accept U.S. dollars and traveler's checks for payment, they will *not* change traveler's checks into Guatemalan quetzals.

Footnote About The Road Between Belize And Guatemala:

Readers often write and ask why I don't mention driving between the Cayo District and Tikal more frequently. Well, it isn't that we haven't traveled it; we have, many times. It can be an interesting, though bumpy, drive. When raining the road becomes a quagmire of very deep mud; we have seen it when the road was so scattered with cars that we just could not make it the entire way. But more to the point, often around Christmas, people traveling by car (and sometimes buses) on their way to or from Belize have been stopped by bandits and robbed of money and watches. I know of *no* case when the bandits caused injuries, but some of them have been known to carry guns, making it a scary experience.

Many of the small cottage resorts offer escorted trips in vans, and they keep their ears open for any rumbles. At the first hint of a problem they will cancel the trip. In some cases drivers run their vans in tandem with other resort vans—safety in numbers! In spring of '92, after several robberies, we traveled in one van while another rode shotgun, both with Guatemalan license plates and tinted glass. As many times as we have traveled that road, we have not been robbed, but we have spoken to those who have.

the road to Guatemala through Benque Viejo

SAN JOSE SUCCOTZ

For a good meal across from Xunantunich ruins, stop at the **Crystal Skull Restaurant,** tasty Belizean food in clean and neat surroundings, run by Teresita Cocum. As you make your way south on the Western Highway past the Xunantunich turnoff and before you arrive at Benque Viejo, the Mopan River runs alongside the road—more than likely you'll see women under shady trees scrubbing the family laundry on the rocks. Close by the kids have a good time playing and splashing around in the cool water. These are Mopan Maya from San Jose Succotz.

Ancestors of the Mopan Maya migrated from San Jose (located in Guatemala's Peten) and throughout the years have preserved the ancient Maya culture and folklore they brought with them to the isolated small village. In Succotz the first language is Mopan, and the people still wear the bright-hued fabrics that the women weave on their back-strap looms. The most colorful time to visit is during one of their fiestas. The two biggest celebrations are 19 March, feast day of St. Joseph, and 3 May, feast day of the Holy Cross. If you're interested in local art, check out the **Stone Maiden Arts & Crafts Shop** at the entrance to San Jose Succotz village, not too far from the Xunantunich ferry. You'll find local woodcarvings, baskets, jewelry, and stone (slate) carvings unique to Belize. Open from 9 a.m.-4 p.m., the shop is run by artist John Roberge, a transplanted Canadian.

CAYO DISTRICT SIGHTS

While traveling in Belize you'll pass through many quaint-sounding towns: **Roaring Creek, Black Man Eddy, Holdfast, Double Head Cabbage, Washing Tree, Gallon Jug, Teakettle,** to name a few. But let's back up for a little side trip; travel west on the Western Highway from Guanacaste Park through the small town of Teakettle and you'll soon get a glimpse of what you might mistake for the countryside of Europe. As you pass through Teakettle, take a right turn up Young Gal Road.

Drive through Black Man Eddy and when you get to Mile 59, follow the sign to **Spanish Lookout.** It's always a surprise for the tropics, but the landscape changes and you see neat barns and rolling green countryside. This is one of the Mennonite communities that brought a small bit of Europe with them and over the years have developed a fine agricultural industry supplying a large part of the milk, cheese, and chicken for the country.

Cross to the other side of the river to rejoin the Western Highway (continuing west) close to the British military camp at Holdfast. At Mile 62 on the right, **Caesar's Place** is a lovely spot to sit in the shade under the vines and trees; have a glass of wine or wander through the gift shop.

The impressive **Hawksworth Bridge** links the highway between Santa Elena and San Ignacio. As the only suspension bridge in Belize, it's a high-tech dot on the landscape of the low-key Belize countryside. It even has one of the few traffic lights in the entire country. In the past, whoever reached the center of the one-lane bridge first had the right of way, and the other vehicle had to back off the bridge; occasionally the local gendarme had to come along and measure car distances in order to settle the drivers' arguments. But that's a thing of the past now with a neat line of traffic waiting patiently at the red light. Old-timers say the water rose as high as this bridge during Hurricane Hattie!

Maya Art
In Cayo District check out the various art shops. Of the 14 art houses that you are apt to hear about in Belize, seven are located in Cayo; a couple of them are really outstanding. In Belmopan, Carolyn Carr paints and has created some lovely canvases. Animals are cherished subjects of hers, but my personal favorite is the painting she did that reminds us of what the old marketplace was like back in the early days of Belize. You can see her work in many Belizean shops; her studio is at her ranch in Belmopan, **Banana Bank Ranch,** Box 48, tel. (8) 22-677. (See "Cottage Resorts In The Cayo Countryside.")

Another shop to look into in Belmopan is **El Caracol Gallery & Gifts** (32 Macaw Ave., Belmopan, Belize, C.A.; tel. 8-22-394). **Caesar's Place** at Mile 62 on the Western Highway is noted for its fine woodwork, especially a uniquely designed folding hardwood chair that many visitors have shipped home. You'll also find beautiful black-coral jewelry (Box 48, San Ignacio, Belize, C.A.; tel. 92-2341). The **New Hope Trading Co.** specializes in exotic woodcrafts (Buena Vista Rd., San Ignacio, Belize, C.A.; tel. 92-2188).

Arts And Crafts
In San Jose Succotz Village, the Magana family business has grown into a fine shop called **Stone Maiden Arts & Crafts.** David Magana has begun working with the youth of the area, encouraging them to continue the art and crafts

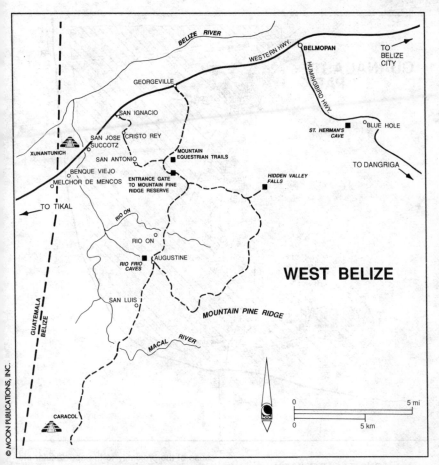

© MOON PUBLICATIONS, INC.

of their ancestors. In San Ignacio, you can't miss the sign for the **Arts And Crafts of Central America** shop on 1 Waight St., San Ignacio, tel. (93) 2351.

Probably the most famous Maya art gallery and museum is **Tanah Mayan Art Museum,** featuring the well-known Garcia sisters. Five young women with Maya heritage have begun recreating slate carvings reminiscent of their ancestors. The Tanah Museum building itself is built in the old Maya way with limestone and clay walls; the floor is a parquet of logs and limestone, and the roof is typical thatch of bay and palm leaves, picked and placed on the nights of the full moon to give them a longer life. These sisters are charming ambassadors of the San Antonio neighborhood, as well as clever artists who make hand-drawn art cards depicting the wildlife of Belize, Belizean dolls, native jewelry, and medicinal herbs (who more qualified than the nieces of Don Eligio Panti, Belize's most renowned bush doctor? See p. 196). If traveling to the **1,000 Foot Falls, Rio Frio Cave,** or the falls of the **Rio On,** stop by and visit the Garcias in San Antonio (Box 75, San Ignacio, Belize, C.A.).

© MOON PUBLICATIONS, INC.

GUANACASTE PARK

On the Western Highway at the junction of Hummingbird Highway, the road leads either south to Belmopan or north to Guanacaste Park. If going to Guanacaste, pack a lunch, bring a swimsuit, and take some time out at this quiet spot where the Belize River and Roaring Creek meet—it takes very little coaxing to cool off with a swim. The 56-acre park was originally the home of the former British city planner (who was commissioned after Hurricane Hattie in 1961 to relocate the capital). It's said that he chose the spot because of the proximity to the spectacular old guanacaste tree (also known as a tubroose). The official decided almost immediately that the meadow should be set aside as a government reserve for future generations to enjoy. The huge tree, well over 100 years old, is more than 25 feet in diameter and host to more than 35 species of exotic flora, including orchids, bromeliads, ferns, philodendrons, and cacti, along with a large termite nest and myriad birds twittering and fluttering in the branches—a tree of life! When rivers were the main method of transport, travelers stopped here to spend the night under the protection of its wide-spreading branches.

The only thing that saved the tree from the dreaded loggers was its crooked trunk.

As you enter the park, walk across the grassy field; go left to get to the trail that brings you to the guanacaste. Beyond the tree there's a looter's trench—someone long ago thought there was treasure buried here—which demonstrates how a looter excavates and works a would-be treasure site (including Maya structures). Continuing, the path meets the shore of **Roaring Creek,** the westernmost boundary of the park. This is a wonderful (and easy) trail; you may or may not see another hiker, but you'll certainly see unique birds, delicate ferns, flowers, and long parades of wiwi ants—"cutters" on the trail carrying their mini green umbrellas (really pieces of leaves that they're carrying back to their nest). From the entrance to the park, cross the meadow and veer to the right for the steps that lead down to the **Belize River.** Along the shore nature quietly continues its creation and subsistence pattern. The amate fig grows profusely on the water's edge and is an important part of the howler monkey's diet. In the middle of the whole scheme is the tuba fish, which eats the figs that fall into the water, dispersing the seeds up and down the river—starting more amate fig trees. And so it goes—on and on. At dusk on a quiet evening, howler monkeys roar the news that they're having dinner—keep your distance, world! The Belize River makes up the park's northern boundary. Its eastern section is the site of mahogany, sapodilla, bullet, and other hardwood trees—many covered with orchids and bromeliads. Picnic tables, benches, restrooms, and trash cans all are appearing slowly on the site, which is under the jurisdiction of the Belize Audubon Society, and most of the work is done by Peace Corps volunteers; the warden of the park is a soft-spoken Maya gentleman named Martin Auk.

XUNANTUNICH

This impressive Maya ceremonial center is located on a natural limestone ridge and provides a grand view of the entire Cayo District and Guatemala countryside. The tallest pyramid on the site, **El Castillo,** has been partially excavated and explored, and the eastern side of the structure displays a unique stucco frieze. The plaza of the ceremonial center houses three carved stelae.

Eight miles past San Ignacio on the Western Highway going toward Benque Viejo and the Guatemala border, you'll reach the turnoff and the Succotz Ferry (there's a small wooden sign on the side of the road). After another mile you'll reach Xunantunich. You can park here, hop on the free hand-cranked ferry that shuttles you across the river, and you have about a mile's hike up gentle hills to the site. If you wish, drive your car on the ferry (which operates daily 8 a.m.-5 p.m.) and then on to Xunantunich (still free).

TODD CLARK

Xunantunich

There's a small fee to enter the grounds, and a guide will explain the site: the history, what's been restored, and what's in the future. For more details about Xunantunich, see "Maya Archaeological Sites of Belize."

PANTI TRAIL

Not too far from Xunantunich and a short walk from Chaa Creek is **Ix Chel Farm** and the **Panti Trail.** Visitors are welcome to take part in a walking tour through the forest where they will see examples of plants and trees that can cause damage (scratches, rashes, poison) and then, close by, the antidote. Rosita Arvigo and husband Greg Shropshire are both graduates of Chicago National College of Naprapathy. Anyone interested in holistic medicine will be fascinated with the Panti Trail, named for the elderly Maya bush doctor, Don Eligio Panti, good friend, teacher, and mentor of Rosita's. It's a

OZ MALLAN

Rosita's fascinating Panti Trail at Ix Chel Farm

fun trip that can start in San Ignacio with a canoe ride down the placid Macal River to the docks at Ix Chel, by car (next door to Chaa Creek), or with any number of tour operators. From there, after checking in with Rosita, Greg, or one of her assistants, enjoy the stroll along the shady, tree-lined trail. Expect a fee, and if you want Rosita to escort you, the fee is more (*if* she is even available; there are other knowledgeable guides as well). Her lively, informative talk and nature walk takes about an hour. Around the house, small garden plots produce fresh vegetables and a pineapple or two, and fruit trees are scattered about. This is a highly recommended way to spend a day; everyone enjoys Rosita and her assistants. Research groups from around the world frequently come to huddle with Rosita and Don Eligio in their quest for a possible solution from the jungle-apothecary for both the AIDS virus and cancer. For more information about the herbs and roots, and details about the Panti Trail and Don Eligio Panti, the 96-year-old Mayan healer, write to Rosita Arvigo (General Delivery, San Ignacio, Cayo District, Belize, C.A.; tel. 92-2267). See also p. 56.

MOUNTAIN PINE RIDGE

For some travelers to Belize this area is the highlight of the trip. **Mountain Pine Ridge Forest Reserve** covers almost 300 square miles and only controlled logging is allowed. The road winds through the tropical foothills of the Cayo district, and gradually the terrain changes—it's always a surprise to discover this different look of sand, rocky soil, and tall pine trees. At first growth is sparse, but as you continue the pines are thick, and high roads and trails abound. As the road rises and the terrain begins to change, you are surrounded by tall granite boulders with rushing streams, small and large waterfalls, and patches of thick forest with the echoing calls of the *chachalaca* and tinnamou. Creases of land within narrow river valleys are rich with stands of tall hardwood trees, many covered with orchids and bromeliads. At certain times of the year bright-colored clouds of flamboyant butterflies float from tree to bush. Here and there small clearings have been carved out of the jungle by *milperos* (slash-

MAP: MOUNTAIN PINE RIDGE AREA

BELIZE RIVER — GEORGEVILLE — TO BELMOPAN
WESTERN HWY
SAN IGNACIO
CRISTO REY
CHIQUIBUL RD.
ROARING CREEK
TO BELMOPAN
HUMMINGBIRD HWY
TO DANGRIGA
BLUE HOLE
CAVES BRANCH
ST. HERMAN'S CAVES
SAN ANTONIO
BARTON CREEK
HIDDEN VALLEY FALLS
BALDY BEACON RD.
PRIVASSION CREEK
RIO ON
RIO FRIO CAVES
RIO ON PICNIC SITE
GRANITE CAIRN RD.
NAVEL RD.
AUGUSTINE
MACAL RIVER
RASPA RD.
SAN LUIS
GUACAMALLO BRIDGE

© MOON PUBLICATIONS, INC.

0   5 mi
0   5 km

and-burn farmers), and picturesque clusters of thatch huts surrounded by banana and cohune trees with delicate blossoms show Belizean life in the slow lane. A new breathtaking scene awaits around each bend.

Getting There
On the Western Highway from Belize City the turnoff for Mountain Pine Ridge is at Mile 65 at Georgeville. From here you head south up toward the mountains. These are not the smoothest roads to travel—unless you like to ride a horse, are a great trekker, or have access to a 4WD jeep, and it isn't raining. **Mountain Equestrian Trails** is just a few miles away and provides great horseback trips into Mountain Pine Ridge (tel. 82-3180, fax 82-3235). From the U.S. and Canada you can make arrangements with **International Expeditions** for tours

of this area; you'll be escorted by a naturalist who knows his/her way around not only the Mountain Pine Ridge but also the adjacent Chiquibul Rainforest and the Maya archaeological site of Caracol.

If driving, bear in mind that while part of the road is fine, the rest is rocky, uneven, and bumpy, and will shake even the sturdiest vehicle till the bolts drop out. Certain sections are impassable during the rainy season; if it's been raining ask before you head up. Those interested in camping check with the forest guard at the entrance of Douglas De Silva Reserve (formerly called Augustine); camping is permitted both at the entrance to the reserve and at Augustine Village, about 10 miles south; neither spot is particularly scenic. But traveling the circular route will take you past beautiful scenery and to the falls and the caves.

Waterfalls And Natural Pools

Follow the reserve's main road for about two miles beyond the entrance and you'll come to the turnoff for **Hidden Valley Falls.** From the turnoff the road keeps going down for about four miles, then you'll come to the falls and a picnic area. These spectacular falls plunge about 1500 feet over the granite edge down to the jungle. Hikers should be experienced if they decide to climb the rocks to the falls.

Pine Ridge offers other fascinating locales to explore. Continuing south toward Augustine Village you will cross the **Rio On** river, and climbing over an assortment of worn boulders and rocks will bring you to a delightful site with waterfalls and several warm-water pools; don't forget your camera.

The Cave System
Of Mountain Pine Ridge

At **Douglas DeSilva** (the western division of the Forestry Department) turn right and continue for about five miles. Follow the signs to the parking lot. From here visitors have a choice of exploring nature trails and two small caves on the road or continuing to the largest and most well-known river cave in Belize, the **Rio Frio,** with an enormous arched entryway into the half-mile-long cave. Filtered light highlights ferns, mosses, stalactites, and geometric patterns of striations on rocks. Each step stirs up the musty smells of the damp rocky cave. Watch where you walk; there are sinkholes here and there,

and a narrow stream flows along the gravel riverbed.

Accommodations

Travelers will find only a few places to stay nearby. For the moderate budget, the **Pine Ridge Lodge** is a small group of cement structures near the river with a total of eight rooms. Very simple, these cottages have private bathrooms with cold water showers and flush toilets, no electricity, screened windows, and screened porches. The open-air cafe serves good home cooking, fresh juices and fruits, eggplant parmigiana, and, as Gary (the owner) says, the best French toast in Belize (he makes it). The kitchen staff is in the process of building a large outdoor grill for barbecues. Owners Vicki and Gary Seewald advertise the **Pine Ridge Tavern** as being the "last stop for a cold beer before heading off to Caracol." Room rates are US$45 d for forest view, and US$85 for river view. The lodge is located 79 miles from Belize City, 19 miles from San Ignacio, seven miles north of the Rio On pools, and south of the Western Highway within the Mountain Pine Ridge Reserve. Write or call for more information (Box 2079, Belize City, Belize, C.A.; tel. 92-3310, 216-781-6888).

For the larger budget take a look at the lovely **Hidden Valley Inn.** It's always a surprise to find this upscale resort in the midst of tall sparse pine trees in the middle of nowhere. Set on 18,000 acres of private reserve, this is really a "getaway" vacation. The main house is the gathering

Rio On River cascades through the mountains.

OZ MALLAN

OZ MALLAN

Hidden Valley Inn

place for guests in several spacious public rooms: a comfortable lounge, card room, TV room, library filled with good reading material, and the dining room where dinner is served in candle-lit splendor. The 12 cottages have *saltillo* tile floors, vaulted ceilings, cypress-paneled walls, fireplaces, and picture windows, ceiling fans, screened louvered windows, comfy beds, and private baths with hot water. When the main electricity goes out at night, 12 volt bedside lamps and night-lights are available. For those who enjoy hiking, well-tended trails on the property lead past **Tiger Creek Pools and Falls, King**

Vulture Falls (where the king vulture nests), **Dragonfly Pool, Butterfly Falls and Crystal Pools, Lake Lollyfolly,** and the famous **Hidden Valley Falls** (also known as **1,000 Foot Falls**). For birders, bird blinds are set up where you may glimpse such beauties as orange-breasted falcons, rose-breasted grosbeak, indigo bunting, and the oscellated turkey. Picnic lunches provided. Bed and breakfast rates are US$77.50 s, US$105 d; lunch US$7.50, dinner US$17.50. Located on Cooma Carin Rd. (Mountain Pine Ridge, Box 170, Belmopan, Belize, C.A.; tel. 8-23-320, fax 8-23-334; in the U.S. 800-334-7942).

KATHY ESCOVEDO SANDERS

STANN CREEK DISTRICT

For those looking for the *real* rainforests of Belize, a trip to the Stann Creek District in southern Belize is in order. This section of the country has not been high on the list of advertised destinations, but that is all beginning to change. Of course this means more and more resorts will come along, changing life here ever-so-slightly at first—however, as more people arrive in response to the Mundo Maya movement, many new doors of financial opportunity are opening for the locals. This southern district of the country has a lot to offer, especially those who are looking for Mundo Maya ("World of the Maya"). As well as being one of the richer rainforests in the country (with more than 120 inches of rain per year), southern Belize offers the best beaches, waterfalls, jungle pools, vine-edged trails, and a plethora of hidden Maya cities of the past. More and more divers are discovering the southern cayes and their opulent undersea life.

DANGRIGA

The town of Dangriga, a Garifuna word meaning "standing waters," was formerly called Stann Creek. The small community is located on the coast, 36 miles south of Belize City as the crow (or Maya Airways) flies. However, the trip is much longer (100 miles) along the twisting, climbing road by car from Belmopan. The city of Dangriga is a bustling, though easygoing, place that is thriving because of the successful citrus industry that has finally begun a healthy growth (after more than 50 years). Tourism today attracts a moderate number of curious citizens-of-the-world, especially divers, because of Dangriga's location near the sea, its scenic beauty, and its rich cultural heritage. Both Stann Creek and Toledo districts are considered by some to be the most "Caribbean" sections of Belize.

THE PEOPLE

Dangriga, as all of Belize, is a rich mix of cultures,

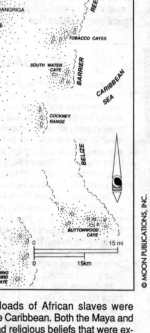

STANN CREEK DISTRICT

TO BELMOPAN &
BELIZE CITY

HUMMINGBIRD HWY.

MAYA MOUNTAINS

COLESON CAYE

NORTH STANN CREEK

POMONA

DANGRIGA

COMMERCE BIGHT

SITTEE RIVER

KENDAL

HOPKINS

TOBACCO CAYES

REEF

VICTORIA PEAK
(3675 ft)

COCKSCOMB RANGE

SOUTH WATER CAYE

BARRIER

KUCHIL BALUM

JAGUAR RESERVE

COCKSCOMB BASIN
FOREST RESERVE

RESERVE HEADQUARTERS

MAYA CENTER

CARIBBEAN SEA

COCKSCOMB BASIN

SOUTH STANN CREEK

COCKNEY RANGE

ALABAMA

SOUTHERN HWY.

RIVERSDALE

BELIZE

SWASEY BRANCH

MAYA BEACH

SEINE BIGHT

RUM POINT

BUTTONWOOD CAYE

MANGO CREEK

PLACENCIA

BIG CREEK

0   15 mi

0   15km

TO PUNTA GORDA

LAUGHING BIRD CAYE

© MOON PUBLICATIONS, INC.

including Garifuna, East Indians, whites, and Maya. The indigenous people of southern Belize are the Maya, from as far back as 3,600 years ago.

Dangriga Maya

Small villages of Maya still practicing some form of their ancient culture dot the landscape. Little is known of their early history except what has been learned from the amazing structures that are continually uncovered in the thick jungle. In more recent times (soon after Columbus visited the New World), records show that many of the Maya moved away from the coast to escape hostile Spanish and British intruders who arrived by ship to search for slaves. The independent Maya refused to be subjugated, so, as

a result, boatloads of African slaves were brought into the Caribbean. Both the Maya and the Africans had religious beliefs that were extraordinarily inconsistent with Christian lifestyles and both were considered subhuman at that time. As a result the Maya and the Garifuna for years kept to themselves.

Even now, the Mopan, Yucatec, and Kekchi continue to live much like their ancestors. Most of them practice some form of Christian religion integrated with ancient beliefs—in southern Belize the Kekchi have their own Mennonite church. But ancient Maya ceremonies are still quietly practiced in secluded pockets of the country, many in southern Belize, by the gentle unassuming Maya people. Curiously, today's

Maya have little connection with the Maya structures that remain. Not too far from Dangriga, many of these ceremonial centers have been discovered with indications that many more lie waiting under thick jungle growth.

Garifuna

The earliest Black Caribs were farmers, fishermen, trappers—and warriors—originating on St. Vincent Island in the West Indies. Here, escaped West African slaves mixed with the aboriginal people called Red Caribs.

Though the Black Caribs were dominated by the Europeans and confined to the islands of St. Vincent and St. Dominica, they never stopped their fight for freedom. They were persistent warriors, and under the leadership of a valiant fighter, Joseph Chatoyer, they continued the battle. But with European firepower against their bows and arrows, they were no match. The Caribs were put down in 1796, and in order to try to contain them, about 5,000 captives were moved once again to the Bay Islands off the coast of Honduras.

(CONTINUED ON PAGE 204)

GARIFUNA SETTLEMENT DAY

The hour before dawn we made our way through the darkness along the edge of the sea heading toward the persistent beat of distant drums. Orange streaks began to widen across the horizon as we climbed over a half-fallen wooden bridge spanning a creek, cutting a muddy path to the Caribbean. We were on our way to Dangriga on Garifuna Settlement Day, one of Belize's lively national holidays, celebrated each year on 19 Nov. to commemorate the arrival of the Garifuna people to Belize.

The ancestors smiled. Rains that had been pouring down for a week subsided, and by the time we reached the center of town and the river shoreline, crowds of revelers were beginning to gather in the breaking dawn. This was a day of reflection and good times in Belize; a severe contrast to Garifuna beginnings that for decades were filled with misery and tragedy.

Settlement Day is a happy celebration. Everyone dresses in colorful new clothes; and while waiting for the "landing," family, friends, and strangers from all over Belize catch up on local gossip, make new acquaintances, and enjoy the party. Sounds of beating drums emanate from small circles of people on both sides of the river; from the backs of pickup trucks and from rooftops. In lieu of drums, young men push through the

crowds shouldering giant boom-boxes that broadcast the beat. Excitement (and umbrellas) hang in the air as the assemblage waits for the canoes and the beginning of the pageant.

Garifuna history really began more than 300 years ago when two ships filled with African slaves were wrecked on the Caribbean's Windward Islands. The next century is shadowy and the only certainty is that with the passage of time they intermarried with the Carib people, creating the Garifuna. They were defeated and controlled over the years by the Spanish and British, the latter deporting them to the inhospitable island of Roatan off the coast of Honduras.

But now, in the early dawn, a cheer is heard from the crowd. Two dugout canoes are spotted paddling from the open sea into the river. Years ago, the first refugees from Roatan—men, women,

OZ MALLAN

and children—crowded into just such boats along with a few meager necessities to start a new life in a new land. Today's reenactment is orchestrated according to verbal history handed down through generations. Leaves and vines are wrapped around the arrivals' heads and waists. Drums, as well as baskets that carry simple cooking utensils, young banana trees, and cassava roots, are all among the precious cargo they originally brought to start their new life in Dangriga.

The canoes paddle past cheering crowds; no matter that this pageant is repeated every year (like the U.S.A.'s Fourth of July); each November is a reminder of the past, and even this outsider is swept along in the excitement and thoughts of what this day represents to the Garifuna citizens of Belize.

Like a winning athlete passing in review, the canoes travel up the river and under the bridge and back again so that everyone lining the bank and bridge can see them. When the "actors" come ashore they're joined by hundreds of onlookers. The colorful procession then proceeds through the narrow streets with young and old dancing and singing to the drumbeats; they proudly lead the parade to the Catholic church where a special service takes place. Dignitaries from all over Belize attend and tell of the past and, most important, of the hopes of the future.

The Catholic church plays a unique part in the life of the Garifuna. Some years back the church reached an unspoken, working agreement with the Garifuna: nothing formal, just a look-the-other-way attitude while their Garifuna parishioners mix Catholic dogma with ancient ritual. It wasn't always this way. For generations the people were forced to keep their religion alive in clandestine meetings or suffer severe punishment and persecution.

Rain, much like time, has not stopped the Garifuna celebrations nor the dancing that is an integral part of the festivities. Street dances traditionally held along village streets for many nights leading up to Celebration Day continue and are moved indoors to escape the flooded streets. Small bars and open *palapa* (thatch) structures are crowded with fun lovers and reverberate with the pounding of exotic triple drums (always three). Drums bring their magic, and parties continue with both modern *punta rock* and traditional dances into the early hours of the morning. The Garifuna are a people filled with music. The songs sung in the Garifuna language tell stories—some happy, some sad—and many melodies go hand-in-hand with daily tasks.

At an open *palapa* hut, three talented drummers begin the beat. Garifuna women who have lived through a past era, heavily influenced by their African beginnings, insist on marshaling the dances—the old way. The first tempo is the *paranda,* a dance just for women. A circle is created in the dirt-floored room and the elderly women begin a low-key, heavy-footed, repetitive shuffle with subtle hand movements accompanied by time-worn words that we don't understand but are told tells a tale of survival from the past.

Every few minutes a reveler filled with too much rum pushes through the circle of people and joins the dancing women. He's quickly chased out of the ring by an umbrella-wielding elder who aims her prods at the more vulnerable spots of his body. If that doesn't work she resorts to pulling the intoxicated dancer off the floor by his ear—a little comic relief that adds to the down-home entertainment.

The *paranda* continues, and little kids energetically join in the dances on the outside of the "circle" or watch wide-eyed from the rafters near the top of the *palapa* roof, entranced by the beat, dim light, and music—the magic of the holiday.

OZ MALLAN

The recurring rain adds an extra beat to the exotic cadence of the drums; dance after dance continues.

The *huguhugn* dance is open to everyone, but the sexy *punta* is the popular favorite, one couple at a time in the ring. Handsome men and beautiful women slowly undulate their bodies with flamboyant grace and sexual suggestion. From their African roots this is the courtship dance. In case you miss Settlement Day parties, stop by a bar or nightclub anywhere in Belize and you'll see locals doing a modern version called *punta rock*.

Living in a matriarchal society, the elder Garifuna women are trying hard to keep the old traditions alive. While English is the language of the country and taught in the classrooms of Belize, one of the concerns of the elders is the preservation of the ethnic language of the Garifuna.

Most of the older Garifuna women wear brightcolored dirndl skirts and kerchiefs tied low over their forehead, symbolic of days spent in the fields. Only a few wear the traditional costumes trimmed with shells; today's young females prefer T-shirts and jeans or modern tight skirts—and none wear a kerchief. The men wear jeans and years ago they traded their straw hats for baseball caps.

Freedom and integration into Belize in the 1800s was not easy. And though the Garifuna were allowed to settle in the Stann Creek District when they first arrived, the British isolated them from the rest of the country. They allowed them into Belize City only with 48-hour passes in order to let them sell their harvest. City dwellers who did no farming and for years were forced to exist on limited imported food welcomed this fresh produce.

The populace in general was frightened of the Garifuna in that early era, believing the lies that they ate babies and would cast evil spells; these stories were spread by slave owners who were convinced that their own slaves would run off and live with the outsiders if they got the chance to see the relative freedom that the Garifuna enjoyed in southern Belize. Eventually the Garifuna were accepted and given a voice in government affairs at the public meeting in Belize City.

During Settlement Day, a walk down the narrow streets takes you past small parties and family gatherings under stilted houses where dancing and singing is the rule, others enjoy holiday foods (including cassava bread), and drinks. If invited to share a cup of coffee dipped from an old blue porcelain kettle heavily laced with rum, join in!—it could turn out to be the best part of the celebration!

From the time that ships flying the Spanish flag began using the ocean to export the riches of the New World to Spain, the Bay Islands (because of their location) were thrust into the middle of the fight over who would control these sea-lanes. At one time or another the fight included Dutch, English, French, and U.S. ships, either pirating or smuggling goods in and out of what Spain considered its own personal territory. The Bay Islands off Honduras shifted ownership regularly as all of those countries vied for control of the sea-lanes.

After arriving in the Bay Islands, the Caribs, still seeking peace, began wandering in their dugout canoes and over the years began to settle in coastal areas of Honduras, Guatemala, Nicaragua, and southern Belize. In 1802 the beginnings of a settlement took hold in Stann Creek with 150 Garifuna. They were an isolated band that supported themselves by subsistence

TODD CLARK

local produce market

fishing and farming. In 1823 a civil war in Honduras forced more Caribs to leave and they headed for Belize. On 19 Nov. 1823, they landed in Belize under the leadership of Alejo Beni and began what has been a peaceful, poor community. Only recently, after more than 150 years, has Dangriga become a thriving agricultural center thanks to the efforts of the whole community, including the Maya and the Caribs.

The Black Caribs are known today by the language they speak, referred to as both Garifuna and Garinagu. According to Phylis Cayetano, who devotes much of her time and effort into preserving the Garifuna culture and language, the group is a mixture of Amerindian, African, Arawak, and Carib, but the mothers were mostly Arawakan. They developed their own language, and, according to a dictionary that dates back to the 1700s, very few words are African; most are Carib.

The Garifuna continued to practice what was still familiar from their ancient African traditions—foods, dances, and especially music (consisting of complex rhythms with a call-and-response pattern that was an important part of their social and religious celebrations. An important person in the village is still the drum maker who continues the old traditions, along with making other instruments used in these often night-long singing and dancing ceremonies.

One of the most enduring customs, the practice of black magic known as *obeah,* was regarded with great suspicion and concern by the colonialists in Belize City. Even after laws were enacted that made it illegal for any man or woman to take money or other effects in return for fetishes or amulets, ritual formulas, or other magical mischief that could immunize slaves from the wrath of their masters, the practice continued—though in more secretive ways. (No doubt, if you have a need and have established a trust with the Garifuna, you can find an *obeah* man today.) The *obeah* works through dances, drumbeats, trances, and trancelike contact with the dead. Small, black, *puchinga* (cloth dolls), stuffed with black feathers can strike dread into the hearts of the Garifuna; if buried under the doorstep of an impending victim the doll can bring marital problems, failure in business, illness, or death. It's not unusual for sacrifices to involve the blood of live chickens and pigs. Small Garifuna children occasionally are seen with indigo blue crosses drawn on their foreheads to ward off evil spirits.

Shortly after the Garifuna established themselves in southern Belize they brought their produce in dugouts to sell in Belize Town where the people were delighted to have fresh vegetables. But because of the fear generated by the slave owners of Belize Town, when these southern people tried to become part of the Town Public Meeting, they were ostracized. The fear pervaded the colonial town for many years.

Now, each year on 19 Nov., the whole country remembers the day the Garifuna arrived in Belize, and **Settlement Day** is celebrated with a reenactment of the landing in 1823—a happy celebration and an opportunity for the curious to witness the exotic tempos of Garifuna dancing and singing. Be adventurous and taste the typical, though unusual, Garifuna foods. If you drink too much "local dynamite," (rum and coconut milk), have a cup of the strong chicory coffee said by the Garifuna "to make we not have *goma*," (a Garifuna hangover).

Recognizing that schooling is essential, the Garifuna, along with the entire country of Belize, are staunch advocates of education—every desk in the classrooms of Dangriga is filled. In many schools across the country, Garifuna women excel as teachers.

The people are, generally, still farmers; their plots often are located 5-10 miles outside of town. In the early days they walked the long distances; today they take a bus, tending their fields from early morning to late afternoon. The district's leading crop is citrus, and the people of Dangriga figure strongly in this production.

Traditionally and continuing today, the Garifuna raise cassava to make *eriba,* a flat bread made from the meal of the cassava root. The large bulbous roots of the shrubby spurge plant are peeled and grated (today mostly by electric graters, but formerly by hand—a long, tedious job on a stone-studded board). The grated cassava is packed into a six-foot-long leaf-woven tube that is hung from a hefty tree limb, then weighted and pulled at the bottom, squeezing and forcing out the bottom the poisonous juices and starch from the pulp. The coarse meal that remains is dried and used to make the flat bread that has been an important part of the Garifuna culture for centuries.

Today's Garifuna are still aloof and seldom marry out of their group. Most are still superstitious; however, a friend is treated warmly. The women are extremely hard-working, the central influence of the family, and generally the caretakers of the family farm.

White Settlers

The earliest white settlers were Puritans from the island of New Providence in the Bahamas. These simple people implemented their knowledge of raising tobacco on nearby offshore cayes (today called Tobacco Cayes), began a trading post (also known as a "stand," that over time

deteriorated to "Stann"), and spread south into the Placencia area. The trading post ultimately faded away, and Dangriga continued its almost stagnant existence. During the American Civil War, arms dealers became familiar with the Belizean coast. In the 1860s British settlers in Belize encouraged Americans to come and begin a new life in Belize. Hundreds of Confederates did arrive after the Civil War and began clearing land to develop. However, it was not to last. Most of the American settlers returned to the U.S., though one group of Methodists from Mississippi stayed in Toledo District long enough to develop 12 sugar plantations. By 1910 most of the Mississippians were gone. During U.S. Prohibition, boats decked out as fishing crafts ran rum from Belize to Florida.

Despite its slow start, today's Dangriga is a community, population about 9,000, with a bright future of growth.

AGRICULTURE

Over the millenia, rivers and streams gushing from the Maya Mountains have deposited a rich layer of fertile soil, making the coastal and valley regions ideal farming areas. The banana industry, once vital in the area, was wiped out by a disease called "Panama Rot" many years back. However, with new technology, a strain of bananas has been developed that appears to be surviving and promises to grow into a profitable operation.

Stann Creek's citrus industry produces Valencia oranges and grapefruit, which are then processed (on-site) into juice—one of Belize's most important exports. The business center of the citrus industry, Dangriga has rebounded with vigor since being wiped out by Hurricane Hattie in 1961. The town itself bears little resemblance to its big brother, Belize City. Dangriga has a bright potential in agriculture.

SIGHTS

Caves

On the way to Dangriga from Belize City via the Hummingbird Highway, go 11 miles past Belmopan and look for a sign that says St. Herman's

WADE BEYER

Blue Hole on the Hummingbird Highway

Cave. Take the turnoff to the right (at Mile 44) and after about two miles you'll come to the long steep stairway (to the right) leading to the **Blue Hole,** with gushing water that soon disappears into the earth. Tall shade trees surround the hole and vines dangle into the water; don't try to play jungle boy and swing on these vines since they pull from shallow roots with the slightest tug. **Note:** Don't confuse this inland Blue Hole with the famous diving Blue Hole in the Caribbean.

This entire area is a labyrinth of caves where the ancient Maya once lived and roamed; some of the caves still show signs of rituals long past. A variety of caves lie in the hilly limestone country and can be cathedral-like with ceilings hundreds of feet high or narrow passages that go on for miles—some with spots of sunlight beaming through holes from the outside and reflecting on stalactites and stalagmites, others with underground streams. And while you won't likely find any Maya living in the caves, you will find fascinating bats. Expect lots of company at these sites on weekends and holidays; during the week you'll usually have the place to yourself! Bring a flashlight and wear sturdy walking shoes. The surrounding lush rainforest is thick with tropical plants, delicate ferns, bromeliads, and orchids. As you get closer to Dangriga, the rainforest gives way to vast groves of citrus.

The Hershey Factory

Continuing on the Hummingbird Highway south toward Dangriga you'll begin to see cleared

patches where farms are thriving. The road takes you past the **Hummingbird Hershey Factory.** Anyone interested in how Hershey makes chocolate is welcome to take a look. If it's the right time of the year, the aroma of roasting cacao will drive chocoholics mad. Just beyond the factory are acres of cacao trees; notice the unusual yellow-green pods growing from the trunks of the trees.

Dangriga Art

Dangriga is home to the well-known **Warribaggabagga Dancers** and the **Turtle Shell Band.** This is the heart of Garifuna folk culture. The music and dancing are an enchanting mixture of the various cultures of southern Belize, including syncopated African rhythms. Some of Belize's most accomplished artists make Dangriga their home. Benjamin Nicholas invites the public to visit his studio (27 Oak St.).

The drums and other typical musical instruments are favorite souvenirs to take home. Women make charming purses woven from reeds. Another unique momento is a mask, carved and painted by an artisan, used during various ceremonies in the south of Belize, both in Maya and Garifuna ceremonies. **Note:** There have been a couple of complaints from readers who have commissioned artwork with payment in advance. Some of these people did not receive exactly what was expected. Perhaps only a partial advance payment would be better.

ACCOMMODATIONS

Along the beachfront just out of town, one of the more modern hotels in Dangriga, **Pelican Beach Resort,** offers fine services, including private bathrooms, a restaurant/bar, a fine beach location, and telephones; credit cards and traveler's checks are accepted. The rooms are simple but clean, and we've just heard that several new rooms may be finished by the time you read this. A Full American Plan is available. Sightseeing trips to the Cayes or to the Jaguar Preserve can be arranged through the hotel. You can walk to Dangriga town (about 15 minutes) along the shore. Rates are with meals, US$65-82 s, US$100-125 d, without meals US$38-49 s, US$48-63 d. Write or call the Pelican Beach Resort for reservations (Box 14, Dangriga, Stann Creek District, Belize, C.A.; tel. 5-22-044, fax 5-22-570).

Downtown Hotels

Along the river, look for an unexpected surprise, **Jungle Huts Hotel,** run by the local dentist, Arthur Usher and his wife, Beverly. You'll find hot water, tiled private bathrooms, pleasant furniture, and two double beds in each of the four rooms in the hotel. The hotel is very secure (located behind their home). They also have four cabañas, but they aren't nearly as nice as the hotel rooms. At last report the Ushers were dredging the river to create a nice beach for their guests. Price per room is US$63.

The Hub guesthouse has five (usually clean) simple rooms with private baths, two with shared bath; some rooms have picturesque river views (look at the rooms before you check in and make certain security on windows, privacy, etc., satisfies you). Room service is available during restaurant hours; breakfast, lunch, and dinner are served. Rates are US$25 s, US$40 d. It is run by Gasper Martin, who is always willing to offer tourist info (573A 8th, Riverside, Dangriga, Stann Creek District, Belize, C.A.; tel. 5-22-397). The bus for Placencia (uncomfortable) leaves daily from the Hub at 3 p.m.

The **Bonefish Hotel,** located on Mahogany Rd., is a pleasant little place with eight rooms, private baths, a/c, and a restaurant and bar—moderate prices, call (5) 22-165/22-447.

Leo Stanley's **Rio Mar Hotel** is a budget guesthouse with tiny clean rooms and paper-thin walls for about US$10 s, US$15 d. For those interested in exploring the offshore cayes, the manager at Rio Mar can arrange trips to South Water Caye. Trips to these cayes are usually more expensive than trips to the more well-known cayes, such as Caye Caulker. For more info write or call the Rio Mar Hotel (977 Waight St., Box 2, Dangriga, Stann Creek District, C.A.; tel. 5-22-010).

Other basic hostelries are **Catalina's Hotel,** US$13 s (35 Cedar St.; tel. 5-22-390), and **Riverside Hotel,** simple and comfortable with shared baths and fans, US$10 s (5 Commerce St.; tel. 800-256-7333, 5-22-168, fax 5-22-296).

Pelican Inn

TODD CLARK

Hub Guest House

TODD CLARK

FOOD

In Dangriga town don't forget what time it is; the small cafes are only open during meal times. **The Hub** serves good traditional Creole dishes of rice and chicken for about US$2. For a change of pace try the **Burger King.** Yes, the Burger King—maybe not *the* Burger King, but they serve great burgers, fries, shakes, ice cream—oh yes, and conch soup. The **Rio Mar Hotel** also has a bar and restaurant.

GETTING THERE

It pays not to be in a big rush when meandering the highways and byways south of Belize City. If driving, you must first travel west to Belmopan and then double back going southeast on Hummingbird Highway—the area directly south of Belize City is swampy and marshy. Building roads through swamps and marshes takes lots of money so up until now it's just been easier to go around the problem areas. Also, "highway" doesn't necessarily denote a smooth, paved road. Most of the highways in southern Belize are graded, potholed, dirt roads that can be impassable during the rainy season (June-Oct.). If you're looking for "fast," the quickest way to get to the southern end of Belize is either by plane or by boat (36 miles from Belize City to Dangriga). Because there isn't a scheduled boat trip to

Dangriga, ask around—either at the Belize City docks by the Shell station, your hotel, or the Belize Tourist Office (53 Regent St.) in Belize City. Flights are available from Belize City to Dangriga Mon.-Saturday. Check with Maya Airways for current schedules and fares; tel. (2) 77-215, (2) 44-032, fax (2) 30-585.

Those inclined to drive will do best with a 4WD vehicle (available to rent) for the 100 rough miles; the reward is a chance to see the countryside, tropical scenery, small villages, large tracts of citrus fruits that smell wonderful, and the people. **Drivers:** Remember to fill up your gas tank whenever you run across a gas station; a fill-up at Belize City should get you to the next gas at Dangriga.

From Belize City's Pound Yard Bridge the **Z-Bus** offers several departure times daily: 10 a.m., 12 p.m., 2 p.m., and 4 p.m. (fare US$4); departure times from Dangriga daily: 5 a.m., 5:30 a.m., 9 a.m., 10 a.m. (US$4). Call for schedule changes; in Belize City call (2) 73-937, in Dangriga call (5) 22-211.

NEARBY DESTINATIONS

Hopkins

Hopkins is a low-key Garifuna fishing village about eight miles south of Dangriga. Wooden boats are dragged onto the beach when fishermen are finished for the day, making for picturesque photos. Craftsmen carve dugout canoes out of one large tree trunk and weave their own nets—life is simple here. The small seaside village, four miles from the main road, has about 800 people and gets only occasional visitors.

However, the **Hopkins Women's Cooperative** at Sandy Beach at the end of the village offers three buildings with nine rooms for rent: Four have private baths; others share a bathroom, outhouse-style. These accommodations are *extremely* basic, but generally clean. Meals are served. Prices start at US$7 twin, outside bath, and the most expensive is US$27.50 d, private bath. Don't expect too much and you'll enjoy your stay in the village. Though located right on the beach, sometimes the shoreline looks pretty trashy, although the women said they were going to start having someone clean it regularly.

Ask around; some women in the village are happy to have a guest at the table for a small fee; the same goes for pitching a tent along the beach.

Hopkins is one of the best places to join in the festivities for Garifuna Settlement Day. You can probably safely drop in and find a room most of the year, *except* around Garifuna Settlement Day (19 November). Or you can make a couple of phone calls in advance. I say a *couple* because Hopkins has only a community phone. The procedure is to call (5) 22-033 and tell whomever answers what time you will call back and that you want to talk to Marleen Castillo, Alberta Coleman or someone from the Women's Co-op for information about rooms.

Cockscomb Basin

The land rises gradually from the coastal plains to the **Maya Mountains;** the highest point in the Cockscomb Basin range is **Victoria Peak** (3,675 feet). Heavy rain along the granite peaks of the Maya range (as much as 160 inches a year) runs off into lush rainforest thick with trees, orchids, palms, ferns, abundant birds, and exotic animals, including peccaries, anteaters, armadillos, tapirs, and jaguars. Until recently, the jaguar was a prize for game hunters. Today the beautiful cat is protected in the Cockscomb Basin Jaguar Preserve.

For the archaeology buff, check out the following ruins found in the vicinity of Cockscomb Basin: **Pomona** on North Stann Creek, **Kendal** on the Sittee River, and **Pierce** on South Stann Creek.

Cockscomb Basin Jaguar Preserve

A large tract of approximately 155 square miles of forest was declared a forest reserve in 1984, and in 1986 the government of Belize set the region aside as a preserve for the largest cat in the Americas, the jaguar. The area is alive with wildlife, including the margay, ocelot, puma, jaguarundi, tapir, deer, paca, and hundreds of bird species. And though you probably won't see the large cats roaming during the day (they hunt at night), it's exciting to see a paw print (they're large!) or signs that the cat does indeed exercise ownership of this jungle. The

Dangriga coastline

TODD CLARK

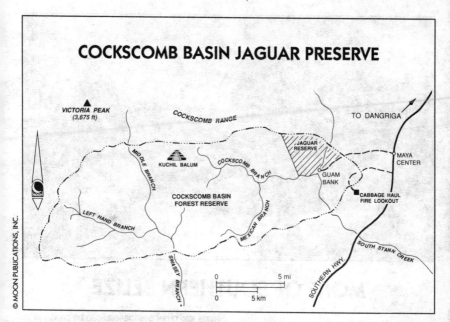

COCKSCOMB BASIN JAGUAR PRESERVE

peccary is said to be the jaguar's preferred diet, but according to locals the jaguar enjoys a love/hate relationship with the animal. Indian legend has it that the jaguar learned to climb trees in order to get away from the peccary because, as large and feared as the jaguar is, a group of the pig-like peccaries can tear the great cat apart. The jaguar prefers to search from its tree branch for a single peccary. Most of the hotels in southern Belize provide transportation and guided tours of the wildlife preserve, or you can make arrangements with your hotel in other parts of the country for a side trip to southern Belize.

Maya Center Village
This small town's claim to fame is the office of the **Cockscomb Basin Jaguar Reserve.** Check in here if you're interested in seeing the reserve (or the remains of the Maya ceremonial site called **Kuchil Balum**). It's easy to get lost without a guide (available at Maya Center).

TODD CLARK

MORE OF SOUTHERN BELIZE

SOUTHERN CAYES AND VICINITY

Blue Marlin Lodge is a short trip from Dangriga at South Water Caye. Here guests will find fishing, diving, and snorkeling the main events, along with a sandy beach, blue sea, private baths, and good food served in a dining room built over the sea. The dome units are unique with a/c, beautiful furniture, and immense bathrooms, phone service at the office and well-kept grounds. Seven-night packages, including room, meals, and diving or fishing, range from US$1195 to US$1950 pp. Nondivers and nonfishermen start at US$1100 s to US$975 d pp p/d. Packages also include a roundtrip flight from Belize City and the ongoing boat trip from shore to the caye. Dome units are US$500 s or d for seven nights. The trip alone is a modern-day expedition. Diving classes for certification are available.

South Water Caye is one mile from the **Smithsonian Marine Biology Institute Laboratory** located on **Carrie Bow Caye** (visitors welcome) and two miles from **Twin Cayes** where manatees play in the sea. Trips to both is-

lands and other destinations can be arranged at the lodge. Write or call for more information (Box 21, Dangriga, Belize, C.A.; tel. 5-22-243, fax 5-22-296).

A British organization called **Coral Caye Conservation** has a group of volunteers headquartered at South Water Caye doing a study on how tourism is affecting the cayes and their environment. The volunteers (fewer than 30) are all divers and study the fish, sea grasses, algae, currents, and tides, and test seawater samples regularly looking for changes. Volunteers also investigate the culture of the people, lifestyle changes, and their boating activities.

GALES POINT

A small village originally established by logwood cutters is located on a two-mile-long peninsula that juts into the Southern Lagoon; both called Gales Point. Gale's Point is about 15 miles north of Dangriga and 25 miles south of Belize City. The Southern Lagoon is part of an extensive estuary surrounded by thick mangroves. Their tangled roots provide the perfect breeding grounds for sport fish, crabs, shrimp, lobster, and a host of other marinelife. Rich beds of sea grass line the bottom of the lagoon and support a population of manatees. These gentle mammals are often seen basking on the surface of the water, or coming up for air (which they must do about every four minutes).

Access from Belize City in the dry season can be by road (during the rainy season the road becomes a quagmire), or by boat, winding through the mangrove-lined canals and across the Sibun River before going through the Northern and Southern lagoons. The only accommodations available are at **Manatee Lodge.** This lodge caters almost entirely to fishermen on week-long package tours; however, they will rent to overnighters for a minimum of two nights. The lodge is really a fishing camp with a tropical ambience, situated on the northern end of Gales Point. Staff are descendants of the original settlers of the village. Rooms are spacious, have private bathrooms, and are connected to the main buildings by elevated walkways. Along with outstanding fishing (in 1989 the largest tarpon caught weighed in at 188 pounds, along with a 28-pound snook and a 45-pound cubera), expeditions to all the exciting nature reserves can be arranged. Bring your favorite rods and lures (limited supplies are available at the lodge). Rates are based on one-week stays, Sat.-Sat., and include roundtrip ground/water transport between Belize International Airport and Gales Point, meals, double room, boat, and guide. Rates are US$1065 pp double occupancy, US$1265 s. Independent travelers must book a minimum of two nights, US$90 d, US$60 s; meals not included. For more information contact Manatee Lodge (Box 1242, Belize City, Belize, C.A.; tel. 800-334-7942, 904-222-2333, fax 904-222-1992).

PLACENCIA PENINSULA

Belizeans and visitors alike agree that the finest beaches in the country are along this 11-mile slender strip of land called the Placencia Peninsula. It feels like an island with the Caribbean on one side and the Placencia Lagoon on the other. It is predicted that eventually this will be the next big tourist development *(Come quickly!)*. Placencians will tell you that the best time to vacation here is *anytime* (although more rain falls May-Nov.). There's an informality and relaxed atmosphere that's very special and highly contagious. Nature provides white sand fringed with waving green palms and the azure sea; the reef can be seen in the distance. The water is clear enough to watch fish through the glasslike surface only occasionally rippled by gentle breezes. And from the Placencia coast you can hoist anchor and within a short time find a score of idyllic offshore cayes.

PLACENCIA TOWN

Located at the southern tip of the palm-dotted peninsula Placencia Village is more than 100 miles south of Belize City. To get there you can travel by land, sea, or air. Placencia has been a fishing village from the time of the Maya, outside of the intrusion of a pirate settlement now and

then. Even with the arrival of tourists, it is still home to many fishermen. Modern conveniences (including electricity) also have arrived!

The town itself is about a mile long. A few delightful guesthouse resorts have developed in the area along the coast, and the people who run these isolated resorts offer a warm pioneer spirit of cordiality. Fortunately (for now at least) they all fit into the environment—Placencia hasn't been spoiled by high-rise, jet-set, hundreds-at-a-time tour groups that have filtered into and transformed many other once-placid Caribbean locations.

"Downtown" Placencia

In Placencia, there really isn't a main road through the "downtown business section," but there *is* a "main sidewalk" about 20 inches wide with houses and businesses located on both sides. The townsfolk better keep this sidewalk forever; it receives almost as much publicity as Beverly Hills' Rodeo Drive. If I had to pick a "central downtown" or "heart" of Placencia town it would probably be the post office. Cancel that image of a staid business-type structure with hustling clerks rushing to and fro. Placencia's post office is an open-air affair near the sea and is manned by one of the most well-known characters in town, Doris Lesie. Here, you not only

The Placencia post office is really a gathering spot for many services besides the mail; it's a great place to sniff out current activities and local gossip.

OZ MALLAN

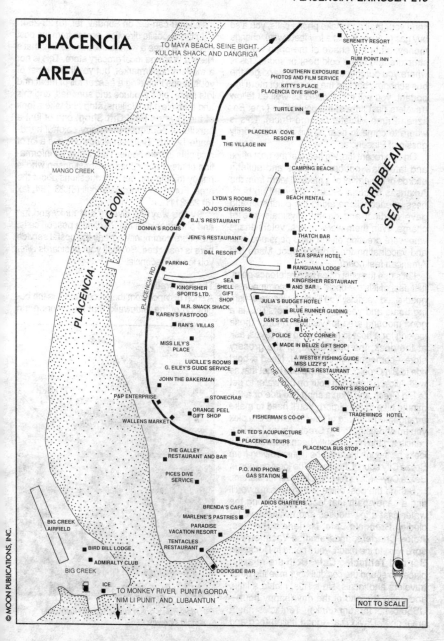

send your mail and make phone calls, you also buy gas (a pump is just a few feet away), change money, sit in the shade of the open wooden structure and buy a cold beer or soda. This is where you purchase airline tickets and get the bus schedule back to the big city; but more important, you will meet locals as well as fellow travelers (last time at the post office I met Belizean Prime Minister George Price). This is where to come to hear all the news and daily gossip of Placencia.

On one recent trip, we heard at the post office and later saw notices on trees and bulletin boards of the arrival of a medical team from the Arkansas National Guard. They set up business at each village along the peninsula and gave medical and dental physicals free of charge. With them were several veterinarians who were greeting all the local dogs and cats and vaccinating them on the spot. Made this American feel *good!*

Let's use the post office as a reference point; just east of it is the dock, which accommodates good-sized vessels. You'll see a mixture of fishing boats and yachts in the harbor. This is a good mooring area for visitors, and for those looking for a boat to head out to the cayes, ask at the dock, the post office, or the grocery store—someone will direct you. Need a boat ride to Big Creek? This is the place to get that as well. Allow a good half hour on the water to get to Big Creek and then a short taxi ride or a 20-minute hike to the airport. You'll need to make arrangements ahead of time to have a taxi pick you up shoreside in Big Creek. **Note:** The Placencia airstrip has recently been repaved and it looks as though there will be flights arriving from Belize City soon. Check with the local airlines in Belize City—Maya Air and Island Air for starters.

Behind the post office (southern side) you'll find a sandy path that leads south along the water past a few houses and businesses, including **Brenda's Cafe, Marlene's Pastries, Adios Charters,** and **Paradise Vacation Resort.** Next to the resort, you'll come to **Dockside Bar** and **Tentacles Cafe.** Both are relaxing places to spend the cocktail hour meeting other travelers and locals; sip a little, nibble a little, and enjoy the end of the day (happy hour—US50 cents for rum drinks). Tentacles has a great chef, David Dial—good Italian food and

it's all-you-can-eat on Sunday, tel. (6) 23-254.

In the opposite direction, across from the post office, you'll see a warehouselike building; that's **Harald Wallens** local grocery store. This is not a modern supermarket, but you'll find most of your needs including a freezer full of meat and lots more, plus produce and sundries, and this and that. Next to Wallens, stop and take a look at the **Orange Peel Gift Shop,** one of just a handful of boutiques that carry colorful handmade T-shirts, Belizean woodwork, and a lot of nice gifts to take home. This is also an information center run by Joanne Christiansen who is happy to help you out with questions about the area. For more information call (6) 23-184, fax (6) 23-211.

By the way: As diverse and funky and fun and photogenic as the Placencia post office is, the entire community agrees the postal service here is really bad. So, mail your postcards *after* you leave Placencia.

The Sidewalk
A short distance from the grocery store is the beginning of the "sidewalk" that meanders north

Placencia's "main street," the 20-inch-wide main sidewalk

lined with small businesses. Just off the sidewalk you'll find the **fishermen's co-op, ice, guide services, fishing services,** and **Made in Belize,** a cute little gift shop, where you'll find a lending library, hand-painted T-shirts, hand-embroidered Maya calendars, baskets (made by Guatemalan women just across the border), beads, and earrings. And if you need them, this is where you'll find the **police.** If you're hungry check out **Cozy Corner, Jene's** and **Kingfisher Restaurant and Disco.** At the end of the sidewalk you'll be at the beach designated for campers, tents and all.

Seine Bight

Seine Bight is a Garifuna village of simple one-room wooden houses on stilts and about 550 people. Most of the men are fishermen and the women tend the family garden, which they depend on for their basic food needs. Visitors will not find overnight lodgings here, and it takes a while for the locals to strike up a friendship. In fact, unless you make the first move, about all that happens is that people will look you over, especially the kids.

The people here are different; they have a carefree intact culture that smacks of ancient tribal customs. Men and women have a major split; the women have their own language that they say the men don't understand. The men will do absolutely nothing that might be construed as women's work. According to the women, the men lounge around in hammocks and drink most of the day. However, they have been known to help a stranger with car trouble. Ask before you take pictures, and accept "no" graciously.

However, in Seine Bight (2.5 miles from Maya Beach), be sure to take an evening and go native; discover the one-of-a-kind **Kulcha Shack** (pronounced "shock"). By day it's just another small forlorn structure on the beach with some friendly people serving drinks and snacks. But at night it takes on magic. You'll hear the haunting drums of the Garifuna accommpanied by melodies from the past. If you're lucky enough to have a translator with you, you'll learn a bit of Garifuna melodrama. The drummers know their craft well, and with reservations on the weekends, you'll see modern entertainment (such as *punta rock*) as well as the traditional fare.

The lamp-lit cafe serves authentic Garifuna food, good entertainment, and for a great souvenir to take home, ask to see Darlene's (the owner's wife) handmade Garifuna dolls (about US$20). For the special dinner and show, minimum of four people, the price is US$25 pp; make reservations and call before 6 p.m., tel. (6) 22-015.

KULCHA SHACK MENU— A FEW GARIFUNA DISHES

Hudut: fish simmered in thick coconut milk with herbs and cooked over an open fire—served with *fu-fu* (beaten plantain).

Tapow: green banana cut in wedges and simmered in coconut milk with fish, herbs, and seasonings—served with white rice or *ereba* (cassava bread).

Seafood Gumbo: a combination of conch, lobster, shrimp, fish, and vegetables, cooked in coconut milk, herbs, and grated green banana or plantain—served with rice or *ereba* and Irish Moss (a seaweed shake).

SIGHTS

When visiting Placencia allow yourself to be lolled into a lazy funk with the beautiful sea, sandy beaches, and a chance to meet the friendly people of Placencia. Once you've relaxed and you're ready to go again, this is a great hub to investigate the surrounding countryside. In Placencia you can be as busy as you desire with snorkeling, beachcombing, scuba diving, or land trekking to the Maya Mountains, the Jaguar Preserve, Maya ruins, or birdwatching and photographing the rich wildlife of the region. This is not to be missed. Consider yourself fortunate; you made it here before the crowds!

ACCOMMODATIONS

Budget Lodgings

Most of these budget lodgings are located within the central part of Placencia Town, and many are close to the "sidewalk." Check out **Ran's**

PLACENCIA ACCOMMODATIONS

BUDGET

D&L Resort, (6) 23-175, US$18 s, US$55 d
Julia's Budget Hotel, no phone, US$9 s, US$11 d
Lucille's Rooms, (6) 23-190, US$5.50 dorm, US$7.50 s, US$13 d
Lydia's Rooms, (6) 23-117, US$7.50 s, US$11.50 d
Paradise Vacation Resort, (6) 23-118/23-119, shared bath US$13, private bath US$23
Ran's Villas, (6) 22-027, US$25 s, US$32 d

MODERATE

Kitty's Place and Placencia Dive Shop, (6) 23-227, US$30-50 s, US$40-60 d
Sea Spray Hotel, (6) 23-148, US$25-35 s, US$50-60 d
Sonny's Resort, (6) 23-103, US$35 s, US$45 d, cabañas US$58
Tradewinds Hotel, (6) 21-322, US$50 four persons

EXPENSIVE

Placencia Cove Resort, (6) 22-024, US$75 pp d, includes meals
Rum Point Inn, tel. (6) 22-239, fax (6) 23-240, 32 Traminer Dr., Kenner, Louisiana 70065,
  (800) 747-1381, (504) 465-0769, fax (504) 464-0325, US$160 s, US$195 d, includes meals
Turtle Inn, 2190 Blue Bell, Boulder, Colorado 80302, (6) 22-069, (303) 444-2555, US$77 s, US$133 d,
  includes meals
Serenity Resort, tel./fax (6) 22-305, (800) 331-3797, US$75 s, US$85 d, extra adult US$25, child
  US$10. Meals available

If you wish to write for information, the address is:
  Placencia Village
  Stann Creek
  Belize
  Central America

Villas, two, simple one-bedroom apartments. Weekly rates are US$175-225, tel. (6) 22-027. **D&L Resort** prices range from US$18 s, US$55 d, to US$75 for four; tel. (6) 23-175. **Lucille's Rooms** offers five rooms; four share a bathroom for US$5.50 dorm, private bath for US$7.50 s, US$13 d; tel. (6) 23-190. **Julia's Budget Hotel** offers prices of US$9 s, US$11 d, no phone. **Lydia's Rooms** are US$7.50 s, US$11.50 d; tel. (6) 23-117. **Paradise Vacation Resort** is a newly renovated hotel with large rooms, king beds, private baths, and ceiling fans downstairs, and smaller rooms with two twin beds, shared baths, and free-standing fans upstairs. Rate for shared bath is US$13, for private bath US$23. Contact owner/host Dalton Eiley, (6) 23-118/23-119, for more information.

Moderate Lodgings

Conveniently located **Sonny's Resort** is a slightly worn but comfortable beachfront hotel. Bar and restaurant, as well as fishing, snorkeling, diving, and beachcombing, are available. Rates are US$58 cabañas, US$35 s, US$45 d; tel. (6) 23-103.

South of Sonny's look for **Tradewinds Hotel** on five acres near the sea. Three cabañas with spacious rooms, fans, refrigerators, coffee pots, and private yards are US$50 per night for four people; tel. (6) 21-322.

The **Sea Spray Hotel,** 30 feet from the beach, has both shared and private bathrooms. Attached to the hotel find the **Thatch Bar.** Rates for rooms with a community bath, US$25-35 s, with a private bath US$50-60 d; tel. (6) 23-148.

Kitty's Place and Placencia Dive Shop is owned and operated by Kitty Fox and Ran Villanueva. This is a small and comfortable spot, with rooms and apartments available. Kitty's offers all-day restaurant (three-course dinner each evening) and bar service, bicycle rentals, gift shop, and day-long trips. Rates for rooms are from US$30-50 s to US$40-60 d. The beach apartment sleeps two and rents for US$70-90 d daily. Ask for the combination weekly price for apartment and rooms. Kitty no longer offers camping. (Check at the post office for camping information.) For more information on Kitty's Place call (6) 23-227) or fax (6) 23-226.

More Expensive Lodgings
Serenity Resort is a new cabaña destination north of Rum Point Inn. Twenty-one acres extend from the white sandy beach on the sea to the lagoon. Currently six cabañas are complete (with six more on the drawing board), complete with a dining room with blue tablecloths and blue-upholstered chairs, and a thatched veranda that faces the sea. Rooms have tiled floors, hot water, ceiling fans, private bathrooms, and patios. There's no bar or alchoholic beverages. Rates are per cabaña US$75 s, US$85 d; tel. (6) 23-232, fax (6) 23-231; in the U.S. (800) 331-3797.

Placencia Cove Resort is a half mile north of Placencia on a 1,000-foot private strip of white beach. The resort has six waterfront cabins, each with two queen-size beds, private bathrooms, and home-cooked meals (try the delicious coconut pie made from coconuts grown on their own trees!). Many activities (including equipment) are available for the asking: snorkeling, scuba diving, fishing, and trips to the Jaguar Reserve and the Maya Mountains. A tennis court and rackets are an example of the amenities offered to guests. Rates are US$75 pp, double occupancy, including three meals (price is a little less in the summer). Boat transport from Big Creek is provided with a fee; if staying one to four days, cost is US$25, five to six days US$12.50, seven days gets it free; tel. (6) 23-233, (800) 662-3091, fax (6) 23-224.

The **Turtle Inn,** run by Americans Skip and Chris White, offers the best in adventure travel and ecotourism. Owners are versatile campers, hunters, divers, and general adventurers. The curious will find excursions to far-off cayes, the reef, and deep into the Maya Mountain jungles, where few outsiders have gone. Skip offers eight- to 10-day jungle tours in the heart of the jungle, river trips, dive and camping trips, and

Kitty's Place

TODD CLARK

trips to the Maya ruins. The Turtle Inn has six quaint thatch-roof cabañas on the beach, US$77 s, US$133 d, meals included. A fully equipped two-bedroom beach house is also available along the 700-foot waterfront, US$450 weekly. Both boat (US$35) and truck (US$10) transport is available from Big Creek. All electricity is solar-powered. For more information contact Turtle Inn (Placencia, Stann Creek District, Belize City, C.A.; tel. 6-22-069) or Dr. Lois Kruschwitz (2190 Blue Bell, Boulder, Colorado 80302; tel. 303-444-2555).

An Almost-luxury Hotel

Though it might change with the Placencia airstrip generating new business, a stay at **Rum Point Inn** is like a safari from the moment your plane from Belize City lands on the jungle strip at Big Creek. A van waits to transfer you to a shoreside dory. The dory rumbles through the placid lagoon and winds through mangrove-lined canals with beautiful tropical

Rum Point Inn

birds swooping and fishing; others watch you from nearby branches. Small signs and white arrows point the way (the canals all look alike!). When you step off the boat, your luggage is whisked away by the waiting staff, and just a short walk from the lagoon you'll get your first look at Rum Point Inn.

Rum Point is an anomaly; from a distance it looks like a mistake—a flock of igloos under the palms, but only for a moment. Probably the most modern and unusual hotel in Placencia, Rum Point Inn is operated by George and Corol Bevier. The beautifully stylized ferroconcrete cabañas somehow fit into the landscape—or don't, according to the beholder. But no one quibbles over the cool, beautiful, tropical atmosphere of each spacious cabaña; attractively furnished with two queen beds, brightly woven Guatemalan fabrics, rich hardwood furniture, tropical plants, roomy bathrooms, tile floors, and fans. Each dome-shaped cabaña is pristine white inside and out, with artfully shaped openings of glass cut into the walls and ceilings to let in the light, moon, and stars—viewing stations from bed during a tropical lightning storm. The warmth and conviviality at the resort is bested only by its outstanding gourmet cooking (according to some, the best food in all of Belize). Each night the table linens are a different color and design, and in a week the daily menu never repeats itself. Foods are fresh and innovative, and a lovely dining room and veranda overlook the water for long evenings under the stars. The Beviers make you feel as though you're a guest in their lovely home, perfect hosts at candle-lit family-style dinners each evening.

George is a medical entomologist and the perfect guide to accompany visitors into special places in the Belize jungle or on boat trips to the reef to snorkel or dive. A new dive boat will soon be taking divers on special trips with qualified dive instructors. Fishing is great, but relaxing on the porch in a hammock is a must. An alluring beach and sea are just a few steps from the cabañas, perfect for beachcombing. Recently a guest discovered a bottle—yes, with a message in it from a sailor who had thrown it overboard three months previous from a ship off Granada! Granted, it wasn't as traditional as our daydreams would conjure—the bottle was a two-liter plastic job with a screw-on lid instead of glass with a cork, but nevertheless an exciting discovery. In the main house, Corol runs a nice little gift shop, and the lounge has a wonderful library with a huge variety of books about Central America, mammals, invertebrates, Mayans, plants, mammals—you name it. The cozy bar is a great gathering place for cocktails and delicious toasted coconut chips before dinner. Town is about a 20-minute walk. Each cabaña rents for US$160 s, US$195 d, including meals; European Plan is available. Summer prices are lower. Tours to the cayes and reef for up to four people start at US$150 and up. Trips for up to four people to the Maya ruins, the rainforest, and rivers start at US$150. Credit cards are accepted. For more information write to Rum Point Inn (Placencia, Stann Creek District, Belize, C.A.; tel. 6-23-239, fax 6-23-240; in the U.S. contact the Belize specialists at Toucan Travel, 32 Traminer Dr., Kenner, Louisiana 70065; tel. 800-747-1381, fax 504-464-0325).

FOOD

Some of the finest Creole cooking in Belize is found in Placencia. Most of the cafes are low-key and the real "stuff" includes fresh seafood cooked in coconut milk and local herbs, with liberal amounts of plantain or banana. However, if something less daring sounds good, you'll find sandwiches, tamales, hamburgers, and great Italian food.

Try the **Galley Restaurant and Bar,** tel. (6) 23-133, and **Stonecrab** restaurant. For excellent Creole food go to **Brenda's,** (very ethnic), and if you want to make sure she's open, make a reservation and for sure she'll be there. For about US$12-15 you'll get a good (ample) meal; tel. (6) 22-137. **Sonny's** also serves everything from seafood to burgers. **B.J.'s Restaurant** is located on Placencia Rd. and offers fresh orange juice and good fried chicken in a screened dining room with wooden tables. Simple fare, open 7 a.m-10 p.m., tel. (6) 23-108. **Dockside Bar** hosts a popular Saturday-afternoon happy hour, 4-6 p.m. They serve hot dogs and ceviche (and rum drinks for US50 cents). The owners here operate a VHF radio for the convenience of boaters. This a great gathering place for visitors and local boatmen, and the current rumor is

that Placencia will soon be a port for visa renewals. Close by, **Tentacles** is a large cafe with a grand thatch roof over a rich hardwood deck where you can watch the sea. Here you can expect good seafood, Italian food, and hamburgers, cooked by David Dial, formerly of Que Pasta, Mon! This is a welcome dimension to commonly found Belizean foods. Try his fettuccines, Italian-style seafood, and great pastries.. A lobster dinner is about US$15. Open 8 a.m.-2 p.m. and 6-10 p.m., tel. (6) 23-254.

Sweet Stuff

Got a sweet tooth? The Belizeans will fix that. Downtown, ask where to find Miss Lily's; she's a great baker and makes delicious powder buns to sell from her house (under the stilts). Like all of the ladies (following), she works on Belizean time—when she sells out, she closes up. They all make the favorites of the villagers (and visitors): Creole bread (with shredded coconut), cinnamon rolls, Johnnie cakes (journey cakes), and other favorite snacks. Anyone will point you to these local bakers: **Miss Elsie's, Miss Lydia's, Miss Lizzy's, Miss Cuncu,** and, to these lady bakers, let's add **John the Bakerman** (great breads!). Along the sidewalk look for **D&N's** (for Daisy and Nadine), a tiny little ice-cream/pastry shop with a few tables. The tasty ice cream here is hand cranked in a variety of flavors, including local papaya and rum raisin, selling for US50 cents or US$1 a cup; open 11 a.m.-5 p.m., 7-9 p.m.

ACTIVITIES

Jungle Explorations

Placencia is a good base for exploring some beautiful jungle areas. A one-hour boat ride to the mouth of the **Monkey River** is a good picnic spot with noisy howler monkeys, tall trees, toucans, oropendulas (birds that nest in hanging bags that they weave), and wading birds. By boat you'll float through a labyrinth of mangrove channels. If possible go to **Golden Stream** this side of Nim Li Punit. Go by boat across Mango Lagoon to more lush forest, small pools, and waterfalls—these can be chilly, although a higher waterfall is warmed as it goes across hot rocks into an eight-foot-deep pool, complete with tiny aquarium fish to keep you company. Nearby, stop at a small craft shop where you'll find carved slate, small baskets, embroidery, and other crafts of the area; there's an outhouse here. If you have a chance while visiting in Placencia, take a trip out of town to the banana packing plant—very interesting. Ask one of the locals for directions.

Diving And Snorkeling

From the **Placencia Dive Shop** trips can be designed to take in the Reef and Inner Cayes, with camping on the reef, lagoon fishing, and deep-sea fishing. Dive trips to the cayes usually include two tanks, dive equipment, lunch, and guide, and scuba divers must bring their "C" cards. Rates to the inner cayes are US$65 pp, outer cayes US$75, based on four passengers. For more information contact Kitty Fox (Placencia, Stann Creek District, Belize, C.A.; tel. 6-22-027).

Fishing

Placencia is considered the "permit capital of the world." And **Kingfisher Sports LTD** is noted for a good fishing operation. Fishing guide Charlie Leslie has a reputation for being *the* best fly fisherman anywhere. He has 16 years experience in these waters and there are those that have been returning almost that long because of Charlie.

Kingfisher Sports takes you to a wide variety of fishing spots, from inshore fishing spots that include nearby flats to **Tarpon Caye** to the remote area of **Ycacos.** Fishermen will find schools of bonefish, tarpon, snook, snapper, and permit that weigh in at up to 30 pounds.

Offshore fishing will take you outside the reef where the depth increases dramatically and it's common to find wahoo, sailfish, marlin, kingfish, and dolphin fish. Sightseeing trips inland, as well as diving and picnicking trips on the nearby cayes, are available. Ask about package prices, which include room, food, boat, guide, and fishing. For more information contact Robert Hardy in the U.S. (107 Lafayette Ave., San Antonio, Texas 78209; tel. 512-826-0469, fax 512-822-6415). In Placencia, contact Charles Leslie, tel. (6) 23-104/23-175, fax (6) 23-204.

Another great place to catch bonefish to your heart's desire is at **Big Creek,** a short skiff-ride away from Placencia. Fishermen can expect "good bones," as well as wily permit and torpedo-size tarpon. Come prepared; there's little choice of equipment in Placencia. For bonefishing, experienced fishermen suggest a sturdy reel, a good nine-foot fly rod, and a No. 8-weight, floating, saltwater, tapered fly-line. Ask about boat charters to Guatemala.

Fishermen Hints

A few hints for the newcomer to tropical fishing locations; bring good polarized glasses with side shields and a heavy-duty sunscreen (don't forget the ears, nose, and lips). Wear a long-sleeved shirt to keep out the sun, and lightweight ripstop nylon pants for wading as the sun's rays will go right through the water and burn your legs. For even more protection, wear a hat—those funky, double-billed, fore- and aft-style hats with bandanas are excellent sun shields. You will need shoes for wading knee-deep along the coral flats; sneakers or Patagonia Reef Walkers serve the purpose. Standing in the shallow water with the sun's reflection for three or four hours can burn your skin to a crisp unless precautions are taken. Above all have fun and remember, fishermen, *catch and release!*

Exploring The Cayes

Find a boat and captain either through your hotel or around the dock or post office. Take a morning to cruise around the southern sea and discover tiny little islands scattered about, including **Laughing Bird Caye.** This mini-atoll is a narrow S-shaped caye with three small harbors and easy access for snorkelers to discover, just offshore, a crystalline underwater world of fascinating corals and beautiful tropical fish. Clumps of palm trees offer a tiny bit of shade, and the sea around the caye is brilliant turquoise, no lie!

Along the way you'll see a tiny little house that from a distance looks like it's floating on the water. On closer inspection, you'll see that it's set on a tiny sand bar that locals say gradually started rising from the sea about 15 years ago. This prompted a Belizean entrepreneur to haul out to the bar the materials to build this tiny unusual little house. The caye is called **Lazy Caye,** and my theory is that the gentleman who built the house is squatting and hoping that the land will continue to rise large and broad from the sea, and he will have his own personal estate someday. Along the way you'll pass other private cayes with lovely homes and small resorts.

Sailing

For a great sailing day aboard the **Adios,** contact Bonnie or Mike Cline (ask at the Dockside Bar, tel. (6) 23-154). This 36-foot catamaran is equipped with all safety equipment, a diesel engine, marine radio, bathroom facilities, and a sun awning. You have a choice of sailing on 16 miles of calm Placencia Lagoon, or sailing and snorkeling on a nearby island. Owners Bonnie and Mike are friendly folk who take good care of their passengers without being overbearing. For two people fare is about US$75, for three or more about US$45 pp. This includes on-board ice, rum punch, and lunch.

Placencia Tour Guides

A number of guides are available in Placencia to take you to the surrounding area. Local Sam Burgess drives a taxi in town, but his main occupation is as a guide for his company, **Jaguar Tours.** He has a good-running, clean, 12-passenger van and escorts guests to Garifuna villages, nearby caves and rivers, as well as to the Jaguar Reserve and Maya ruin sites. He can be reached at his **Sea Shell Giftshop,** (6) 23-139.

   Placencia Tours (tel./fax 6-23-186) does a fine job. Owner Ellis Burgess takes visitors to Cockscomb Basin Wildlife Sanctuary for day or overnight trips, and if you really want to look for the nocturnal stroll of the jaguar he will take you on a night walk through the forest (overnight trip with a night stroll including food, US$67 pp). Ellis tells us that howler monkeys are being translocated to the Jaguar Preserve and are now being sighted about every third trip. He also travels to the Maya sights of Lubaantun, Nim Li Punit, Uxbenka, and Blue Creek; daytrips (US$60). Pick up (or drop off) in Cayo, Belize City International Airport, with optional stops

like the zoo, Belmopan, parks, etc. along the road to Placencia. At US$60 pp, it's a good deal! Placencia Tours is located in Placencia Village, across from the ball field; Ellis says, "drop by the veranda for information." Other guide services are available through most of the hotels and guesthouses.

PRACTICALITIES

Photo Processing

Southern Exposure is a photo lab/image bank located at Rum Point Inn, with talented photographer **Wade Bevier** available. He will set up blinds in nature reserves and knows the area well; he also processes film and takes passport pictures, tel. (6) 23-239.

GETTING THERE

If driving, continue past the Dangriga turnoff (can it be possible that this strip of road to Placencia is worse than other southern roads? Yes!). Four-wheel-drive is a necessity, especially for the last five miles from the small village of **Seine Bight** to **Placencia Town** on the very tip of the peninsula. However, an alternative is to fly on Maya Airways, landing and departing from **Big Creek** airfield. Or take the **Z-Line** bus to Mango Creek, US$7.50; ask at the post office about the boat to Mango Creek, or the mail boat for Big Creek. The buses also continue to Punta Gorda, US$8.50. A bus leaves from Dangriga at **The Hub** guesthouse going to Punta Gorda at 3 p.m.; fare is around US$5. This particular bus ride gets three goose eggs for discomfort. From Mango Creek you travel by dory across the lagoon to Placencia. Flying is easier, quicker, and gentler to the body. For current schedules and fares call **Maya Airways** in Belize City, tel. (2) 77-215. From Placencia small boats take passengers across the lagoon to the airport in Big Creek. Make reservations at the post office for both the boat and Maya Airways.

BIG CREEK

This small community is growing into the banana center of Belize. Planes land at **Big Creek Airfield,** the third busiest airport in Belize after Belize City and Ambergris Caye. Mango plantations are becoming more common and shrimp farming is a new successful industry. When flying between Belize City and Dangriga you'll get a bird's-eye view of **Laguna Madre,** a shrimp farm and processing plant. Note the 12 large ponds next to the sea. This could be an invaluable asset for the fishermen.

But it's bananas that are putting Big Creek on the map. Somehow it was a surprise to see a bright yellow crop duster doing its thing in the surrounding green banana groves. It seemed so high tech! After traveling around southern Belize, the high-tech world seems far distant. But the growing banana industry of southern Belize is changing the scene. Small and large banana ranches are springing up, many run by Americans who see the entrepreneurial potential of Belize.

The Big Creek dock also shows signs of successful development with a new deep channel port. For years small container boats and barges were loaded with bananas by cranes and hauled through the shallow harbor. The fruit then was transferred into seagoing container ships that headed across the Atlantic to England and Ireland. With the new deep harbor, bananas, as well as citrus products, arrive at their destination in Europe in 15 days rather than in 21 days. This represents a big savings in fruit, time, and, hence, money.

The deep port will also enable cruise ships to make stops along Belize's southern coast someday, in turn encouraging more locals to open tourist attractions, mainly hotels and restaurants. It's easy to understand why the government refers to the brisk banana business as "yellow gold." Thriving industry is providing jobs for workers, both men and women, and the future of the area is happening now.

Practicalities
Big Creek has a couple of hotels. One is newish, called **Bird Bill Lodge,** formerly the **Toucan Hotel.** Inside you'll find the **Admiralty Club** bar and restaurant. Another, more Spartan hotel is the **Hello Hotel.** Try **Cardie's Restaurant** for simple meals.

Placencia Beach

TODD CLARK

TODD CLARK

TOLEDO DISTRICT

Toledo is the most southerly district in Belize and shares a border with Guatemala. As in the Stann Creek District, the Garifuna were the first to make homes in this detached area in the 1800s. In 1866 they were followed by Americans—Southerners who'd been buying guns from the British during the American Civil War. When their side lost, they asked for and received refuge and land grants from the British—

then tried their hand at raising sugarcane. Most Americans eventually returned to the United States. Over the years laborers from distant parts of the world were brought into the country for logging and sugarcaning and made Toledo District their permanent home. Today the district is an equal blend of many unrelated cultures—Caucasian, Kekchi and Mopan Maya, mestizo, Garifuna, Creole, Chinese, and East Indian.

PUNTA GORDA

Punta Gorda is the last sizable town you'll come to before reaching the Guatemala border. Most folks are English-speaking; the majority of inhabitants are Garifuna and East Indian. Don't miss the colorful Saturday market; many Guatemalans offer rich weavings from across the border—though basically it's a produce market. Fishing was the main support of the local people for centuries; today the industry has added high-tech shrimp farming. Agricultural activity is successful with rice, mangoes, bananas, sugarcane, and beans—all important food crops. While exploring the countryside, re-

member that most of the small outer villages are either Mopan or Kekchi Maya. Do your best to respect their ways; if you're backpacking bring your own food and water.

Another Face Of Ecotourism

It used to be that Toledo District's only accommodations were in Punta Gorda, except for one tiny guesthouse in San Antonio, **Bols Hilltop Hotel,** 15-20 miles away. However, that's slowly changing with a new program of small Maya guesthouses coming to life in the ethnic villages in Toledo. More than anything, this program is to

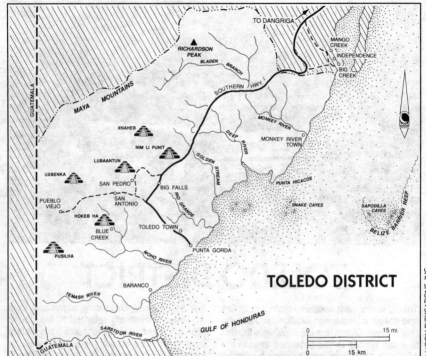

TOLEDO DISTRICT

© MOON PUBLICATIONS, INC.

help the villagers find a safer economy—another way to support their families besides total dependency on the meager subsistence farming that entails slashing and burning the rainforest. And though this is a much-discussed subject worldwide, it's becoming a vital problem in southern Belize because of the growth of the various Maya communities. Not only will this project protect natural resources, it is designed to preserve an ancient culture that is now in danger of becoming diluted by outside influences and lifestyles, especially with the increased interest from tourism.

Visitors, please note: It's best to be very flexible when visiting Punta Gorda. Although accommodations can be as described one day, they can change overnight—especially those in the outback. In many cases these are new small guesthouses, still ironing out the kinks in a whole new industry for most of these people.

So to really enjoy the experience, be ready for *anything*.

Tourism

Tourism is on the rise even though the infrastructure of southern Belize lags far behind. More and more travelers are passing up generic highrise hotels and luxury accommodations in exchange for a chance to peer into another time and culture, and in Toledo it is in its purest form. Obviously this is not a vacation for everybody. But for those with a curiosity about old traditions and the beauty of the rainforest creatures, a world of adventure awaits. Concern includes the preservation of jungle growth where so many of the pharmaceutical world's biggest discoveries have been made (with the promise of many more).

In southern Belize programs are in various states of progress, perhaps nurtured by the promise of the biggest program of all, **Mundo Maya** (see p. 74), originally known as La Ruta Maya. Since Mundo Maya is already bringing in visitors, the number of people traveling to Central America and southern Mexico is expected to grow. Because all of these travelers will be looking for the most culturally preserved areas of Maya culture, Toledo will undoubtedly get a big hit from the outside world. A few programs are on the drawing board; some have already been implemented and are highly successful. Some have been called "too controlled," where tourists must stay in the villages that are chosen for them. However, these choices are seen as ways to keep the Maya villages from being rapidly infiltrated and changed. Yes, this is a form of "Big Brother," but it's what the village fathers feel is best for their villages right now.

MAYA GUESTHOUSE HOMESTAYS

Education

By some city standards, the **Maya Guesthouse Homestays** would be small potatoes, since there are seldom more than four people per guide per village at one time. But for a society of people who have stayed pretty much to themselves for hundreds of years, and who in modern times have had an annual income of about US$500, the sudden influx of people and money is a real boon for the villages. With education the people can now see a reason to care for and nurture the environment that attracts the visitors.

GUEST VILLAGES OF TOLEDO DISTRICT

Santa Cruz	San Jose	San Pedro Columbia
San Miguel	Laguna	Barranco

Some of these villages are within an hour's walk of each other. Most of them are surrounded by thick forest, and if not already, eventually the paths between them will also be thick forest; reforestation is a viable part of this program.

Visitors

Visitors spend a 24-hour period in one of the villages and a local guide takes them through jungle trails to show them growing roots and herbs used for medicines and food still gathered and used in the villages. They have the opportunity to see arts and crafts being made, enjoy Maya dances and music, visit the farmlands, and observe local wildlife in a small zoo maintained on each of the trails at the villages.

Benefits

This is a communal affair, and everyone in each village benefits, even though he/she may not be directly employed as either a guide, arts and crafts demonstrator, dancer, singer, or one of the other positions needed to provide service to the visitors. The money goes into a general fund in the village, salaries are first paid and the balance is then used for either education or health.

Where To Go

Interested travelers in Punta Gorda should check in at the **Toledo District Maya Guest House** office and ask for Ted Schmidt (for now the office is located at **Nature's Way Guest House,** 65 Front St., tel. 7-22-119). Here you will receive all information about a scheduled 24-hour stay, an orientation for your visit to a village, and a bag that contains the eating utensils you will use (cup, fork, spoon, bowl, plate) for your entire stay. Whichever village is next up on the list will be the one you are assigned to visit. The orientation will give you some basic information about the Mopan and Kekchi Maya, how the program began, what you can expect during your visit, and an explanation about the **Food Providers Workshop** that each village participant must attend; visitors can be assured of safely boiled water. Visitors will have each meal in a different home; this spreads the visitors around, and keeps the event fresh and welcome to the villagers. In addition to paying the fee, the visitor has one other obligation: to give a written report about their visit. The village elders want the truth; the good things, the bad things, anything that will help them improve this new project. Thanks to visitors' comments, the meals went from too small to too big, and now the villagers are trying to hit a happy medium.

Guesthouses are designed after the local style: thatch roof, wooden walls, and built on a cement platform. So far there is one guesthouse in each village that will accommodate eight people. Each room has beds with clean linens, mosquito netting, and male and female showers and outhouses.

Meals

Breakfast generally consists of eggs, homemade tortillas, and coffee or cacao drink. All meals are ethnic and lunch is the largest meal of the day; it is often chicken *caldo* (like a stew cooked with Maya herbs) and fresh tortillas. Supper is the lightest meal of the day, and generally includes "ground" food (a root food like potatoes) that the guide and visitors might "harvest" along the jungle trail. The *comal* is always hot and if you're invited to try your hand at making tortillas, go ahead—this is a wonderful way to break the ice with the usually shy Maya women.

OTHER PUNTA GORDA PROGRAMS TO LOOK FOR

Garifuna Village Project

Garifuna people make up the largest ethnic group in Punta Gorda. Life has never been easy for the Garifuna, and in recent years there's been a real danger of old traditions slipping away entirely. Fortunately, a group of Garifuna volunteers have used 40 acres of a 1,000-acre plot (a legacy from their ancestors) to recreate an early Garifuna village at St. Helena Block. Farming is part of the project, and this recreated village is a small living museum. Something good usually is bubbling on the stove, and the workers in the field become docents, showing the visitor around and serving them lunch Garifuna style.

Punta Gorda Nature Trail

On the drawing board is another project that just needs a little funding to complete. It's a trail that starts at the edge of town and meanders through mangrove swamps and other examples of Punta Gorda's flora and fauna. Eventually it will be an education center for agricultural reform, showcasing methods to revitalize the land (one way is to plant nitrogen-fixing shrubs),

thereby eliminating the need to move a farming area to new and usually freshly cleared rainforest lands in order to plant successful food crops.

Jungle Adventure Accommodations

Near **Chano Creek**, the **Jose and Amelia Oh** family has opened a small jungle hostel with a few rooms with bathrooms and showers (solar-heated water), 12 volt lanterns, and an upstairs open-air porch for meals. For the backpacker they've built a hammock hut, all pretty basic. This is a family affair with their son Rolando as the head guide (after his father!). Mom does the cooking and prepares good Kekchi specialties like *caldo* (chicken cooked with Maya spices and vegetables) and always lots of handmade tortillas. This is really discovering nature's wonders. By day Rolando will take you upriver about three or four miles to the Rio Grande Cave. You'll go in one side and all the way through to the other side, about two miles from Lubaantun. For a day-trek through tall primary forest, bring your hiking boots and Rolando will give you a unique look at the jungle (never on the same trail twice), lunch, and a swim by the riverside. You'll see orchids, mahogany trees, and the yellow-head parrot. A trip downriver from the Ohs' takes you through lower, secondary forest where you'll find fig trees, ceiba, howler monkeys, spiny-tailed wish-willy iguana, six- to seven-foot-long iguanas that turn bright orange during the mating season. At the Rio Grande waterfall you'll swim and have lunch. You can also take a day-long canoe trip along the Rio Grande River, about 12 miles downriver where you'll be met by vehicle to take you back home. When we went to press these trips were all priced at about US$12, but Rolando suggests that his father will be raising the prices soon. Rolando is full of down-to-earth facts that come only from someone who has lived around the jungle. As he points out, the days spent in the primary jungle will not be burdened with mosquitoes, but in the secondary jungle you'll definitely need bug repellent. His eyes are trained to see every little camouflaged creature in the jungle. He explained that the traditional thatch roofs built by the Kekchi are of bay palm, and by the Mopan, cohune thatch. This type of adventure is not for everyone, but if you're looking for a *natural* expedition, ask around Punta Gorda for Rolando or Jose Oh. Remember, this is pretty basic, but an experience of a lifetime.

Another jungle experience is at **Safe Haven Hotel** not too far away. A Safe Haven representative, Lloyd, also called Sandman, will pick you up at the airport in Punta Gorda and drive you to the river (about six to seven miles), where he'll take you across in a motorized dory to the hotel. In a jungle clearing right near the Rio Grande riverbank, guests will find a three-bedroom house, with electricity and two private bathrooms. A Maya couple takes care of the grounds and does the cooking. This is a pleasant getaway with comfortable beds. From here several guided trips are offered: **Blue Creek Caves, Lubaantun, Santa Cruz Falls, Nim Li Punit,** rafting on the **Rio Grande,** and (this one is worth it just to roll the words around in your mouth) **"Dem Dats Doin."** Yeah, I asked what that was also, and I'm still not sure! I am told it is a visit to "a self-sufficient, appropriate-technology farm, including a piggery, methane-gas digester, local and exotic plants, wide variety of fruit trees, Lorraine stove, solar power, perfume-making demo." Rooms are available in **Nim Li Punit;** rates, including meals, are US$68 pp d. Call for more information in the U.S., (800) 552-3419, (218) 847-4441, fax (218) 847-4442.

and local bus station. It's centrally located with a bakery across the street. Rates are US$70 and up. I get the feeling they're still working out the prices and logistics of a hotel. For information call (800) 552-3419, (218) 847-4441, fax (218) 847-4442.

St. Charles Inn has rates from US$14.50-25, depending on shared or private bath; it's located at 21 King St., tel. (7) 22-149/22-197. Take a look at the **Mira Mar Hotel;** it's so-so for US$18 s, US$25 d, (95 Front St.; tel, 7-22-033). Mira Mar also has a Chinese restaurant. Two others to check out are **Mahung's Hotel,** with hot and cold water (on the corner of North and Main streets, tel. 7-22-044), and **Verdes Guest House** (22 Main St.; tel. 7-2069). For more information about Punta Gorda, write to the Toledo branch of the Belize Tourism Industry Association (Punta Gorda, Toledo District, Belize, C.A.; tel. 7-22-119).

ACCOMMODATIONS AND FOOD

Accommodations are simple in Punta Gorda. Several small guesthouses in town have received good comments. **Nature's Way Guest House** is simply furnished, clean, and fan cooled; rates are about US$15.50 s, US$25.50 d. It has a fine little restaurant that serves only breakfast in the low season (about US$2-4); during the high season it serves three meals a day. Jungle and Maya-site trips are available. Write or call for information (65 Front St., Box 75, Punta Gorda, Toledo District, Belize, C.A.; tel. 7-22-119).

The **Travelers Inn** is a pleasant new hotel just on the edge of town. Six rooms each have private baths, hot water, a/c, fan, and of all the things you'd least expect, cable TV. The rooms are upstairs, and downstairs is the dining room

Dining
We've recently had a couple of different readers tell us about the **Morning Glory Cafe;** the food is good, the staff has a sunny disposition, and prices are low. A couple more to try are **Shaiba Cultural Restaurant,** tel. (7) 22-370, and **The Airstrip Cafe.**

One Reader's Experience
I recently recieved a letter from a reader who gave us a little insight into one Maya family in the

village of Santa Cruz. Our traveler had a chance meeting in Punta Gorda with a gentleman named Marcus Sho. From that meeting he received an invitation to visit the village of Santa Cruz and spend the night in a hammock in the family cottage. This was a great cultural exchange and the American traveler was impressed with the family, Marcus's English, and the ideas that they discussed on subjects from slash-and-burn agriculture to how the Maya construct their huts. He paid Marcus US$5 for accommodations, US$2.50 for both meals, and US$15 for a day's guide service.

Marcus made ongoing arrangements for the traveler to visit the nearby village of San Jose for an overnight jungle trip. He described the trip as very simple, spending the night on the ground, and seeing small wildlife and a jaguar's footprints. Again, he was most influenced by the ideas the Maya have for tourism in their area. He went on to say:

I have traveled in Guatemala and Honduras and even spent time in the refugee camps in the latter country. It was really satisfying for me to have a chance to interact with Mayans who do not live in fear, and who have a chance to take control of their own destinies. For that reason alone, my visit with these people was well worth it!

GETTING THERE

You always see more when driving. In this area a 4WD vehicle is the only way to go, especially if you like investigating out-of-the-way villages and small hidden roads. Southbound flights from Belize City to Dangriga continue to Big Creek and then to Punta Gorda. This is really the most comfortable way to get to Punta Gorda—compared to the bus! Your body will thank you for days. For a current schedule and fares call Maya Airways in Belize City's downtown office, tel. (2) 77-215/72-312, at the airport office, tel. (2) 44-032/45-968, fax (2) 30-585. Check with Venus and Batty buses for current schedules. The James Bus Line waits for the ferry arrival from Guatemala on Tuesdays and Fridays (bus departure time about 1 p.m.). Figure about eight to nine hours on the road.

DIANA LASICH-HARPER

VICINITY OF PUNTA GORDA

SAN PEDRO AND SAN ANTONIO

These are some of the Maya villages taking part in the **Toledo District Maya Guest House** program. But for those interested in wandering the countryside on their own, Punta Gorda is a good starting point to wander off in many different directions. For a step back in time, a visit to **San Pedro** is fascinating. To get there, take the main road in town that goes inland about 10 miles toward San Antonio. Just before you get to San Antonio, a dirt track to the right breaks off to the village of San Pedro. If you're without a vehicle, take the bus, which makes this trip about three times a week, or you can hire a cab by day—a bit pricey, but the most convenient way to come and go according to your personal schedule. After leaving San Pedro and returning to the main road, make a right turn and you'll soon be in **San Antonio.**

Inhabitants of these thatch-hut villages, Kekchi and Mopan Maya, are people who fled to Belize to escape from oppression and forced labor in their native Guatemala. The old folks continue to maintain long-time traditional farming methods, culture, and dress. No modern machinery here—they use a simple hoe to till the soil, and water is hand-carried to the fields during dry spells. The village of San Antonio is famous for its exquisite traditional Kekchi embroidery. However, the younger generation is being whisked right along into 20th-century Belizean society.

Surprisingly, a local tourism representative lives in San Antonio. He is friendly and happy to give helpful advice about the area, and can direct you to local guides in town willing to take you to archaeological zones, including a trip to the caves called **Hokeb Ha** and **Blue Creek** (bring your swimsuit). This is great birdwatching country. From here the road is passable as far as **Aguacate** ("Avocado"), another Kekchi village. But if you intend to visit the ruins at **Pusilha,** near the Guatemala border, you must travel either on foot or horseback. Another ruin, **Uxbenka,** is west of San Antonio near the

village of Santa Cruz, easy to get to by trucks that haul supplies a couple of times a week. Not known by anyone but locals until 1984, this is where seven carved stelae were found, one dating back to the early Classic period. In San Antonio check out a tiny clean guesthouse, **Bol's Hilltop Hotel,** with rates approximately US$9.50 pp.

LUBAANTUN

North of the Columbia River and one mile beyond San Pedro is the Maya ruin of **Lubaantun** ("Place of the Fallen Stones"). It was built and occupied during the late-Classic period (A.D. 730-890). Eleven major structures are grouped around five main plazas—in total 18 plazas and three ball courts. The tallest structure rises 50 feet above the plaza, from which you can see the Caribbean Sea, 20 miles distant. Lubaantun's disparate architecture is completely foreign to Maya construction in other parts of Latin America. Maya buffs will want to examine this site. For more detailed information see "Maya Archaeological Sites of Belize."

NIM LI PUNIT

At Mile 75 on the Southern Highway near the village of Indian Creek, 25 miles north of Punta Gorda, you'll find **Nim Li Punit** (expect a 15-minute walk from the highway). The site was briefly surveyed in 1970, and about the only thing known for sure is that it held a close relationship with nearby Lubaantun. One of the memorable finds was a 29.5-foot-tall carved stela, the tallest ever found in Belize—and in most of the rest of the Maya world. It's best to make arrangements to see these ruins and the villages prior to your arrival in Punta Gorda if you don't have your own car. In any case, if you plan on visiting these ruins, check with the Department of Archaeology in Belmopan before you go, tel. (8) 22-106.

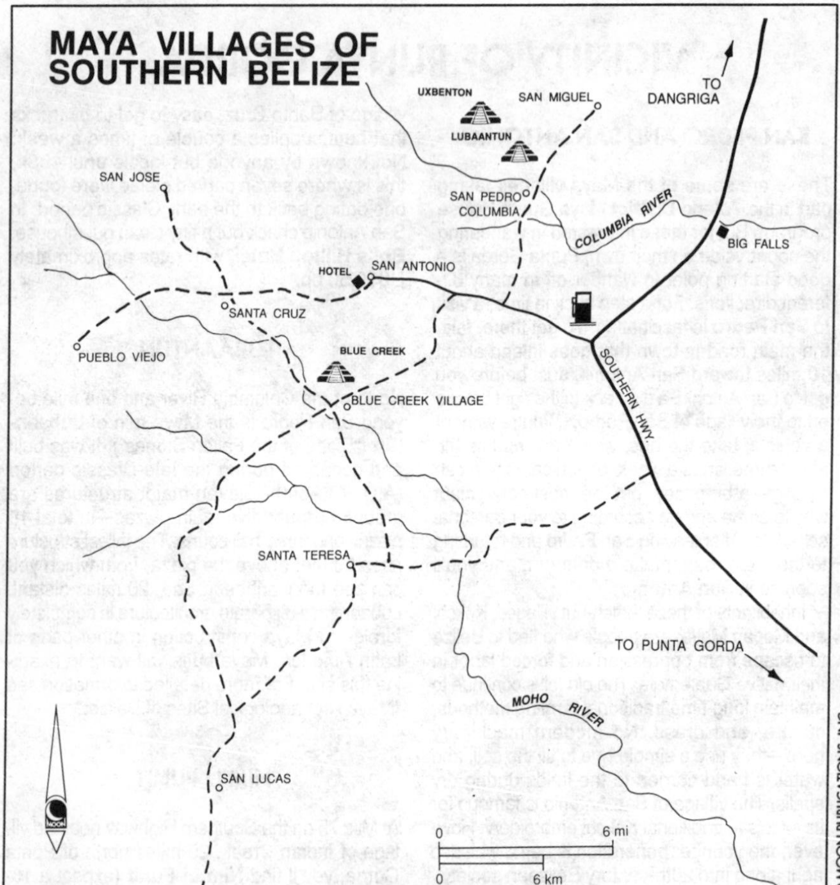

MAYA VILLAGES OF SOUTHERN BELIZE

UXBENTON

SAN MIGUEL

TO
DANGRIGA

LUBAANTUN

SAN JOSE

SAN PEDRO
COLUMBIA

COLUMBIA RIVER

BIG FALLS

HOTEL   SAN ANTONIO

SANTA CRUZ

PUEBLO VIEJO

BLUE CREEK

BLUE CREEK VILLAGE

SOUTHERN HWY

SANTA TERESA

TO PUNTA GORDA

MOHO RIVER

SAN LUCAS

0   6 mi
0   6 km

© MOON PUBLICATIONS, INC.

INTO GUATEMALA

Across the bay from Punta Gorda is Livingston, Guatemala, mostly inhabited by Caribs. For those interested in doing a little exploring across the border, the ferry, a large motorized dory, takes passengers two to three times a week. Sit toward the back (near the driver) for the driest ride. At other times ask around the docks; you can usually hitch a ride in a dugout. Either way, check with the local police to have your passport stamped before leaving.

To get the latest information about the ferry (a Guatemalan government ship) between Punta Gorda and Guatemala, Livingston and Puerto Barrios, call (7) 22-495. Once in a while it doesn't run at all, and when it does it has an unpredictable schedule. A lot of the hotels rely heavily on the business of Guatemalans who come to Belize to sell goods. However, smaller boats still make the trip to Livingston.

Note: See the "Travel Advisory" in the "Guatemala" chapter, p. 250.

TOMMY THOMSON

TOURS ORGANIZED IN THE U.S.

TOURING WITH AN EXPERT WHO KNOWS WHERE HE'S GOING

Have you finally decided to do it? Is this the first time you've ever left the border of the good old United States? Did your curiosity about the world of Belize take hold when you watched Morley Shafer on "60 Minutes?" Are you having heart palpitations because you don't know where to start to plan this once-in-a-lifetime trip? You can stop worrying now. The first time out is a good time to book a tour with an experienced group. I know, I know—you don't want to be a bus-window looky-loo! You won't be. Today's tour travelers have a world of possibilities. You can get as involved as you want in any way you wish— all with the help and encouragement of an experienced escort. The tours will include real involvement, which can be snorkeling, diving, or climbing the tall Maya ruins (there's no way possible to see the Belizean Maya sites from a bus window). Okay, on the other hand you don't want to commit to a lot of hiking—just leave it to the expert escort. Plenty of magical places are just right for *you*. The escort can be a scuba diver, an archaeologist, a naturalist, or a zoologist. Plan your own trip with the help of one of these experienced operators.

Tours

One reason people choose a tour over independent travel is the luxury of having someone else handle all the details—especially the first time out—someone who knows about passports, visas, reservations, airline schedules, time changes, the tastiest food, the safest water, the most comfortable beds plus the experience to be able to show you the best of what you wish to see.

Trip Choice

If you've chosen to visit Belize you must be someone who's interested in jungles, diving, the Caribbean, nature, wild animals, flowers, trees, history of the West Indies, the Maya, archaeology, exotic cultures, or—just Belize. Following are descriptions of some of the adventures available and a few itineraries. If any of them sound good, remember, this is just the tip of the you-know-what. In most cases telephone numbers are toll free; call them and you'll have a live human to answer all the questions you've *ever* had about Belize—and a few of its neighboring countries. We have chosen the following operators on the basis of their knowledge; all of them have a sincere feeling for the country, maybe even a love affair. All have been dealing with Belize for some time, and as in the case of **Sea & Explore,** they are transplanted Belizeans who maintain close ties. If you need more tour operators to choose from, call **Belize Tourist Board** in New York at (800) 624-0686 and ask for the *Belize Sales Planner.*

TOUR OPERATORS

International Expeditions, Inc.

One of the finest tour companies in the U.S. with an intimate knowledge of Belize is International Expeditions, Inc. They have planned itineraries to suit all tastes. If you have one or a dozen interested in something out of the ordinary, give them a call and they will work with you in every way possible.

Escort/guides have been trained in their field, and most of them are either native Belizeans or have lived in Belize for some time and know their way around the country. Expeditions run from 7-14 days with two- and three-day add-ons available. A few itineraries offered are **Naturalist Quest,** an 11-day overview of the natural wonders of Belize, including an in-depth look at the unique fauna, the rainforest, or a concentrated study of the island and reef ecology. This program is available in many combinations that include snorkeling and scuba diving—or even a workshop with the **Nature Conservancy.** The **Maya Heartland** expedition focuses on the ruins of the once-great ceremonial centers built by the sophisticated, ancient Maya, escorted by an informed archaeologist.

Special expeditions are planned with a variety of schemes, one taking in the **Garifuna Settlement Day** celebration (see pp. 202-204). Shorter excursions (three and four days) are planned for **Tikal** (see p. 250), **Mountain Pine Ridge** (see p. 196), the fabulous archaeological site of **Caracol,** (see p. 85), and the **Cockscomb**

DIANA LASICH-HARPER

Basin Jaguar Preserve (see p. 210). Hotels and restaurants are well chosen for comfort and adaptation to the area. For more information and prices call or write International Expeditions (One Environs Park, Helena, Alabama 35080; tel. 800-633-4734, 205-428-1700, fax 205-428-1714). **Note:** International Expeditions, Inc. is known for sponsoring and supporting various programs in the country to help the Belizean people, including the new Belizean Performing & Visual Arts Consortium.

Great Trips

Specializing in offering Great Trips to Belize for over 10 years, they provide custom foreign independent travel to experienced travelers, selective vacationers, and serious sportspeople. They provide expert counseling and personal service and use carefully selected hotels and resorts, emphasizing Maya ruins, nature and wildlife, jungle river tours, diving, fishing, and just plain old sunning. Write or call for more information (1616 W. 139th St., Burnsville, Minnesota 55337; 800-552-3419, tel./fax 218-847-4441.

Sea & Travel

Owners Sue and Tony Castillo, native Belizeans, take pleasure and pride in sharing their country with visitors. They know every out-of-the-way destination, and go out of their way to match a client with the right area of the country to suit their interests. Susan worked with the Belize Ministry of Tourism before coming to the United States. Whether you wish to see the Cayes or the Maya sites, contact Sea & Travel (1809 Carol Sue Ave., Gretna, Louisiana 70056; 800-345-9786, 504-366-9985).

Tropical Travel

Located in Houston, Texas, **Tropical Travel** can direct you to the perfect diving and fishing trip—including live-aboard dive-boat trips for a week at a time. The boat cruises to the offshore reefs and atolls where the diving is without equal. For the past four years, Tropical Travel (formerly **Belize Promotions**) has been a one-stop representative of the tourism industry in Belize, with excellent packages and guides who will take you to the most fascinating parts of Belize, whether on land, in the jungle, or on the reef.

Tropical Travel is now taking tours to **Honduras Bay Islands** (see p. 237), one of the Caribbean's best-kept secrets. Fishing and diving packages are planned as well as tours for those interested in the rich history that revolved around the pirates who fought over these strategically located islands—pirates from France, Holland, Spain, and England. And if you just want to worship the sun, they can help you out there also. For more information and prices, write or call Tropical Travel (720 Worthshire, Houston, Texas 77008; tel. 800-451-8017, 713-688-1985, fax 713-869-2540).

Slickrock Adventures, Inc.

For those interested in ocean kayaking, **Slickrock Adventures, Inc.** offers a nine-day kayak adventure based on a private island at Glover's Reef. This includes charter flights from Belize City, sailboat transfers to the reef, all guides (one American, one Belizean), hotel accommodations upon arrival and departure, all meals (daily fresh seafood), all kayak and camping equipment (bring your own sleeping gear), rustic cabins on Glover's Reef, and overnight trips to neighboring cayes by kayak. Experience is recommended but not required; weather can sometimes make for strenuous days. Although the trips are made during the dry season, tropical squalls can come along at anytime, delaying the ongoing passage. Conditioning before the excursion is encouraged; kayakers can expect to paddle no more than nine miles per day, often only three or four. Prices are US$1195 pp, nine days. For more information and a color brochure, contact Slickrock Adventures (Box 1400, Moab, Utah 84532; tel./fax 801-259-6996).

Far Horizons Cultural Discovery Trips

Mary Dell Lucas is known throughout the Maya world for her excellent archaeological knowledge and insight. Her company provides trips into the most fascinating Maya sites regardless of location. Although Dell Lucas is an archaeologist herself, she often brings specialists along with her groups. For more information call Far Horizons, (800) 552-4575.

Toucan Travel

This company is run by Dulce, another transplanted Belizean. She specializes in Placencia.

Maya vessels
discovered recently in
Vaca Cave system

OZ MALLAN

Call or write for more information (32 Traminer Dr., Kenner Louisiana 70065; 800-747-1381).

Best Of Belize
This growing company has been bringing visitors from the U.S. to Belize for some years. For information about all parts of the country, call in the U.S., (800) 735-9520.

Vagabond Tours
A terrific way to see both Belize and Mexico's Yucatán coast is to travel with **Vagabond Tours of Belize.** They offer great escorted trips that begin with a stay along Mexico's Caribbean coast, just south of Cancun at **Kai Luum, Shangri La,** or **Capitan Lafitte,** aptly called **Turquoise Resorts.** They range in style from "tents with a touch of class" to conventional bungalows to thatch cabañas. At all three resorts you'll find good food, pools, dive shops and instructors, water sports, car rentals, and best of all, pure white sand beaches and the crystal-

clear sea. From here you'll join the custom Vagabond Tours of Belize. These are offered in three versions keyed to your interests: diving and snorkeling, Maya archaeology, or nature and wildlife. Depending on your choice, the price includes a guide, most meals, all transportation from Cancun, Mexico, through Belize and back, hotel accommodations, admission fees to nature reserves, horseback riding, boats and diving equipment, and an excursion into Tikal—the fabulous Maya ceremonial center across the Belize border in Guatemala. For more details and reservations, contact the CVI Group (Box 2664, Evergreen, Colorado 80439; tel. 800-538-6802 or 303-674-9615).

Belize Specialists
For travelers who want a little more independence but still need help with planning, reservations, and suggestions, call or write Belize Specialists (Box 1722, Palo Alto, California 94302; tel. 415-641-9145, fax 415-326-3557).

KATHY ESCOVEDO SANDERS

NEARBY COUNTRIES TO VISIT

Several neighboring countries offer further exploration of the Caribbean Sea and its coral reef, as well as a chance to see more of the Maya countryside. Once in Belize, many travelers combine their trip with a visit to another nearby country. The gateway to Honduras, **San Pedro Sula,** should be explored. Enjoy delicious (inexpensive) food at the **Gran Hotel Sula** across from the Plaza.

HONDURAS—BAY ISLANDS

The Caribbean coast has many well-kept secrets. One that divers have kept to themselves for years is the Bay Islands of Honduras. Unspoiled and untouched by time, it's like living in your own private island world. Geologically the islands are an extension of the renowned barrier reef that runs from the tip of Mexico's Isla Mujeres south into the Honduras Bay, 35-70 miles off the Honduras coast. Reaching heights of 1,300 feet, the Bay Islands' spiny pine-covered hills drop to coconut-fringed, powder-fine sand beaches washed by the crystal water of the Caribbean. The reef is so close to many of the islands that often it just means a short swim from the beach to discover the flamboyant marine spectacle.

It's exhilarating to find a world without the interruptions of TV, fast-food hangouts, five-lane highways, glass-encased malls, or crowds of tourists. Geographically the island group includes **Utila, Morat, Barbarat, Roatan,** and **Guanaja,** along with some spectacular cayes. Whether snorkeler or scuba diver, each is a diver's ecstasy. Add the pleasures of the '90s to the rich history of the island, which gives Honduras its "other" dimension, and you can't miss having a memorable vacation.

History

The first inhabitants of the islands were the pre-Columbian **Paya,** whose relationship to the mainland Maya is not completely understood. Some archaeologists say the Paya predated the Maya, but there's little left of these first inhabitants to really know—except for the *yapa ding dongs,* as the locals call the few artifacts remaining. A more recent (and exciting) history begins in the 1700s. The past of the Bay Islands includes the British colonial government of 1741, pirate attacks, kidnappings, and a 300-year fight between the Spanish and the British for control of the islands.

The strong connection that remains between Belize, the Cayman Islands, Roatan, and the Mosquito Coast (the mainland across the bay from Roatan) began in the 1700s with settlers moving from one region to another while fleeing first from Spanish attacks and then from British attacks. The musical chairs rotation of government takeovers in the strategically located islands was dominated by the British due to its proximity to Belize and its British government. As a result, particularly English family names are common to all four areas, and despite the mixture of cultures, English has remained the commonly used language of the people on the islands, even though Spanish is the official language of Honduras. After traveling through the islands, you'll get the feeling that most islanders consider themselves separate from mainland Honduras.

Safety

An important question on everyone's mind planning a trip to this part of the world is, "How safe is it to travel here?" I don't claim to be a political expert, but I feel comfortable enough to drop everything and go to the Bay Islands at any opportunity.

After looking into the safety issue, which means we have talked to ordinary residents of the islands (expats and locals), business people, government officials, and returning visitors, including divers and nondivers that come back year after year, we have not encountered even one report of a problem. All of these people describe a very peaceful environment.

As far as the Honduras mainland is concerned, after tracking down news reports in U.S. papers, in almost every case the problems were along the Nicaragua border and included the Sandinistas who were ducking behind the peaceful Honduras border to "hide out" for a while. Again, we have not been able to locate a problem in the areas that we recommend: Copan, Tegucigalpa, or San Pedro Sula. However, if I were in the U.S. military, I would not wear my uniform and go for a hike along the Honduras/Nicaragua border until Pres. Violetta Chamorro gets her soldiers under control. So, my answer is, I believe traveling to the aforementioned places in Honduras is safe. Pitfalls await the unwary everywhere in life—travelers, like everyone, must take their steps carefully.

ROATAN

Shortly after Columbus's visit in 1502, during his last trip to the New World, the islands were either scenes of bustling activity or they were

San Pedro Sula

OZ MALLAN

completely deserted. At the beginning of the 17th century buccaneers made the Bay Islands their hangout and Henry Morgan established his operations in the deep-water harbor of **Port Royal** on the southern coast of Roatan. Over the years, timber was harvested, small villages of diverse cultures maintained their purity, and eventually outsiders began to discover the tranquility and beauty of the islands. The largest island is 30-mile-long Roatan. **Tan Sahsa, Western Caribbean Airlines,** and **TACA Airlines** make frequent trips to the international airstrip at the town of **Coxen's Hole** at the southwestern end of Roatan. Roundtrip from Belize City costs about US$160, and from Houston, New Orleans, or Miami, approximately US$350; the best deals are packages available from Tan Sahsa and Tropical Travel.

The long slender island has a multitude of small bays, inlets, and cayes—and low-key rustic accommodations at each. The alluring water between sunrise and sunset displays multishades of blue, green, and purple. The marinelife is rich with lobster, conch, a variety of turtles, and colorful coral. The offshore reef, decorated with a constant ruffle of white foam, has boats of all sizes scattered about.

The people of Roatan seem happy with their lives. No one really wants to see a highrise, and most are already concerned that too much development will spoil the low-key lifestyle they enjoy. Talk circulates of condominiums, retirement villages, and more beach resorts. So far it is *just* talk.

Expats
About 600 Americans are living on the island, many involved in the hotel business, some just enjoying the idyllic life of the tropics.

Coxen's Hole
Coxen's Hole is a bustling community whose streets are filled with people all going somewhere in various modes of transport: cars, buses, bicycles, taxis, and, of course, lots of pedestrians. If you're a shopper you'll enjoy a stop at super-store **Casa Warren,** where you can buy everything from groceries to sunglasses to junior's underwear. At **Joanna's,** visitors will find the perfect gift to bring home to remember Roatan.

Not too far from Anthony's Key is the small village of **Sandy Bay.** This isn't much more than a group of stilted dwellings. From here visitors who can tear themselves away from the sea trek up the steep twisting path about a mile to the tree-covered spine of the island where the view takes in the southern and northern coasts of Roatan, with Anthony's just below. Divers will find excellent walls, pillar corals, fluffy yellow gorgonian, and reaching sponge.

Bailey's Key
At **Bailey's Key** you'll find a program involving diving with dolphins. Still in the experimental stage, only six divers at a time are permitted to dive with the dolphins and only in the holding pen; eventually this will expand to become an open-water experience—under supervision, of course.

ROATAN ACCOMMODATIONS

Anthony's Key Resort
Five miles from the airport the lovely Anthony's Key Resort climbs the steep hillsides of its island. This 50-room complex is on a private eight-acre island that caters mostly to divers year-round. Most of the guest bungalows are set in a grove of coconuts (this small island was formerly a coconut plantation). Anthony's has learned the secret of good service, and the resort lures visitors back year after year. Divers can explore the sea as often as they wish, day or night. Lectures and slide shows inform newcomers of what to expect. Tennis, horseback riding, and sailboarding give a variety of breaks from diving. At Anthony's you'll climb four flights of steps to get to the lobby where the view is breathtaking.

Accommodations are available in a variety of styles and prices. Seven-day packages are available from US$500-650 pp plus seven-percent tax. For more information contact Anthony's Key Resort (1385 Coral Way, Ste. 401, Miami, Florida 33145; tel. 800-227-3483 or 305-858-3483).

Coco View Resort
A cozy secluded retreat with private beachfront bungalows and two guesthouses, this

Fantasy Island Hotel

TROPICAL TRAVEL

charming resort offers unlimited diving on a beautiful reef right off the beach. After your arrival on Roatan Island, you'll be taken to Old French Harbor where the hotel shuttle picks you up and takes you on a 10-minute ride up the coast. Winding through the cayes you'll suddenly realize you've left civilization in the following wake. Forget about the world you left behind; give your return airline tickets to Evelyn and you can forget everything until she taps you on the shoulder when it's time to go.

Along with **Zinger,** "super dive dog," mask and all, you'll enjoy the cozy ambience, especially over a cold beer in the "sunset-enhancing station" (sometimes called the bar) when the sky is splashed with golden reds. This is the time when diving folk hash out the day's discoveries and nondivers enjoy once again the experience of doing "whatever feels good."

Divers come to Coco View to enjoy the wall just 100 yards off the beach, as well as **Mary's Place,** an immense volcanic crack where the delights of the underworld flourish. And there's more—the 140-foot tanker wreck of the *Prince Albert* awaits exploration in 25-65 feet of clear water. **Would-be divers:** Expect PADI and SSI American instructors, two dive boats with equipment lockers on-board, freshwater dunk tanks everywhere, and plenty of air. Complete gear rental and repair are available. Five- to seven-day package trips start at US$375-700,

depending on whether you are a diver or an "Islander." For more information and reservations contact Coco View Resort (Box 877, San Antonio, Florida 33576; tel. 800-282-8932). Accommodations include two guesthouses and four over-the-water luxury bungalows. You'll find them clean and comfortable with hot water and private baths, overhead fans, 120-volt electricity, and each with its own porch to gather in the beautiful views of the sea.

Fantasy Island

For those who enjoy being pampered in luxurious surroundings or who think that living the life of the "rich and famous" is okay, check out **Fantasy Island,** the newest resort in the Bay Islands. Visitors will find 39 beautiful, a/c, beachfront rooms luxuriously appointed on a 15-acre private island just off Roatan. You name it, all water sports are available, from blue-water fishing to snorkeling and scuba diving to private yacht charters; don't forget the water toys, from wind-driven to mechanical. Excellent meals are served in a lovely tropical dining room. And for those who like to stay in touch, you'll find telephones and satellite TV. For more information call (800) 676-2826; in Roatan call (504) 45-1222, fax (504) 45-1268.

French Harbor

Named for a couple of French families who moved to Roatan from the Mosquito Coast in

1823, **French Harbor** is the largest town on the island and the most industrialized. The chief industry revolves around seafood (no surprise there) with a large fleet of boats that work the coastal areas as far south as Nicaragua. Conch, lobster, and shrimp are processed and frozen for world export.

While wandering around the city, check out the **Buccaneer Inn,** owned by Rita Silvestri, who is very much involved with the environmental protection of Roatan as well as a pro-development association that helps low-income citizens with a development bank. The Buccaneer Inn is a great beachfront hotel that some claim has the best chef on the island. Also at French Harbor have a talk with transplanted American Eric Anderson, who first tried his hand at farming at Port Royal (until it was obvious the farm was not making it) and today owns and operates (with his wife Teri) **Hotel French Harbor Yacht Club.** Set on a hill overlooking French Harbor, 12 rooms offer an intimate resort with private baths, ceiling fans, cable TV, direct-dial telephones, some a/c (extra), porches with a view, boat rentals, island tours, and car rental. Dockage facilities are available for boaters. For more information call (504) 45-1478 in Roatan, fax (504) 45-1459; in the U.S. contact Tropical Travel, tel. (800) 451-8017.

Oak Ridge

Another Roatan harbor, Oak Ridge, is also totally engrossed in catching and processing seafood for export. The key is recognized by the seagoing world as the site of the original **Cooper Boatyard,** set up in 1870 and where in 1919 the 700-ton *Rubicon* was built—the largest ship ever built on the Caribbean side of Central America. This is a haven for historical tidbits that include the past events of the French, Dutch, English, Spanish, and Americans.

One of the oldest Bay Island dive resorts, the **Reef House,** is located on a small caye at the entrance of the harbor and is still as popular as ever. A small unpretentious tropical hideaway designed for 30 divers, it has just been remodeled and enlarged. When not diving you'll be pampered with excellent Creole, Caribbean, or American food served in your choice of candlelight dining room or at the terrace edge. Outdoors you'll find a poolside patio, bar, and a

120-foot blue lagoon with a sandy white bottom where protected swimming is only steps from your room.

Divers have access to a 37-foot diesel cruiser and a fully equipped dive shop. Five- to seven-day packages for nondivers, divers, and fishermen range from US$375-550 pp, plus seven-percent tax. Workshops and seminars are offered by the **Caribbean Institute** located at the Reef House Resort. These seminars explore a variety of areas of information including marine biology, ecology, anthropology, and folklore of the islands. The programs provide a pleasant way to learn about the world around us, past, present, and future. For more information contact Tropical Travel; tel. (800) 451-8017.

Live-aboard Boats

Two popular live-aboard dive boats roam the waters of the Bay Islands making the dive experience convenient and luxurious. The *Isla Mia* is a 75-foot floating dive resort perfectly suited for exploring all the waters of the Bay Islands. The boat has five double cabins plus a

A San Pedro businessman—the oranges look green on the outside but are orange, sweet, and juicy on the inside.

cabin for six. Completely air-conditioned, the boat provides unlimited diving. A seven-day, six-night package is US$1195 pp.

The classy *Reef Runner* is 44 feet long, entirely self-contained, and equipped to handle six divers in style—a/c, with a large salon, sun deck, and good food. A six-night charter is US$600 pp. For more information about both boats call (800) 451-8017, (713) 298-2238, fax (713) 298-2335.

GUANAJA ISLAND

Posada Del Sol
On the island of Guanaja, the discriminating traveler will find a relaxed elegance at the Posada del Sol, with gourmet food and perfect service. The luxurious Spanish hacienda is set in a beautiful mountainside location with more than 1,600 feet of waterfront. Besides the usual diving and deep-sea and light-tackle fishing, the visitor will enjoy tennis and horseback riding. Divers come to dive sites that include five shipwrecks, 10 miles of deep vertical coral walls (in 28-50 feet of water), and four miles of coral barrier reef. The resort has three dive boats and complete dive equipment. For a change of pace the Posada offers waterfall jungle trips, hiking, water-skiing, and charter sportfishing plus lots more. Amenities include 24 Spanish-style rooms with a choice of poolside, hillside, or oceanfront accommodations. Package prices include three meals. Rates range US$730-1395 pp, depending on your activities. For more information contact Posada del Sol (1201 U.S. Highway One, Ste. 220, North Palm Beach, Florida 33408; tel. 800-624-DIVE, 407-624-DIVE, fax 407-624-3225).

Bayman Bay Club
This rustic resort of wooden bungalows built into a mountainside jungle offers a tropical retreat for anyone who really wants to get away from it all—and the diving is great. Lodging is about as close to staying in a treehouse as you can get and still be termed a guesthouse, with the amenities that make traveling fun. Close to all diving activities on Guanaja Island, guests enjoy great food, offshore trade winds, and a feeling of being in another world. Seven-day

packages start at US$650 nondiver, US$675 diver. For more information contact Tropical Travel; tel. (800) 451-8017.

MAINLAND HONDURAS—COPAN

With an interest perhaps stronger than we had ever felt in wandering among the ruins of Egypt, we followed our guide . . . to fourteen monuments of the same character and appearance, some with more elegant designs, and some in workmanship equal to the finest monuments of the Egyptians.

Although these are the words of John Lloyd Stephens describing his first view of Honduras, they could easily be mine—and probably yours as well. Anyone who has visited archaeological monuments of ancient societies around the world

Maya stelae at Copan site

will mõre than likely come to the same conclusion as the erstwhile explorers Stephens and his fellow-traveler, artist Frederick Catherwood.

The Maya

For a thousand years Copan lay covered by trees, embraced by roots of the tall strangler ficus amid layers of dust, dead-plant material, and loose particles that floated on the Honduran breeze and gradually covered most of this archaic wonderland. Since Stephens's and Catherwood's visit, much has happened. Astounding carvings of immense heads, stairways lined with stone jaguars rearing up on their hind legs, and many plazas have been uncovered and revealed to the sunlight once again. Stephens describes a colossal stone figure:

The front was a figure of a man curiously and richly dressed, and the face, evidently a portrait, solemn, stern, and well fitted to excite terror. The back was of a different design, unlike anything we had ever seen before, and the sides were covered with hieroglyphics.

Maya ruins at Copan

OZ MALLAN

Maya Sites

Copan is located on the Copan River in a valley about 2,000 feet high. Stonework continues to be revealed throughout the valley. In its 1,500 years of existence, the Maya moved Copan's centers from one place to the other, building impressive structures at each site, perhaps each improving over the other until the middle of the 8th century when it would seem that they reached the pinnacle of their accomplishments. Scientists believe Copan's beginnings were during the early Classic period (A.D. 400), and these Maya continued in their advancements and structural designs until the late-Classic period (A.D. 700).

While wandering through the site with your guide (a guide is the way to go for good info), you will learn when the various structures were built and what archaeologists have learned about them over the years. The Acropolis, for example, is the largest complex at 130 feet high. This is where you'll find the well-known **Hieroglyphic Stairway,** covered with the longest "book" of hieroglyphics—2,500 glyphs on 63 steps. No, you cannot climb the steps; in fact, the public is not allowed to get too close. The Maya glyphs at Copan are considered the finest Maya art found to date. Look at the **Eastern** and **Western courts.** At the Eastern Court you'll find **Temple 22,** the most breathtaking structure in Copan. Though much of the intricate carving has been destroyed, enough is left that visitors can see what complicated, tedious work was devoted to this temple—believed to have been the most sacred of Copan. The **Great Plaza** is located at the northern end of the **Main Structure,** and those who have visited Tikal will notice the similarities between this one and the Great Plaza at Tikal.

Don't miss the museum on the main plaza in town; you'll see a booth to buy your ticket to both the archaeology zone and the museum (about US$2.50). At the museum you'll find the usual collection of stelae, a tomb, and other artifacts from the site. From the museum expect about a half-hour walk to the site. It's best to plan at least one full day to take in the site; one and a half days is even better. Several very simple hostelries are close by for an overnight stay.

PRACTICALITIES

Getting There

Tan Sahsa provides 727-737 service to the Honduras mainland and Bay Islands from U.S. gateways in Houston, Miami, or New Orleans. If you opt for an escorted two- or three-day tour from the Bay Islands (the most efficient way to go the first time), transportation, meals, and overnight hotel stay are arranged for you.

Miscellaneous Information

A valid passport is needed to enter Honduras; U.S. citizens do not need visas, but they are required in advance for those traveling on Canadian passports. The official currency in Honduras is the **lempira,** referred to locally as the "lemp." Currently the exchange rate is US$1 to two lemps. Not all resorts accept **credit cards,** but **traveler's checks** are accepted almost every place, and most resorts on the islands and the mainland are happy to take U.S. dollars. **Departure tax** of US$20 pp must be paid at the airport when leaving. Only a few hotels offer **car rentals;** as the roads improve, more are becoming available. **Hotel tax** has just

risen to seven percent. **Divers,** remember to bring your certification card; PADI or SSI certification courses are available. Spearfishing is not permitted, and removing coral, shells, or fish is prohibited without express permission from the Honduran government. Bring whatever film you think you might use, as it is much more expensive on the islands and all types are not sold.

Medical Concerns

Emergency **medical treatment** is available at a clinic in French Harbor and good hospitals are 35 miles away (about 20 minutes away by plane) on the Honduras mainland. Although malaria is rarely encountered in the islands, you may wish to ask your doctor or contact the Disease Center in Atlanta, Georgia; tel. (404) 639-2888, before leaving the United States. A recompression chamber with trained staff is located on Roatan. Prescription drugs are unavailable so bring any necessary medicines in your carry-on luggage. Bring a bug repellent; though mosquitos are a rarity, "no see-ums" and occasional sandflies can be a nuisance—Avon's Skin-So-Soft works great for *some* people (if you can stand the strong smell)!

AIRLINES SERVING HONDURAS

Name	From	Tel.
Sahsa	Miami	US (800) 432-9818
	New Orleans	US (800) 452-7589
TACA	New Orleans	US (800) 535-8780
Lacsa	New Orleans	US (504) 469-5618
		US (504) 464-0001/0002
Continental	Houston	US (713) 290-3337

CHETUMAL

This is a good base to visit the many archaeological sights in the southern section of Quintana Roo and the gateway to Mexico's well-known Caribbean resorts: Cancun, Cozumel, Playa Del Carmen, and Akumal. The capital of this young state, also named Chetumal, is without the bikini-clad, touristy crowds of the north and presents the businesslike atmosphere of a growing metropolis. A 10-minute walk takes you to the waterfront from the marketplace and most of the hotels. Modern sculpted monuments stand along a breezy promenade that skirts the broad crescent of the bay. Also explore the back streets, where worn, wooden buildings still have a Central American/Caribbean look. The largest building in town—white, three stories, close to the waterfront—houses most of the government offices.

Wide, tree-lined avenues and clean sidewalks front dozens of small variety shops. The city has been a free port for many years and as a result has attracted a plethora of tiny shops selling a strange conglomeration of plastic toys, small appliances, exotic perfumes (maybe authentic?), famous-label(?) clothes, and imported foodstuffs. Because the tax in Chetumal is only six percent instead of the usual 15, it's a popular place for Belizeans and Mexicans to shop. The population is an exciting mixture of cultures, including Carib, Spanish, Maya, and British. Schools are prominently scattered around the town.

CLIMATE

Chetumal is hot and sticky. Though sea breezes help, humidity can make the air terribly uncomfortable. High temperatures in August average 100° F, in Dec. 86° F. In the last 34 years, three destructive hurricanes have attacked the Mexican Caribbean coast, and Hurricane Janet all but destroyed Chetumal in 1955. Not something to be too concerned about though—these devastating blows are infrequent. The most comfortable time to visit is the dry season Nov.-April.

FLORA AND FAUNA

Chetumal is noted for its hardwood trees, such as mahogany and rosewood. (Abundance of wood explains the difference in rural housing between the northern and southern ends of the peninsula. Small houses in the south are built mostly of milled board, some with thatch roofs; structures with circular walls of slender saplings

Spujil in Mexico's state of Campeche

OZ MALLAN

set close together are still common in the north.) Copious rainfall in the Chetumal area creates dense jungle with vine-covered trees, broadleafed plants, ferns, and colorful blossoms. Orchids grow liberally on the tallest trees. Deer and javelina roam the forests.

SIGHTS

Calderitas Bay
On Avenida Heroes five miles north of the city is Calderitas Bay, a breezy area for picnicking, camping, and RVing. The trailer park is one of the few in the state that provides complete hookups for RVs, including a dump station and clean showers, toilets, and washing facilities. Right on the water's edge, the spotless camp is in a parklike setting, fringed with cooling palm trees. Even amateur divers will find exotic shells, and the fishing is great. Nearby public beaches have *palapa* shelters that are normally tranquil, but on holidays they're crowded with sun- and fun-seekers.

Isla Tamalcas
Tiny Isla Tamalcas, 1.5 miles off the shore of Calderitas, is the home of the primitive capybara. This largest of all rodents can reach a length of over a meter and weigh up to 50 kilograms; it's found in only a few other places in the world (South America and Panama). The shaggy animal is covered with reddish yellowish brown coarse hair, resembling a small pig or large guinea pig, has partially webbed toes, and loves to swim, even underwater. It's referred to by the locals as a water hog and is a favorite food of the jaguar. Because it's been a favorite food, it's seldom seen anymore. Isla Tamalcas is easily accessible from Calderitas Beach.

ACCOMMODATIONS

Although Chetumal is not considered a tourist resort, its low taxes and location on the Belize border make it a desirable marketplace and busy stopover for both Mexicans and Belizeans. If traveling without reservations, arrive as early in the day as possible to have your choice of hotel rooms. During the holiday season it's wise to reserve in advance. Most of the hotels listed are within walking distance of the marketplace, downtown shops, and waterfront.

Higher Priced
Chetumal doesn't have a true luxury hotel. The **Hotel Los Cocos** (formerly the Del Prado) comes closest with pleasant rooms, cleanliness, a/c, pretty garden, and a large, clean swimming pool. You'll also find a bar with evening disco music and a quiet dining room with a friendly staff serving a varied menu. Rates are about US$80 d, and Los Cocos is on Avenida Heroes con Chapultepec; tel. (983) 2-05-44. The **Hotel Continental-Caribe** promotes itself as a luxury hotel (perhaps in the past it was), has a/c, restaurant, pool, bar with evening entertainment, and though the rooms are clean the overall appearance is not. Prices start at about US$48; it's located at Avenida Heroes #171; tel. (983) 2-11-00.

Moderate To Budget
The moderately priced hotels for the most part are friendly (some clean, some not; look before you pay), usually fan-cooled, some with a/c, and they have hot water. Prices range US$24-35 d. **Hotel Marlon** is a newish hotel with a very pleasant staff. Rooms are comfortable and clean, with a/c, hot water, telephone, and color TV. There's a pool, a good restaurant, and the **Marquis** is a neat little piano bar. Rates start at about US$25 s, US$29 d. The address is Avenida Juarez #87; tel. (983) 2-95-22, fax (983) 2-10-65. **Hotel Principe** offers ample rooms, a/c, hot water, a pleasant courtyard, and the **El Arlequin** restaurant. Rates are US$25 s, US$29 d; it's at Avenida Niños Heroes #326, tel. (983) 2-47-99, fax (983) 2-51-91. **El Marques Hotel** is on Avenida Lazaro Cardenas #121, and rooms come with servibar, private bathrooms, and hot water; tel. (983) 2-29-98, rates US$28; **Restaurante El Marques** is on the premises. **Hotel Caribe Princess** is very clean and has a/c, hot water, and TV; Avenida Alvaro Obregon #168; tel. (983) 2-05-20. A real budget spot is **Hotel Jacaranda**, Avenida Alvaro Obregon #201; tel. 2-14-55. Rooms come with fan or a/c, simple and cheap; rates start at about US$11. Very reasonably priced food is available at their simple cafe.

FOOD

It's easy to find a cafe to fit every budget in Chetumal. Walk down the street to Avenida Alvaro Obregon for several fast-food cafes. On the same street, try **El Pez Vela** for seafood; for chicken go to **Pollos Sinaloa.** On the corner of Avenidas Efrain Aguilar and Revolucion is **Los Pozos,** a regional cafe serving typical Yucatecan dishes. Eat great tacos at **El Taco Loco** at Morelos #87, open 6 a.m.-3 p.m.; **Sergios Pizza** on Obregon and Cinco de Mayo is good. **Mandinga** serves good seafood on Belize St., usually busy, reasonable prices. **El Grill** at Hotel Los Cocos is great for a special night out. The **public market** has just about everything you could need; three **Conasuper** markets can provide the rest.

SPORTS

A yearly event in Chetumal is the auto road race. Open to drivers from all over the globe, it's gaining prominence in the racing world. This event takes place in December and hotel reservations should be made well in advance.

A popular sport in both Chetumal Bay and Bacalar Lagoon is sailboarding. State competitions are held yearly in both areas. What a great place to fly across the sea! Make reservations early, since many others will have the same idea. For more information, write to the Secretaria de Turismo (Palacio de Gobierno #20, Chetumal, Quintana Roo 77500, Mexico).

SERVICES

The **post office** is on Calle 2A. You can send a telegram from **Telegrafos Nacionales,** Avenida Cinco de Mayo. For any **medical** emergency, several hospitals and clinics are available. Ask at your hotel for a doctor who speaks English. One **pharmacy** is on Carmen Ochoa de Merino y Heroes; tel. (983) 2-01-62. Four **gasoline stations** and at least seven mechanics are in town. Several **banks** will cash traveler's checks Mon.-Sat. 9 a.m.-1 p.m. First- and second-class buses use the new bus station on the outskirts of town.

TRANSPORT

By Air

Chetumal's small modern airport still has only a few commuter flights each day. An airport van provides transportation to hotels or downtown. Check with Aerocaribe for flights in and out of Chetumal.

By Bus

Buses from Belize arrive throughout the day at the new modern Chetumal bus station located on the highway, 20 blocks south of town. Taxis are available from the station into town. With the expanding road system, bus travel is becoming more versatile and is the most inexpensive public transportation to the Quintana Roo coast. Buses from Chetumal make frequent trips to Playa del Carmen and Cancun. New express buses are appearing in many parts of Mexico. They are modern and clean, with bathrooms, a/c, and airline-type seats. Each bus has an attendant who will serve you coffee and cookies, and some buses have earphones for music—the 747s of the road. Chetumal is part of the loop between Campeche, Cancun, and Mérida. Check with a travel agent or Belize Transfer Service, tel. (415) 641-9145, fax (415) 326-3557, for a pickup point in Chetumal, usually at one of the hotels. Fares and schedules change regularly: to Cancun the fare is about US$30. Frequent bus service into Belize can be aboard the **Batty Bus** or the **Venus Bus,** US$1-4, depending on whether or not you take an express. You will have to get off the bus when you go across the border into Belize. Have your passport handy; sometimes this takes a while.

By Car

A good paved road connects Chetumal with Mérida, Campeche, Villahermosa, and Francisco Escarcega; Highway 307 links all of the Quintana Roo coastal cities. Expect little traffic, and gas stations are well spaced if you top off at each one. Car rentals are scarce in Chetumal; go to the Hotel Los Cocos for Avis. Chetumal is an economical place to rent your car (if they have one available), since the tax is only six percent. If you're driving watch out for "No Left Turn" signs in Chetumal.

BACALAR

Twenty-four miles north of Chetumal (on Highway 307) lies a beautiful multihued lagoon called **Las Lagunas de Siete Colores** ("Lagoon of Seven Colors"). Bacalar, complete with 17th-century Fort San Felipe, is a small town founded by the Spanish to protect themselves from the bands of pirates and Maya that regularly raided the area. Today, part of the fort has a diminutive museum housing metal arms used in the 17th and 18th centuries. A token assortment of memorabilia recalls history of the area. The stone construction has been restored, and cannons are still posted along the balustrades overlooking beautiful Bacalar Lagoon. The museum is open daily except holidays, and a small entry fee is charged.

Close by, built into the side of a hill overlooking the colorful Bacalar Lagoon, is **Hotel Laguna,** moderately priced, with clean rooms and private baths. Rooms each have a fan and a view of the sea. The dining room serves tasty Mexican food at moderate prices. Special touches make it an out-of-the-ordinary stopover: local shells decorate walls and ceilings, and ornate fences are neatly painted in white and green. A small pool (filled only during high season) and outdoor bar look out across the unusually hued Lagunas de Siete Colores. A diving board and ladder make swimming convenient in the lagoon's sometimes-blue, sometimes-purple, sometimes-red water; fishing is permitted and you can barbecue your catch on the grounds. Rates are about US$36 d. Ask about a bungalow that includes kitchen facilities. Reserve in advance during the tourist season and holidays. To find the hotel, turn left off Bacalar's main street and follow the shore south. For reservations phone (983) 2-35-17 in Chetumal, (99) 27-13-04 in Mérida, or write to Avenida Bugambilias #316, Chetumal, Quintana Roo. Allow plenty of time for the mail to reach its destination.

Close by is the **Laguna Milagros Trailer Park** with tent camping also permitted, about US$2-3 pp. Restrooms, showers, sun shelters, a narrow beach, small store, and open-air cafe combine to offer an exotic milieu on the edge of the lagoon.

Rancho Encantado

Thirty-five miles north of Chetumal (200 miles south of Cancun), an enchanting small resort lies on the edge of Bacalar Lagoon. Specializing in laid-back, relaxing vacations, this mini-resort includes six casitas built with native hardwoods and Mexican tile. They sit in a lush Eden of tropical shrubs, coco palms, and fruit trees—all just a few steps from the shore of Bacalar Lagoon. Each unit contains a small sitting room, ceiling fan, convenience kitchen/dining room, bathroom, stove, refrigerator, and deck with a view of the garden or lagoon. A 40-foot palapa-roofed structure is the social center of the resort. Here visitors enjoy a tropical buffet breakfast and candle-lit dinner (both included in the room rate).

If you don't wish to "do nothing," you can be as vigorous as you desire with a variety of activities. The archaeology buff has the rarely visited **Kohunlich** Maya site with its giant masks close at hand. Take an excursion through the Quintana Roo savanna to tour Mexico's southern Caribbean coastline, or plan a scuba trip to the Caribbean's **Chinchorro Banks.** Rancho Encantado offers a variety of sporting equipment. Ask about the private villa with three bedrooms, 2.5 baths, and private dock located on the waterfront a short distance from Rancho Encantado. Car rentals are available through Hertz at Hotel Los Cocos in Chetumal. Rates in premium season, Nov.-April, are US$110 d and drop to US$88 May-Oct., including breakfast and dinner. Phone for reservations (800) 221-6509, fax in Mexico (983) 8-04-27 (Box 1644, Taos, New Mexico, 87571).

PLACES TO VISIT

Cenote Azul

Twenty-one miles north of Chetumal (on Highway 307) is a circular *cenote* 61.5 meters deep and 185 meters across filled with brilliant blue water. This is a spectacular place to stop for a swim, lunch at the outdoor restaurant, or just have a cold drink.

Kohunlich

Forty-one miles west of Chetumal on Highway 186, turn right and drive five miles on a good

OZ MALLAN

Mask of Kohunlich

Though not totally restored nor nearly as grand as Chichen Itza or Uxmal, Kohunlich is worth the trip if only to visit the exotic **Temple of the Masks,** dedicated to the Maya sun god. The stone pyramid is under an unlikely thatch roof (to prevent further deterioration from the weather), and unique gigantic stucco masks stand two to three meters tall. The temple, though not extremely tall as pyramids go, still presents a moderate climb. Wander through the jungle site and you can find 200 structures or uncovered mounds from the same era as Palenque. Many carved stelae are scattered throughout the surrounding forest.

Walking through luxuriant foliage, you'll discover a green world. Note orchids in the tops of trees plus small colorful wildflowers, lacy ferns, and lizards that share cracks and crevices in moldy stone walls covered with velvety moss. The relatively unknown site attracts few tourists. The absence of trinket sellers and soft-drink stands leaves a visitor feeling that he or she is the first to stumble on the haunting masks with their star-incised eyes, mustaches (or are they serpents?), and nose plugs—features extremely different from carvings found at other Maya sites. Even the birds hoot and squawk at your intrusion as if you were the first. Like most archaeological zones, Kohunlich is fenced and opens 8 a.m.-5 p.m.; entrance fee. Camping is not allowed within the grounds, but you may see a tent or two outside the entrance.

side road to this unique Maya site. The construction continued from late pre-Classic (about A.D. 100-200) through Classic (A.D. 600-900).

GUATEMALA

TRAVEL ADVISORY

As we go to press, a military coup ousted former Guatemalan president Jorge Serrano. The congress then elected Ramiro de Leon Carpio as his successor. The coup was in response to Serrano's attempted suspension of Guatemala's constitution and the dissolution of its congress and supreme court. It is advised that travelers check with the Guatemala Embassy in Belize City (see p. 109) concerning safe onward travel into Guatemala.

An important part of **Mundo Maya** is Guatemala. The hilly country offers numerous villages with populations of Maya descendants who continue their primitive lifestyle, closely imitating that of their ancestors of thousands of years ago. **Tikal,** one of the most magnificent ceremonial sites of the original Maya, should not be missed by any self-respecting Mayaphile.

Tikal

On Belize's Western Highway from the Xunantunich turnoff the road leads to Benque Viejo, an old town with aged wooden houses. It's a good place to stop and have a cold drink before the ride into Guatemala, where the culture changes immediately. For Americans (with passports) crossing the border is usually no problem. First you must stop at the Belize side, show your passport, and fill out a departure form. At the Guatemala side you stop again, show your passport, and fill out some more papers for your visa. You'll be asked how long you expect to stay in the country; allow an extra couple of days just in case you are delayed. Expect to pay US$5 (unless you got the visa previously in Mérida, Belize, or the U.S.). You should not have to pay to have your passport stamped here, but as border guards often do, they may ask for more money. You can try and play dumb, act as if you don't hear or don't understand—it *sometimes* works—but be prepared to pay a few dollars! If you're driving your own car make sure you have all the necessary papers of ownership, which they *will* want to see. You are required to have your tires fumigated (by law), for which the cost is a few Belizean dollars.

Once across the border it's pretty easy sailing, but keep a couple of things in mind. When passing military camps (and you will pass several on the way to Tikal), do not take *any* photos (even of the large vicious sign of a soldier pointing his gun at you saying *I dare you*). If you're aiming your lens at the lovely river and the water happens to flow in front of the guard station,

Tikal in all its glory

OZ MALLAN

you can get into difficulties no matter how innocent it seems to you. The Guatemalan military (and they will be in uniform) is very touchy. Don't be surprised if you're stopped by the military and asked for your papers; keep your passport and visitor's permit handy, smile and answer all questions, and you'll soon be on your way.

Yes, a trip to flamboyant Tikal is worth the border crossing and the terrible road you'll be on once you leave the Guatemalan border town of Melchor de Mencos. Expect another two-hour drive before you reach **Tikal National Park.** From the park it's another 30 miles, and from there the road is excellent.

Note: If backpacking and taking public buses, be aware that no public transportation is available from the Belize border to Tikal. The only bus that runs from the Belize/Guatemala border is a Guatemalan public bus that goes to Flores. You can spend the night here and take the morning bus to Tikal (in front of the **San Juan Hotel.**) The border/Flores bus is usually very crowded with chickens and the works. If you wish to bypass Flores and take your chances of hitching a ride straight to Tikal, ask the bus driver to drop you off at the crossroad (about US$3), that leads to Tikal, some 30 miles away. You won't find any stores or restaurants here, and you may wait quite a while for a car or taxi headed for Tikal. Many hotels from the Cayo District and Belize City run minibuses to Tikal. If you see one flag it down; they'll pick you up if there's room. From the Belize border fare is about US$40-50.

Flores

Many visitors opt to come by plane to Flores; flights are available from Belize, Guatemala, and Mexico cities. The airport in Flores is newish and modern; much more so than the town it services. Several hotels are around the area; most are very simple and very cheap. **Westin Hotels** is the most upscale in the area, located in Remate (about a 45-minute drive from the Tikal site).

Site Entrance

At the gate to Tikal expect a fee (about Q$35). Hang on to your ticket; you may be asked to show it. If you want to have a really memorable experience, have the ticket man stamp yours

Tikal

for an after-hours stay; it's good till 8:30 p.m. Otherwise you must be out of the park by 5 p.m. Watching the sunset from the top of a Tikal pyramid is memorable—and who knows? It might be a moonlit night besides. Someone will probably offer to sell you a Tikal guidebook; after purchasing the book at the entrance, I found a later edition of the same book inside at a cafe gift shop.

Within the Tikal grounds you'll have the choice of staying overnight at three locales or camping (about US$6 pp). Accommodations are very simple; most do not have 24-hour electricity or hot water, and some have shared baths.

When you enter Tikal note the large visitor's center. Take a look at the scale model of the site and you'll get an idea of where everything is. The visitor's center has photos of the reconstruction, as well as some fine artifacts. Clustered around the visitor's center you'll find a few cafes, and nearby is a bazaar of Guatemala artisans selling mostly items made from their colorfully woven fabrics.

The Ruins

Unless you have a week to really explore Tikal, it pays to hire a guide. Official guides are available at the site and the fee is fairly standard (about US$30), varying according to the size of your group and the length of your tour. Try negotiating if the price is not to your liking. These ruins are among the more outstanding in the Maya world. They have been excavated and restored nearly to perfection, mostly by archaeologists and students from the University of Pennsylvania. What you'll see is only a small part of what is still buried and unexplored in the rainforest. It's been a national park for over 30 years, so the forest has been protected from loggers—and parts of it are considered virgin. This is a *don't-miss* site. **Note:** The airstrip at Tikal is no longer used since the coming and going of planes was found damaging to the park's ecology. Now flights from Guatemala City and other points in the country land in nearby

An orphaned ocelot at Jaguar Inn in Tikal gets lots of TLC, and is seen here with Belizean archaelogical guide Tessa Fairweather.

OZ MALLAN

Flores (about a one-hour drive—buses are available to Tikal).

As is the case with most Maya ceremonial centers, archaeologists are learning more and more about life in Tikal and its 3,000 structures (with 10,000 more foundations). They left behind 250 stelae that have been mapped by archaeologists. Wear good walking shoes to cover the six square miles of excavated sites. Near the old airstrip you'll find vendor stalls selling colorful weavings and farther on a good little museum displaying some excellent pieces of Maya history. Don't miss the fascinating tomb exhibit, including a skeleton and funerary offerings, just as they were found.

Tikal is not only a treasure trove for the archaeology buff but also for nature lovers. You'll hear and, with luck (if up very early in the morning), see the howler monkeys that live in the treetops on the site. You'll see and hear hundreds of parrots squawking at you as you wander through **Twin Complex Q and R**—this is their domain. And while wandering the **Great Plaza** and the **Lost City,** colorful toucans fly between ancient stone structures and tall vine-covered trees.

Several twin complexes with identical pyramids facing each other across a central plaza are seen throughout the site. No one knows the reason for this. At Twin Complex Q and R, one pyramid has been excavated and restored while its opposite is just as it was when found—covered with vines and jungle growth. You'll see this frequently throughout Tikal; perhaps that's what gives it its special feeling of mystery, antiquity, and the lingering presence of the Maya.

The Great Plaza

Note: Only VIPs of the park are allowed to drive on most of the roads; expect to walk a lot. It's one mile from the museum to the **Great Plaza.** This plaza, considered the heart of ancient Tikal, is almost unbelievable in design. Terraces and stairways lead up and down into a plethora of architecturally intense buildings. Most of these palaces were ceremonial centers, but a few are believed to have been apartments. If you climbed and poked around into every structure at the Great Plaza alone, it would take at least an entire day.

Temple I

Because of its grace, form, and balance, this is probably the most photographed temple at Tikal. Also known as the **Temple of the Giant Jaguar** (named for a carving on one of its lintels), it rises 172 feet above the **East Plaza,** offers nine sloping terraces, and its roof comb is 145 feet above the Great Plaza floor. It's believed to have been built midway into the late-Classic period, about A.D. 700. Photographers, bring lots of film because you'll become maniacal with your camera trying to capture it all—the white-gray stone buildings with the vibrant green of the grass and surrounding jungle.

Temple IV

It's another long walk, but follow your map and visit challenging **Temple IV.** The platform itself has not been excavated and those in good physical condition will want to climb the ladders to the top (the steps are in poor condition). To date, Temple IV is the tallest surviving Maya structure from pre-Columbian history—212 feet from the base of its platform to the top. (William Coe, prominent archaeologist, suggests that perhaps the Aztec **Pyramid of the Sun at Teotihuacan** may have been slightly higher since there is nothing left of its temple on top.) From the summit of Temple IV, the sight of the entire area is beyond breathtaking.

In the spring a vendor sells breadnut tortillas at Temple IV. Try them; the taste is quite unusual. Usually a youngster will have an ice chest filled with beer and soda for sale, quite welcome after a hike up and down the tall pyramid.

There's so much to see and experience in this lovely jungle—a lazy walk through one of many dirt pathways will bring you up close to striking orchids of all colors, bromeliads, exquisite ferns, delicate blossoms, and myriad trees of every variety. One of the Maya guides told a story of when he was just a young boy hunting for a week at a time with his grandfather. The game was wrapped in a particular jungle leaf (that kept it in "good health") and buried in the ground at a convenient spot; on the return trip home it was dug out, still fresh and ready for cooking. Talk to every local you can; these folks are filled with stories—okay, who knows how accurate they are? But in each there is a seed—a feeling of what life is like in the *peten* (jungle) of Guatemala.

Temple IV is a challenge even for the hardy climber.

To get the most out of a visit to Tikal, do some reading first. An excellent book to read and then carry with you to read again at the site is William Coe's book, *Tikal, Handbook of the Ancient Maya Ruins,* available through the University Museum at the University of Pennsylvania (be sure to carry the map from the book with you—it's easy to get lost in this large complex). If you don't get it before you leave home, it's available at the site.

Accommodations

The **Jaguar Inn** offers rooms in the main building, as well as several bungalows around the pool. All beds have mosquito netting and you *do* need it. Rooms have private bathrooms and cold-water showers. Electricity (private generator) is on until about 10 p.m., candles for later. If you're a reader, bring a mini book light, and do bring a flashlight to light your way to the bathroom at night. Remember, you are in the middle of the jungle. Rates include three meals;

Q$150 s, Q$200 d, Q$275 t. The dining room is a low-key, screened-in porch with tile floors. Two additional on-site lodgings are the **Jungle Lodge** and **Tikal Inn**.

A Little Nicer

For those who want something a little nicer, go along the highway about 15 minutes. Before you reach the park stop at Remate Peten, just across from Lake Peten-Itza. Take a look at a charming hotel called **Mansione del Pajaro Serpiente.** This is a group of cottages stepped up the side of a hill, giving wonderful views of the lake and the *peten*. The 10 rooms are really small suites with sitting rooms, tile bathrooms, a double bed, hot water, electricity and an open-air dining room close by. The buildings are built of stone with *palapa* roofs and furnished with a flair. Across the road, a small group of shops sell wood carvings, jade jewelry, and more. Pickup at the Flores airport (no charge), and transportation to and from the park is available along with guided tours. Room rate is US$75 d; ask about two tiny rooms on the property without all the amenities, no sitting room, US$15 s, US$20 d. Add 17% tax to all prices. For more information, contact Nancy at Mansione del Pajaro, fax (502) 0500-662. If you're in a hurry and want to talk by phone, you'll have to follow these instructions: Call the only phone in Remate (500-269) and ask for Nancy at the hotel—someone will go get her. Then you call back five minutes later and she'll be there.

Maya Man Triathlon

At the village of Remate, usually in the first week of March, the yearly triathlon begins. It consists of a one-km swim, 34-km bike ride (to Tikal Park) and a seven-km run (through the park). For more information fax Nancy at Mansione del Pajaro.

Camino Real Tikal

Another upscale hotel, the Camino Real Tikal, is located a little farther from the Tikal site, but also in the village of Remate. The hotel is situated on 220 acres that overlook Lake Peten-Itza and the *peten*. The hotel offers a wide selection of sporting options, including hiking, swimming, fishing, scuba diving, canoeing, bicycling, sailboarding, and sailing. In keeping with the area's environmental standards, no motor vehicles are permitted on Lake Peten-Itza. In 12, tri-level, thatch-roof bungalows, 72 attractive rooms provide luxurious bathrooms, a/c, minibars, international telephone service, cable TV, and individual balconies overlooking the lake. In the main building guests will find a full-service restaurant, swimming pool, snack bar, lounge, and lake-view bar open till midnight. For more information and reservations, call (800) 327-373, (800) 228-3000, (9) 500-204.

LOUISE FOOTE

BOOKLIST

Barry, Tom. *Belize: A Country Guide*. Alburquerque: Inter-Hemispheric Education Resource Center, 1989.

Bernal, Ignacia. *The Olmec World*. Berkeley: University of California Press, 1969.

Bolland, O. Nigel. *Belize: A New Nation in Central America*. Boulder: Westview, 1986.

Burgess, Robert. *Secret Languages of the Sea*. Dodd, Mead, and Company.

Bynum, Richard, et al. *Manston's Before You Leave on Your Vacation*. The Globe Pequot Press.

Carrasco, David. *Religions of Mesoamerica: Cosmovision and Ceremonial Centers*. San Francisco: Harper & Row, 1990.

Coe, Michael D. *The Maya*. New York: Thames and Hudson, 1984.

Coe, William R. *Tikal, A Handbook of the Ancient Maya Ruins, with a Guide Map*. Philadelphia: University Museum at the University of Pennsylvania, 1967. 123 pages.

Cousteau, Jacques-Yves. *Three Adventures: Galapagos, Titicaca, the Blue Holes*. Garden City, NY: Doubleday, 1973.

Edgell, Zee. *Beka Lamb*. London: Heinemann Educational Books Ltd., 1982.

Freidel, David. *Archaeology at Cerros, Belize, Central America*. Dallas: Southern Methodist University Press, 1986-1989.

Garvin, Richard. *The Crystal Skull: The Story of the Mystery, Myth and Magic of the Mitchell-Hedges Crystal Skull Discovered in a Lost Mayan City During a Search for Atlantis*. Garden City, NY: Doubleday, 1973.

Gifford, James. *Prehistoric Pottery Analysis and the Ceramics of Barton Ramie in the Belize Valley*. Cambridge: Peabody Museum of Archaeology and Ethnology, Harvard University, 1976.

Grant, C.H. *The Making of Modern Belize*. Cambridge: Cambridge University Press, 1976.

Highwater, Jamake. *Journey to the Sky: A Novel About the True Adventures of Two Men in Search of the Lost Maya Kingdom*. New York: Thomas Y. Crowell, 1978.

Kelly, Joyce. *The Complete Visitor's Guide to Mesoamerican Ruins*. Norman: University of Oklahoma Press, 1982.

Kerns, Virginia. *Women and the Ancestors: Black Carib Kinship and Ritual*. Urbana: University of Illinois Press, 1983.

King, Emory. *Belize 1798, The Road To Glory*. Belize: Tropical Books, 1991.

Kuhlmann, Dietrick. *Living Coral Reefs of the World*. New York: Arco Publishing, 1985.

Lewis, Scott. *The Rainforest Book: How You Can Save the World's Rainforests*. Living Planet Press, 1990.

MacKinnon, Barbara. *Common Birds of the Yucatán Peninsula*. Cancun, Quintana Roo: Amigos de Sian Ka'an (Apto. Postal 770, Cancun, Quintana Roo, 77500, Mexico.) 1989. 220 pages.

Mercer, Henry Chapman. *The Hill-Caves of Yucatán: A Search for Evidence of Man's Antiquity in the Caverns of Central America*. Norman: University of Oklahoma Press, 1975.

Meyer, Franz. *Diving & Snorkeling Guide to Belize: Lighthouse Reef, Glover Reef, and Turneffe Island*. Houston: Gulf Publishing, 1990.

Poisonous Snakes of the World. Superintendent of Documents, U.S. Government Printing Office, Washington D.C.

Rabinowitz, Alan. Jaguar: A Struggle and Triumph in the Jungles of Belize. New York: Arbor House, 1986.

Sawatzky, Harry. They Sought a Country: Mennonite Colonization in Mexico. With an Appendix on Mennonite Colonization in British Honduras. Berkeley: University of California, 1971.

Schroeder, Dirk. Staying Healthy in Asia, Africa, and Latin America, 3rd edition. Chico, CA: Moon Publications, Inc., 1993.

Setzekom, William David. A Profile of the New Nation of Belize Formerly British Honduras. Ohio: Ohio University Press, 1981.

Shuman, M.K. The Maya Stone Murders. New York: St. Martin's, 1989.

Snakes of Belize. Audubon Society, drawings by Ellen MacRae, 29 Regent Street, Box 100, Belize City. 54 pages.

Tiptree, James Jr. Tales of Quintana Roo. Sauk City, WI: Arkham House, 1986.

Westlake, Donald. High Adventure. New York: Mysterious Press, 1985.

Wood, Leberman, and Weyer. Checklist of the Birds of Belize. Pittsburgh: Carnegie Museum of Natural History, 1986. 22 pages.

Wright, Ronald. Time Among The Maya. New York: Weidenfeld & Nicolson, 1989.

RESTAURANT INDEX

HOTEL INDEX

INDEX

Page numbers in **boldface** indicate the primary reference. *Italicized* page numbers indicate information in captions, callouts, charts, illustrations, or maps.

Chicki Mallan

About The Author

As a child Chicki Mallan discovered the joy of traveling with her parents. The family would leave their Catalina Island home yearly, hit the road and explore the small towns and big cities of the U.S. Traveling was still an important part of Chicki's life after having a bunch of kids to tote around. At various times Chicki and kids have lived in the Orient and Europe. When not traveling, lecturing, or giving slide presentations, Chicki and photographer husband Oz live in Paradise, CA, a small community in the foothills of the Sierra Nevada. She does what she enjoys most, writing newspaper and magazine articles in between travel books. She has been associated with Moon Publications since 1983, and is the author of *Yucatán Peninsula Handbook, Catalina Island Handbook, and Cancun Handbook*. In 1987, Chicki was presented the Pluma de Plata writing award from the Mexican Government Ministry of Tourism for an article she wrote about the Mexican Caribbean which was published in the *Los Angeles Times*. Chicki is a member of the SATW, Society of American Travel Writers.

About The Photographer

Oz Mallan has been a professional photographer for the past 40 years. Much of that time was spent as chief cameraman for the *Chico Enterprise-Record*. Oz graduated from the Brooks Institute of Photography, Santa Barbara, in 1950. His work has often appeared in newspapers across the country via UPI and AP. He travels the world with his wife, Chicki, handling the photo end of their literary projects, which include travel books, newspaper and magazine articles, as well as lectures and slide presentations. The photos in *Belize Handbook* were taken during many visits and years of travel on the Yucatán Peninsula. Other Moon books that feature Oz's photos are *Yucatán Peninsula Handbook, Catalina Island Handbook, and Cancun Handbook*.

About The Illustrators

Most of the banner art at the start of each chapter was done by Kathy Escovedo Sanders. She is an expert both in watercolor and stipple (excellent for black-and-white reproduction). Kathy is a 1982 California State University Long Beach graduate with a BA in art history. Her stipple art can also be seen in Chicki Mallan's *Catalina Islands Handbook, Yucatán Peninsula Handbook*, and *Cancun Handbook*.

Bob Race, illustrator and cartographer, has always been interested in maps, especially the technique and material used to draw them. After receiving his BA in art in 1974, he earned an MA in painting and drawing one year later. For 14 years he taught fine art at the college level, and in 1989 he began working at Moon Publications.

Diana Lasich-Harper received her degree in art from San Jose State University and continued studying as she traveled through Japan, where she learned wood-block printing, *sumie*, and kimono painting.

Louise Foote is a talented illustrator and cartographer. She has also worked on archaeological digs around Northern California.

MOON HANDBOOKS—THE IDEAL TRAVELING COMPANIONS

Open a Moon Handbook and you're opening your eyes and heart to the world. Thoughtful, sensitive, and provocative, Moon Handbooks encourage an intimate understanding of a region, from its culture and history to essential practicalities. Fun to read and packed with valuable information on accommodations, dining, recreation, plus indispensable travel tips, detailed maps, charts, illustrations, photos, glossaries, and indexes, Moon Handbooks are ideal traveling companions: informative, entertaining, and highly practical.

To locate the bookstore nearest you that carries Moon Travel Handbooks or to order directly from Moon Publications, call: (800) 345-5473, Monday-Friday, 9 a.m.-5 p.m. PST.

THE PACIFIC/ASIA SERIES

BALI HANDBOOK by Bill Dalton
Detailed travel information on the most famous island in the world. 428 pages. **$12.95**

BANGKOK HANDBOOK by Michael Buckley
Your tour guide through this exotic and dynamic city reveals the affordable and accessible possibilities. Thai phrasebook. 214 pages. **$10.95**

BLUEPRINT FOR PARADISE: How to Live on a Tropic Island by Ross Norgrove
This one-of-a-kind guide has everything you need to know about moving to and living comfortably on a tropical island. 212 pages. **$14.95**

FIJI ISLANDS HANDBOOK by David Stanley
The first and still the best source of information on travel around this 322-island archipelago. Fijian glossary. 198 pages. **$11.95**

INDONESIA HANDBOOK by Bill Dalton
This one-volume encyclopedia explores island by island the many facets of this sprawling, kaleidoscopic island nation. Extensive Indonesian vocabulary. 1,000 pages. **$19.95**

MICRONESIA HANDBOOK: Guide to the Caroline, Gilbert, Mariana, and Marshall Islands
by David Stanley
Micronesia Handbook guides you on a real Pacific adventure all your own. 345 pages. **$11.95**

NEW ZEALAND HANDBOOK by Jane King
Introduces you to the people, places, history, and culture of this extraordinary land. 571 pages. **$18.95**

OUTBACK AUSTRALIA HANDBOOK by Marael Johnson
Australia is an endlessly fascinating, vast land, and *Outback Australia Handbook* explores the cities and towns, sheep stations, and wilderness areas of the Northern Territory, Western Australia, and South Australia. Full of travel tips and cultural information for adventuring, relaxing, or just getting away from it all. 355 pages. **$15.95**

PHILIPPINES HANDBOOK by Peter Harper and Evelyn Peplow
Crammed with detailed information, *Philippines Handbook* equips the escapist, hedonist, or business traveler with thorough coverage of the Philippines's colorful history, landscapes, and culture. 587 pages. **$12.95**

SOUTHEAST ASIA HANDBOOK by Carl Parkes
Helps the enlightened traveler discover the real Southeast Asia. 873 pages. **$16.95**

SOUTH KOREA HANDBOOK by Robert Nilsen
Whether you're visiting on business or searching for adventure, *South Korea Handbook* is an invaluable companion. Korean glossary with useful notes on speaking and reading the language. 548 pages. **$14.95**

SOUTH PACIFIC HANDBOOK by David Stanley
The original comprehensive guide to the 16 territories in the South Pacific. 740 pages. **$19.95**

TAHITI-POLYNESIA HANDBOOK by David Stanley
All five French-Polynesian archipelagoes are covered in this comprehensive guide by Oceania's best-known travel writer. 235 pages. **$11.95**

THAILAND HANDBOOK by Carl Parkes
Presents the richest source of information on travel in Thailand. 568 pages. **$16.95**

THE HAWAIIAN SERIES

BIG ISLAND OF HAWAII HANDBOOK by J.D. Bisignani
An entertaining yet informative text packed with insider tips on accommodations, dining, sports and outdoor activities, natural attractions, and must-see sights. 347 pages. **$11.95**

HAWAII HANDBOOK by J.D. Bisignani
Winner of the 1989 Hawaii Visitors Bureau's Best Guide Award and the Grand Award for Excellence in Travel Journalism, this guide takes you beyond the glitz and high-priced hype and leads you to a genuine Hawaiian experience. Covers all 8 Hawaiian Islands. 879 pages. **$15.95**

KAUAI HANDBOOK by J.D. Bisignani
Kauai Handbook is the perfect antidote to the workaday world. Hawaiian and pidgin glossaries. 236 pages. **$9.95**

MAUI HANDBOOK by J.D. Bisignani
"No fool-'round" advice on accommodations, eateries, and recreation, plus a comprehensive introduction to island ways, geography, and history. Hawaiian and pidgin glossaries. 350 pages. **$11.95**

OAHU HANDBOOK by J.D. Bisignani
A handy guide to Honolulu, renowned surfing beaches, and Oahu's countless other diversions. Hawaiian and pidgin glossaries. 354 pages. **$11.95**

THE AMERICAS SERIES

ALASKA-YUKON HANDBOOK   by Deke Castleman and Don Pitcher
Get the inside story, with plenty of well-seasoned advice to help you cover more miles on less money. 384 pages.   **$13.95**

ARIZONA TRAVELER'S HANDBOOK   by Bill Weir
This meticulously researched guide contains everything necessary to make Arizona accessible and enjoyable. 505 pages.   **$14.95**

BAJA HANDBOOK   by Joe Cummings
A comprehensive guide with all the travel information and background on the land, history, and culture of this untamed thousand-mile-long peninsula. 356 pages.   **$13.95**

BELIZE HANDBOOK   by Chicki Mallan
Complete with detailed maps, practical information, and an overview of the area's flamboyant history, culture, and geographical features, *Belize Handbook* is the only comprehensive guide of its kind to this spectacular region. 263 pages.   **$14.95**

BRITISH COLUMBIA HANDBOOK   by Jane King
With an emphasis on outdoor adventures, this guide covers mainland British Columbia, Vancouver Island, the Queen Charlotte Islands, and the Canadian Rockies. 381 pages. **$13.95**

CANCUN HANDBOOK   by Chicki Mallan
Covers the city's luxury scene as well as more modest attractions, plus many side trips to unspoiled beaches and Mayan ruins. Spanish glossary. 257 pages.   **$12.95**

CATALINA ISLAND HANDBOOK: A Guide to California's Channel Islands
by Chicki Mallan
A complete guide to these remarkable islands, from the windy solitude of the Channel Islands National Marine Sanctuary to bustling Avalon. 245 pages.   **$10.95**

COLORADO HANDBOOK   by Stephen Metzger
Essential details to the all-season possibilities in Colorado fill this guide. Practical travel tips combine with recreation—skiing, nightlife, and wilderness exploration—plus entertaining essays. 422 pages.   **$15.95**

IDAHO HANDBOOK   by Bill Loftus
A year-round guide to everything in this outdoor wonderland, from whitewater adventures to rural hideaways. 275 pages.   **$12.95**

JAMAICA HANDBOOK   by Karl Luntta
From the sun and surf of Montego Bay and Ocho Rios to the cool slopes of the Blue Mountains, author Karl Luntta offers island-seekers a perceptive, personal view of Jamaica. 213 pages. **$12.95**

MONTANA HANDBOOK   by W.C. McRae and Judy Jewell
The wild West is yours with this extensive guide to the Treasure State, complete with travel practicalities, history, and lively essays on Montana life. 393 pages.   **$13.95**

NEVADA HANDBOOK by Deke Castleman
Nevada Handbook puts the Silver State into perspective and makes it manageable and affordable. 400 pages. **$14.95**

NEW MEXICO HANDBOOK by Stephen Metzger
A close-up and complete look at every aspect of this wondrous state. 375 pages. **$13.95**

NORTHERN CALIFORNIA HANDBOOK by Kim Weir
An outstanding companion for imaginative travel in the territory north of the Tehachapis. 759 pages. **$16.95**

OREGON HANDBOOK by Stuart Warren and Ted Long Ishikawa
Brimming with travel practicalities and insider views on Oregon's history, culture, arts, and activities. 422 pages. **$12.95**

TEXAS HANDBOOK by Joe Cummings
Seasoned travel writer Joe Cummings brings an insider's perspective to his home state. 483 pages. **$13.95**

UTAH HANDBOOK by Bill Weir
Weir gives you all the carefully researched facts and background to make your visit a success. 445 pages. **$14.95**

WASHINGTON HANDBOOK by Dianne J. Boulerice Lyons and Archie Satterfield
Covers sights, shopping, services, transportation, and outdoor recreation, with complete listings for restaurants and accommodations. 433 pages. **$13.95**

WYOMING HANDBOOK by Don Pitcher
All you need to know to open the doors to this wide and wild state. 495 pages. **$14.95**

YUCATAN HANDBOOK by Chicki Mallan
All the information you'll need to guide you into every corner of this exotic land. Mayan and Spanish glossaries. 391 pages. **$14.95**

THE INTERNATIONAL SERIES

EGYPT HANDBOOK by Kathy Hansen
An invaluable resource for intelligent travel in Egypt. Arabic glossary. 522 pages. **$18.95**

MOSCOW-ST. PETERSBURG HANDBOOK by Masha Nordbye
Provides the visitor with an extensive introduction to the history, culture, and people of these two great cities, as well as practical information on where to stay, eat, and shop. 260 pages. **$13.95**

NEPAL HANDBOOK by Kerry Moran
Whether you're planning a week in Kathmandu or months out on the trail, *Nepal Handbook* will take you into the heart of this Himalayan jewel. 378 pages. **$12.95**

NEPALI AAMA by Broughton Coburn

A delightful photo-journey into the life of a Gurung tribeswoman of Central Nepal. Having lived with Aama (translated, "mother") for two years, first as an outsider and later as an adopted member of the family, Coburn presents an intimate glimpse into a culture alive with humor, folklore, religion, and ancient rituals. 165 pages. **$13.95**

PAKISTAN HANDBOOK by Isobel Shaw

For armchair travelers and trekkers alike, the most detailed and authoritative guide to Pakistan ever published. Urdu glossary. 478 pages. **$15.95**

STAYING HEALTHY IN ASIA, AFRICA, AND LATIN AMERICA
by Dirk G. Schroeder, Sc D, MPH

Don't leave home without it! Besides providing a complete overview of the health problems that exist in these areas, this book will help you determine which immunizations you'll need beforehand, what medications to take with you, and how to recognize and treat infections and diseases. Includes extensively illustrated first-aid information and precautions for heat, cold, and high altitude. 200 pages. **$10.95**

**New travel handbooks may be available that are not on this list.
To find out more about current or upcoming titles,
call us toll-free at (800) 345-5473.**

TRAVEL MATTERS

Travel Matters is Moon Publications' biannual newsletter. It provides today's traveler with timely, informative travel news and articles.

You'll find resourceful coverage on:

- **Money**—What does it cost? Is it worth it?

- **Low impact travel**—tread lightly travel tips

- **Special interest travel**—cultural tours, environmental excursions, outdoor recreation, adventure treks, and more

- **Travel styles**—families, seniors, disabled travelers, package and theme tours

- **Consumer reviews**—books, language aids, travel gadgets, products, and services

- **Facts and opinions**—reader's letters and Moon Handbook author news

- **Moon Handbook booklist**—the latest titles and editions, and where and how to purchase them

To receive a free copy of *Travel Matters*, write Moon Publications Inc., P.O. Box 3040, Chico, CA 95927-3040, or call toll-free (800) 345-5473.

IMPORTANT ORDERING INFORMATION

FOR FASTER SERVICE: Call to locate the bookstore nearest you that carries Moon Travel Handbooks or order directly from Moon Publications:

(800) 345-5473 • **Monday-Friday** • **9 a.m.-5 p.m. PST** • **fax (916) 345-6751**

PRICES: All prices are subject to change. We always ship the most current edition. We will let you know if there is a price increase on the book you ordered.

SHIPPING & HANDLING OPTIONS: 1) Domestic UPS or USPS first class (allow 10 working days for delivery): $3.50 for the first item, 50 cents for each additional item.

Exceptions:
- **Moonbelt** shipping is $1.50 for one, 50 cents for each additional belt.
- Add $2.00 for same-day handling.
- UPS 2nd Day Air or Printed Airmail requires a special quote.
- International Surface Bookrate (8-12 weeks delivery):
  $3.00 for the first item, $1.00 for each additional item. Note: Moon Publications cannot guarantee international surface bookrate shipping.

FOREIGN ORDERS: All orders that originate outside the U.S.A. must be paid for with either an International Money Order or a check in U.S. currency drawn on a major U.S. bank based in the U.S.A.

TELEPHONE ORDERS: We accept Visa or MasterCard payments. Minimum order is US$15.00. Call in your order: (800) 345-5473, 9 a.m.-5 p.m. Pacific Standard Time.

MOONBELTS

Made of heavy-duty Cordura nylon, the Moonbelt offers maximum protection for your money and important papers. This all-weather pouch slips under your shirt or waistband, rendering it virtually undetectable and inaccessible to pickpockets. One-inch-wide nylon webbing, heavy-duty zipper, one-inch quick-release buckle. Accommodates traveler's checks, passport, cash, photos. Size 5 x 9 inches. Black. **$8.95**

ORDER FORM

Be sure to call (800) 345-5473 for current prices and editions or for the name of the bookstore
nearest you that carries Moon Travel Handbooks • 9 a.m.–5 p.m. PST
(See important ordering information on preceding page)

Name: _____ Date: _____

Street: _____

City: _____ Daytime Phone: _____

State or Country: _____ Zip Code: _____

QUANTITY	TITLE	PRICE

Taxable Total_____
Sales Tax (7.25%) for California Residents_____
Shipping & Handling_____
TOTAL_____

Ship: ☐ UPS (no PO Boxes)   ☐ 1st class   ☐ International surface mail

Ship to: ☐ address above   ☐ other _____

_____

_____

Make checks payable to: **MOON PUBLICATIONS, INC**. P.O. Box 3040, Chico, CA 95927-3040
U.S.A. We accept Visa and MasterCard. **To Order**: Call in your Visa or MasterCard number, or send
a written order with your Visa or MasterCard number and expiration date clearly written.

Card Number: ☐ **Visa**   ☐ **MasterCard**

☐☐☐☐ ☐☐☐☐ ☐☐☐☐ ☐☐☐☐

Exact Name on Card: _____

expiration date:_____

signature_____

SP/93

WHERE TO BUY THIS BOOK

BOOKSTORES AND LIBRARIES:
Moon Publications Handbooks are sold worldwide. Please write
our sales manager for a list of wholesalers and distributors in
your area that stock our travel handbooks.

TRAVELERS:
We would like to have Moon Publications Handbooks available
throughout the world. Please ask your bookstore to write or
call us for ordering information. If your bookstore will not order
our guides for you, please write or call for a free catalog.

MOON PUBLICATIONS, INC.
P.O. BOX 3040
CHICO, CA 95927-3040 U.S.A.
TEL: (800) 345-5473
FAX: (916) 345-6751